Diplomacy and the Making of World Politics

This book examines world politics through the lens of diplomatic practice. It argues that many global phenomena of our time, from the making of international law to the constitution of international public power, through humanitarianism and the maintenance of global hierarchies, are made possible and shaped by evolving forms of diplomacy. The study of diplomacy is largely dominated by firsthand accounts and historical treaties, with little effort at theoretical discussion. This book shows how diplomatic studies can benefit from more explicit theorizing, and argues that the study of world politics should pay more attention to what goes on in the diplomatic "engine room" of international politics.

OLE JACOB SENDING is Director of Research at the Norwegian Institute of International Affairs (NUPI).

VINCENT POULIOT is Associate Professor and William Dawson Scholar in the Department of Political Science at McGill University.

IVER B. NEUMANN is Montague Burton Professor of International Relations at the London School of Economics and Political Science, and an Associate of the Norwegian Institute of International Affairs (NUPI).

Cambridge Studies in International Relations: 136

Diplomacy and the Making of World Politics

Cambridge Studies in International Relations is a joint initiative of Cambridge University Press and the British International Studies Association (BISA). The series aims to publish the best new scholarship in international studies, irrespective of subject matter, methodological approach, or theoretical perspective. The series seeks to bring the latest theoretical work in International Relations to bear on the most important problems and issues in global politics.

Cambridge Studies in International Relations

135 *Barry Buzan and George Lawson*
The global transformation:
History, modernity and the making of international relations

134 *Heather Elko McKibben*
State strategies in international bargaining:
Play by the rules or change them?

133 *Janina Dill*
Legitimate targets?
Social construction, international law, and US bombing

132 *Nuno P. Monteiro*
Theory of unipolar politics

Series list continues after index

Diplomacy and the Making of World Politics

Edited by

OLE JACOB SENDING, VINCENT POULIOT, AND IVER B. NEUMANN

CAMBRIDGE
UNIVERSITY PRESS

CAMBRIDGE
UNIVERSITY PRESS

University Printing House, Cambridge CB2 8BS, United Kingdom

Cambridge University Press is part of the University of Cambridge.

It furthers the University's mission by disseminating knowledge in the pursuit of education, learning and research at the highest international levels of excellence.

www.cambridge.org
Information on this title: www.cambridge.org/9781107492004

First published 2015

Printed in the United Kingdom by Clays, St Ives plc

A catalogue record for this publication is available from the British Library

Library of Congress Cataloguing in Publication data
Diplomacy and the making of world politics / edited by Ole Jacob Sending, Vincent Pouliot, Iver B. Neumann.
pages cm. – (Cambridge studies in international relations ; 136)
ISBN 978-1-107-49200-4 (paperback)
1. Diplomacy. 2. World politics. I. Sending, Ole Jacob.
JZ1305.D54416 2015
327.2–dc23

2015007317

ISBN 978-1-107-09926-5 Hardback
ISBN 978-1-107-49200-4 Paperback

Contents

Contributors

Rebecca Adler-Nissen, University of Copenhagen
Tarak Barkawi, The London School of Economics and Political Science
Lieutenant Commander Shannon L. C. Souma, Georgetown University
Ian Hurd, Northwestern University
Captain Miriam Krieger, Georgetown University
Cecelia Lynch, University of California, Irvine
Jennifer Mitzen, Ohio State University
Iver B. Neumann, The London School of Economics and Political Science, Norwegian Institute of International Affairs
Daniel H. Nexon, Georgetown University
Vincent Pouliot, McGill University
Leonard Seabrooke, Copenhagen Business School, Norwegian Institute of International Affairs
Ole Jacob Sending, Norwegian Institute of International Affairs

Acknowledgments

This book started as a rather loose conversation among the three editors about the future of diplomacy. Our plan was to explore the diplomatic work being done by a host of different types of actors. We assembled a team of authors for an initial workshop, financed by the Centre for International Peace and Security Studies (CIPSS) at McGill University in Montreal in March 2011 and organized by Vincent Pouliot. Generous financial support from Kjetil M. Stuland, former chairman of the board at the Norwegian Institute of International Affairs (NUPI), enabled us to organize what turned out to be a highly significant second workshop at the New School University in New York City in September 2012. Tarak Barkawi, then at the New School, made all of this practically possible by making conference facilities and logistical support available. Through two days of intense and highly productive discussions, we expanded the scope and rationale of our project – to bring social theory to bear on diplomacy, and to bring diplomacy to the core of debates about world politics. At the New School workshop, we received extremely productive feedback from Marcus Holmes, Frederic Merand, and Carne Ross on the overall direction of the project as well as on individual chapters. Minda Holm and Nuraida Abdykapar kyzy have provided excellent assistance with references, copy editing, and formatting. Big thanks go to John Haslam at Cambridge University Press for his support and for his efforts to identify two reviewers whose comments on the book have greatly improved its quality. Thanks also to Carrie Parkinson for help in the production. Lastly, the contributors to this volume have pushed us editors to rethink and adjust our initial ideas and arguments and for making this book a truly collective project.

OJS, VP, IBN

Introduction

OLE JACOB SENDING, VINCENT POULIOT, AND IVER B. NEUMANN

This book examines world politics through the lens of diplomatic practice. We argue that many global phenomena of our time, from international law to world order, through humanitarianism, global hierarchies, and public power, are made possible by evolving forms of diplomacy. In that sense, this book is not about diplomacy per se, but rather about the constitution of world politics in and through diplomatic practice. To shed new light on the making and remaking of international relations, we bring social theory to bear on diplomacy. Our starting point is simple: as we enter the twenty-first century, everybody seems to agree that diplomacy is changing, yet few people can specify exactly how – and with what effects on world politics. Our goal is to produce new knowledge about the evolving character of diplomacy and the ways in which it (re)constitutes significant facets of world politics.

In this Introduction, we accomplish two main goals. First, we provide theoretical tools to better grasp the role and character of diplomacy and how it may be changing in the contemporary era. We develop a relational framework focused on two dimensions: the evolving configurations of state and non-state actors and the competing authority claims that underpin diplomatic practices on the world stage. Second, we begin to theorize the ways in which diplomacy makes and remakes world politics. The remainder of the book offers rich case studies to empirically substantiate our broad argument about the constitution of world politics in practice. In this Introduction, our more limited objective is to explain the significance of our argument for key debates in international relations (IR).

All in all, by bringing theory to bear on diplomacy and, reciprocally, by bringing diplomacy back into the study of world politics, this book clears new grounds in IR. While diplomatic studies would greatly benefit from a more concerted effort at theorizing, the rest of the discipline should also pay careful attention to the larger effects of what is actually going on in the engine room of global politics. This Introduction supplies the building blocks for both of these contributions. But first, we make the case for a renewed effort at theorizing diplomacy.

Theorizing diplomacy and change

In the first edition of the *Handbook of International Relations*, Jönsson makes the rather harsh but substantively accurate judgment that so far, the study of diplomacy has been "long on typologies" but "short on theory."[1] With some exceptions,[2] most of the existing literature in diplomatic studies has a very hands-on flavor, detailing the purposes, tactics, and procedures of diplomacy. This work is important, in that it specifies how certain kinds of topics are handled through diplomacy, establishes what kind of traditions for handling them exist, and draws some generalizations from comparative case studies. Studies of this type are also valuable for their focus on what actors who are up against a certain historical circumstance actually do.

The dominance of empirics in diplomatic studies probably stems from a combination of two factors. First, the study of diplomacy was traditionally the province of practitioners more than academics. Diplomats such as Sir Ernest Satow and Harold Nicolson as well as

[1] Christer Jönsson, "Diplomacy, Bargaining and Negotiation," in Walter Carslnaes, Thomas Risse, and Beth Simmons, eds., *Handbook of International Relations* (London: Sage, 2002), 215.

[2] James Der Derian, *On Diplomacy: A Genealogy of Western Estrangement* (Oxford: Blackwell, 1987); Costas Constantinou, *On the Way to Diplomacy* (Minneapolis: University of Minnesota Press, 1996); Iver B. Neumann, "Returning Practice to the Linguistic Turn: The Case of Diplomacy," *Millennium* 32(3), 2002, 627–652; Christer Jönsson and Martin Hall, *Essence of Diplomacy* (London: Palgrave, 2005); Rebecca Adler-Nissen "Late Sovereign Diplomacy," *The Hague Journal of Diplomacy*, 4, 2009, 121–141; Vincent Pouliot, *International Security in Practice: The Politics of NATO-Russia Diplomacy* (Cambridge: Cambridge University Press, 2010); Paul Sharp, *Diplomatic Theory of International Relations* (Cambridge: Cambridge University Press, 2009); and Iver B. Neumann, *At Home with the Diplomats: Ethnography of a European Foreign Ministry* (Ithaca: Cornell University Press, 2011); Corneliu Bjola and Markus Kornprobst, *Understanding International Diplomacy: Theory, Practice and Ethics* (London: Routledge, 2013); and Vincent Pouliot and Jérémie Cornut, "Practice Theory and the Study of Diplomacy: A Research Agenda," *Cooperation and Conflict* 50(2), 2015.

budding statesmen such as Henry Kissinger have written key texts.[3] This helps explain why diplomacy has often been seen as the "art" of resolving negotiations peacefully or, more generally, of identifying the national interest beyond the constraints and lack of vision expressed by elected politicians. Based on their first-hand engagement with diplomacy, these authors were primarily concerned with defining the purposes and ideal functions of diplomacy, from negotiation through information gathering to communication.

This prescriptive bent relates to the second reason why diplomatic studies have often stayed clear of theorization. In his famous IR textbook, Hans Morgenthau suggested a hermeneutic study of statesmen:

> We look over his shoulder when he writes his dispatches; we listen in on his conversations with other statesmen; we read and anticipate his very thoughts. Thinking in terms of interest defined as power, we think as he does, and as disinterested observers we understand his thoughts and actions perhaps better than he, the actor on the political scene, does himself.[4]

Nowhere in the IR literature have people stuck closer to Morgenthau's methodology than in diplomatic studies.[5] The result is that we now have a sizeable literature focusing on how states pursue diplomacy rather than on theories of diplomacy. These literatures concentrate on problem solving rather than on the social and political processes that make issues emerge as diplomatic tasks in the first place. Existing studies also tend to treat the attributes of the state and of diplomats as constant.

At the conceptual level, the implication of the specific way in which diplomatic studies have evolved is that seminal definitions usually focus

[3] Sir Ernest Satow, *Satow's Guide to Diplomatic Practice*, 6th edn (London: Longman, [1917] 2009); Harold Nicolson, *Diplomacy*, 3rd edn (London: Oxford University Press, [1939] 1963); Henry Kissinger, *Diplomacy* (New York: Simon & Schuster, 2004). For a critique, see Neumann, *At Home with the Diplomats*.

[4] Hans J. Morgenthau (with Kenneth W. Thompson), *Politics among Nations: The Struggle for Power and Peace*, 6th edn (New York: Alfred A. Knopf, [1948] 1985), 5.

[5] Note, however, that Morgenthau identifies the practice of diplomacy as the central empirical site for the study of world politics. This equally important part of his approach has unfortunately not been followed very well, in part because the theory he proposed saw diplomacy as a medium for the application of power. This selective reading has made the study of diplomacy strangely marginal to broader debates about world politics.

on a set of core functions of diplomacy, typically physical and symbolic representation. For example, a classic view owed to the English School of IR holds that diplomacy is "the process of dialogue and negotiation by which states in a system conduct their relations and pursue theirs purposes by means short of war."[6] As useful as it may be to distinguish diplomacy from other social forms, such a definition ends up fixing so many features of diplomacy that it makes the study of change impracticable.[7] To circumvent this obstacle, a lot of the works that delve into recent developments in diplomatic practice tend simply to add a prefix: there is new diplomacy (in many flavors) – paradiplomacy, small states diplomacy, non-governmental organization (NGO) diplomacy, business diplomacy, public diplomacy, twiplomacy, multilateral diplomacy, polydiplomacy, catalytic diplomacy, celebrity diplomacy, real-time diplomacy, triangular diplomacy, and the list goes on.

Our strategy differs in two respects. First, we move from diplomacy as a category of practice to diplomacy as a category of analysis.[8] Too often, there seems to be a conflation of the two: the "folk-models" and self-understandings of diplomats have been codified and described at length in historical treatises and books, over time also becoming part of the scholarly attempt to unpack and account for the nature and functioning of diplomacy. For example, while Kissinger's account of diplomacy[9] is important, it is more so because of its influence on the ideal, typical self-understanding of diplomats and more generally of "diplomatic culture"[10] than as a source from which to try to unpack and account for diplomatic culture. We strongly believe in the value of inductively restoring categories of practice in social analysis; as such,

6 Adam Watson, *Diplomacy: The Dialogue between States* (London: Routledge), 11.

7 One notable exception is Jan Melissen, ed., *Innovation in Diplomatic Practice* (London: Palgrave Macmillan, 1999).

8 Pierre Bourdieu, *The Logic of Practice* (Stanford: Stanford University Press, 1990); Morten Skumsrud Andersen and Iver B. Neumann, "Practices as Models: A Methodology with an Illustration Concerning Wampum Diplomacy," *Millennium*, 40(3), 2012, 457–481.

9 Henry Kissinger, *A World Restored: Metternich, Castlereagh and the Problem of Peace, 1815–1822* (Boston: Houghton Mifflin, 1957).

10 Hedley Bull, *The Anarchical Society: A Study of Order in International Politics* (New York: Columbia University Press, 1977); James Der Derian, "Hedley Bull and the Idea of Diplomatic Culture," in Rick Fawn and Jeremy Larkins, eds., *International Society after the Cold War: Anarchy and Order Reconsidered* (Houndsmills: Macmillan, 1996), 84–100.

many of the classics in diplomatic studies are of great value, but then not as theoretical propositions (analytical categories) but for what they tell us about how diplomats themselves categorize the world. We therefore take great pains to treat diplomats' (practice) categories as a prelude to theoretically and historically informed accounts of where these categories come from, how they were made possible, and what effects they produce. The categories used by people to be studied should not be the end point of social inquiry.[11]

Second and related, we problematize the contours of what diplomacy is and is not by conceiving of it as a profession. What makes a diplomat is a claim to jurisdictional control over certain tasks that are sanctioned by the state and recognized in international law.[12] In this regard, diplomats form what Ashley once termed a mutually recognized "community" that "administers the recognized public sphere of international life."[13] Very importantly, we do not treat the tasks over which diplomats claim jurisdictional control as givens, nor do we limit the tasks that we may define as diplomatic to official diplomats. Rather, the extent to which diplomats actually "administer" or control the "recognized public sphere" between states is something to be assessed empirically, not taken as a definitional starting point. To be able to assess diplomacy empirically as a set of durable practices, we need to cast our net wider to capture the relationships between diplomats and a broader array of actors who are engaged in practices that have conventionally been defined as core diplomatic tasks to analyze how new tasks emerge and become more or less recognized as constituting

[11] Note that there is nothing inherently problematic in using a practice category as an analytical category. For example, if a central self-understanding of diplomats is their ability to "keep a bracket" during negotiations, then this must surely be included in the analysis. But analytical tools are needed to capture the institutional conditions for why this is so, how it affects what diplomats do, and how this feature of diplomacy affects the making of world politics. In the next three sections, we begin to carve such tools.

[12] Andew Abbott, *The System of Professions* (Chicago: University of Chicago Press, 1988), chap. 1.

[13] Richard K. Ashley, "The Poverty of Neorealism," *International Organization*, 38(2), 1984, 225–286, p. 275. Diplomats form a community of practice; see Emanuel Adler, *Communitarian International Relations: The Epistemic Foundations of International Relations* (London: Routledge, 2005, chap. 1). For an analysis of diplomats as an epistemic community, see Mai'a Davis Cross, *The European Diplomatic Corps: Diplomats and International Cooperation from Westphalia to Maastricht* (London: Palgrave Macmillan, 2007).

"diplomacy." We believe that this move is of crucial importance, for it allows us to theorize diplomacy as an emergent phenomenon whose form changes over time. This way, not only do we embed diplomacy in broader institutional changes, we also gain perspective on how much diplomacy matters in defining the infrastructure through which world politics is produced and reproduced.

As a category of analysis premised on a particular kind of jurisdictional claim, diplomacy may be defined, in the broadest possible terms, as a claim to represent a given polity to the outside world. Pitched at this level of abstraction, the concept reduces to three key dimensions: first, diplomacy is a process (of claiming authority and jurisdiction); second, it is relational (it operates at the interface between one's polity and that of others); and third, it is political (involving both representation and governing). To study diplomacy, then, we need analytical categories that offer distance and clarity, as well as sufficient analytical flexibility to allow for the analysis of change. Indeed, if we are to understand the social processes through which diplomacy is central to the making and remaking of world politics, we need analytical tools that can unpack diplomacy as a set of durable social practices. Using a relational perspective, we propose two such theoretical lenses: configurations and authority claims. These two analytical tools allow us to specify what, if anything at all, is actually changing in contemporary diplomatic practices. To situate our focus on configurations and on authority claims, we first discuss in some detail what we mean by a relational perspective.

Relational analytical tools

It is generally admitted that an actor's identity is defined by its relationship with other actors. As such, there is an implicitly relational view in so-called actor-centric accounts: to analyze diplomacy by adding a prefix of "business diplomacy," say, is to define it in terms of its relationship to, and differentiation from, diplomacy. Moreover, inasmuch as diplomacy is often equated with "diplomatic relations," one may easily conclude that the practice of diplomacy invites a focus first and foremost on relations, as that is the stuff from which and on which diplomats work. This is true: there is something distinct about diplomatic practice that invites a focus on relations (see also Conclusion, this volume). Yet, our point is a more fundamental one: the social world as a whole is made up of relations. By this we mean that agents, objects, and structures emerge from transactions and connections, that is, relations. Our task as analysts is to grasp the processes through which such relations are appropriated and used to stabilize and reify some other relations as making up an entity or thing.[14] This means that diplomacy is not merely a practice that deals in relations between pre-constituted political entities. Rather, these relations are seen as constitutive of, and ontologically prior to, these entities. With Abbott, we may say that a relational perspective looks for "things of boundaries" rather than the boundaries of things.[15]

Our focus is therefore on the processes through which diplomacy is made and remade through practices whose characteristics must be treated as contingent and open to change. This follows from our choice to see diplomacy as defined through the practices that are socially recognized as such. Diplomats and others engage one another in both competitive and cooperative ways to produce what counts as competent diplomatic practice. Conversely, in our efforts to analyze the effects of diplomacy on world politics, we focus on how diplomacy is involved in generating agents (e.g., states), objects (e.g., treaties, embassies), and structures (sovereignty). Take the state for instance: diplomatic work is organized around, and helps reproduce, the state as the naturalized political arena for the generation of meaning and belonging. It follows that if the constituent contents of diplomatic practice change, then the meaning of statehood changes with it.

Our frequent invocation of the concept of (diplomatic) practice now becomes more readily understandable: from a relational perspective, it does not make sense to say that an institution – such as international law or multilateralism or sovereignty – structures or secures a certain order. It is the continual use or performance of the material and symbolic resources that are recognized as being vested in these institutions that helps produce and reproduce certain orders. Indeed, one central virtue of focusing on diplomacy as an infrastructure for the making of world politics is that it opens up oft-neglected causal pathways through which particular orders are continually reproduced. As Barkawi

14 See Patrick Jackson and Daniel H. Nexon, "Relations before States: Substance, Process, and the Study of World Politics," *European Journal of International Relations*, 5(3), 1999, 291–332.

15 Andrew Abbott, "Things of Boundaries," *Social Research*, 62(4), 1995, 857–882.

explores in his chapter, for example, diplomacy emerges as a central vehicle for the continued reproduction of hierarchies between states, and as Hurd argues in his chapter, diplomatic practices of public reason giving and justification are crucial to how international law shapes states' behavior. We explore this in more detail later, but before we do, we must put meat on the bones of our relational perspective.

Configurations

In a lively exchange dating back to 1998, Sharp and Cooper gave new scholarly prominence to the ways in which state-to-state diplomacy is being challenged by new actors.[16] Since then, a number of books announcing the age of a "new diplomacy" document the arrival *en force* of an array of new actors on the diplomatic stage.[17] Various non-state actors, from NGOs to celebrities, are analyzed as new actors and forces in world politics.[18] Essentially, the new diplomacy literature describes the effects that globalization is having on the diplomatic crowd. It usefully shows how the social and political fabric of diplomats is evolving. If globalization means the gradual de-territorialization of some social relations and politics,[19] then the

16 Paul Sharp, "Who Needs Diplomats? The Problems of Diplomatic Representation," *International Journal*, 52(4), 1997, 609–632; Andrew F. Cooper, "Beyond Representation," *International Journal* 53(1) 1997/1998, 173–178.

17 Andrew F. Cooper, John English, and Ramesh C. Thakur, eds., *Enhancing Global Governance: Towards a New Diplomacy* (New York: United Nations University Press, 2002); Shaun Riordan, *The New Diplomacy* (Cambridge: Polity, 2003); Andrew F. Cooper, Brian Hocking, and William Maley, eds., *Governance and Diplomacy: Worlds Apart?* (New York: Palgrave Macmillan, 2008); Andrew F. Cooper, *Celebrity Diplomacy* (Boulder: Paradigm, 2008).

18 One intriguing aspect of this literature is that it seems not to have been integrated with the parallel literature in IR theory more generally, which showcased the role and power of a range of non-state actors, such as epistemic communities, transnational advocacy networks, and more generally civil society organizations. See, for example, Peter M. Haas, "Knowledge, Power and International Policy Coordination," *International Organization*, 46(1), 1992, 385–387; Margaret Keck and Kathryn Sikkink, *Activists Beyond Borders: Advocacy Networks in International Politics* (Ithaca: Cornell University Press, 1998); Manuel Castells, "The New Public Sphere: Global Civil Society, Communication Networks, and Global Governance," *The Annals of the American Academy of Political and Social Science*, 616(1), 2008, 78–93.

19 Jan Aart Scholte, *Globalization: A Critical Introduction* (New York: Palgrave Macmillan, 2001).

nature and role of the diplomat – whose traditional function precisely is to represent at a distance, that is, to span geographic space – must be changing as well. While we should be careful in stating that "the present international system is on the verge of acquiring the same level of social density that characterized the nation state at the end of the nineteenth century," the depth and scope of cooperation and communication are certainly unprecedented.[20] The global stage, in other words, is becoming home to social and political relations that are more intense and numerous, although the jury is still out as to whether this trend is pointing in the direction of further political integration.[21]

Because of its actor-centric focus, however, the new diplomacy literature tends to engage in "explanation by naming": a set of actors is defined – a transnational advocacy group, say – and these actors are then analyzed with a view to demonstrating their ability to shape policy outcomes and state interests. For instance, Betsill and Corell try to measure how and under what conditions NGOs may influence negotiations over international environmental policy. Finding evidence of such influence, they label it "NGO diplomacy" and posit it as a challenge to traditional interstate diplomacy.[22] When it comes to explaining change in diplomatic practices, we find this perspective of limited use. By hanging the causal story on one set of actors – defined by the analyst – Betsill and Corell say little about the relative significance of other groups and the relationship between different types of actors. It is one thing to demonstrate the newly acquired power of a certain type of actors; it is quite another to account for the process by which they become authoritative or important relative to other and more entrenched actors in controlling and performing certain tasks that were previously the province of diplomats.[23] While non-state actors

20 Bertrand Badie, "The European Challenge to Bismarckian Diplomacy," *International Politics*, 46(5), 2009, 519.

21 For a discussion that introduces a teleological argument around this development, see Alex Wendt, "Why a World State is Inevitable," *European Journal of International Relations*, 9(4), 2003, 491–542.

22 Michelle Betsill and Elizabeth Corell, eds., *NGO Diplomacy: The Influence of Non-governmental Organizations in International Environmental Negotiations* (Cambridge: MIT Press, 2007).

23 On this, see Ole Jacob Sending, *The Politics of Expertise: Competing for Authority in Global Governance* (Ann Arbor: University of Michigan Press, 2015).

are important, they make their influence felt, directly or indirectly, through the medium of state-run diplomacy.

Put differently, even if we find that some non-diplomatic actors are powerful in some sense, that still does not tell us much about the relative significance of traditional diplomats, or about the institutional environment in which diplomats and non-diplomats both operate. More importantly, it is by analyzing in some detail the processes through which some relations are mobilized and appropriated rather than others that we can account for the particular configuration between diplomats and other actors. What, concretely, do these non-diplomatic actors bring to bear to amend, challenge, or extend established diplomatic practices in significant ways? Which elements of diplomatic work do these other actors target or seek to emulate? What is their claim to authority compared to that advanced by diplomatic actors? How does it change diplomatic practice?

The challenge is to avoid the tendency that characterized some of the early work on globalization, where the empirical demonstration of the power of global financial markets or of any particular type of non-state actor was used as an argument for how the sovereign state was being circumvented, undermined, or rendered less powerful under conditions of globalization. More recent contributions to this debate challenge this view, arguing instead that we are seeing a reassemblage of state practices, involving a reconfiguration of the strategies employed by states and non-state actors alike.[24] What these more recent studies have in common is their taking stock of contemporary shifts in practices thanks to a focus on the relations inside a given social configuration.

Instead of focusing solely on new actors, then, this book casts a wider net to locate both traditional and nontraditional diplomatic agents as part of an evolving configuration of social relations. Only through such an analysis can we make good on our promise to explore the relations between diplomats and other actors. It is through these relations that we find instances of cooperation as well as competition as to what

[24] Saskia Sassen, *Global Transformations: Authority, Territory, and Rights* (New York: Columbia University Press, 2007); Rita Abrahamsen and Michael C. Williams, *Security Beyond the State: Private Security in International Politics* (Cambridge: Cambridge University Press, 2010); Iver B. Neumann and Ole Jacob Sending, *Governing the Global Polity: Practice, Rationality, Mentality* (Ann Arbor: University of Michigan Press, 2010).

constitutes diplomatic practice, thereby illuminating how diplomacy is changing (or not) with reference to how purportedly new actors engage diplomats over what to do, how, and by whom. Overall, the picture that we draw shows an intriguing combination of the diplomacy inherited from a state-centric world with various heterodox forms of political intercourse made possible by globalization. In the changing diplomatic landscape, we argue, old and new practices coexist in a mutually constitutive relationship.[25] We chart how the tasks that nontraditional diplomatic actors perform add to and change ways of doing things for diplomats, and how non-diplomatic actors model their operations on the institution of diplomacy. Humanitarian organizations, for example, have "resident representatives" (ResReps) in their core partner countries who perform the same set of tasks as diplomats. And the setup for reporting to humanitarian organizations' headquarters mirrors that traditionally performed by embassy staff. Meanwhile, in multilateral settings such as the World Trade Organization (WTO), one can find "diplomats" for hire from special-purpose law firms for developing countries. As WTO negotiations are highly technical, the skills of generalist diplomats quickly become irrelevant without specialized knowledge. Finally, military officials rely on core diplomatic practices as they build and maintain an infrastructure for war making with other states, but nonetheless they depart from it by bringing to bear their distinct professional backgrounds and assessments of what matters for them.

As new relationships develop between an increasingly heterogeneous cast of diplomatic actors, therefore, the nature and function of diplomacy also evolve. Of course, today's diplomacy, just like yesterday's, remains primarily concerned with the ways in which states deal with the external world. But emerging practices also indicate efforts on the part of states to enroll various non-state actors in their action just as nontraditional agents seek to act globally through the state's diplomatic outreach. Observe, for instance, how foreign ministries have bankrolled historically non-diplomatic practices such as development and disaster relief, and how nontraditional agents use public resources toward their ends. As soon as one scratches a little, in fact, examples

[25] See also Andrew F. Cooper and Vincent Pouliot, "How Much Is Global Governance Changing? The G20 as International Practice," *Cooperation and Conflict* 50(2), 2015.

of new forms of diplomatic relations abound. Globalization and increased interdependencies have caused line ministries to interact directly with their counterparts in other countries, thereby challenging the position of foreign affairs ministries. In multilateral settings, the practice of diplomacy is being reshaped by recent changes in the global distribution of power, often in unexpected ways. NGOs have become more visible in world politics through delegation and indirect rule, thereby opening new state-society interfaces at the global level.

Authority

As we have argued, a relational view treats the identity and attendant resources of actors as inhering in the relations that they have with others – a process in which authority claims play a prominent role.[26] For example, diplomats derive their strength relative to others engaged in global governance not only from representing a particular territorial unit but also from their contacts inside and ability to work with other territorial units. Similarly, economists may have authority over an issue, but the recognition of a position of authority is itself a product of the relationship that economic actors have established between themselves and other actors, notably the market over which they claim jurisdiction. In the same vein, lawyers are authoritative interpreters of the law by virtue of the position so accorded them by the state.

As far as authority is concerned, what sets diplomats apart from other types of actors is not that they exclusively engage in representation, but that they claim – usually with success – jurisdictional control over it. It seems useful here to treat diplomats as the members of a profession – that is, as "professional strangers," as Sharp calls them.[27] From the sociology of professions, we know that professions are defined by efforts to establish and maintain jurisdictional control over certain tasks.[28] Thanks to this insight, it becomes possible to grasp the changing character of diplomacy by asking which tasks are

[26] We focus on authority claims, as opposed to the social fact of authority, to give preeminence to politics in our account. On the notion of authority, see Rodney Bruce Hall, "Moral Authority as a Power Resource," *International Organization*, 51(4), 1997, 591–622.

[27] Sharp, *Diplomatic Theory*, 100, building on Der Derian.

[28] Abbott, The System of Professions; James Faulconbridge and Daniel Muzio, "Professions in a Globalizing World: Towards a Transnational Sociology of the Professions," *International Sociology*, 27(1), 2012, 136–152.

considered central to diplomacy, and which ones are considered more peripheral. For example, line ministries with technical expertise are forging direct links with their regulatory counterparts in other countries, often joined by non-state actors and the staff of international organizations (IOs), to form transnational networks through which negotiations on behalf of states take place, thus undermining the jurisdictional control over some tasks by traditional diplomats. In another illustration, with the current trend toward the legalization of world politics, law has become a central diplomatic resource in its own right, with lawyers providing authoritative interpretations of other actors' room to maneuver. Religious actors are often powerful by virtue of the capacity to mobilize transnational constituencies. Economists, for their part, shape diplomatic practice through claims to expertise that go beyond the technical details of economic governance.

That being said, non-territorially defined authority claims are neither new nor necessarily something that undermines, in and of itself, the position of traditional diplomacy. Authority is a political process made of never-ending symbolic struggles. As much as there is a diffusion of authority and new roles for heterodox diplomatic agents, we are not moving toward a world where diplomats are rendered obsolete.[29] For as long as there is contact between polities, there is diplomacy at work; when the character of the relations between these polities changes, so, too, does diplomatic practice. An example of this is Seabrooke's analysis in this book of the emergence of "private" diplomats for hire, such as Independent Diplomat. Even in a globalizing era, hardly any other group than traditional diplomats perform all of those tasks that are typically associated with diplomacy. For instance, an NGO involved in environmental negotiations or a transnational corporation being involved in setting up global transparency standards can be said to perform some elements of diplomatic practice, but not all of them.[30] Moreover, diplomacy being a deeply institutionalized feature of the global system, it remains significant even when it is being supplanted and changed by new practices and new actors. Indeed, established diplomatic practices – summits, preparatory committees charged with

[29] George Kennan, "Diplomacy without Diplomats?" *Foreign Affairs*, 76(5), 1997, 198–212.

[30] Iver B. Neumann, "Globalization and Diplomacy," in Andrew F. Cooper, Brian Hocking, and William Maley, eds., *Global Governance and Diplomacy* (London: Palgrave, 2008), 15–28.

drafting, and so on – provide the infrastructure for other actors to partake in representation and governing when different polities are involved.

State diplomats are in a powerful position that enables them to draw on and use different types of actors to advance particular interests in different contexts. States now typically include key non-state actors in negotiations when these can offer advice and input, and when they are seen to represent powerful domestic constituencies. By virtue of how the institution of sovereignty sets up states as primary interlocutors – codified in international law and practice – the interesting question is less whether diplomacy is being pressured from the outside than how diplomatic practices are changing over time and how new social configurations develop at the global level. An adequate understanding of evolving diplomacy necessitates a closer look at variation and similarities in the character of the relation between diplomats and the territorially defined unit they represent, on the one hand, and other types of representatives whose constituencies differ in that they are not territorially defined, on the other hand.

If we want to account for changes in diplomatic practice by virtue of the proliferation of actors involved in diplomatic work, the question of how and why different actors do diplomacy must be central. For example, an actor representing a religious community is expected to represent that constituency in a different way than an actor representing a territorial unit, and both will differ from an actor who claims to represent professional expertise. Besides the constituency per se, it is primarily the source of authority that is shifting or, in many cases, deterritorializing. In her analysis of economics as a global profession, for instance, Fourcade shows how economists, while still located within a national professional setting, are able to rely on technical knowledge and language whose universalistic tone makes it possible to claim global jurisdiction.[31] Expertise, which is in fast-increasing demand in contemporary diplomacy, is shifting the principle of representation away from territoriality toward virtual forms of authority grounded in symbolic systems. Note, however, that the distinction between territorial and non-territorial representation often blurs in practice.

[31] Marion Fourcade, "The Construction of a Global Profession: The Transnationalization of Economics," *American Journal of Sociology*, 112(1), 2006, 145–194.

Economists who perform regulatory work with counterparts from other countries make both territorial and non-territorial claims to representation and authority. Conversely, as Hurd demonstrates, state diplomats deploy moral arguments and expert-based legal interpretations produced by non-state actors as they debate whether or not state behavior conforms to international law.

The de-territorialization of diplomatic representation is attributable not only to expertise but also to older symbolic forms embedded in value systems. We have already mentioned the dually territorial and virtual nature of religious constituencies. Here, too, value systems intersect with territoriality. Lynch shows how different loyalties and constituencies intersect to constitute the *sui generis* character of Christian humanitarian organizations. Similarly, the de-territorialized character of representation is seen in the diplomacy – or good offices – functions of the UN Secretary General (SG) as a neutral, cosmopolitan arbiter. This representation is distinct in type and scope because it is performed on behalf of an international organization, with all the symbolic pomp of the international community. This difference stems from the character of the relation between the representative and the constituency: the nature of the constituency that is represented by the SG is in part the UN Charter, for which the SG acts as the highest international civil servant, but it is also in part the member states themselves, whose approval is ultimately necessary for forceful action. Moreover, there is the shored-up moral authority that an SG may be able to build over time.

Similarly, many NGOs advocating on behalf of humankind (e.g., in favor of a right to migrate) also claim an authority that is not territorially bounded. An actor representing Amnesty International is communicating with others, gathering information, and engaging in negotiations in a way that will differ from that of representatives of states or other actors. Amnesty's effort to build and institutionalize its authority as representatives of certain values (human rights) affect both what it does and how: Amnesty is torn between two competing claims to authority – one moral, the other political – and this tension runs through the organization, shaping its identity and mode of operations.[32] There is reason to believe that this dynamic also goes for other actors, but

[32] Stephen Hopgood, *Keepers of the Flame: Inside Amnesty International* (Ithaca: Cornell University Press, 2006).

representatives of states are distinct in this regard by virtue of the institution of sovereignty.

Taken together, the relationships between diplomatic and non-diplomatic actors tell us something significant about how their respective authority is produced and maintained. But the transnationalization of specific professions and the advancement of claimed universal values by advocacy networks are nonetheless parasitic on the practice of diplomacy. To put the matter differently, given the institutionalized features of diplomacy in world politics, it carries a level of institutional authority that can be used by diplomats and non-diplomats alike in furthering specific projects. Barkawi (this volume) shows how the idea of diplomacy as being about peaceful modes of interaction is used to legitimize and couch in a non-offensive language the strategic positioning of military capabilities. Similarly, Hurd is able to recast the workings of international law by observing how states commit to it in an effort to be part of the process of (re)interpreting and developing it. In so doing, Hurd brings out the extent to which law has a level of authority and binds states, but also that diplomacy is a condition of possibility for the law to function in this way by virtue of states offering public reasons for their positions. This dovetails with Mitzen's work on the "forum effects of talk" in world politics, in which the language and practices of diplomacy render possible this form of interaction (see also Chapter 4 in this volume).[33] Diplomatic claims of being in authority, as representative of a polity, must be couched in the language of public reason.

All in all, a relational perspective helps specify, at the analytical level, to what degree and in which ways diplomacy is changing. On today's global stage, social configurations and authority claims appear to be shifting. These evolutions produce significant effects on the larger picture of world politics.

Diplomacy's constitutive effects on world politics

This book builds on the premise that diplomacy is constitutive in that it makes other social processes possible. Diplomacy is not reducible to an epiphenomenon of systemic imperatives, as in neorealism or, to a lesser

[33] Jennifer Mitzen, "Reading Habermas in Anarchy: Multilateral Diplomacy and Global Public Spheres," *American Political Science Review*, 99(3), 2005, 401–417; and *Power in Concert: The Nineteenth Century Origins of Global Governance* (Chicago: University of Chicago Press, 2013).

extent, the English School.[34] Instead, diplomacy is a socially emergent phenomenon and as such it produces effects of its own on world politics. This all-important point is often lost in IR literatures. Sharp rightly observes that IR theories are often systemic in orientation, leaving little room for diplomacy in their causal stories. His aim is to reverse this sorry state of affairs: instead of formulating an IR theory of diplomacy, he develops a diplomatic theory of international relations. By contrast, our objective is not to replace IR theory with a diplomatic one, but rather to bring social theoretical insights to bear on the study of diplomacy, with the aim of identifying how diplomacy is implicated in the making of world politics.

Following Bull, diplomacy is often defined as a core institution of international society. What sets it apart from other institutions is that it is the place where other institutions are acted out and brought to bear – making diplomatic practices the site where these institutions are reproduced and may change over time. To return to our relational argument, a particular political order or institutional arrangement anchored in sovereignty does not regulate the behavior of pre-constituted political actors. Rather, sovereignty is produced and reproduced (and transformed) through changing diplomatic practices, whereby recognition as a competent participant (diplomat) hinges on deploying or enacting some strategies and roles that reproduce the state as a recognized sovereign.[35]

Broadly speaking, we argue that diplomacy is about much more than representation. In today's world, diplomacy is also concerned with governance, understood as a system of rule and control. Theoretically, representation differs from governing in that the former is organized around the idea of advancing the interest of a group, which necessitates communication with others, whereas governing involves changing other actors' behavior to achieve certain objectives. Arguably, imperial diplomacy was always more about governing than representation. Today, this shifting balance takes new forms. As an example, consider the military. There has always been a strong connection between a

[34] Kenneth N. Waltz, *Theory of International Politics* (New York: McGraw-Hill, 1979); Bull, *The Anarchical Society*.

[35] Richard K. Ashley, "Untying the Sovereign State: A Double Reading of the Anarchy Problematique," *Millennium – Journal of International Studies*, 17, June 1988, 227–262; and Emanuel Adler and Vincent Pouliot, "International Practices," *International Theory* 3(1), 1–36.

polity's diplomatic and military capabilities. For example, in the Middle Ages, diplomats were frequently tucked away in the train of both sides when the military went into battle, only to emerge to begin negotiations when the new status quo had been decided on the battlefield.[36] Alternatively, diplomatic threats have implicitly and explicitly hovered in the background of diplomatic negotiations. If we consider the situation on the ground in places such as Afghanistan today, however, the soldier and the diplomat are working in tandem, both partaking in governing and deploying distinct claims to authority by virtue of what they represent. Barkawi's chapter shows how military-to-military relations between states – legitimated in the language of diplomatic representation – are very much about governing and the constitution of hegemonic relations. Indeed, he demonstrates how the system of diplomatic representation in other states offers a territorial access point and thus gives form to the "advice and support" that has been central to US imperial governance after World War II.

The general point here is that such transnational links between professionals – representing the state or other forms of constituency – are assuming an institutionalized form.[37] When states meet in the World Health Organization (WHO) or the International Monetary Fund (IMF), representatives from line ministries (i.e., health and finance), whose claim to authority is linked both to the territorial unit being governed and to the specific expertise over the issue-area in question, typically dominate delegations. We interpret this trend as having to do with governing becoming a central frame of reference for representation and thus for traditional diplomatic work. A case in point is the degree to which the performance of the task of representation in the making of new international law or in setting up new financial regulations necessitates in-depth technical expertise. As such, a condition of being recognized as a competent interlocutor qua sovereign state is to be able to engage in governing – to be an actor that can and will engage in efforts to act on transnational issues and therefore to invest diplomatic practices with substantive expertise that take us beyond representation.

[36] Donald E. Queller, *The Office of Ambassador in the Middle Ages* (Princeton, NJ: Princeton University Press, 1967).

[37] Anne-Marie Slaughter, *A New World Order: Government Networks and the Disaggregated State* (Princeton, NJ: Princeton University Press, 2004).

If governing becomes progressively more important in the realm between and beyond borders, then not only will diplomats have to bring skills in representation to bear on the task of governing, but their effectiveness as diplomats will also depend to a large degree on their ability to work with and through other actors. And to the extent that diplomacy is constitutive of international society and that diplomats produce, through the practice of diplomacy, an international system that would otherwise be different, then it is important to pinpoint and account for how diplomatic practice may change.[38] While state actors remain in a powerful position with regard to governing, arguably a growing number of actors – those claiming to represent expertise, values, civil society, or affected populations – are also becoming more important. This evolution is largely due to the fact that governing is concerned with acting on an external social reality, the contents of which must be assessed and known to be ruled and controlled effectively.

Taking diplomacy's constitutive effects seriously would significantly improve our understanding of global governance. It is quite remarkable how diplomacy has been largely neglected in the literature so far. In what is arguably the most comprehensive review to date, Avant, Finnemore, and Sell advance (as we do here) a relational view, seeing those involved in global governance as defined by the relations of authority forged between "global governors" and their constituencies.[39] However, missing from their account is a sustained treatment of the distinctive features of diplomacy as an institutionalized practice within which (and on which) these governors operate. Broadly understood, diplomacy is the infrastructure of global governance, and as such, both levels are likely to evolve hand in hand.

Claims that non-state actors are powerful actors are a mainstay in global governance studies, and they are typically based on accounts that focus on a particular type of actor, such as advocacy groups, civil society organizations, or expert groups.[40] In singling out one set of actors and hanging the causal story on their doings, analysts of non-state actors have marginalized the practice of diplomacy and the actions of diplomats in these processes. This also holds, we believe,

[38] Sharp, *Diplomatic Theory*, 11, 105–107.

[39] Deborah Avant, Martha Finnemore, and Susan Sell, eds., *Who Governs the Globe?* (Cambridge: Cambridge University Press, 2010).

[40] For example, Keck and Sikkink, *Activists beyond Borders*.

for accounts that are chiefly concerned with measuring the relative significance of state and non-state actors, as they see the relationship between these actors as a zero-sum game. We opt for a different strategy, asking instead how changes in the cast of actors involved affect diplomatic practice, and how, in turn, diplomatic practice itself conditions and structures non-state actors' strategies. Both Lynch's and Sending's contributions suggest that diplomatic practices are central structuring sites for the actions of others, such as humanitarian and development actors engaged in global governance. At the same time, as diplomats are increasingly engaged in representation in the context of global governance efforts, distinct relations of dependence and information sharing are being developed between diplomats and other actors.

Diplomacy's role in the making and remaking of world politics also has implications for the study of globalization. If diplomacy is about mediation between the inside and the outside of distinct polities, and the character and relationship between these polities change so that the boundaries between them become blurred, then changes in diplomatic practices are likely to impact globalization, and reciprocally. Lynch's contribution makes the case that diplomacy is constitutive of the very boundaries between war and politics, since diplomacy is always implied in the processes by which decisions are made to use or not use force and to give public reasons for actions taken. Similarly, Seabrooke's argument is in part that the rise of consultants can be attributed to a distinct style on the part of diplomats that the latter have to appropriate to succeed in an emerging market where diplomats are for hire. Neumann's analysis of how small and medium powers increasingly invest in systems maintenance suggests that this new practice may be a response to the rise of new great powers. Mitzen similarly identifies the international order as possibly having an internal source in the practice of diplomacy understood as the production of international public power and collective intentionality. In the end, we need not go all ontological to see why it makes sense to adopt a relational position in analyzing how diplomacy may be changing. We agree with Wight that diplomacy is the master institution of international relations.[41] It is by studying diplomatic practice that we come closest to the actions that accumulate to make up the international system.

[41] Martin Wight (ed. Hedley Bull), *Systems of States* (Leicester: Leicester University Press, 1977).

If, as we argue, diplomacy constitutes world politics, then IR theorists ignore it at their peril. An interesting illustration is the current debate on the rise of a new world order, which centers on the nature of power, the role and character of balancing, and the sources of strength of great powers, notably the United States and China.[42] What is the role of diplomacy in this transformation? A key issue here is whether to treat the anarchical features of world politics as defining for the analysis of the role of diplomacy. Our view (echoed by Mitzen in her chapter) is that diplomacy produces effects that mitigate the impact of the lack of central authority, and as such the practice will be determinant in shaping coming transformations. The reversed question is equally important: how will diplomacy change in response to the new distribution of power? At one extreme is the view that diplomacy is so stable and institutionalized – an unmoved mediator – that it does not change in the face of a transforming international environment. The opposite view, to which we adhere, is that diplomacy reflects the underlying distribution of power, leading us to expect changes in diplomatic practice when the distribution of power shifts.

Indeed, the constitutive relationship between diplomacy and world politics works both ways: diplomacy produces global effects beyond representation, but it is also significantly shaped by the evolution of governance structures and modes. That is why a focus on social configurations is so important. As Pouliot argues in his contribution, for instance, the rise and spread of multilateral governance in recent decades has enabled, but also constrained, the diplomatic practices of permanent representatives at international organizations. Krieger, Callahan Souma and Nexon, on their part, document how bureaucratic practices at the Pentagon transform everyday diplomacy in Washington. There is an interesting recursive loop between what diplomacy constitutes, in world politics, and how it is also constituted by higher-order phenomena.

The substantive chapters in this book document in detail how – that is, through what social processes – diplomacy constitutes a number of key facets of contemporary world politics. Hurd shows how diplomacy provides justificatory resources for states' foreign policies, thereby

[42] Stephen G. Brooks and William C. Wohlforth, *World out of Balance: International Relations and the Challenge of American Primacy* (Princeton, NJ: Princeton University Press, 2008); Charles Kupchan, *No One's World: The West, the Rising Rest and the Coming Global Turn* (Oxford: Oxford University Press, 2012).

creating the normative structure of international law. Seabrooke theorizes "epistemic arbitrage" as the key mechanism by which diplomacy evolves in response to larger changes in management practices. Pouliot identifies the distinctive relational features of permanent representation, such as a clique structure and internal clustering, as constitutive of the peculiar logic of multilateral diplomacy. Barkawi focuses on military-to-military relations, which often run parallel to diplomacy, to explain the making of North-South hierarchies. Krieger, Callahan Souma, and Nexon investigate how bureaucratic practices at the Pentagon transform the nature of the hegemon's foreign relations. Lynch looks into how ethical concerns, once built into diplomatic practices, mediate but also transform the tension between the universal and the particular in global politics. Neumann uses the diplomacy of small, status quo–oriented countries to explain larger dynamics of order and systems maintenance. Mitzen theorizes the ways in which diplomacy, because it involves collective problem solving, generates a structure of "public power" that alters the nature of international commitments. Finally, Sending studies the complex relationship between diplomats and humanitarians and sheds light on how they both trade practices and how the configuration of what constitutes diplomacy and humanitarianism is itself a highly political question.

At a more general level, a number of particular features of diplomacy help explain why and how it participates in the making and remaking of world politics. First, diplomacy is a communicative channel. It provides a frame for meaning making through which others' views may be taken into account. In its modern form at least, diplomacy rests on a commitment to continue talking and to keep lines of communication open even in conflict situations. In practical terms, we see this process on display when difficult negotiations break down and headlines tell us that "diplomacy failed." Conversely, we hear calls for giving diplomacy a chance if there is a risk of war and about the importance of "shuttle diplomacy" to avert international crises. In more theoretical terms, diplomacy is where the logic of recognition is most clearly put into the system: sovereignty depends on recognition from others.[43] When diplomats engage in meaning making, whether through cables to the home office or speeches to diplomatic peers in multilateral settings, they continually assess other states' views and

[43] Wendt, "Why a World State Is Inevitable."

likely courses of action. In this interpretation, the "other" is not an antithesis against which one's own identity and interests are formed, but an entity that becomes part of how states reflect on and formulate their identities and their interests. This process is clearly on display in the contributions by Mitzen, Hurd, and Neumann, which show that diplomacy thrives on the inclusion of the other as a subject with agency rather than an object to be acted on. For Mitzen, this is based on the identification of a *Grundnorm* in international politics that can be found in different historical periods of a premium on, and expectation that, other states follow through on their commitment. Hurd, for his part, demonstrates that international law is constituted by states engaging in the diplomatic practice of reason giving as a tool to shape the application and interpretation of international law. And Neumann shows how not only great powers, but also some small states take the whole (the system) as their frame of reference as they think through what their interests are. In all these cases, the practice of diplomacy is central as the actors in question think from and with diplomacy as they reflect on, negotiate, and advance their interests vis-à-vis those of others.

Second, diplomacy reduces transaction costs, with order-producing effects. In his seminal book on interdependence and international cooperation, Keohane argued, based on rational choice theory, that international regimes (and organizations) are created because they functionally reduce transaction costs. We would submit, however, that without the active force of diplomacy, regimes would hardly be enough to shape international cooperation on their own. Acknowledging diplomacy's role here also helps solve a question raised by Keohane's argument, about what enabled sustained international cooperation – even collective problem solving – prior to the advent of modern-day international organizations.[44] If anything, Mitzen's argument about the Concert of Europe suggests that beyond functional efficiency, other mechanisms are at work generating trust and joint action that cannot be reduced to institutional features. As Pouliot notes, multilateral diplomacy has become an end in itself with key constitutive effects for the ordering

44 Robert O. Keohane, *After Hegemony: Cooperation and Discord in the World Political Economy* (Princeton, NJ: Princeton University Press, 1984). See also Brian Rathbun, *Trust in International Cooperation: International Security Institutions, Domestic Politics and American Multilateralism* (Cambridge: Cambridge University Press, 2012).

of world politics, including mutually recognizable patterns of action and problem solving.[45]

Third, diplomacy provides a permanent infrastructure stretching beyond state boundaries. Diplomats are physically present in most capitals of UN member states to maintain close knowledge of recipient countries and steady contact. This infrastructure helps explain how and why diplomacy is constitutive of world politics. For example, Barkawi argues that the American imperial form of governance during the Cold War was made possible by diplomacy, in two distinct ways. First, diplomacy was (and is) central to the legitimation of military presence in subordinate states, grounding forms of rule under "advice and support" with reference to diplomatic representation among sovereign equal states, as stated in the 1961 Vienna Convention on Diplomatic Relations. Second, diplomacy more fundamentally enabled a vast presence of US citizens, with diplomatic immunity, on other states' territory. As Sending also shows in his chapter, the system of representation on other states' territory forms the default structure from which non-diplomatic actors also operate. Indeed, diplomacy is arguably central not only to efforts to govern beyond the state but also in reproducing and maintaining the boundary of the state vis-à-vis the market and society more generally. In this vein, Seabrooke shows how diplomatic practices are central to the continual reproduction of statehood vis-à-vis other actors – it is the practice par excellence through which the inside/outside boundary is continually drawn. For Hurd, diplomacy is productive of international law, as it is the practice through which states commit to yet retain the right to exercise judgment and advance their particular interests. Finally, Lynch demonstrates how diplomacy is not only about the mediation between the universal and the particular but also very much the key mechanism through which war is differentiated from politics.

In the limited framework of this introduction, our exploration of diplomacy's constitutive effects on world politics can only be suggestive. The real substantiation comes in the rest of the book, where contributors were challenged to specify the processes by which (changing) diplomatic practices partake in the making of global dynamics. Their case studies

[45] Vincent Pouliot, "Multilateralism as an End in Itself," *International Studies Perspectives*, 12(1), 2011, 18–26.

demonstrate why the IR discipline needs to take diplomacy much more seriously than it has in recent times.

Plan of the book

The chapters in Part I focus on the relationship between diplomacy and fundamental international institutions of law, war, and multilateralism. In Chapter 1, Hurd offers a novel interpretation of the role and functioning of international law by linking it explicitly to states' diplomatic practice. For Hurd, states use international law to justify and explain their behaviors and interests vis-à-vis other states. The practice through which this process of explaining and justifying state behavior takes place is that of diplomacy. Hurd demonstrates that while there is a shared commitment to the idea of the international rule of law, states exploit the meaning of legal rules to bring their interpretations into conformity with state behavior. Since there is no external standard to fix the meaning of law, international law evolves and expands – but is never fixed – through diplomatic practice. In adopting an explicitly relational perspective on the practice of international law and the practice of diplomacy, Hurd shows how our ability to understand and account for both is considerably improved.

In Chapter 2, Barkawi looks at an ignored but essential dimension of diplomacy: how the symbols and practices of diplomacy enable the successful presentation of imperial forms of rule as mere diplomatic relations between formally equal sovereigns. The chapter draws on a rich array of historical and present-day examples to not only question the formal legal – and diplomatic – categories of war and peace but also to establish what Barkawi refers to as a sociologically informed, empirical study of the "international administration of war" in which diplomacy plays a key part. In this analysis, scholars of world politics are also to be faulted for reproducing a distinction between war and peace, and diplomacy as a political project "short of war." Here, then, diplomacy constitutes an infrastructure that both practically (through embassies and international legal rules for diplomatic presence) and symbolically (through the ideal of peaceful relations and representation) makes possible and legitimizes war and imperial forms of governing.

In Chapter 3, Pouliot argues that multilateral diplomacy has become a key vehicle of global governance. In the twenty-first century, the practice of permanent representation to international organizations is not only increasingly prevalent but also significant, because its peculiar morphology and practical rules push multilateralism beyond strict representation toward a logic of governing. The chapter analyzes how the network form of permanent representation, including its clique shape and clustered structure, enables distinctive rules of the game, from esprit de corps to chain reactions through pecking orders. The local and partly autonomous dynamics of permanent representation mean that the everyday practice of multilateral diplomacy is deeply constitutive – as opposed to merely reflective – of global governance and state interests.

The chapters in Part II focus on the relationship between diplomacy and international cooperation. In Chapter 4, Mitzen discusses the difference between diplomacy as representation and diplomacy as governing. While the former is organized around estrangement, the latter is organized around obligation. Put differently, governing, which is necessarily performed "together," presumes the production of international public power, which in turn hails from states jointly committing to doing something together. Diplomacy here emerges in a qualitatively new and hitherto underappreciated form, exhibiting collective intentionality. Mitzen makes the important point that collective intentionality is not directed toward substantive values but toward a thinner "normative value of action itself," which helps us understand, in a significantly new way, how the authority to govern beyond the state is established and advanced through the practice of diplomacy.

In Chapter 5, Neumann looks at diplomacy through a functional lens – diplomacy as a response to systemic requirements – to offer a novel interpretation of an important transformation in international cooperation. Conventional wisdom holds that great powers invest in so-called systems maintenance, which they value in order to exert control over that system, but also – the argument goes – for the order and stability provided to smaller states. By contrast, Neumann analyzes the increase in peace and reconciliation efforts by smaller states and non-state actors and links their investment in this area to systems maintenance. The contents of these tasks not only push diplomacy beyond representation toward governance, but their performance also amounts to a considerable maturing of international anarchy.

In Chapter 6, Lynch unearths how religious (particularly Christian) actors continue to shape modern diplomacy. She compares two periods (the 1930s and 1940s versus the 1990s to this day) to demonstrate that although the configurations of state and non-state actors were different, the universalist pretensions of Christian actors have been central in shaping both diplomatic practice (such as multilateralism) and direct forms of governance (such as humanitarian relief and peace building). In so doing, Lynch also captures how the universalist drive of many Christian actors, though often presented in an image of secularized rights, generates tensions as it confronts a pluralist religious and moral landscape in which they seek to govern directly.

Part III is focused on diplomacy as a contested terrain, where new practices, and also new actors, are forged out of both collaborative and competitive relations between diplomatic actors and others. In Chapter 7, Seabrooke analyzes a set of actors that fills voids between transnational and international networks. Observing that there is a wide array of tasks that sit at the interstices of the private and the public, Seabrooke demonstrates how relations between economic profit, humanitarian principles, and the traditional world of diplomacy offer fertile ground for the conduct of diplomacy by a distinct breed of actors, whose hallmark is an ability to draw on and wield together skills and expertise from different social spaces. Economic consultancies, the chapter shows, can engage in "epistemic arbitrage" to successfully claim authority over what type of professional approach is appropriate to deal with distinct problems that are part of or have direct bearing on diplomats' work. Empirically, Seabrooke discusses the role of Independent Diplomat and the consultancy firm STATT to demonstrate how these organizations practice a form of diplomacy wedding management expertise and economic analysis related to humanitarian concerns.

In Chapter 8, Krieger, Callahan Souma, and Nexon draw on their respective backgrounds from the US Air Force, US Navy, and the Department of Defense to compare military diplomacy with other, more conventional diplomatic practices. At the heart of the analysis is how the different strands of the US military not only have distinctive ways of engaging others but also – as a result of a different professional background – they use different avenues for wielding power. Citing the many mechanisms through which US military actors engage foreign counterparts – including training of aviators at US flight schools, military education, and permanent presence of US command structures on foreign soil – they show the heterogeneity of what amounts to diplomacy. But they also note that what counts as diplomacy for these actors is highly variable, suggesting that for military practitioners, diplomatic work may be less valued precisely because it is of little use or relevance.

In Chapter 9, Sending explores the relationship between humanitarian actors and diplomats by comparing their relationship in institutional and practical terms. He argues that while diplomacy is defined by a thin culture (held together by the fact that states are particular and different), humanitarian action is defined by a thick culture (held together by shared substantive values). Sending explores how diplomacy forms an infrastructure that shapes what non-state actors are and what they do, as when they negotiate with states on behalf of suffering individuals, or when they collect and use information to advance particular interests. Finally, he explores how diplomacy reproduces states as naturalized venues for political action and mobilization, even when – as in humanitarian crises – the very capacity of states as sovereign agents is in question.

In her concluding chapter, Adler-Nissen explores the sources of the epistemic gap between the theory and practice of diplomacy. While IR scholarship tends to view diplomacy in substantialist terms – pre-formed states bumping into one another, so to speak – practitioners cling to the relational notion that states are made and remade in and through the practice of diplomacy. By adopting a relational perspective too, the chapters in this volume narrow the gap between theory and practice: the development, consolidation, and weakening of states make sense only in terms of continuous processes of diplomatic relations. As a practice, diplomacy is all about social entanglement and a perpetual exchange of views. Using the grease-in-the-wheel analogy, Adler-Nissen explains that diplomacy is more than keeping the conversation going; it is also about managing relations and, thus, shaping the process of world politics. She concludes by raising a few limitations of a relational approach to diplomatic practice, including the reliance on the native point of view to unearth power relations on the world stage.

PART I

Making of international institutions

1 International law and the politics of diplomacy

IAN HURD

Diplomacy is the social practice by which states interact with other states. It takes place in the medium of international law as states use international law to explain and justify their policies to other states and other audiences and to understand them themselves. It is clear to see that in practice, states invoke law to strengthen their positions relative to other states by constructing justifications that situate their policies and preferences as consistent with international laws and norms. This is a ubiquitous practice in contemporary international politics. It can also be used to inform a theory of diplomacy as the intersection of international law and international politics.

This chapter advances two substantive points about diplomacy: first, that it is a social practice of states, and second, that the practice consists of reconciling state behavior with international law. The first section explains what is entailed in seeing diplomacy both as a practice and as state centric, including the dynamic between state officials and "new actors" in diplomacy such as activists, media, and non-state actors. The second section examines diplomacy's connection to compliance, contestation, and the rule of law in world politics. Diplomacy makes state behavior sensible by explaining it in terms of existing international legal forms. It is therefore productive of foreign policy and international law. The contemporary international order rests on a widely shared commitment to the international rule of law – the belief that the primary virtue of states and the main machinery of international stability depend on compliance with international law.[1] Public diplomacy operates in the

For comments on earlier versions of this article, I am grateful to Holger Niemann, Peter Spiro, the anonymous reviewers, and the editors of this volume. I also wish to thank the participants at workshops at McGill University (2010) and the New School for Social Research (2012) where this work was discussed.

[1] For instance, Anne-Marie Slaughter and Kal Raustiala, "International Law, International Relations and Compliance," in Walter Carlsnaes, Thomas Risse, and Beth Simmons, eds., *Handbook of International Relations* (Thousand Oaks, CA: Sage, 2002).

context of this commitment. States strive to be seen as acting consistently with their legal obligations, and public diplomacy is to substantiate and defend that position. In doing so, however, it is shaped by the tendency for states to see international rules as naturally consistent with their own interests and desires. As a result, competing claims about compliance are standard fare, and they cannot be resolved by recourse to either legal formalism or deliberative procedures. I end the chapter by presenting implications for the philosophy of international law, for the concepts of compliance and noncompliance, and for the agent-structure debate in international theory.

The chapter also contributes to contemporary debates about the relationship between international law and international politics, a topic that is receiving a good deal of attention.[2] First, it suggests that international law provides the resources with which states talk about and understand their behavior, and these resources are reinforced and changed in the process. The power of international law lies in its utility to states for explaining their actions and interests. This view of international law is at odds with the philosophy of international law shared by Hobbesian, positivist, and Kantian traditions, as these all presume that legal rules exist independently of the interests and behavior of agents. Instead, I suggest that the practice of diplomacy is the *via media* in the mutual constitution of international law and foreign policy – the "law-in-use" meaning of international legal rules arises from how it is invoked in the diplomacy of states.[3] Second, it implies that disagreements over the interpretation of international law are inherent in the legal project itself. States are naturally inclined to provide legal interpretations that serve their own interests, and as these will conflict the process leads to divergence rather than coherence in the law. The meaning of compliance is up for debate and is not resolved by legalized argumentation.

[2] For instance, Emilie Hafner-Burton, David G. Victor, and Yonatan Lupu, "Political Science Research on International Law: The State of the Field," *American Journal of International Law*, 106(1), 2012, 47–97. Gregory Shaffer and Tom Ginsburg, "The Empirical Turn in International Legal Scholarship," *American Journal of International Law*, 106(1), 2012, 1–46. Also Jeffrey Dunoff and Mark A. Pollack, eds., *Interdisciplinary Perspectives on International Law and International Relations: The State of the Art* (Cambridge: Cambridge University Press, 2013).

[3] See also Ingo Venzke, "Is Interpretation in International Law a Game?" in Andrea Bianchi, Daniel Peat, and Matthew Windsor, eds., *Interpretation in International Law* (Oxford: Oxford University Press, 2015).

Diplomacy generates competing opinions about the content of compliance and noncompliance with international law.[4] The process of diplomatic interaction does not necessarily increase consensus, and its success cannot be measured in its contribution to public order or avoiding violence. Finally, this view sees diplomacy as a process of exchange between agents (states and others) and structures (international legal resources) in international relations. Studying the practice of diplomacy provides an example of how the interactive process between agents and structures can be modeled for international relations theory.

This approach to diplomacy draws on more conventional models but charts a distinct conceptual route through the practice. One traditional approach understands diplomacy primarily as a mechanism for reconciling (or failing to reconcile) the clashing interests of states (usually powerful states): for instance, when Germany wanted to take over Czechoslovakia in the 1930s, the various European powers sent their diplomats to Berlin to negotiate with Hitler's government; the result was an agreement that allowed Germany to annex the Sudetenland – a classic episode of diplomacy.[5] Similarly, Russia's annexation of Crimea in 2014 was widely reported as a "failure" to bridge states' differences through diplomacy.[6] This narrative assumes that diplomacy exists when representatives of the state carry instructions and interests from home and discover where, if at all, these interests overlap.[7] Diplomacy in this view is a function of interests, bargaining space, and representation – what Eyffinger calls "the juggling and balancing of the competing interests of these state-champions of autonomy."[8] Relative state power

[4] Ian Hurd, "The International Rule of Law: Law and the Limits of Politics," *Ethics and International Affairs*, 28(1), 2014, 39–51.

[5] Frank McDonough, *Hitler, Chamberlain and Appeasement* (Cambridge: Cambridge University Press, 2002). This also fits how many in IR treat diplomatic encounters, for instance, Lloyd Gruber, *Ruling the World: Power Politics and the Rise of Supranational Institutions* (Princeton, NJ: Princeton University Press, 2000).

[6] For instance, "Ukraine Crisis: Diplomacy Fails to Yield Result as Russia Stays Put in Crimea," *The Guardian*, March 5, 2014, www.theguardian.com/world/2014/mar/05/ukraine-crisis-russia-nato-talks-live, accessed May 21, 2014.

[7] This is the model clearly explained and thoroughly critiqued in Carne Ross, *Independent Diplomat: Dispatches from an Unaccountable Elite* (Ithaca, NY: Cornell University Press, 2007).

[8] Arthur Eyffinger, "Diplomacy," in Bardo Fassbender and Anne Peters, eds., *The Oxford Handbook of the History of International Law* (Oxford: Oxford University Press, 2012), 813.

mixes with diplomatic skill to determine where within the win-set the outcome rests. An alternative tradition of scholarship sees diplomacy as a function of discourse and argumentation – that is, as a process of communicative action. In this view, diplomacy involves parties using a common language to exchange competing interpretations of the situation;[9] a filtering device, which might be public reason,[10] an epistemic community,[11] internal consistency, or something else, selects for the better argument.[12] State interests might change in the course of argumentation, and the outcome might be unimaginable at the outset. The end result is that the parties come to a shared understanding around one interpretation, and this both settles the dispute and invests a new legal-political element into the discursive context for public order into the future.

I take a different starting point from both these approaches: I begin from the need of states to give meaning to their actions and those of others, which I see as a necessary implication of the constructivist insight that states and their actions are socially constructed. The meaning of state acts is neither self-evident nor fixed by material conditions; thus, actors are always involved in the process of interpreting and constructing their interests, their relations, and their ideas about the interests and relations of other actors. Diplomacy takes place as states (and other actors) invoke ideas and concepts to explain their needs and their actions to other states. International law provides a ready and socially legitimated pool of such ideas and concepts – these include ideas and rules around sovereignty, intervention, self-defense, humanitarian rescue, self-determination, and much more. Legal resources are useful, and powerful, instruments in the process of "sensemaking" for states.[13] The practice of making sense of the world through legal categories presumes both argumentation and competing interests; so as a scholarly attitude it implies both of the more conventional

9 Dino Kristiotis, "The Power of International Law as Language," *California Western Law Review*, 34, 1998.

10 For example, John Rawls, *Political Liberalism* (New York: Columbia University Press, 1996).

11 Ian Johnstone, *The Power of Deliberation: International Law, Politics and Organization* (Oxford: Oxford University Press, 2011).

12 Thomas Risse, "'Let's Argue!' Communicative Action in World Politics," *International Organization*, 54(1), 2000, 1–39.

13 On sensemaking, see the classic Karl E. Weick, *Sensemaking in Organizations* (Thousand Oaks, CA: Sage, 1995).

approaches to diplomacy mentioned earlier. It is by reference to international legal rules and categories that states understand, explain, and justify their actions and policies to themselves and others. The process does not necessarily lead to agreement over either how the issue will be resolved or how it will be understood, but it consumes, produces, and is limited by international legal resources.

Diplomacy as a practice

The interaction among sovereign states inevitably produces diplomacy, that is, the dialogue of states talking to states about the business of states. This is the "infrastructure of world politics,"[14] and it is made necessary by what Paul Sharp calls the "relations of separateness" that define sovereign states.[15] Diplomacy is a subset of these dialogues, where the broader set also includes private negotiations and secret interactions. Negotiation involves trading interests toward an agreement, where reaching a point of agreement is essential to moving forward on a common project.[16] It requires several actors in pursuit of their private interests where coordination with the other(s) carries the possibility of a greater payoff than does independent action. Secret interactions are defined by the state's failure to provide a public justification for its action – the public justification being the crucial component of diplomacy. The absence of a public justification may have many reasons, one being that the state finds itself outside the bounds of the available resources of justification, that is, outside of existing international law. In studying diplomacy, I am interested in the pattern of public justification of state policy or action, undertaken by leaders, diplomats, and other government officials as well as by the professional staffs of foreign offices and other bureaus. Non-state actors participate in these processes as well.

Diplomacy is a social practice. It is a form of interaction among social actors that is framed by the existing social structures of rules, norms, and habits, and that is in turn productive of these structures.

14 Ole Jacob Sending, Vincent Pouliot, and Iver B. Neumann, "Introduction," this volume.

15 Paul Sharp, *Diplomatic Theory of International Relations* (Cambridge: Cambridge University Press, 2009), 84.

16 Vincent Pouliot, "Multilateral Diplomacy," *International Journal*, Summer 2011.

These rules define and constrain the practice of diplomacy, and they are in turn reproduced and changed in the course of being deployed or invoked. The new literature on practice in international relations (IR) is unified around the idea that there exists "a sociality that always interconnects, constrains, and enables the 'particles' of social life throughout their motion."[17] This insight can lead in many directions. For my purposes, states are the "particles," and I focus on the macro effects of their motion in relation to international law, that is, on the interaction between states around and through international law, including the reproduction of law by means of those interactions.

The practice of diplomacy is defined by three elements: it is social, it is state centric, and it uses and produces the legal resources of the international system. The following section outlines these aspects of the formal system of diplomacy, and the subsequent section addresses its substantive content in relation to international law.

Social component of diplomacy

Diplomacy is, first of all, a social activity. It connects a public language to the business of the state, giving meaning, reasons, and explanations for state action. It is embedded in a social context of reasons, rules, and meanings that exists before the interaction.[18] The primary component of the contemporary legalized international order is the notion of an international rule of law in which states are expected to abide by the legal commitments that they take on. Through treaties, custom, and other mechanisms, the content of these commitments might be subject to competing interpretations, but the underlying idea of the rule of law and the importance of compliance are universally espoused and are presented as morally, legally, and politically good by states and publicists.[19] The pervasiveness of the rule-of-law ideology in world politics is evident in the absence of critical contestation over it and in the degree to which compliance with international obligations is

[17] Theodore R. Schatzki, *Social Practices: A Wittgensteinian Approach to Human Activity and the Social* (Cambridge: Cambridge University Press, 1996), 17. For international politics, see Emmanuel Adler and Vincent Pouliot, eds., *International Practices* (Cambridge: Cambridge University Press, 2011).

[18] Sending, Pouliot, and Neumann, "Introduction," this volume.

[19] I do not attempt to defend this view of international order fully here. For suggestions in this direction, see Hurd, "The International Rule of Law."

identified as the solution to a wide range of political problems – from human rights abuses to international conflict to economic development.[20] The presumption of its inherently progressive character is on display in the long tradition of international legal promotion by scholars and activists.[21]

Diplomacy puts these resources to work to explain, justify, or change the actions of the state. Frederick Schauer describes giving reasons for behavior in society as "the practice of engaging in the linguistic act of providing a reason to justify what we do or what we decide."[22] These reasons make action meaningful to the self, and potentially to others. Public reasons are among what Allen Buchanan calls the "epistemic requirements for justified action."[23] They are conceptually essential to action: agents cannot operate without the resources with which to explain and understand their actions. Diplomacy is the international variant of this activity. It draws on international rules, norms, and concepts to construct state action that is meaningful to the actor and its audience.

It is my contention that today the language of legality dominates the field of interstate discourse and thus that law constitutes the practice of

20 On the international rule of law as an ideology and practice, see Simon Chesterman, "An International Rule of Law?" *American Journal of Comparative Law*, 56, 2008, 331–361. Shirley V. Scott, "International Law as Ideology: Theorising the Relationship between International Law and International Politics," *European Journal of International Law*, 5, 1994, 313–325.

21 Among recent works, see Ruti G. Teitel, *Humanity's Law* (Oxford: Oxford University Press, 2011). The work of Martti Koskenniemi puts this into historical perspective, showing its limits and its politics. See inter alia *From Apology to Utopia: The Structure of International Legal Argument* (Cambridge: Cambridge University Press, 2006), and "A History of International Law Histories," in Fassbender and Peters, eds., *Oxford Handbook of the History of International Law*. More generally on the political implications of legal frames, see Judith N. Shklar, *Legalism: Law, Morals, and Political Trials* (Cambridge, MA: Harvard University Press, 1964/1986).

22 Frederick Schauer, "Giving Reasons," *Stanford Law Review*, 47, 1995, 633–659, at 634. For international organizations and law, see Simon Chesterman, "Who Needs Rules? The Prospects of a Rules-Based International System," discussion paper for the Institute of International Law and Justice, New York University, 2006.

23 Allen Buchanan, *Justice, Legitimacy, and Self-Determination: Moral Foundations for International Law* (Oxford: Oxford University Press, 2007), cited in Henry Shue and David Rodin, *Preemption: Military Action and Moral Justification* (Oxford: Oxford University Press, 2007), 21.

diplomacy. This was not always the case – the legitimating discourse for state affairs has not always been the discourse of law and legality. I do not examine here how this came to pass, but among historians of international politics, the growth of legalization is the subject of increasing study. Several scholars chart the behavioral manifestations of this process, including the growth in formal international organizations with explicit legal personality or with a mandate to adjudicate disputes through law;[24] others account for the intellectual foundations on which these institutions rest – specifically, the historical developments that bring us to a generalized belief that legal institutions are the natural, appropriate, or expeditious means to accomplish international relations.[25] Law and interests are today necessarily connected through the process of diplomacy.

The public, social quality of diplomacy arises because the resources for making these justifications come from the wider social setting in which the actor finds itself, from the legal concepts and rules that make up the corpus of international legal argument. These are the raw materials of state policy that the state uses to suggest, for example, that its use of force is an instance of humanitarianism rather than imperialism,[26] that it is expropriating foreign assets for security reasons rather than to enrich the state,[27] or that its aerial drones are part of a lawful war against a non-state enemy rather than an assault on the

[24] For instance, G. John Ikenberry, *After Victory: Institutions, Strategic Restraint, and the Rebuilding of Order after Major Wars* (Princeton, NJ: Princeton University Press, 2000); Ruti Teitel, *Humanity's Law* (Oxford: Oxford University Press, 2013); Karen J. Alter, *The New Terrain of International Law: Courts, Politics, Rights* (Princeton, NJ: Princeton University Press, 2014).

[25] For instance, Martti Koskenniemi, *The Gentle Civilizer of Nations: The Rise and Fall of International Law 1870–1960* (Cambridge: Cambridge University Press, 2004); Christian Reus-Smit, *The Moral Purpose of the State: Culture, Social Identity, and Institutional Rationality in International Relations* (Princeton, NJ: Princeton University Press, 2009); Mark Mazower, *Governing the World: The History of an Idea, 1815 to the Present* (New York: Penguin, 2013). Further back, see Carl Schmitt, *The Nomos of the Earth in the International Law of Jus Publicum Europaeum* (New York: Telos Press, 2006).

[26] On France in Mali in 2012, see François Hollande's address to the UN General Assembly, September 25, 2012, www.franceonu.org/france-at-the-united-nations/geographic-files/africa/mali-1202/article/mali, accessed February 25, 2013.

[27] See, for instance, the resources on targeted sanctions and international law compiled by Thomas Biersteker and Sue E. Eckert in the UN Targeted Sanctions Consortium at the Watson Institute at Brown University, www.watsoninstitute.org/pub/Watson%20Report%20Update%2012_12.pdf, accessed March 18, 2015.

sovereignty or territory of another country.[28] When France sent its military to Cote D'Ivoire in 2011, it explained itself in relation to the international rules and norms on humanitarian intervention, and especially the actions of the United Nations.[29] The power of this diplomacy came from its ability to distinguish between the image of humanitarian intervention and images of imperialism and neocolonialism. The competing narratives of humanitarian intervention, colonialism, and imperialism are like the "symbolic tokens" described by Zygmunt Bauman – resources deployed by agents that signal membership in groups or ways of thinking.[30] These concepts have content because of how they have been used in the past, sometimes in treaties or legal texts but always in the practice and discourse of states. How they have been used and understood and argued over in the past shapes how they can be used today.

With the use of these tokens, diplomacy involves both internal and external processes in the state. Internal deliberation draws on the conceptual resources that exist in the external legal environment and may be done with an external audience in mind. As the state deliberates within itself about the meaning of its interests, obligations, and behavior, the connection between these interests and their international legality is never irrelevant, and so the power of legal resources to define legality is consequential even without an external audience. The internal effect of international law may be "performatively sufficient" (in the sense defined by Nicholas Onuf from Jürgen Habermas)[31] – it may operate within individual agents to organize their understanding of the world and their place in it, independent of any audience effect. The deliberation within the Bush administration prior to invading Iraq in 2003 shows some of this: a behind-closed-doors consideration of the complexity among interests, rules, and actions, which included a need

[28] Eric Holder, "Remarks to Northwestern University School of Law," March 5, 2012, www.justice.gov/iso/opa/ag/speeches/2012/ag-speech-1203051.html, accessed February 25, 2013.

[29] For instance, "Situation Critique à Abidjan, Laurent Gbagbo se Terre Toujours," *Le Monde*, July 4, 2011, http://bit.ly/OnMqUi, accessed September 11, 2012.

[30] Quote is from Zygmunt Bauman, *Intimations of Postmodernity* (London: Routledge, 1992), 196, discussed in Schatzki, *Social Practices*, 17.

[31] Nicholas Onuf, "Do Rules Say What They Do? From Ordinary Language to International Law," *Harvard International Law Journal*, 26(2), 1985, 385–410, at 406. Also Jutta Brunnée and Stephen J. Toope, "An Interactional Theory of International Legal Obligation," *Legal Studies Research Paper*, University of Toronto, 2011, #08–16.

to reconcile the invasion with a self-understanding of the US government as a peaceful rather than an aggressive actor. The prohibition against aggression under international law forced the war's planners to define their policy as something other than that. The result was a series of attempts to associate the invasion with American self-defense, humanitarian rescue for people in Iraq, and a defense of the UN Security Council's resolutions against the Iraqi government.[32] This narrative, constructed in opposition to the concept of aggression, was then sent out as a quantum of international public discourse where it was widely disparaged by governments, academic lawyers, and others.[33] It failed to convince its external audience, but the urge to construct a legal frame for the invasion was inseparable from the US government's internal deliberations on the war itself.

Rules and norms define the possible actions available to states, and states articulate those rules and norms by making reference to them in their explanations of their interests and behavior. This suggests that international diplomacy bridges between state interests and their external environment in two ways: first, states make use of legal resources and contribute through that use to remaking them, and second, states exercise agency in the construction of their legal positions but within constraints set by the history and politics of their context. The first suggests the mutual constitution of states and rules (or interests and international law), and the second suggests the interconnection between structure and agents. International diplomacy can show the way for IR scholars in the empirical study of mutually implicating phenomena.[34]

Diplomacy and state centrism

The second feature of international diplomacy is that as a practice, it is necessarily connected to *states* rather than to other kinds of actors. This

[32] For instance, John Yoo, "International Law and the War in Iraq," *American Journal of International Law*, 97(3), 2003, 563–575; Charles Hill, "Remarks by Charles Hill," *ASIL Proceedings*, 98, 2004, 329–331.

[33] Among governments, see the debates at the UN Security Council ahead of the invasion, including in Holger Niemann, "Justification as a Discursive Practice in the UN Security Council during the 2002/2003 Iraq Crisis," manuscript. Among international lawyers, see, for instance, the International Commission of Jurists, March 18, 2003, http://jurist.org/paperchase/2003/03/international-commission-of-jurists.php, accessed March 18, 2015.

[34] Sending, Pouliot, and Neumann, "Introduction," this volume.

does not mean that non-state actors cannot engage in the practice – rather, it means that when they do, they are engaged in an activity that is directed toward states, in a process of using international social resources to influence state behavior. This follows naturally from the formal structure of the activity and its connection to the state-centric framework of public international law: only states are obligated under public international law, and only states find themselves in a position to claim credit or earn demerits for following or breaking international law.[35] The politics of international law center on claims about compliance or noncompliance, and non-state actors are not in a position to comply or violate it. This does not mean that non-state actors may not engage in diplomacy, nor is it a challenge to the widely held view that non-state actors are taking a larger role in diplomacy than they previously had.

The interposition of new kinds of actors (i.e., non-state actors) into public diplomacy has dramatically increased the density of interaction, but it remains a state-centric social field. Non-state actors contribute to diplomacy despite not being subject to the rules of international law: they can invoke international rules, provide interpretations of behavior and of rules, and construct arguments using the resources of public international law. This can be consequential in constructing the field in which diplomacy takes place and in contributing resources to it. However, this is ultimately directed toward influencing states, by either forcing them to act in certain ways or giving them resources to pursue the policies preferred by the non-state actors. For instance, the Center for Constitutional Rights, a US non-governmental organization (NGO), provided legal briefs to states regarding George W. Bush's responsibilities for torture.[36] Its documents are designed to assist, indeed to provoke, national prosecutors' offices in initiating criminal investigations regarding violations of the Convention Against Torture. It also implicitly threatens states with being seen as noncompliant with their own obligations under that treaty. Similarly, the Global Compact program at the United Nations encourages firms to adopt voluntary

[35] There are exceptions, of course, including public international organizations and individual persons in relation to certain international crimes.

[36] Center for Constitutional Rights, "CCR Announces Bush Indictment for Convention Against Torture Signatory States," 2011, http://ccrjustice.org/newsroom/press-releases/human-rights-groups-announce-bush-indictment-convention-against-torture-sign, accessed February 8, 2011.

standards of labor and environmental practices, and then it enlists NGOs to monitor them. It builds a pseudo-legal structure out of international norms and uses the imagery of compliance and noncompliance with those norms to induce firms to improve their behavior.[37] The environmental group Sea Shepherd International explains its interference with Japanese whaling boats in the southern ocean on the grounds that Japan is violating the International Convention on the Regulation of Whaling and that Sea Shepherd is acting as that treaty's enforcement agent. It refers to itself as "the only organization whose mission is to enforce these international conservation regulations on the high seas."[38] Many other examples exist. Activists, scholars, investigative commissions, and media, among many other actors, use diplomacy to shape the environment in which states operate.[39] Thereby, they hope to change what states do or are.

The essentially state-centric nature of diplomacy could conceivably change if non-state actors become more central to public international law, and specifically if non-state actors were able to commit violations of international law. Two trends hint at this possibility: first, international criminal law may be developing in such a way that individuals can begin to make meaningful claims to compliance with international law, and second, non-state groups that aspire to be recognized as governments increasingly publicize their adherence to international rules (which under international law cannot apply to them) to support their claims to statehood. This is exemplified by the transitional government of Libya, which, while still fighting Gaddafi in the spring of 2011, declared its support for "all international and regional agreements" relevant to Libya, at a time when the vast majority of countries

[37] Ian Hurd, "Labor Standards through International Organizations: The Global Compact in Comparative Perspective," *Journal of Corporate Citizenship*, 11, 2003.

[38] Sea Shepherd International, www.seashepherd.org/whales/, accessed February 25, 2013.

[39] See, for instance, Kenneth Anderson, "The Ottawa Convention Banning Landmines, the Role of International Non-governmental Organizations and the Idea of International Civil Society," *European Journal of International Law*, 11 (1), 2000, 91–120; Roberta Cohen, "From Sovereignty to Responsibility," in W. Andy Knight and Frazer Egerton, eds., *The Routledge Handbook of the Responsibility to Protect* (New York: Routledge, 2012); Charlotte Epstein, *The Power of Words in International Relations: Birth of an Anti-Whaling Discourse* (Cambridge, MA: MIT Press, 2008).

continued to recognize Gaddafi's government in Tripoli as the formal representative of the country.[40]

Productive aspect of diplomacy

As states use international law to explain their behavior, they contribute to remaking and reinforcing those rules. Diplomacy therefore has a "productive" effect in the sense of the term defined by Barnett and Duvall:[41] it produces the public, social, and legal resources with which future state behavior is understood, justified, and argued over. This is the effect identified by Sending, Pouliot, and Neumann by which "forms of diplomacy come to constitute the basic political fabric of world politics."[42] The productive effect of diplomacy provides one dynamic for change in international law and international relations since the content of international law at any point in time is a function of how it has been deployed by actors in the past.

The productive elements of diplomacy can be seen in many recent cases where international law has developed through practice. Humanitarian intervention, for instance, is increasingly seen as legal under certain circumstances, despite its tension with the ban on war and other rules of the UN Charter.[43] This process was largely driven by governments using the language of legalized humanitarianism to justify their positions on intervention, and the effect has been to change the prevailing definition of the laws on the use of force.[44] Similarly, one cannot explain the content of the laws on preemptive war without making reference to the moments of state practice in the past when these laws were invoked and argued over in practice. These span from the *Caroline* incident in 1837 to the Six-Day War in 1967, the Osirak

[40] See Libyan Interim Transitional National Council statement, cited in Monday Dickson, "Nigeria's Recognition of the Transitional National Council of Libya: Exploration and Critical Assessment," *British Journal of Arts and Social Sciences* 14(1), 2013, 66–82, at 68.

[41] Michael Barnett and Raymond Duvall, "Power in Global Governance," in Michael Barnett and Raymond Duvall, eds., *Power in Global Governance* (Cambridge: Cambridge University Press, 2005).

[42] Sending, Pouliot, and Neumann, "Introduction," this volume.

[43] Ian Hurd, "Is Humanitarian Intervention Legal? The Rule of Law in an Incoherent World," *Ethics and International Affairs*, 25(3), 2011, 293–313.

[44] Christine D. Grey, *International Law and the Use of Force*, 3rd edn (Oxford: Oxford University Press, 2008).

attack in 1981, and on to the 2002 US *National Security Strategy*. Determining what is or is not allowed as preemptive force depends on a close reading of these and other incidents.[45] Even though states generally present their legal interpretations as seamlessly continuous with past practice, the reproduction of law through its use means the content of the rules is dynamic.

The interpretive exercise of understanding the law relies on these historical moments for its raw materials, where acceptable state practice defines what is legal rather than the other way around. This is precisely what some legal theorists most fear: that self-interested and ad hoc interpretations might become formal pieces of law.[46] And yet, in international law this is something like the normal condition of being; the use of legal arguments is motivated by their congruence with actors' interests. This is neither an indictment of the law nor an abuse of it by states. Indeed, it accounts for the possibility that diplomacy can be a source of change for international law as these references to the rules can shift their meaning. Long-standing doctrine on customary law is that it changes when states change their behavior and their beliefs regarding what constitutes lawful behavior, and so law *follows from* behavior rather than leading it. This is the inverse of the conventional rule-of-law model that says that states should narrow their behavior according to their legal obligations. It holds true for treaty law as well as customary law.

The productive effect of diplomacy is not dependent on a consensus around the meaning of the new claims, only on the fact that the rules were deployed and interpreted to fit the case. Arguments about the epistemic community of international lawyers go too far when they presume that this community is in a position of authority over states or over the construction of legal arguments.[47] This overstates the position of international legal experts and understates both the public and the variegated qualities of the diplomatic process. The most politically

45 See, for instance, Michael Doyle, *Striking First: Preemption and Prevention in International Conflict* (Princeton, NJ: Princeton University Press, 2008); Ian Hurd, "Breaking and Making Norms: American Revisionism and Crises of Legitimacy," *International Politics*, 44, 2007; Henry Shue and David Rodin, eds., *Preemption: Military Action and Moral Justification* (Oxford: Oxford University Press, 2010).

46 Brian Tamanaha, *Law as a Means to an End: Threat to the Rule of Law* (Cambridge: Cambridge University Press, 2006).

47 See, for instance, Sending, Pouliot, and Neumann, "Introduction," this volume.

important legal concepts do not have a settled meaning governed by the community of lawyers – they are open to competing interpretations serving competing political purposes in the hands of governments and other actors. Thus, when the US argued in its "war on terror" that its detainees were illegal enemy combatants and therefore not covered by the Geneva Conventions, it was generally seen as having made an error of legal interpretation.[48] But its claims nonetheless entered the public sphere and interacted with existing international law and shifted the boundaries for future arguments about these issues. Whether the US claims were successful in legalizing US behavior in the eyes of the international community of legal scholars is not crucial to the political impact that it sought to accomplish – or, at a minimum, the two outcomes are somewhat independent of each other. States often aspire to use their diplomacy in an activist manner to change international rules or situations but may or may not end up with the desired effect. The social nature of diplomacy ensures that these changes are never fully under the control of any single actor, and that the strategic direction of diplomatic activism is always uncertain. The meaning of precedents depends on how states and others choose to use them.

As a social practice, diplomacy has these three formal qualities: sociality, state centrism, and a productive effect. The substantive content comes from its connection with international law, and especially with the ideology of the rule of law, which I discuss next.

Diplomacy and law

Diplomacy operates at the boundaries between politics and law and between the internal needs or interests of the state and their explanation in an external language. It translates state policies and needs into the language of international law. It is therefore deeply bound to the idea of rule following, and the practice of diplomacy is constituted by the political appeal invested in the idea of compliance: diplomacy means providing rule-following explanations for the choices of the state.[49]

[48] Michael P. Scharf, "International Law and the Torture Memos," *Case Western Reserve Journal of International Law*, 42, 2009, 321–358.

[49] One could imagine other moral schedules for diplomacy at other times and places, where the primary value involved reconciling state needs to, say, justice or natural law or sustainability or some other good. Rule following is the

Diplomacy and compliance

It is often said that the modern era of international politics is characterized by the idea of the rule of law. Ikenberry, for instance, suggests that the post-1945 "liberal international order" is distinct for being "relatively open, rule-based, and progressive."[50] The principle of *pacta sunt servanda* ("agreements should be honored") is the central norm of international law and politics. Academics argue about the foundations of that obligation (or lack thereof),[51] but the premise of all this discussion is the shared commitment to the view that states are required to comply with the rules that they have accepted. The conventional approach has it that *pacta sunt servanda*, consent, legal obligation, and the ordering power of the rule of law are fundamental to international society, and that effective law is law that states choose to follow despite holding an interest in noncompliance.

This is uncontroversial to many scholars of international law and politics, but it is contradicted by the practice of diplomacy, where all states claim to be uniformly complying with their own interpretation of the rules. The preceding discussion leads instead to the conclusion that the idea of compliance is built into the practice of diplomacy and so cannot be modeled as a matter of choice. States face an international environment in which complying with international law is valued and noncompliance is in almost all situations a negative. They therefore engage in diplomacy to present their interests and behaviors as consistent with the terms of international law. This is evident in the degree to which states do not admit to violations of the law.[52] It also suggests that compliance and noncompliance are not structural equals in the process of international law and politics. Compliance occupies a privileged position as the default self-interpretation of state behavior, and noncompliance is a term of diplomatic attack used against opponents.

This is sometimes taken as evidence that international rules are inconsequential or non-binding or epiphenomenal. This is the view of

defining feature of modern diplomacy. See Christian Reus-Smit, *The Moral Purpose of the State: Culture, Social Identity, and Institutional Rationality in International Relations* (Princeton, NJ: Princeton University Press, 1999).

50 G. John Ikenberry, *Liberal Leviathan: The Origins, Crisis, and Transformation of the American World Order* (Princeton, NJ: Princeton University Press, 2011).

51 For a summary, see Brunnée and Toope, "An Interactional Theory."

52 Nathaniel Berman, "Legitimacy through Defiance: From Goa to Iraq," *Wisconsin International Law Review*, 23(1), 2005, 93–125.

the "new sovereigntists" in US public discourse and neorealists in academic international relations.[53] These conclusions are mistaken because, among other things, they conflate the writers' policy preferences (i.e., that the United States *should* ignore international rules) with empirical research (e.g., on how states *actually behave* toward rules in practice). Diplomacy is ubiquitous precisely because there are political gains to be earned by portraying oneself as compliant and one's opponents as noncompliant; these payoffs are as appealing to revisionist states as they are to status quo powers, and to nationalists and cosmopolitans alike. The power of law is evident in the eagerness of states to make use of it, and in the consequences one can imagine should a state fail to make use of it when others expect it to.

Diplomacy generates a constant stream of claims regarding compliance. States' references to law and lawfulness in explaining their actions often mask rule violation and also often construct new law, and often do both at the same time. The function of international law in these cases is to provide the resources for diplomacy, and individual rules are consequential only insofar as they are invoked by actors and deployed in the public domain. The law-making capacity of diplomacy points to a philosophy of international law along the lines suggested by Hans Morgenthau, following Carl Schmitt, that law emerges from the struggle among social forces rather than from formal legislation.[54] It contradicts Hedley Bull's suggestion that the role of the international lawyer is to "state what the rules of international law are."[55] This is impossible when the content of the rules depends on how they have been used by states in past practice – the meaning of past practice is not fixed and stable. It depends on the political goals of those who draw on it. Peter

[53] See, for instance, Peter Spiro, "What Happened to the New Sovereigntism?" *Foreign Affairs*, July 28, 2004.

[54] Hans J. Morgenthau, "Positivism, Functionalism and International Law," *American Journal of International Law*, 1941. See the discussion in Martti Koskenniemi, "Carl Schmitt, Hans Morgenthau, and the Image of Law in International Relations," in Michael Byers, ed., *The Role of Law in International Politics: Essays in International Relations and International Law* (Oxford: Oxford University Press, 2000).

[55] Hedley Bull, *The Anarchical Society: A Study in World Order* (New York: Columbia University Press, 1977), 150. Stephen J. Toope, "Emerging Patterns of Governance and International Law," in Byers, ed. *The Role of Law in International Politics* (Oxford: Oxford University Press, 2001), 91–108.

Lindseth arrives at a similar point in relation to the development of law in the EU:

> The very nature of public law has itself deeply evolved. It has become less a system of rules marking seemingly clear lines between "valid" and "invalid" exercises of authority, as classical understandings of . . . the rule of law have demanded. Instead, public law has evolved toward something more focused on "the allocation of burdens of reason-giving," or, as European scholars are increasingly calling it, "accountability."[56]

Diplomacy and contestation

This view presents diplomacy as inherently relational, but it suggests that the relation is between the state and the international environment of legal resources rather than between one state and another. Actors draw on these resources to conduct diplomacy and in doing so they remake them. Their presentations of lawfulness do not need to be accepted by their audience to be legally and politically powerful; disagreements over what it means to comply with a given international law are endemic to the international legal field, and it is a rare exception when an international dispute is resolved by determining the true meaning of compliance. The key relation in diplomacy is not between the speaker and the audience but rather between the actor and the structure of international legal resources.

The fact that the audience for diplomacy need not agree with the claims being made by the state suggests that the most important product of diplomacy is not persuasion or consensus or agreement or socialization or learning or acculturation.[57] Each of these may indeed be important in international politics in various and interesting ways, but they are generally presented as means for overcoming disagreement, as embodying a means for reducing or eliminating divergent views. This makes them less relevant for thinking about the contestation around diplomacy and international law where disagreement is endemic and is not resolved by the process of interaction. Much of the

[56] Peter Lindseth, *Power and Legitimacy: Reconciling Europe and the Nation-State* (Oxford: Oxford University Press, 2010), 21–22.

[57] Jeffrey T. Checkel, ed., *International Institutions and Socialization in Europe* (Cambridge: Cambridge University Press, 2007) on socialization; on acculturation, see Ryan Goodman and Derek Jinks, "Toward an Institutional Theory of Sovereignty," *Stanford Law Review*, 55, 2005.

literature on deliberation and communication in international relations and international law carries the assumption that the end point of diplomatic interaction is a consensus or shared understanding of either the rules in question or the interests and needs of the other party. Versions of this argument are well known in the international legal literature, from the Yale School through Abram Chayes and Antonia Chayes and Harold Koh, and in IR in Thomas Risse, Corneliu Bjola, Jennifer Mitzen, and others dealing with communicative action. Most rest on a variant of the idea that public reasoning over differences of opinion drives toward new shared understanding, consensus, and legitimation, all of which conduce to compliance with the rules. Chayes and Chayes suggest that argument and persuasion can lead to compliance as "good" legal arguments carry more force than "bad" ones.[58] Koh sees repeated transnational interaction over a rule as gradually clarifying it so that it becomes increasingly compelling to states.[59] This is commonly applied to international diplomacy and is often suggested as a key feature of the UN and other places where states gather to deliberate on their relations. Michael Doyle and Ian Johnstone, among others, argue that the persuasive process by which Security Council decisions are made helps winnow out unreasonable claims and can therefore reduce the incidence of unnecessary wars.[60] The diverse membership of the Security Council is an important component of this argument, as it means that persuasion must be targeted to a variety of interests and identities, and the filtering function of the process is therefore stronger.[61]

My view suggests instead that the argumentation that makes up diplomacy does not move toward consensus. Inherent in the concept of diplomacy is the possibility that the audience will disagree with the legal representations that one makes, and the formal structure of public

58 Abram Chayes and Antonia Handler Chayes, *The New Sovereignty: Compliance with International Regulatory Agreements* (Cambridge, MA: Harvard University Press, 1995), 25–26, 119.

59 Harold Hongju Koh, "Why Do Nations Obey International Law?" *Yale Law Journal*, 106(8), 1997, 2599–2659.

60 Doyle, *Striking First*; Ian Johnstone, *The Power of Deliberation: International Law, Politics and Organizations* (Oxford: Oxford University Press, 2011).

61 This motivates many of the proposals for increasing the diversity in the Security Council by adding new members. See the discussion in Ian Hurd, "Myths of Membership: The Politics of Legitimation in UN Security Council Reform," *Global Governance*, 14(2), 2008.

diplomacy anticipates contestation over who is or is not complying with the law. There is no teleology toward shared understanding in disputes over law. In any number of cases of international disagreement and deliberation, we can see that the process of interacting around international law bears no necessary relationship to a shared understanding as the result. Indeed, diplomacy adds a language of law to a dispute, but it typically ends with as much disagreement as existed at the start. For instance, the US diplomacy around the Nicaragua case in the 1980s included a detailed legal argument explaining why it had done nothing wrong. This was "exported" to the International Court of Justice (ICJ) through the Departments of State and Justice and other channels despite the US boycott of the proceedings. The court's judgments in that case, which were decisive as a legal matter under the UN Charter and the ICJ Statute, did not solve the problem of competing interpretations of legal terms that was central to the politics of the dispute. Other diplomatic controversies over the law on preemption, from Osirac in 1981 to Iraq in 2003, have likely made the law less clear rather than more, as they are deployed to shift the understanding of the law. Even unsuccessful claims to "legitimacy through legality" have constitutive effects on the rules and norms through which they are presented.

Implications

This has several implications for theories of international law and politics, two of which I examine in this section: law as a resource and the relation between agents and structures. First, all uses of law in this process can be seen as being strategic on the part of states, in the sense of being designed to produce a result that is favorable to the states' interests. It is self-interested and instrumental, though; because it operates with socially constructed legal resources that are not fully controlled by the actor, it cannot be taken as evidence of radical agency or autonomy by the agent. The function of law here is to provide permissive passage of the policy that is preferred by the state or alternately to provide a legal critique of the preferences and actions of an opposing state. Law is a resource. As a tool, it is both empowering and limiting for its users.

This view is at odds with the effort to remove politics from law and legal interpretation, as seen in the work of Brian Tamanaha and other legal scholars. Tamanaha argues that the strategic use of law by instrumental actors, including judges and activists, is a threat to the rule of law, which he understands as necessarily apolitical.[62] It also conflicts with the social-scientific effort to operationalize compliance as a variable and identify the factors that conduce to it across cases. This is exemplified by the recent explosion of literature at the intersection of political science and international law that looks for correlations between features of law, of states, or of the international setting and the rate of compliance with a treaty or rule.[63]

A resource view of law is incompatible with both of these projects because it recognizes the political power of states' self-serving interpretations of the law.[64] Competing interpretations of law are ubiquitous in international law and international relations. They persist precisely because states see a payoff in being on the side of compliance rather than noncompliance, and they will not disappear as a result of arguing through to an end point of agreement. These legal disagreements are important in settings that lack a centralized judicial institution to provide authoritative judgments about competing legal claims. In such situations, arguing over the interpretation of compliance takes the place of arguing over the substantive questions in the dispute. The dispute over sovereignty for Kosovo, for example, took place in part as an argument over the legal fine points of the secession declaration, with both sides claiming to represent the international rule of law – an ICJ advisory opinion added legal resources to the fight but did not resolve questions of compliance and noncompliance.[65] Similarly, disputed claims about self-defense are impossible to resolve without making judgments about matters internal to the identity and security of the state, such as how the military operations relate to national perceptions

62 Brian Tamanaha, *On the Rule of Law: History, Politics, Theory* (Cambridge: Cambridge University Press, 2004).

63 See, for instance, the survey by Emilie Hafner-Burton, David G. Victor, and Yonatan Lupu, "Political Science Research on International Law: The State of the Field," *American Journal of International Law*, 106(1), 2012, 47–97. Also Jeffrey Dunoff and Mark A. Pollack, eds., *Interdisciplinary Perspectives on International Law and International Relations: The State of the Art* (Cambridge: Cambridge University Press, 2013).

64 Among others on this, see Ingo Venzke, "Is Interpretation in International Law a Game?" in Andrea Bianchi, Daniel Peat, and Matthew Windsor, eds., *Interpretation in International Law* (Oxford: Oxford University Press, 2014).

65 ICJ Advisory Opinion, "Accordance with International Law of the Unilateral Declaration of Independence in Respect of Kosovo," www.icj-cij.org/docket/files/141/15987.pdf, accessed February 25, 2013.

of security and to beliefs about threat. Legal claims under Article 51 of the United Nations Charter (on self-defense) can in principle be refuted but require that outsiders make judgments about the dangers perceived by national leaders, judgments that cannot be made conclusively. The issue necessarily remains open for dispute. Controversy over these kinds of issues is the stuff of diplomacy, and it is not amenable to objective judgment; answering the question about compliance versus noncompliance amounts to taking sides in the substantive political content of the dispute.

The situation is different when an institution exists to give authoritative answers to questions of compliance and noncompliance. In those cases (e.g., in the World Trade Organization dispute settlement process), the parties may well continue to disagree with the outcome, but the decision produces a legal fact that shapes the possibilities for future disputes. The legitimacy of the rule-of-law ideology adds power to the legal fact, and a dissenting state will generally organize its diplomacy such that it claims to be accepting that fact while continuing the dispute in other forms.

The second implication follows from the recognition that diplomacy is a domain in which state interests and international rules are ontologically combined. This leads to a new conceptualization of the relationship between states and international rules, norms, and laws. Making sense of the politics around diplomacy requires a method that integrates states and rules (i.e., agents and structures) so that the act of using the rules to justify the state becomes the unit of analysis. Alexander Wendt said, "In the last analysis, agents and structures are produced or reproduced by what actors *do*."[66] Instead of modeling international law as a device for differentiating compliance from noncompliance, we can instead see it as the medium in which state behavior is explained, understood, and argued over in terms of international rules and norms. The perspective of social practices puts the focus on the interaction between states and rules.

This moves away from asking whether or not states are complying with the rules, and away from asking whether the rules serve as a constraint on the actors; these represent the agentic and the structural

[66] Alexander Wendt, "Collective Identity Formation and the International State," *American Political Science Review*, 88(2), 1994, 384–396, at 390. Emphasis in original.

approaches respectively. Instead, one can look at how the actors *use* the rules, and how the rules shape the actors and their possibilities. To borrow a phrase from Thomas Sewell, international law is "both the medium and the outcome of the practices which constitute" this social system.[67] This is what Laurent Thévenot has called the "responsiveness" of the social environment in reaction to actors' behavior, and he suggests framing research toward the ways the actor takes these responses into account when acting: "the dynamics of this material engagement between an agent and his environment is a central issue [in the study of] pragmatic regimes."[68]

A provocative question is raised regarding whether there can be international action in the absence of international rules and norms that define it, and in the absence of the diplomatic process of attaching these rules to state policies. If international rules are the resources with which action is understood and given meaning (both by the actor and by the audience), then it would seem that actions that are not envisioned in the rules could not be taken. This is consistent with the philosophical literature on the essential role of social resources in making possible meaningful action by agents.[69] Can this be true of foreign policy as well? The history of humanitarian intervention, as mentioned earlier in relation to Martha Finnemore, suggests that it might: the invention of the concept of humanitarian intervention made possible something that was not possible before. Without the concept, states were more limited in their policy choices than they were after its invention, which implies that the absence of the concept in the field of international law was effectively a constraint on their power and choices.

Conclusion

Diplomacy occupies a position at the intersections between law and politics, between domestic and foreign affairs, and between agency and structure. It consists of framing the state's needs or choices in the

67 Thomas Sewell, quoted by Ann Swidler, "What Anchors Cultural Practices," in Theodore R. Schatzki et al., eds., *The Practice Turn in Contemporary Theory* (London: Routledge, 2001), 78.

68 Laurent Thévenot, "Pragmatic Regimes Governing Engagement with the World," in ibid., 58.

69 Charles Taylor, "... to Follow a Rule," in Craig Calhoun, Edward Lipuma, and Moishe Postone, eds., *Bourdieu: Critical Perspectives* (Chicago: University of Chicago Press, 1993).

language of international law. This is an example of Adler and Pouliot's broader notion of practices and their place in international relations: "world politics [is] structured by practices" that "give meaning to international action; make possible strategic interaction; and are reproduced, changed, and reinforced by international action and interaction."[70] The state-centric nature of diplomacy is a product of the place of states and state agency in the prevailing framework of the international rule of law: only states are full subjects of international law, able to act in relation to international law, either consistently with it or in contradiction of it. The legalized international society of today validates compliance with international law and is ostensibly committed to punishing violations. The purpose of public diplomacy is to make state policy and desires consistent with the state's legal obligations. The practice depends on the existing stock of legal categories and concepts. It also remakes them as they are invoked in relation to particular cases and policies.

Recourse to international legal explanations is inescapable for states. Its use helps illuminate the political dimensions of the international rule of law, which are often overlooked in international legal theory. States' claims about their compliance with international law are indeed self-serving, but they are not mere cheap talk. The need to see and explain foreign policy as consistent with international law is deeply internalized in states, so much so that states often seem incapable of imagining that their most important policy desires might conflict with existing legal rules. The motivation to interpret international law as permitting what the state wants can be preconscious in the state – that is, occurring before the state is confronted with a choice between complying with or violating its obligations. This does not contradict the idea of the rule of law for world politics or weaken the power of international law. Instead, it shows how profoundly it shapes states and their sense of their interests – states find it impossible to conceive that their deep-seated needs might not be served by law because they have fully internalized the project of an international legal order.

[70] Adler and Pouliot, "International Practices: Introduction and Framework," in Adler and Pouliot, eds., *International Practices*, 5.

2 Diplomacy, war, and world politics

TARAK BARKAWI

What are the relations between diplomacy and war? If diplomats who write about diplomacy are to be believed, diplomacy is both distinct from and opposed to war. It is the "'art' of resolving negotiations peacefully."[1] Similarly, many scholars of diplomacy distinguish diplomacy from war and align diplomacy with peace. For Paul Sharp, diplomacy is about the maintenance of peaceful relations between separate political entities.[2] War marks the "failure of diplomacy."[3] In Adam Watson's account, it is "the process of dialogue and negotiation by which states in a system conduct their relations and pursue their purposes by means *short* of war."[4] Keith Hamilton and Richard Langhorne define diplomacy as "the peaceful conduct of relations amongst political entities."[5] Realists, and certainly strategists, by contrast, do not necessarily align diplomacy with peace. Diplomacy can be about building alliances and delivering threats. But diplomacy is still seen as distinct from war. Even "coercive diplomacy," according to Alexander George, is an "alternative to war."[6]

Thanks to the editors, Jennifer Luff, Andrew Zimmerman, LSE colleagues and students in IR502, and four anonymous reviewers for comments and assistance in writing this chapter.

1 Sending, Pouliot, and Neumann, "Introduction," this volume.

2 Paul Sharp, *Diplomatic Theory of International Relations* (Cambridge: Cambridge University Press, 2009), 10, 103.

3 Ibid., 1.

4 Adam Watson, *Diplomacy: The Dialogue between States* (New York: McGraw Hill, 1983), 11. Emphases added.

5 Keith Hamilton and Richard Langhorne, *The Practice of Diplomacy*, 2nd edn (London: Routledge, 2011), 1. One exception to the tendency to see diplomacy as inherently peaceful is R. P. Barston, who notes that diplomacy can be used to orchestrate violence and that "counter-diplomacy" can be used to continue a conflict. Barston, *Modern Diplomacy*, 4th edn (London: Routledge, 2014), 1, 4–5, 244.

6 Alexander George, *Forceful Persuasion: Coercive Diplomacy as an Alternative to War* (Washington, DC: United States Institute of Peace Press, 1991).

This chapter argues that it is not, in fact, possible to define diplomacy in opposition to war or to see diplomatic activity as necessarily distinct from the administration and conduct of war. It does so by sketching out a postcolonial and sociological approach to the relations between diplomacy, armed force, and war in world politics. It argues that diplomacy is central to the administration and conduct of war, and to the constitution and use of force more generally. In much international relations (IR) scholarship, understandings of diplomacy and war are premised on Eurocentric accounts of the sovereign states system. This chapter, by contrast, draws on the histories and sociologies of small wars and of other forms of violence used to defeat and rule non-European peoples. It uses them to critique and provincialize Eurocentric accounts, and to inform a general discussion about the relations between diplomacy and war in the making of world politics.

The place to begin is with a prior binary: that between war and peace. Only through some version of this binary can diplomacy be distinguished from war or aligned with peace. One must first have an idea of peace as distinct from war to place diplomacy on one side or another. In IR, juridical and Eurocentric ideas inform the determination of states of peace and war. The criteria used elide the forms of violence characteristic of international hierarchies, whether in empires or in other kinds of world order projects that involve armed conflict between the strong and the weak, as in the Cold War in the Third World or the War on Terror. The discussion in the first section that follows breaks down the war/peace binary and maps out a sociology of war and armed force in core-periphery relations. By refusing the question of whether a state of war or peace appertains, the role of organized violence in securing international hierarchies comes into view, as does the diplomatic work involved in constituting armed forces and making war.

Of course there are diplomatic efforts to promote peace as well as to organize fighting. But the point is that it is not possible to *define* diplomacy against war or imagine that diplomacy is in some way inherently opposed to war, or necessarily distinct and apart from the international relations that go into the making of war. In what follows, through Clausewitzian and sociological conceptions of war, diplomacy reappears as the crucial modality of international coordination it is often understood to be. But part of its role is the organization and facilitation of the coercive capacities essential to the construction and maintenance of international and local orders. The second section outlines this role in respect of the administration and constitution of force, and of the conduct of war.

In breaking down the binary between peace and war, it becomes necessary to broach the more general question of the relationship between politics and organized violence. It is not only war, in the sense of the reciprocal organized violence, which is at issue, but the place of organized violence in rule and domination. As Sending, Pouliot, and Neumann point out in the Introduction to this volume, diplomacy in part is about practices of governing, and governing involves coercion and coercive capacities. Diplomacy provides a permanent extraterritorial infrastructure crucial to military, security, and intelligence activities in other states and societies. Where consideration of diplomacy, force, and war leads is to the *international* organization and deployment of coercive capacities for a variety of purposes, from local internal security to interstate alliances. Once this point is made, the intimate relations between diplomacy and war, and the participation of diplomacy in the constitution and use of force, become more or less obvious. The administration and conduct of war often requires complex international coordination and facilitation across many different spheres. This includes more traditional diplomacy between governments, ministries, and militaries as well as multilateral diplomacy at the UN and other international governmental organizations (IGOs). It also includes military and security advice and support programs, the coordination of arms shipments and logistics, the resolution of legal matters, negotiations over strategy and the assembling of alliances, the administrative and planning minutiae of coalition warfare or other uses of force, and so on.

However, in IR theory, where space is made for it, diplomacy is most often associated with peace and negotiation. For liberals, diplomacy is a principal means for achieving peace and progress, and for the realization of normative goals.[7] This raises a final question to consider: what is the damage to understanding of aligning diplomacy with peace? What is obscured by opposing diplomacy to war? Doing so drains war and violence out of theories of international cooperation and multilateralism. Through diplomacy-as-peace, such terms take on a pacific air and seem to signal the opposite of war. But even liberal

[7] See e.g. Christian Reus-Smit, *The Moral Purpose of the State* (Princeton, NJ: Princeton University Press, 1999).

world order projects wage war. They often do so multilaterally in the garb of peace, democracy, and human rights, all of which take a great deal of diplomacy to arrange and conduct. More broadly, constructing and maintaining international hierarchies and the violent practices of domination, exploitation, and expropriation they involve, require much cooperation and coordination, as well as direct diplomatic involvement in governance, security, and military relations. One need only think of US policy in Central and South America in the twentieth century.[8] The chapter concludes by critiquing the imperial politics behind the association of diplomacy with peace and its consequences for IR theory.

Diplomacy, peace, and war

A source of the association of diplomacy with peace concerns communication. Diplomacy is in various ways defined and distinguished by the fact that it involves communication and negotiation. For the practitioner-scholar Harold Nicholson, diplomacy is "the management of international relations by negotiation."[9] Representation, analysis and reporting, and other aspects of formal diplomatic relations are also forms of communication. The idea is that communication, talking, is a distinct activity from fighting or using force. It is a short step from there to the idea that talking is a way out of fighting or a way of avoiding fighting, perhaps altogether. For Costas Constantinou, "diplomacy can be viewed as a response to the possibility of violence ... talking to the enemy about those things we differ in and indeed those we may share."[10] In G. A. Pigman's textbook on diplomatic studies, the chapter on "Managing Military and Security Diplomacy" mainly covers topics such as avoiding, limiting, and mitigating conflict, as well as controlling arms.[11] For G. R. Berridge, war and fighting threaten to sever relations, but a "minimum of diplomatic communication" offers the prospect of preventing escalation and restoring the peace.[12] The problem is not that Pigman and Berridge

[8] See e.g. Greg Grandin, *Empire's Workshop* (New York: Henry Holt, 2006); Walter Lafeber, *Inevitable Revolutions* (New York: W. W. Norton, 1993).
[9] Harold Nicholson, *Diplomacy* (Oxford: Oxford University Press, 1963), 4.
[10] Costas Constantinou, "Between Statecraft and Humanism," *International Studies Review*, 15, 2013, 142.
[11] G. A. Pigman, *Contemporary Diplomacy* (Cambridge: Polity, 2010), 138–179.
[12] G. R. Berridge, *Diplomacy* (Basingstoke: Palgrave Macmillan, 2010), 207–208.

are wrong to discuss these topics. It is that a darker role for diplomacy is ignored almost entirely in what are meant to be comprehensive texts on the subject. As Jeremy Black notes, definitions of diplomacy that emphasize peaceful management through negotiation leave "aside the key role of diplomacy in preparing for war."[13]

Sharp, too, reflects the tendency to leap from talking to peace. He writes, "diplomacy is distinguished by its emphasis on the opportunity for conversations which continue to exist in the worst possible situations."[14] The faulty premise at work here is that "conversations" are necessarily about avoiding or getting out of "the worst possible situations." Conducting invasions and wars and organizing mass murders and genocides, not to mention colonization and empire, also have required conversations between representatives of separate polities. In equating diplomacy with an always present potential path out of conflict, Sharp and others make diplomacy not only the opposite of war but also its antidote.

Contrast this definitional opposition between diplomacy and war with the following two examples. The first concerns the establishment of an air corridor over Iraq through which Iran supplied arms to its embattled ally President Bashar al-Assad of Syria, enmeshed in a civil war since 2011. The air corridor involved some complex diplomacy on the part of the Iraqis, who not only made arrangements for the shipments but also had to fend off US and international pressure. The Iraqis insisted that only humanitarian supplies were sent through their airspace, and they staged inspections of a few aircraft – no doubt closely coordinated with Iran – to prove this point.[15] While here we see Sharp's central point at work – the coordination of relations between separate political entities – we cannot sharply distinguish diplomacy from war in the diplomatic activity surrounding the air corridor. Iran and Iraq assisted Syria in waging war, while the United States, favoring elements of the opposition, used diplomacy to try and stop arms shipments to the Syrian regime. For Syria, Iran, and Iraq, talking was about coordinating and sustaining the fighting, while for the United States diplomacy

13 Jeremy Black, *A History of Diplomacy* (London: Reaktion Books, 2010), 12.
14 Sharp, *Diplomatic Theory*, 186–187.
15 One such inspection was of an aircraft on its way back to Iran from Syria. Michael R. Gordon, Eric Schmitt, and Tim Arango, "Flow of Arms to Syria Persists, to U.S. Dismay," *New York Times*, December 1, 2012.

was a way of boosting the fortunes of the rebels and conducting the struggle against Assad by other means.

The second example concerns the establishment in April 2013 of a UN "peacekeeping" force for Mali. There was no peace to be kept in Mali, but a war between the regime in Bamako, Tuareg separatists, and transnational Islamic militants. The UN force of 11,200 soldiers and 1,440 police officers was built around 6,000 Economic Community of South West African States (ECOWAS) troops already in the country and a French battle group remaining behind after France's January 2013 intervention, which had prevented the Islamist forces from marching on Bamako. UNSC Resolution 2100 directly involves the UN force in the War on Terror. "Terrorists" and "extremists" are identified as the enemy of "stability"; the purpose of the mission is to restore "national unity," and the mandate falls under Chapter VII of the UN Charter, identifying the situation in Mali as a threat to international peace and security. The resolution authorizes the force to "use all necessary means" in carrying out its mandate.[16] Here again is an entire complex of diplomatic activity that cannot easily be separated from war. Under cover of a forest of euphemisms and orchestrated by France, the former colonial power, the UNSC proposed to wage a limited war to reestablish rule over the sovereign territory of Mali.[17] Here, multilateral cooperation (and all the diplomacy it involves) is a means by which one world order project – the liberal society of states – wages war on an alternative world order project – that of the global *jihad*.[18]

While these are but two particular moments in specific contexts, they are in their different ways representative of common classes of diplomatic activity. After all, the waging of war requires all manner of diplomatic coordination, as exemplified by the Iraqi arms corridor, while the UN has been participating in wars in one way or another since its founding. What one really has to wonder about is where the idea that diplomacy is opposed to war came from in the first place. Diplomacy seems to be part and parcel of war. Think, if further

16 UNSC Resolution 2100 (2013), http://www.securitycouncilreport.org/atf/cf/%7B65BFCF9B-6D27-4E9C-8CD3-CF6E4FF96FF9%7D/s_res_2100.pdf, accessed May 22, 2013.

17 Neil MacFarquhar, "U.N. Votes to Establish Peacekeeping Force for Mali," *New York Times*, April 25, 2013.

18 See Faisal Devji, *The Terrorist in Search of Humanity: Militant Islam and Global Politics* (London: Hurst, 2008) for thinking about radical Islam as a global political project.

examples are needed, of the diplomacy involved in assembling and maintaining the coalitions that fought the Persian Gulf War, invaded Iraq, and occupied Afghanistan.

But what of the notion that diplomacy is distinct from fighting, even if it is not necessarily aligned with peace? Is it entirely convincing that facilitating an arms corridor amounts to participating in a war? Is not the arms corridor a good example of the wisdom of Watson's definition of diplomacy as everything *short* of war?

At work in this commonsense reading is not only a binary between war and peace but also one of the core juridical inheritances of IR theory: thinking of the state as a person or unitary actor that is responsible for its actions. War is a particular class of violent acts by a state-person. The Iraq state-person is merely transiting arms, not fighting a war. Strangely, this juridical metaphor derived from political and legal theory is reinforced by efforts to scientifically define war, as in the widely used Correlates of War (CoW) data set. CoW incorporates the legal apparatus of sovereignty into its conceptual and statistical system for the determination of states of war and peace. For example, interstate war is defined as organized violence between two sovereign states involving at least one thousand battle deaths over the course of a year. Legally and scientifically, it would seem, Iraq was not at war in 2012 with Syrian rebels. Moreover, to say that the United States is using diplomacy to pursue its struggle against the Assad regime by "other means" again reinforces the conclusion that the United States is not at war in Syria, either in the terms of international law or those of international theory. The means in question are not those of war but of diplomacy.

War and politics

How might we approach the question of war and peace differently than the model of juridical determination? Carl von Clausewitz helps show the way. For him, the politics of war cloud and confound any clear distinction between peace and war. In discussing the political nature of war, he notes that many people assume that war "suspends" normal intercourse between states and "replaces it by a wholly different condition." Here is a peace/war binary – either normal intercourse appertains or there is a state of war. "[O]n the contrary," Clausewitz writes, "war is simply a continuation of political intercourse, with the addition of other means."[19] Those "other means" are of course violence, but they may take the form of large-scale warfare – a "terrible-battle sword" – or that of more finely applied force – a "light, handy rapier."[20] Clausewitz's focus here is on the political character of uses of force – that political purposes shape the turn to violence – and on the way in which a policy of war "intermixes" force with other kinds of means. It may be necessary, he says, to wage "minimal wars, which consist in *merely threatening the enemy with negotiations held in reserve*."[21] He discusses the play between active and passive phases of wartime operations and the continual, always ongoing calculations of relative advantage coupled with threatening maneuvers and positioning of forces.

The question of the *duration* of war cannot, on this account, be limited to periods of active hostilities. Rather, the distinction between peacetime and wartime is a border zone in which one is not necessarily easily distinguishable from the other. War threatens to "shrivel into prudence" in its passive phases and is sometimes "just a foil for the exchange of thrusts, feints and parries."[22] "This poses," he goes on to say, "an obvious problem for any theory of war that aims at being thoroughly scientific."[23] The political character of war confounds efforts to establish what war is and when it is or is not happening.

To be sure, for Clausewitz, fighting is the essence of war, the possibility and the actuality of reciprocal organized violence. But he is at pains to emphasize the decisive character of politics (as well as of historical context) in shaping fighting, its scale, its manner, how it is organized, to what specific purposes it is directed, and so on. The political purpose determines what mix of violence and other means is appropriate in a given situation. War can shade into coercion when violence is not reciprocated. A short step further and violence sublimates into policing and governance.

Michel Foucault takes up the logic of Clausewitz's position on politics and war in the lectures of *Society Must Be Defended*. If we think of political power as a relationship of force, then why not analyze it in terms of "conflict, confrontation and war?"[24] Foucault explores

[19] Carl von Clausewitz, *On War* (Princeton, NJ: Princeton University Press, 1976), 605.
[20] Ibid., 606. [21] Ibid., 604. Emphases in original. [22] Ibid., 604, 606.
[23] Ibid., 604.
[24] Michel Foucault, *Society Must be Defended* (London: Penguin, 2004), 15.

the inversion of Clausewitz's proposition: that politics is the continuation of war by other means. Instead of force, other levers and means of power are used for political ends. "Peace," he says, "is waging a secret war"; it is "a coded war" by which the victors and defeated of the last war continue to pursue their aims.[25] Foucault looks at nascent national societies emerging from foreign conquest or civil war. Law, history, religion, political theory, what might now be called public administration, become sites of contest between groupings within society: "Law is not pacification, for beneath the law, war continues to rage in all the mechanisms of power, even in the most regular."[26] The outcomes of actual wars, such as the Frankish conquest of Gaul or the Norman invasion, set up relations of power between groups, of defeat and subordination for some, and of dominance for others. The priests maneuver against the nobility in the field of law. Thomas Hobbes spins elaborate philosophical webs in the service of sovereign power, whisking away histories of conquest and colonization to legitimate a Norman monarchy in England. "[B]attle cries," Foucault writes, "can be heard beneath the formulas of right, in the dissymmetry of forces that lies beneath the equilibrium of justice."[27]

However much he might appreciate Foucault's realist approach to politics, Clausewitz would have little trouble in identifying his arguments as metaphorical uses of the concept of war, which at its essence involves fighting. But a point that can be drawn from Foucault's intervention is that to think of war and peace as two separate states of affairs, subject to different ways of knowing, is to misunderstand politics. It is to get "peace" wrong as well as "war" (as Clausewitz tells us); both involve force and violence as well as more pacific means. Organized violence in its many forms is one set of means available to power, and it can be applied, in ways blunt or creative, in combination with other means of domination, internationally or domestically. Strategy is the art of weaving together force with other means in a given social and historical context to achieve political purposes. It is crucial to emphasize the significance of context. What war is, how force might be mixed with other political means, shifts with context.

Context here has to be thought of in the broadest possible terms. For example, in a sovereign states system, sovereignty as a juridical and political construct is part of the context, part of the field on which

[25] Ibid., 50, 51. [26] Ibid., 50. [27] Ibid., 56.

strategy operates. Granting sovereign recognition to a rebel movement and cloaking a state's involvement in a war are forms of strategic maneuver (which, it should be mentioned, require diplomacy). This is why efforts to scientifically define war in terms of sovereign state categories can be confounded by the politics of war.

What is being outlined here is a way of bringing peace and war into the same analytic field, which we might label "politics," and within which organized violence is conceived as an ordinary rather than extraordinary element. In introducing his mature discussion of how politics shapes the use of military force, and of the difficulty of telling war from peace, Clausewitz raises the problem of one state supporting another state that is fighting a war.[28] He uses the example of sending a contingent of soldiers some few tens of thousands strong to support the ally. He highlights the resulting frustrations of what contemporary NATO and UN commanders would recognize as "national red cards," the political limitations that troop-contributing countries put on the use of their forces. He notes as well the unsurprising hypocrisy of official pledges of unstinting support for fraternal allies. Instead, "the affair is more often like a business deal," in light of risks and dividends, each state will "invest about 30,000 to 40,000 men, and behave as if that were all [it] stood to lose."[29] In more contemporary contexts, what investing 30,000 to 40,000 soldiers might mean can take different forms. It might for example take the form of advice and support teams to train host country forces, of special operations groups to raise and direct local militias, of technicians for the complex machinery of war, of the provision of warplanes and pilots, or of manned antiaircraft systems under the flag of the host country, or of privately hired forces, or other clandestine means.

Contexts of hierarchy and small war

All of the examples just given are taken from histories of great power involvement in wars in the Third World and global South from 1945. They are significant for a number of reasons. For one, it is easy to imagine the key role of diplomats and their official and back channels in organizing and facilitating these various exercises of coercive power. For another, they demonstrate the blind spots of Eurocentric images of

[28] Clausewitz, *On War*, 603–604. [29] Ibid., 603.

war as consisting of large-scale clashes of official, national forces, as operationalized in the CoW data set. As I have shown in other work, the statistical artifact of the "democratic peace" is constructed such that covert and clandestine uses of force do not count as "war."[30] Thus, it is possible to maintain scientifically that no two democratic states have ever fought a war, while it is more or less well known that the United States overthrew a number of elected governments during the Cold War through covert uses of force.

The classic example is the way the United States organized the invasion of Guatemala in 1954 to bring down the elected government of Jacobo Arbenz. CoW classifies the resulting fighting as a civil war, but the entire affair was authorized at the highest levels of the Eisenhower administration. It was organized and funded by the CIA, and the fighting conducted by mercenaries, seconded US military personnel, and third-country CIA contractors. The failure to see this for what it is – the use of force by the United States for political purposes, that is, an international war – hinges on the idea that war is a particular, Eurocentric state of affairs that involves large-scale clashes between official, sovereign armed forces. But war sometimes consists of the light, handy rapier Clausewitz wrote of, perhaps wielded at arm's reach by a third party.

Ultimately of greater significance than the covert operations of the 1950s was the use of advice and support to raise, train, arm, supply, and direct (in so far as possible) the military and security forces of anti-communist allies during the Cold War. Large-scale violence took place through such means, although officially and scientifically, the United States was never at war in El Salvador or in Laos until 1964 (after 10 years of armed involvement), or in Vietnam until 1965 (ditto), or in Afghanistan in the 1980s; the same was true for the Soviet Union during the Korean War, the Vietnam War, and the conflicts in Mozambique and Angola. As a result of the threat of escalation, it was crucial during the Cold War that only one of the superpowers be officially involved in any given Third World conflict. Therefore, in this context, cloaking sovereign involvement and working through third parties were crucial dimensions of strategy and the conduct of war.

30 Tarak Barkawi, "War inside the Free World: The Democratic Peace and the Cold War in the Third World," in Barkawi and Mark Laffey, eds., *Democracy, Liberalism and War* (Boulder: Lynne Rienner, 2001), 107–128.

What these examples attest to is that war takes different forms when fought by great powers against lesser ones in peripheral regions of the world. Sometimes it takes less force, is smaller scale, such as the tiny wars of many European colonial conquests, or the continual but small-scale armed revolts the colonial authorities were forever putting down, or the various insurgencies that the superpowers became involved in on one side or the other during the Cold War. Today, one US military command, Africom, is set up almost entirely as an advice and support operation, assisting African countries in fighting "terrorists." Such small war is organized differently and often makes use of foreign military personnel and other third parties. Thus, we cannot read across images of war and diplomacy from the heyday of the European sovereign states system to world politics, whether in historical or contemporary eras.[31] War is different in different contexts, and most of the population of the planet, and any relations of war and diplomacy that are relevant to them, live outside Europe and always have. This turn to forms of great power warfare in the global South is not of value only for understanding small wars. It also can be used to sharpen general concepts, to think through how we might more properly understand and analyze war and the use of force.

Consider the state-person, the juridical fiction of the state as a unitary actor mentioned earlier. Here is Hobbes's Leviathan as an artificial man, wielding military forces as he would a hammer or sword, an instrument of violence. But war is in fact a complex organizational endeavor, which requires all manner of planning, administration, finance, logistics, communications, training, practicing, and so on, not least in organizing and constituting the very forces capable of fighting war. Theorists as well as commanders might like to imagine that armed forces operate like well-oiled machines, and sometimes in some contexts they may indeed approach such a standard. But even for the disciplined armed forces of the Napoleonic era with which he was directly concerned, Clausewitz gave friction and contingency primary roles in his theory of war, while mocking the intellectual products of overly rationalist philosophers of war for ignoring them. How much less like machines are the international, third-party agglomerations of forces found in the kind of small wars described earlier? Might they not require much diplomacy to organize, maintain, and operate? What the

[31] Black makes a similar point about diplomacy in his *A History of Diplomacy*.

image of the state-person neglects is what might be called the *sociological* character of war, which, among other things, requires the raising, organizing, supplying, arming, and directing of armed forces. What this sociological character might consist of changes with historical and political context, a topic that risks obliteration by ahistoric conceptions of the international system as consisting of unitary rational actors. Getting rid of the state-as-person analogy reveals the complex web of social relations, domestic, international, and transnational, required to constitute force and make war. The question then arises of diplomacy's role in creating, sustaining, and directing these webs to certain ends.

A final point needs to be drawn out of the sociological character of war. In liberal thought, war is often conceived as the breakdown of order, while peace is the reestablishment of order. But of course war can also sustain orders, as for example in the regular use of force necessary to maintain European colonial rule or to keep parts of the Free World from going communist during the Cold War, or vice versa in the Eastern bloc. The same is true of forms of organized violence other than war. Secret police, torturers, and concentration camps can protect totalitarian regimes, while contemporary liberal societies rely on well-funded, organized, and trained police and security forces to maintain order. Here is the single analytic field of politics in which force is but one instrument available to power in ensuring continued domination. If we internationalize this insight, we can see that international orders also require for their maintenance complex mixes of pacific and violent means, of police and military, of spies and torturers, of propaganda and prisons, all of which can be orchestrated in foreign societies. War happens when the use of force is reciprocated, but there are many ways in which internationalized forms of violence are created and deployed to sustain the local instantiation of a larger order. The European imperial world needed its colonial armies and police, recruited from the colonized, just as the US-run Free World of the Cold War required its military, police, and intelligence advisors and the indigenous organizations they worked with, as does the war on terror. The larger backdrop against which to think about war is not some beatific state of peace, but the range of forms of organized violence used to pursue political purposes and maintain local and international orders of power. The role of diplomats and diplomacy in facilitating such violence is not too difficult to glimpse. So too is the power of the war/peace binary in *pacifying* our conceptions of social and political order – as if organized violence were not an ordinary feature of politics in times of official "peace."

Diplomacy, force, and war

The discussion of Clausewitz, Foucault, and small war has sought to break down the binary between war and peace and emphasize the centrality of force to politics. It has tried also to suggest a certain cunning in the making of war, especially its imperial varieties, which infects the very categories we use to make sense of war and peace in political life and in scholarship. Among other things, war is a destroyer, manipulator, and creator of truths.[32] Whether or not a state is officially at war, just how it is at war, and with whom, is a political matter, for domestic as for international audiences. How can these insights help rethink diplomacy and war? It is helpful to return to the Iraqi air corridor. The first move is to resist the question of whether or not Iraq is at war or at peace with the Syrian rebels. The second is not to think of "Iraq" as some kind of unitary actor but instead recall the web of relations sustaining the war in Syria, the international flows of money, people, material, arms, munitions, expertise, and so on, and the various configurations they take over time. The arms corridor in question, it turns out, along with the arrival of Hezbollah infantry from Lebanon, seems to have been crucial to the Assad regime's ability to gain the upper hand against the rebels in the spring of 2013.[33]

This web of international relations necessary to sustaining war can be thought of as a kind of "international administration of war," in which Iraq is involved. "Iraq" being here in the first instance its state apparatus, including its diplomatic corps, but also the various interconnections with civil society and communities with sectarian identifications and other aims, within and beyond Iraq's sovereign territory, not least in Iran. Iraq is engaged in its own long and many-sided war, which has reordered the battle lines among its constituent groupings. Publically and privately, inside and outside the state apparatus, different groupings of Iraqis are aiding those on both sides in Syria whom

[32] Tarak Barkawi and Shane Brighton, "Powers of War: Fighting, Knowledge and Critique," *International Political Sociology*, 5(2), 2011, 126–143.

[33] Mark Mazzetti, Michael R. Gordon, and Mark Landler, "U.S. Is Said to Plan to Send Weapons to Syrian Rebels," *New York Times*, June 14, 2013.

they perceive as allies. To the extent the officialdom is caught up in these relations, Iraq is helping sustain and supply the forces involved in the fighting. It is in this sense that Iraqi diplomats among other officials can be said to be participating in war. War cannot occur or be sustained without some such logistical web in the broadest sense. Far from being short of war, diplomacy is often a necessary part of it, especially given the myriad international dimensions of modern warfare, not least the international sourcing of its basic implements, weapons, and munitions. Iraq was neither at peace nor at war, nor was it fighting in Syria, but its officials and their allies were helping sustain and internationally administer the war there.

What is being called here the international administration of war – the web of international relations that makes war possible – is a subject amenable to empirical inquiry, as are the various roles played by state officials including diplomats as well as civil servants and contractors in other ministries concerned with foreign affairs. The proper study of diplomacy and war would investigate this subject in historical and contemporary perspective to arrive at a full account of the relations between diplomacy and fighting. The juridical and social contract theory inheritances of IR would have to be left behind, and a sociological attitude taken toward diplomats and their participation in warfare in the sense outlined here: the empirical study of the international administration of war. Two broad categories for such an analysis suggest themselves: the constitution of force and the use of it. Some discussion and examples for each will give a fuller sense of what the subject of diplomacy and war might consist of.

The constitution of armed force

The state-as-person, as a unitary sovereign actor, often entails an assumption about armed forces: that they are constituted from within sovereign borders, recruited from national subjects, and then projected outward. The idea of the modern state as a territorial monopoly on the legitimate use of force contributes to this assumption, in which state, army, and society are co-located, in isomorphic or "trinitarian" relations with one another. The state-person of social contract theory dovetails with a sovereign nation-state ontology of the international. "War" happens when official, national armed forces are directly involved in fighting, as in CoW's coding rules. In this way, juridical fictions invade the operational definitions of social science: a state's official, national armed forces are the only ones deemed relevant for the determination of whether a state of war or peace appertains. Since the constitution of force is a domestic matter, on this view, diplomats would appear to have no role. It is as if the armed forces were just there, ready and waiting for the state-person to command them.

In fact, modern world politics is replete with many and varied foreign forces, and with an array of historical and contemporary modalities by which states constitute force internationally.[34] These include foreign recruitment for national forces, the raising and maintaining of colonial armies and police forces recruited from colonized populations, the advice and support of the armed forces of subordinate states, and various covert and deniable uses of foreign military personnel, including putatively private forms of armed force. The coercive power of states has international and transnational dimensions that call into question the adequacy of the idea of public, territorial monopolies as a way of thinking about the global organization of force and state power. Once these dimensions are taken into account, the manifold and changing role of diplomats and diplomacy in the constitution of force comes into view.[35]

Perhaps the most obvious examples concern foreign recruitment for national forces, a story that begins with the prominent role of mercenaries in early modern warfare but continues to the current day. Recruiting mercenary companies abroad required an official apparatus of some kind, as did managing them while under contract. Diplomats, civil servants, and ministers became involved in various ways. Such recruiting continued in later eras but took different forms in new historical contexts. In the middle of the American Civil War, the Union found itself in a severe personnel crisis and looked to encourage immigration from abroad to fill the ranks of its regiments and for laborers for its factories and farms. Secretary of State William Seward was a key proponent of such schemes and played a decisive role in establishing a partnership between a private company and the federal government to facilitate immigration. US consulates and embassies

[34] Tarak Barkawi, "State and Armed Force in International Context," in Alex Colas and Bryan Mabee, eds., *Mercenaries, Pirates, Bandits and Empires* (London: Hurst, 2010), 33–53.

[35] On which, see Tarak Barkawi, "'Defence Diplomacy' in North/South Relations," *International Journal*, 66(3), 2011, 597–612.

became heavily involved in these schemes, which involved providing funds for potential immigrants to cover their transportation and other costs. The Irish were a particular focus for military recruits. In addition to poverty and lack of jobs and land in Europe, many Europeans were attracted by the Emancipation Proclamation of 1863, which inspired radicals disappointed in the outcomes of 1848 to join the fight against the Confederacy. It is impossible to know the numbers involved, and the studies available do not focus specifically on the role of the diplomatic corps, although Seward figures prominently.[36] The example gives some idea of the directions the empirical study of diplomacy and war might take.

More contemporary examples include the continuing recruitment of foreign citizens into Western militaries. In some cases, such as the French Foreign Legion, diplomats are only minimally involved in the recruiting process (those interested in joining the legion must first travel to France for which they may require visas), while in others there appears to be a substantial official role. The United Kingdom recruited extensively in Fiji in the past decade and maintains a recruiting relationship with Nepal that dates back to the breakup of the Raj in 1947. Many Commonwealth citizens have served in the ranks of the UK's armed forces, just as tens of thousands of Latin Americans and other foreign citizens served in the US military.[37] How diplomats are involved in facilitating these relationships or in obstructing them – South Africa has passed a law preventing its citizens from serving in foreign militaries[38] – are questions for further research.

If foreign recruitment appears to be a relatively minor way in which diplomats might participate in the constitution of force, far more significant is the question of advice and support. With decolonization, colonial armies and police forces became the sovereign armed forces of the new states, yet they continued their relationships with their former colonial patrons or developed new ones with the superpowers. The

36 See Scott Reynolds Nelson and Carol Sheriff, *A People at War* (New York: Oxford University Press, 2008), 187–213; and Aristide Zolberg, *A Nation by Design* (Cambridge, MA: Harvard University Press, 2008), 166–175.

37 See e.g. Vron Ware, *Military Migrants* (London: Palgrave Macmillan, 2012); Fernanda Santos, "After the War, a New Battle to Become Citizens," *New York Times*, February 24, 2008; Eric Schmitt, "Boom Times for U.S. Military Recruiters," *International Herald Tribune*, September 22, 2003, 8.

38 Michael Wines, "South Africa: Anti-Mercenary Law Passed," *New York Times*, August 20, 2006.

United States, for example, formed the South Korean army and national police around those who had served the Japanese during the colonial period. It took over from the French responsibility for the South Vietnamese armed forces. The Soviet Union fostered the armies of the Warsaw Pact as well as those of its clients in the Third World. Both superpowers developed extensive programs for foreign military training; advising; and the supply, sale, and maintenance of weapons, equipment, and munitions.[39]

The scale of international military relations in the post-1945 world was substantial, as were the requirements for diplomatic coordination, planning, administering, trouble-shooting, and so on. Before armed forces can be used for violent purposes, they have to be constituted, trained, maintained, and exercised. Diplomacy is involved in these processes and participates in key dimensions of the international administration of war. Consider in this regard foreign bases such as Diego Garcia, which has played a significant role in US military operations in both the Cold War and the War on Terror. The atoll is a British Indian Ocean Territory claimed by Mauritius and leased to the United States, originally in exchange for a discount on Polaris SLBMs purchased by the UK. The indigenous islanders were forcibly evicted and resettled in Mauritius and the Seychelles.[40] Here, and as indicated elsewhere in this chapter, a small universe of diplomatic activity comes into view, one necessary for sustaining the very bases from which forces operate on their wartime missions. In nearly all of its military involvements in the post-1945 world, US forces have operated from foreign bases, amid more or less complex diplomatic, legal, financial, and political arrangements.[41] Recently, the United States negotiated a 20-year lease for a base in Djibouti, which serves as a hub for manned and unmanned aircraft, military trainers, and advisors for Africom, and a rapid reaction force to protect US embassies.[42]

The sociological perspective on war has drawn attention to the question of how armed forces are constituted and to the international

[39] See e.g. Chalmers Johnson, *The Sorrows of Empire* (London: Verso, 2004), 131–140; Lora Lumpe, "U.S. Foreign Military Training" (Interhemispheric Resource Center and the Institute for Policy Studies, 2002); Stephanie Neuman, *Military Assistance in Recent Wars* (New York: Praeger, 1986).

[40] David Vine, *Island of Shame* (Princeton, NJ: Princeton University Press, 2009).

[41] Alexander Cooley, *Base Politics* (Ithaca: Cornell University Press, 2008).

[42] Eric Schmitt, "U.S. Signs New Lease to Keep Strategic Military Installation in the Horn of Africa," *New York Times*, May 5, 2014.

dimensions of these processes. Unlike colonial armed forces, subject to the command authority of the colonial powers, the kinds of advised and supported forces discussed earlier often belong, formally speaking, to other sovereign states. Their use on active operations requires all manner of diplomacy, practiced not only by diplomats and foreign ministry officials but also by military officers and others involved. The utility of such forces for the sponsoring power is precisely that they are foreign, and that officially speaking the sponsoring power is not involved in hostilities. Embassies become crucial sites for influence, control, and coordination. The US embassy in San Salvador during the 1980s and the one in Saigon before and after the direct involvement of US forces in Vietnam were major conduits for arranging and controlling military assistance. More recently, the US embassy in Sana'a played a significant role in directing Yemini intelligence and security forces in their fight against local and foreign *jihadis*. The US embassies in Kabul and Baghdad were central administrative nodes in long wars. Diplomacy's permanent, extraterritorial infrastructure remains crucial and takes on new roles in the "colonial present."[43] Coalition diplomats and other officials served as political advisors to wartime commanders, were members of Provincial Reconstruction Teams, and otherwise staffed the administration of occupying forces at war, working as part of a mix of coercive and other means intended to defeat many-sided insurgencies and establish order.

The use of force

In securing permission for forces to operate from foreign bases or in turning embassies into sites for organizing, assisting, and directing third-party forces, we move from the role of diplomats in merely constituting forces to participating in their wartime use. Cold War Laos offers a revealing example of such involvement, in which US diplomats and other civilian, military, and intelligence officials in several countries constituted forces and then coordinated and conducted a "secret" war, a war fought by diplomatic means. The 1954 Geneva Accords prevented the United States and the USSR from deploying their military personnel in Laos, even as advisors. The standard US institutional apparatus for the advice and support of foreign forces, a Military

[43] Derek Gregory, *The Colonial Present* (Oxford: Blackwell, 2004).

Assistance Advisory Group, would violate the agreements. Yet neither the United States nor the USSR and the Democratic Republic of Vietnam (North Vietnam) were willing to abandon their respective clients in Laos. The United States was aware of Soviet and North Vietnamese violation of the accords but decided to maintain the appearance of compliance, while finding other routes through which to conduct its policy.[44]

The result was the creation of what one US admiral wryly referred to as the only "SECSTATE theater of war."[45] US military advice and support was channeled through the "civilian" aid programs of the US embassy in Vientiane to, in Henry Kissinger's words, "avoid a formal avowal of American participation for diplomatic reasons."[46] The innocuously named Programs Evaluations Office (PEO) was created in Laos by the Department of State. It was staffed initially by reserve, retired, or conveniently discharged US military personnel who were given State Department rank as foreign service officers. Later, CIA officers, US Army Special Forces, and third-country personnel on contract, such as Filipino combat veterans of the US-backed counterinsurgency campaign against the Huks, were placed on PEO rolls as well as those of other US civilian aid agencies, such as USAID, and their private contractors.

To support its operations in Laos and elsewhere in Indochina in the wake of the Geneva Accords, the United States developed a military and covert operations infrastructure, much of it based in Thailand. Establishing and maintaining this infrastructure required negotiation and administration, as did the various programs to constitute foreign forces. Training of Laotian, Thai, and other third-country personnel was conducted in Thailand. Later in the war, in response to the continuing disappointing combat performance of the Laotian army, the United States established a Thai Volunteer Program through which Thai military and police specialists were given discharges of convenience, reissued with Laotian identity papers, hired by various US entities, and then sent to Laos as "civilian experts." As the fighting in Laos

44 Timothy N. Castle, *At War in the Shadow of Vietnam: U.S. Military Aid to the Royal Lao Government 1955–1975* (New York: Columbia University Press, 1993), 61.

45 Quoted in ibid., 2. "SECSTATE" is bureaucratic jargon for the U.S. Secretary of State.

46 Quoted in ibid., 57.

intensified after 1960, the United States doubled the size of the Laotian regular army, which it paid the entire cost of, and raised a force of Hmong, which became known as *L'Armee Clandestine* and eventually numbered 30,000.[47] (It was a corps-size force not considered by CoW to amount to US participation.[48]) To support these and other forces in Laos, the United States created a small CIA/State Department Air Force that flew ground attack sorties and supported search and rescue missions for US pilots downed while bombing the Ho Chi Minh Trail.[49]

Throughout the period of US involvement in Indochina, pitched battles as well as guerrilla operations and air strikes were conducted against Pathet Lao and North Vietnamese forces in Laos.[50] Command and control for operations in Laos, both in the air and on the ground, were largely conducted out of the US embassy in Vientiane, with the US ambassador in the role of commanding general.[51] Ambassador Sullivan was known as the "field marshal." Such were the arrangements necessary for the United States to conduct what William Colby termed a "non-attributable war," fought with plausibly deniable army and air forces.[52] The Geneva Accords of 1954 and 1962 and, later, US congressional action had prevented overt US deployments.

Laos shows just how deeply embassies and diplomats can become involved in war, and it demonstrates how much war making CoW's and other sovereign state-based categories can miss. Laos also broaches a final subject for this section. Laos was a frontier zone of the Free World, a world order project of US and Western power, one that required for its maintenance a complex intermixing of means, and not just the violence of war, in its competition with the Soviet-led socialist world order project. The overworked US embassy in Vientiane, with its field marshal ambassador, also had to influence and fix elections in Laos and administer rural development programs designed to discourage peasants from supporting the Pathet Lao, Lao's

47 Bernard Fall, *Anatomy of a Crisis* (Garden City, NY: Doubleday, 1969); Castle, *At War in the Shadow of Vietnam*, 122.

48 Melvin Small and J. David Singer, *Resort to Arms* (Beverly Hills, CA: Sage, 1982), 326.

49 Castle, *At War in the Shadow of Vietnam*, 69–71, 74–76.

50 See e.g. William M. Leary, "The CIA and the 'Secret War' in Laos: The Battle for Skyline Ridge, 1971–1972," *The Journal of Military History*, 59, 1995, 505–518.

51 Castle, *At War in the Shadow of Vietnam*, 55.

52 Quoted in ibid., 94.

communist party.[53] As elsewhere in Indochina, the communists responded with their own intermixing of pacific and violent means characteristic of revolutionary guerrilla warfare and the social, political, and economic contradictions it sought to exploit. Before 1960, pacific means dominated while the reverse was true after that date, but what was at issue were different phases of a long political struggle requiring at various moments different combinations and forms of coercive and non-coercive means.

Today, under guise of the War on Terror, US embassies are again channeling large advice and support programs for states in the global South; they serve as sites for intelligence gathering, coordination, and directing operations, and they are administrative organs for the international carceral apparatus and its practices of rendition.[54] Looked at from Yemen today, Laos is not quite the Cold War relic it may seem. Officially, the United States was not involved in a war in Yemen in 2014. Yet, by April of that year, the Obama administration had conducted more than a hundred drone and other air strikes, killing just under a thousand people.[55] Drones and F-15s fly their missions in Yemen from the base in Djbouti, while other drones operate from Saudi Arabia, Ethiopia, and the Seychelles. US Special Forces were active in Sana'a.[56] Extensive advice and support programs were put in place to "improve the Yemeni military's operational range, tactical proficiency, and response time; build an integrated aerial surveillance and ground mobility capability to monitor and interdict threats along Yemen's coastline; and improve communications between aerial assets and ground forces."[57] Equipment and training included everything from small arms, ammunition, and radios to vehicles, helicopters, patrol boats, and fixed-wing aircraft. Alongside this program of war, orchestrated in no small measure through diplomatic means, is a

[53] Charles Stevenson, *End of Nowhere* (Boston: Beacon Press, 1973), chaps. 1–3; Castle, *At War in the Shadow of Vietnam*, 19.

[54] See e.g. Laleh Khalili, *Time in the Shadows* (Stanford: Stanford University Press, 2012).

[55] Peter Bergen, "Obama's High-Stakes Drone War in Yemen," CNN, April 21, 2014, http://edition.cnn.com/2014/04/21/opinion/bergen-yemen-obama-drone-war/index.html, accessed 13 June, 2014.

[56] Eric Schmitt, "U.S. Officers Kill Armed Civilians in Yemen Capital," *New York Times*, May 9, 2014.

[57] US Department of State, "U.S. Support for Yemen," Fact Sheet, August 20, 2013.

program of imperial governance in the form of the reconstruction of the Yemeni state along lines preferred by the United States, which has allocated more than $600 million in aid to, in the words of a White House official, help "strengthen governance and institutions on which Yemen's long-term progress depends."[58] Initiatives include a national dialogue, constitutional reform, elections, and other capacity- and institution-building efforts.

As with the Cold War, scholarship will take some time to catch up with official secrecy and uncover the extent and nature of the activities in Yemen and elsewhere. In part by recovering older notions of civilization versus barbarism, the War on Terror has taken on the garb of a world order project, in which civilized states cooperate against "terrorism" in the name of progress. As with the Free World, a mix of coercive and non-coercive means is deployed to further this world order project against transnational *jihadi* opponents who seek to further their own visions of global and local caliphates. In Afghanistan, Libya, Mali, and other places, the War on Terror has melded also with the 1990s project of international humanitarian intervention, in which the civilized world exercises its "responsibility to protect" the innocent and furthers the spread of liberal democracy. Here again is a many-sided political struggle, globally and locally, in which force is combined with other means to achieve political purposes. Yet, the international cooperation required for this struggle appears as the opposite of war. The pacific aura of diplomacy dresses it up in the garb of peace and progress, creating an image devoid of violence, domination, and exploitation. The alliance between diplomacy and peace has distorted understanding of world politics.

Diplomacy and the war behind the peace

As the Introduction to this volume explicates, it is an irony of some proportions that IR has failed to engage with diplomacy. The study of it largely has been the preserve of historians and of former practitioners. In place of axiomatic deductions about the relations between diplomacy, peace, and war, this chapter has sought to define the contours of

[58] John Brennan, quoted in Gordon Lubold and Noah Schachtman, "Inside Yemen's Shadow War Arsenal," *Foreign Policy*, 7, 2013, http://www.foreignpolicy.com/articles/2013/08/07/inside_yemens_shadow_war_arsenal, accessed June 8, 2014.

an empirical object of analysis, the international administration of war, and to identify the role of diplomacy and diplomats in it. Another route to integrating IR theory with the study of diplomacy is to turn to those theorists who, while they may not directly address the activities of diplomats, presume a prominent role for diplomacy in their theories. In this way, the subject of diplomacy dovetails with that of international cooperation, and in so doing reinforces the association between diplomacy and peace. It is diplomacy that oils the gears of international society, that makes cooperation happen, and that undergirds multilateralism.[59] In part through the diplomacy-as-peace association, each of these IR theoretic terms takes on a pacific air and seems, like diplomacy, to be the opposite of war. Yet, "international society" has spent some centuries cooperating in snuffing out indigenous peoples, colonizing large tracts of the planet, and fighting total wars. Diplomacy-as-peace has drained war and violence out of theories of international cooperation.

In IR, the problem of international cooperation largely is conceived as a collective action problem among state-persons: how do individuals come to cooperate in a state of nature. Answers to this basic problem of social contract theory can be rationalist or constructivist in nature. For example, in his influential *The Moral Purpose of the State*, Christian Reus-Smit offers a constructivist take that revolves around the idea that in any given international system, a hegemonic belief about the moral purposes of autonomous political entities reigns, one that governs the forms of cooperation that develop between them.[60] The concern is with how states "solve their cooperation problems and achieve coexistence," not with what happens when they do not. War is defined out of the subject of cooperation, much like it was from the idea of diplomacy.[61] In the "stable" societies of states with which Reus-Smit is concerned, contestation occurs only at the "margins."[62] In this way, the fascist and socialist challenges to the West were made to disappear, just as the Persians do not appear in his discussion of ancient Greece.

59 See e.g. Hedley Bull, *The Anarchical Society* (New York: Columbia University Press, 1977); Robert Keohane, *After Hegemony* (Princeton, NJ: Princeton University Press, 2005); Reus-Smit, *The Moral Purpose of the State*.

60 Reus-Smit, *The Moral Purpose of the State*, 26.

61 Ibid., xi. There is a single index entry for war, 14, where it is suggested that war might be a fundamental institution of international society, an idea that receives no further consideration.

62 Ibid., 33.

Cooperation appears in a wholly pacific light. Yet, the melding together of Western military-industrial complexes and the conduct of coalition warfare during the world wars were exemplars of cooperation, as well as of the diplomatic staff work of war.[63]

Also striking in IR approaches to cooperation is the relative absence of empire and other forms of international hierarchy that persisted after decolonization and the expansion of international society.[64] The states of the liberal constitutionalist core, which lie at the heart of IR theories of cooperation, were the most successful imperialists in world history. They grew rich off slavery, indentured labor, conquest, colonization, and expropriation; they developed an array of innovative forms of foreign rule and mechanisms for the maintenance of international hierarchy; and they defeated near-continuous local challenges to their dominance. All of this involved a great deal of diplomacy and cooperation, yet it finds little place in disciplinary debates about the collective action problems of sovereign states. The world appears not as a charnel house of exploitation and death, but as a place where civilized states are committed to norms of "procedural justice."[65]

In this way, international cooperation appears nearly entirely as a matter of peace and coexistence, not of the organization and maintenance of domination, or of the mixing of coercive and non-coercive means in the service of world order projects like liberal civilization. These projects of course encounter resistance and require wars to see through, as in our own day. And wars oftentimes require diplomacy for their making, a truism difficult to keep in focus in a discipline that so readily associates diplomacy and cooperation with peace.

63 William McNeill, *The Pursuit of Power* (Chicago: University of Chicago Press, 1982), chaps. 9–10.
64 Cf. David Lake, *Hierarchy in International Relations* (Ithaca: Cornell University Press, 2011).
65 Reus-Smit, *The Moral Purpose of the State*, 26–27.

3 *The practice of permanent representation to international organizations*

VINCENT POULIOT

– Negotiating multilaterally you are entering a world of its own.

Nyerges, "How to Negotiate," 177

Multilateral diplomacy has come of age – to the point that it now "incontestably dominates international life," according to two prominent observers.[1] Everyday global governance is punctuated by a seemingly endless series of regular international meetings dealing with security, trade, finance, the environment, development, and many other issues. A cursory survey of world news returns a large proportion of G20 summits, UN conferences, Security Council meetings, World Trade Organization (WTO) negotiation sessions, Association of Southeast Nations (ASEAN) forums, and other EU councils. In the past few decades, multilateralism – "an institutional form which coordinates relations among three or more states on the basis of 'generalized' principles of conduct"[2] – has become the ordinary process by which international relations are conducted. Actors and observers usually think from multilateral diplomacy, much less about its opportunity.[3]

[1] Bertrand Badie and Guillaume Devin, eds., *Le multilatéralisme. Nouvelles formes de l'action internationale* (Paris: La Découverte, 2007), 7. All translations from French are the author's.

[2] John Gerard Ruggie, "Multilateralism: The Anatomy of an Institution," *International Organization* 46(3), 1992, 571.

[3] Vincent Pouliot, "Multilateralism as an End in Itself," *International Studies Perspectives*, 12(1), 2011. In this piece, I try to specify Ruggie's definition a little further: "Multilateralism is a global governance practice characterized by an inclusive, institutionalized and principled form of political dialogue. By this definition, multilateral governance stands in opposition to a number of other institutional forms on the global stage, including: (i) unilateralism, bilateralism and "minilateralism," which tend to exclude actors for the sake of efficiency; (ii) coalitions of the willing, whose ad hoc shapes constantly evolve from one issue to the next; and (iii) concert-type organizations, which typically rest on discriminatory rules that set certain self-appointed participants above the others.

Multilateralism is a political process that keeps evolving over time. For heuristic purposes, it is useful to distinguish among three broad forms of multilateral diplomacy – all of which are currently on the rise. First, there is the rapidly emerging form of "complex multilateralism,"[4] a hybrid configuration of heterodox actors (states, NGOs, IOs, corporations, etc.). The Global Compact[5] exemplifies this new kind of "multiscalar," "polycentric," and "diffuse" global governance.[6] Second, the most visible form of multilateral diplomacy is that of summitry, ranging from annual G8 summits to Asia-Pacific Economic Cooperation (APEC) sessional gatherings. These high-level meetings easily catch headlines when they happen, even though their outcomes usually rest on lower-key and often informal transgovernmental cooperation.[7] Third, operating more or less behind the scene (though in a rather formal role) are permanent representatives (PRs), that is, ambassadors posted at various IOs to conduct ongoing negotiations on behalf of member states. Cities such as New York, Brussels, and Vienna host vast numbers of national delegates attached to the UN, the EU, NATO, the Organization for Security and Co-operation in Europe (OSCE), the International Atomic Energy Agency (IAEA), and a plethora of other intergovernmental bodies. Indeed, Kleiner goes as far as to write that "if any form of diplomacy deserves to be called 'modern,' it is the multilateral diplomacy within an international governmental organization."[8] It is on this form of multilateral diplomacy – permanent representation – that this chapter focuses.

Using the lens of political sociology, the chapter argues the following: because permanent representation rests on peculiar practical logics, its rising prevalence is incrementally transforming diplomacy

As a form of collective action, then, the qualitatively distinct nature of the multilateral procedure combines comprehensiveness, routinization, and non-discrimination," ibid., 19.

4 Robert O'Brien et al., eds., *Contesting Global Governance: Multilateral Economic Institutions and Global Social Movements* (Cambridge: Cambridge University Press, 2000).

5 See Jean-Philippe Thérien and Vincent Pouliot, "The Global Compact: Shifting the Politics of International Development?" *Global Governance* 12(1), 2006.

6 Jan Aart Scholte, *Globalization: A Critical Introduction*, 2nd edn (Basingstoke: Palgrave MacMillan, 2005).

7 Anne-Marie Slaughter, *A New World Order* (Princeton, NJ: Princeton University Press, 2004).

8 Jürgen Kleiner, *Diplomatic Practice: Between Tradition and Innovation* (Singapore: World Scientific, 2010), 306.

into a new mode of governing. "Perm reps," as insiders call them, do not simply represent their state inside headquarters, as the traditional image of the conveyor belt would suggest. As a result of powerful though often overlooked social dynamics, perm reps are also implicated in the conduct of global governance itself. As Neumann correctly points out, "very little seems to be known about the standard operational procedures and the everyday routines of diplomacy."[9] And yet, as this chapter shows, the practicality of diplomacy has a considerable import on world politics, not least in transforming the roles played by diplomats in global governance. As a result of relational and practical logics, perm reps occupy a dual role, as country representatives and "global governors."[10] Needless to say, this evolution renders the practice of permanent representation not only increasingly prevalent but also more and more significant for the study of world politics.

My demonstration proceeds as follows. I begin with a brief description of permanent representation to show its rapid expansion in recent history. In the second section of the chapter, I explore the distinctive relational features of the practice. Not only is permanent representation a form of group diplomacy, it is also a diplomacy of groups[11] – a social morphology that generates significant social dynamics. In the third section, I analyze the practical logics and rules of the game that characterize permanent representation, including pressure dynamics, translation games, discipline, a specific tempo, esprit de corps, and pecking orders. These relational and intersubjective structures matter, I conclude, because taken together, they progressively push multilateral diplomacy down the road of governing, with significant constitutive effects on world politics.

I should make one prefatory note about the logical sequence of my theoretical argument, which seemingly implies that the relational structure of permanent representation generates the practical logics of multilateral diplomacy. Theoretically speaking, the connection between relationality and intersubjectivity flows both ways. As Mische aptly puts it, relations, interpretations, and actions are

9 Iver B. Neumann, *At Home with the Diplomats: Inside a European Foreign Ministry* (Ithaca, NY: Cornell University Press, 2012), 3.

10 Deborah D. Avant, Martha Finnemore, and Susan K. Sell, *Who Governs the Globe?* (New York: Cambridge University Press, 2010).

11 The double meaning works better in French: "une diplomatie de groupe" and "une diplomatie de groupes."

"mutually generative."[12] However, in this chapter, I do emphasize relationality as a key determinant of intersubjectivity, primarily because permanent representation takes place within an organizational setting – that is, a social form devised by actors for a purpose. In other words, while some practical logics may be unintended outcomes, most of the institutional features of permanent representation were historically developed through collective processes. Ultimately, one key theoretical payoff of relational analytics is in specifying the non-semiotic processes that inform the social construction of reality.

The increasing prevalence of permanent representation

To say that multilateral diplomacy, including permanent representation, is an increasingly prevalent practice in the twenty-first century should not be too controversial a statement. Several indicators would seem to attest to this evolution. Most remarkably, the sheer number of IOs to which permanent missions are attached is constantly rising. This includes the UN and several of its specialized agencies (e.g., FAO, UNESCO), of course, but also many regional (e.g., the EU, NATO, the OAS) and functional organizations (e.g., the OECD). As Kleiner observes, "IGOs have added new platforms and new functions to diplomacy."[13] In addition, each of these IOs holds an increasing number of meetings at various levels, from ambassadors to experts.[14] Further, the scope of activities and sphere of competence of several IOs seem to know few limits to growth.[15] Indeed, the decision-making power of IOs is made stronger by the day. This is the case, most consequentially, of the Security Council, which now deals with a host of untraditional security issues such as women's rights, but also of an organization such as NATO that currently forays much beyond defense into economics, disaster relief, and the environment.[16] In the

12 Ann Mische, "Relational Sociology, Culture, and Agency," in John Scott and Peter J. Carrington, eds., *The Sage Handbook of Social Network Analysis* (Thousand Oaks, CA: Sage, 2011), 90.

13 Kleiner, *Diplomatic Practice*, 15.

14 E. R. Appathurai, "Permanent Missions in New York," in Geoff R. Berridge and Anthony Jennings, eds., *Diplomacy at the UN* (London: MacMillan, 1985), 96.

15 Michael N. Barnett and Martha Finnemore, *Rules for the World: International Organizations in Global Politics* (Ithaca, NY: Cornell University Press, 2004).

16 Bruce Cronin and Ian Hurd, *The UN Security Council and the Politics of International Authority* (London: Routledge, 2008).

twenty-first century, multilateral IOs play significant roles in almost all aspects of individual citizens' lives.

Politically speaking, international actors also attach more and more importance to the multilateral procedure.[17] In contemporary global governance, multilateralism is less of an item on the restaurant menu than the utensils with which one has to eat. Perhaps the most convincing evidence of this comes in those rare instances when relevant multilateral bodies are bypassed, such as the American invasion of Iraq in 2003. The loud and generalized outcry that such actions unfailingly generate, on a worldwide scale, is proof to the centrality and legitimacy that the practice has now attained. Those who see the demise of multilateralism in such episodes fail to grasp the political significance of contention and public justification in cases of norm breaching. A norm's salience becomes particularly visible precisely when it is violated. As Kratochwil writes: "Norms are used to make demands, rally support, justify action, ascribe responsibility, and assess the praiseworthy or blameworthy character of an action."[18] In contemporary world politics, those who circumvent multilateral diplomacy almost systematically try to justify their behavior and, failing that, usually have to suffer some international outrage.

At the administrative level, considerable changes suggesting the increasing prevalence of multilateral diplomacy, and permanent representation more specifically, are also underway.[19] First, states devote a considerable and growing amount of resources to staffing their missions to IOs. This regards not only funding, but also personnel.[20] It is well known, for instance, that the position of ambassador to the UN, the EU, and NATO "belongs to those of the highest rank in many foreign services and is filled with experienced diplomats."[21] And this tendency is increasing as permanent representative positions multiply.

17 Pouliot, "Multilateralism as an End in Itself."

18 Friedrich Kratochwil, "The Force of Prescriptions," *International Organization* 38(4), 1984, 686.

19 Robert A. Denemark and Matthew J. Hoffmann, "Just Scraps of Paper? The Dynamics of Multilateral Treaty-Making," *Cooperation and Conflict* 43(2), 2008; Mai'a K. Davis Cross, *Security Integration in Europe: How Knowledge-based Networks Are Transforming the European Union* (Ann Arbor: University of Michigan Press, 2011).

20 Alasdair Blair, "Permanent Representations to the European Union," *Diplomacy and Statecraft* 12(3), 2001.

21 Kleiner, *Diplomatic Practice*, 308.

Second, national governmental bodies have undergone significant restructurings to accommodate the rising significance of permanent missions. New departments for multilateral affairs or ministers of European affairs have been created,[22] while some countries are establishing a distinct professional trajectory for "multilateral diplomats" specialized in the practice of permanent representation.[23] Third, many permanent missions have become key hubs of international diplomacy, playing what is sometimes dubbed a "multibilateral role" of coordination and representation that reaches beyond the confines of the particular IO to which they are attached.[24] Permanent representation has become one of the most prevalent forms of modern diplomacy.

It is important to remember that such was not always the case. In fact, the practice of permanent representation is relatively new, and it took a long time to establish. The very first national delegations (to the League of Nations) gradually appeared in the 1920s and 1930s, originally composed of small numbers of delegates – one to four.[25] According to Placidi, between the two world wars major members such France, the UK, Germany, Italy, and the USSR did not even bother to establish a permanent mission in Geneva. [26] The development of permanent representation was slow, to the extent that the 1945 UN Charter contains no provision to that effect. It is only in the 1975 Vienna Convention on State Representation, which has yet to become active, that the practice of permanent representation was legally codified. Since then, however, diplomatic missions to IOs, most notably to the UN and several of its agencies, have "proliferated" to the point of now constituting a universal phenomenon. [27] When he was secretary-general, Dag Hammarskjöld went as far as to suggest that permanent missions "may be considered the most important

22 Pierre Grosser, "De 1945 aux années 1980: Une efflorescence sur fond de Guerre Froide et de décolonisation," in Bertrand Badie and Guillaume Devin, eds., *Le multilatéralisme. Nouvelles formes de l'action internationale* (Paris: La Découverte, 2007), 25.

23 Delphine Placidi, "La transformation des pratiques diplomatiques nationales," in ibid., 104.

24 Victor-Yves Ghebali, "L'évolution du phénomène des missions permanentes à Genève," in Marcel A. Boisard, Evgeny Chossudovsky, and Jacques Lemoine, eds., *Multilateral Diplomacy: The United Nations System at Geneva* (The Hague: Kluwer Law International, 1998), 43.

25 Ibid., 39.

26 Placidi, "La transformation des pratiques diplomatiques nationales," 99.

27 Kleiner, *Diplomatic Practice*, 303.

development in customary law ... within the constitutional framework of the Charter."[28]

Permanent missions to IOs are tasked with conducting multilateral negotiations on behalf of member states. Delegates attend various meetings dealing with directives, treaties, resolutions, budgets, and other official documents that form the textual fabric of global governance. Negotiating is what permanent representatives do day after day, setting them apart from other kinds of diplomats more focused on representation.[29] In that sense, multilateral diplomacy is based on "a kind of give-and-take," according to one NATO perm rep, "that's the spirit of all processes." Intriguingly, this process is a text-based one, composed of writing memos, drafting communiqués, circulating non-papers, refining wording, playing with commas, holding brackets, and so on – various editorial practices that, in a Latourian spirit, involve material artifacts as part of social relationships.[30] The material and institutional environments of permanent representation inside an international organization demand no less than a constant disposition to talk about, show interest in, and inquire into multilateral matters of debate. Perm reps are in a permanent state of negotiations.

In functional terms, the traditional image of permanent representation is that of a conveyor belt or diplomatic intermediary: the mission staff receives instructions from the capital, which are then implemented at the multilateral table. Yet, this picture is incomplete. For various reasons, which I explore in the third section of the chapter, permanent representatives do much more than represent their capital: they also govern the global commons. Given the number of local compromises, creative policy making, and horse trading that happen on the ground, in the practice of permanent representation to represent often is to govern. As a preliminary step to developing this assertion, in the next section I explore the relational sources of this surprisingly understudied dynamic in contemporary world politics.

28 Quoted in Placidi, "La transformation des pratiques diplomatiques nationales," 99.
29 Blair, "Permanent Representations to the European Union," 156.
30 See Vincent Pouliot, "The Materials of Practice: Nuclear Warheads, Rhetorical Commonplaces and Committee Meetings in Russian-Atlantic Relations," *Cooperation and Conflict*, 45(3), 2010.

The relational structure of permanent representation

The practice of permanent representation takes place within a particular kind of social configuration. In this section, I describe some of the key parameters of the relational structure of multilateral diplomacy inside IOs. In tune with Nexon's "relational analytics," I conceive of structures as "ongoing, dynamic patterns of transaction between actors and other social sites."[31] The key insight is that the ways in which social ties are organized in a given social configuration help understand its dynamics, including at the intersubjective level. The goal of this section, then, is to map the specific patterns of relationships that characterize the practice of permanent representation to IOs. My main argument is that permanent representation is, relationally speaking, both a form of group diplomacy and a diplomacy of groups, and it is relatively secluded from other social sites. These characteristics stem from various relational structural features that I describe later and which, as I argue in the following section, go a long way in explaining the non-semiotic origins of the peculiar practical logics of permanent representation.

Group diplomacy

Several of the relational features of permanent representation point to its communitarian form. First, permanent representation generally involves a relatively small number of participants. This is particularly the case of regional organizations such as NATO and the EU, but also of many UN bodies, from the Security Council to the Human Rights Council, which count between one and a few dozen ambassadors (the General Assembly is, of course, the exception to this rule). As network theorists are quick to emphasize: "Size is critical for the structure of social relations because of the limited resources and capacities that each actor has for building and maintaining ties."[32] By implication, size often correlates with a second relational feature, density, defined as

31 Daniel H. Nexon, *The Struggle for Power in Early Modern Europe: Religious Conflict, Dynastic Empires, and International Change* (Princeton, NJ: Princeton University Press, 2009), 40.

32 Robert A. Hanneman and Mark Riddle, "Concepts and Measures for Basic Network Analysis," in John Scott and Peter J. Carrington, eds., *The Sage Handbook of Social Network Analysis* (Thousand Oaks, CA: Sage, 2011), 341.

"the sum of the ties divided by the number of possible ties."[33] In permanent representation configurations, the density ratio equals (or is very close to) 1; that is to say, (nearly) all PRs have ties with (nearly) all the others. This maximum density also implies, by definition, high levels of reachability and connectivity across nodes. It also means that ties are generally characterized by high reciprocity and few to no structural holes. As Kadushin observes: "Other things being equal, the greater the density, the more likely is a network to be considered a cohesive community."[34]

A third characteristic helps explain the high density of permanent representation configurations: propinquity. Physical proximity matters in social relations: "nodes are more likely to be connected with one another, other conditions being equal, if they are geographically near to one another."[35] In the clearest cases, such as NATO, national missions are physically located inside the organization's headquarters building. As one Alliance permanent representative put it:

> This is a microcosm . . . we spend all the time together. We have our bank, our restaurant, our café, post office and hairdresser, and so it's this microcosm where, of course, you use your time outside the meetings to network and have contacts with colleagues, with the military side, and I think that's a very important factor, also, in the decision making, that we have a very close interrelationship.

Inside the building, delegations are located a few doors, corridors, or stairways away from one another. The overwhelming majority of meetings take place inside the headquarters, which offers all the required facilities for formal and informal exchanges. The IO and its permanent missions become a kind of extraterritorial bubble, which partially lives in parallel to its surroundings, and from which there is little (professional) need to exit. Even in cases such as the UN, where national missions are spread over a portion of the city (mostly midtown Manhattan), the relative closure of the social configuration is striking. Comings and goings concentrate on the headquarters, with some visits to other delegations and a limited set of tested restaurants and coffee

[33] Ibid., 342.

[34] Charles Kadushin, *Understanding Social Networks: Theories, Concepts, and Findings* (New York: Oxford University Press, 2012), 29.

[35] Ibid., 18.

shops. Missions staffers also interact with other actors, including in some cases the media or civil society organizations, but most of their daily intercourse is confined to their peers.[36] In fact, the one major link that national missions entertain with the outside world is the busy communication channel with the capital.

Fourth and related, high social density often produces what network theorists call "content multiplexity," which characterizes relational environments where "there are a number of different flows between a pair of persons, for example, advice, friendship, and work on common tasks."[37] Given the particularly intense level of social intercourse involved in permanent representation, PRs and their teams entertain multiple contacts and exchanges on a daily basis. These transactions are obviously based on formal positions and titles, but they often reach much more informal levels as well. Inside IO headquarters, for example, there is a lot of back and forth, in various venues, from official meetings to coffee breaks. An organization such as NATO is particularly exemplary of this social intensity: one only needs to watch the mixed crowds at the cafeteria during lunchtime to understand the social depth of the interpersonal ties involved. Similar patterns can be observed on Manhattan's First Avenue, where swarms of diplomats can be seen, at all times, having informal discussions in the corridors, sharing a meal or a coffee at a favorite restaurant, or running together to one of the many meetings taking place simultaneously. National delegates have a special budget for "wining and dining," because "networking is crucial," said one deputy PR to the UN. Being a multilateral diplomat is a profoundly social profession, and no workday is worth its name without its load of regular interpersonal exchanges. Mostly run at a professional level, several contacts often parallel more informal flows.

Taken together, small size combined with high density, propinquity, and multiplexity means that permanent representation resembles a peculiar relational structure that network theorists call a clique – a

[36] As a result of space constraints, this chapter focuses on the social configuration composed of state representatives only. But relational analytics could also be used to analyze the social ties between permanent representatives and non-traditional diplomatic agents. On the UN case, see Geoffrey Wiseman, "Diplomatic Practices at the United Nations," *Cooperation and Conflict* 50(2), 2015.

[37] Kadushin, *Understanding Social Networks*, 36.

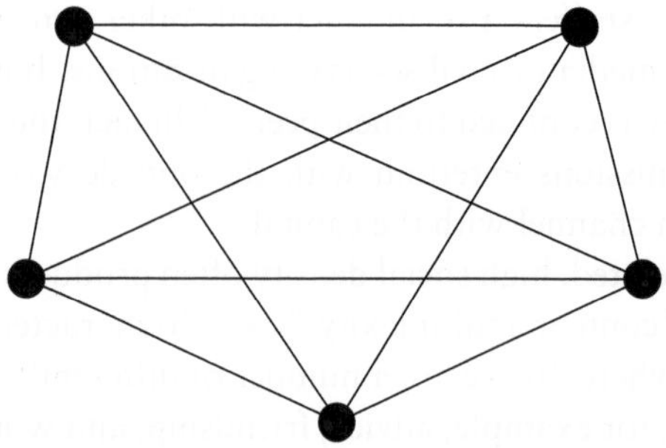

Figure 3.1 The Clique Structure of Permanent Representation

dense configuration in which each node is connected to (almost) every other.[38] And because "cohesiveness defines 'cliques,'"[39] this relational structure generates – and rests on – a thick social fabric. Tilly describes such relational structures as "communities":

> Networks qualify as communities to the extent that: 1. They have well-defined and complete perimeters; 2. those perimeters correspond to or define categorical differences: us vs. them, insiders vs. outsiders, members vs. non-members, and so on; 3. a substantial proportion of all ties within their perimeters fall into triads, in the sense if A has a given relation to C and B has a similar relation to C, A and B also have such a relation; 4. all sites within them connect, however indirectly.[40]

As Figure 3.1 illustrates, permanent representation meets all five of these criteria.

In sum, as a social form permanent representation consists largely of group diplomacy, meaning that it takes place within more or less tightly knit communities of delegates. These configurations often meet as a whole: a significant portion of transactions happens in the open, in front of all members. Of course, corridor and bilateral negotiations also abound. But permanent representation, as a form of diplomacy, is characterized by the sustained and direct presence of a group of

[38] Alexander H. Montgomery, "Proliferation Networks in Theory and Practice," *Strategic Insights*, 5(6), 2006.

[39] Kadushin, *Understanding Social Networks*, 47.

[40] Charles Tilly, "International Communities, Secure or Otherwise," in Emanuel Adler and Michael Barnett, eds., *Security Communities* (New York: Cambridge University Press, 1998), 404–405.

interlocutors: without being public, its diplomacy necessarily has to engage an audience of multiple nodes. I analyze the intersubjective consequences of this relational structure in the third part of the chapter, including "forum effects."[41] The important point, from a relational perspective, is that permanent representation as a form of group diplomacy enables distinctive social dynamics. In effect, network theory underscores the key difference between a dyad and a triad: "Triads are the true start of a social system."[42] As a practice, multilateral diplomacy at IOs is fundamentally "multiparty"[43]: it cannot be reduced to a set of bilateral ties – an all-too-common mistake made in bargaining theory.

For instance, a small-society configuration "'embeds' dyadic relations in a structure where 'other' is present along with 'ego' and 'alter.'"[44] This relational feature introduces fundamental third-party dynamics. In permanent representation, third parties are those representatives from states that do not have a direct stake in a given negotiation and yet often hold the balance of power to decide where the collective wind shall blow. In the practice of multilateral diplomacy, when two delegates disagree, the dispute is often not settled by them, as in a duel, but by the other members around the table, who observe, ponder, and adjudicate the reasons given by each to take a given stance. They may remain neutral in appearance, but in actuality through corridor conversations they are likely to tip the balance to one side. Even those who are not directly concerned will be pushed to take sides, altering the postures of everyone else. Tilly reminds us that in communities, "third parties frequently have interests, and some power to intervene, in a given paired relation." Thus, the pluridimensionality of multilateral diplomacy means that actors are not only defending their interests but also arbitrating those of others.[45] This adds to the complex social dynamics at work. As Thuysbaert sums up nicely: "Negotiation being a collective exercise, everyone adjusts to the

[41] Jennifer Mitzen, "Reading Habermas in Anarchy: Multilateral Diplomacy and Global Public Spheres," *American Political Science Review* 99(3), 2005.

[42] Kadushin, *Understanding Social Networks*, 204.

[43] I. William Zartman, ed., *International Multilateral Negotiation: Approaches to the Management of Complexity* (San Francisco: Jossey-Bass, 1994).

[44] Hanneman and Riddle, "Concepts and Measures for Basic Network Analysis," 345.

[45] Tilly, "International Communities, Secure or Otherwise," 406.

others, anxious never to be cantilevered compared to the whole's movement."[46]

I should add that another type of third party is involved in permanent representation: the presence of a chair acting as a neutral arbiter. These may be elected or rotating member states or international officials such as secretaries-generals and their representatives. Clearly, the presence at the table of an agent with a distinctive political status has a few critical implications, such as opening the possibility of "good offices" functions, which introduce a non-territorial basis of authority for diplomacy. All in all, the key relational insight here is that "[t]he addition of a third member to a dyad . . . vastly increases the complexity of relationships."[47]

Relative seclusion

As far as its external environment is concerned, permanent representation is a relatively closed social configuration. Although far from isolated from the external world, in many ways the multilateral clique is a world onto itself or, in one practitioner's words, "a microcosm." Physical propinquity is, obviously, a key factor here, but there is more than that. Compounding the seclusion of national missions is the fact that they entertain exclusive and strong ties with their respective capitals.[48] Beyond the boundaries of the clique itself, by far the most intense and significant relationship that perm reps enjoy is that with their direct superior from the Ministry of Foreign Affairs or related agency in the government. Communications along that channel are repeated and bidirectional, consisting of instructions from the capital to the mission and reports on negotiations flowing the other way. This singular and exclusive tie really sets permanent representation apart from other forms of representation and delegation. What is more, while permanent missions are connected only to their own capital, governments on their part entertain parallel relations with other head offices. That is to say, permanent missions' contact points in the

[46] Prosper Thuysbaert, *L'art de la diplomatie multilatérale* (Brussels: Vander, 1994), 86.

[47] Kadushin, *Understanding Social Networks*, 23.

[48] Even if one entertains the hypothesis of "complex multilateralism," it is quite clear that the strength of the ties between perm reps and civil society actors consistently pales in comparison to that of the links to the capital.

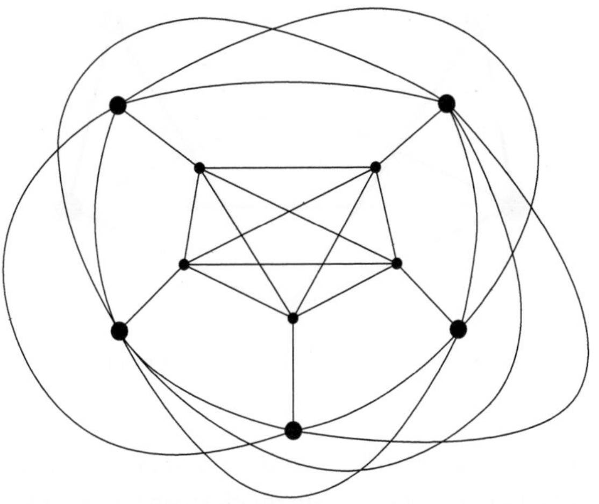

Figure 3.2 The Star-Shaped, Dual-Layered Structure of Permanent Representation

government apparatus tend to have their own set of ties that circumvent permanent missions themselves.

We thus find ourselves with an odd relational structure, with the perm reps clique in the middle and a series of individual ties to a surrounding network of agencies in relevant capitals. Graphically, we may picture this structure as a star-shaped network of ties originating from the permanent representation clique, with the particularity that the stars also enter in variably intense, parallel interaction (see Figure 3.2). This peculiar morphology introduces information asymmetry between the members of the clique and the nodes that form the outer layer (i.e., the network of foreign ministries). Perm reps are aware of a number of internal dynamics that escape capitals' knowledge; but central government also has valuable information about what other governments think (beyond what perm reps state at the IO). As we shall see in the third section of the chapter, this feature is at the source of intriguing diplomatic practices.

A diplomacy of groups

Although multilateral configurations often approximate density ratios of 1 (see earlier discussion), it does not mean that all ties in the network

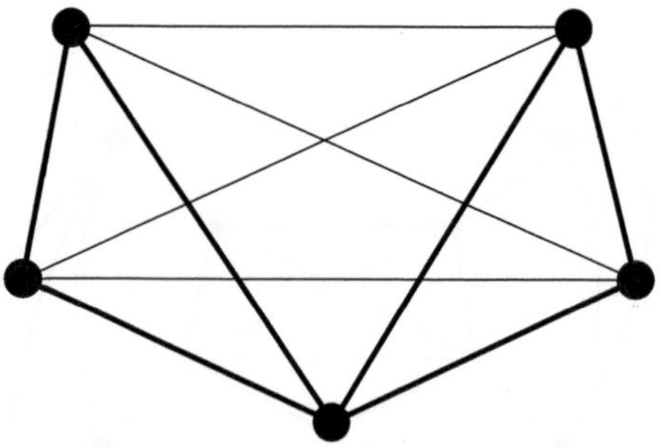

Figure 3.3 The Cluster Structure of Permanent Representation

have the same strength. In other words, a number of subgroups within the clique have nodes that entertain much stronger ties with each other than with the rest of clique members. Recall that "the strength of a tie is conceptualized as a combination of the magnitude and frequency of interactions between the nodes."[49] Whatever their shape and name, permanent representation subgroups are characterized by stronger ties between members, a relational feature that opens the door to coalition dynamics. A few brokers usually spearhead communication and interaction between the subgroups. Thus, not all members of the social configuration enjoy the same level of popularity and centrality. The practice of permanent representation is prone to social clustering (see Figure 3.3), usually for political reasons attributable to the countries that they represent (converging interests, special relationships, geographical proximity, etc.), but also because of personal and technical factors on the ground.

Generally speaking, the larger the membership, the stronger is the need to build more or less shifting groups of member states to advance one's agenda. For instance, clustering exists inside NATO, but it is fluctuant and remains mostly informal. Subgroups do not wear names, they do not have an organizational structure, and their meetings are not heralded. Because of tradition or conjuncture, PRs from certain subgroups do entertain much closer relations (e.g., the Balts, the United States and the UK, France and Germany, the

[49] Emilie M. Hafner-Burton, Miles Kahler, and Alexander H. Montgomery, "Network Analysis for International Relations," *International Organization*, 63(3), 2009, 536.

Mediterranean members), but most of the time the drive for consensus ultimately trumps coalition politics. By contrast, at the UN, subgroups of various guises constitute the "energizing force"[50] and "kingpin" of multilateral negotiation.[51] This includes regional groups, which were formalized in the mid-1960s, but also manifold other coalitions ranging from the Non-aligned Movement (NAM) to various groups of topical friends of the secretary-general. In fact, in New York the subgroup is the social site where most decisions find their roots.[52] As one longtime PR put it: "The only sin at the UN is to be isolated." In functional terms, this feature is both an advantage and a disadvantage. In Laatikainen's words: "Groups may facilitate international dialogue and help overcome lowest common-denominator and consensus decision-making by building consensus among the like-minded first, locking in positions and reducing the number of possible objections; at the same time, they may also introduce rigidity into decision-making and prevent coalitions among potential partners."[53] The latter dynamic often creates particularly vexing deadlocks, as the case of the reform of the Security Council shows. Once a subgroup finds a common position, it is often less flexible given the compromises that have already been made internally.

In sum, the multiparty structure of permanent representation generates a rather peculiar diplomacy of groups. In practice, multilateral diplomacy generally takes place on two fronts simultaneously: within the group, and among the groups.[54] At the intersubjective level, permanent representation as diplomacy of groups yields a number of remarkable dynamics: "these groups create patterns of diplomatic interaction at the UN, and those patterns suggest an organisation of multilateral diplomacy that scholars have not yet fully analysed."[55] It is to this analysis that I now turn.

[50] Appathurai, "Permanent Missions in New York," 102.

[51] Jean-Pierre Vettovaglia, "De la coordination comme instrument essentiel de la négociation multilatérale intergouvernmentale," in Boisard, Chossudovsky, and Lemoine, eds., *Multilateral Diplomacy*, 251.

[52] Subgroups also foster informality, as gatherings are usually held in a looser format, for instance on the premises of one leading national mission.

[53] Katie V. Laatikainen, "Group Politics at the UN: Conceptual Considerations." Paper presented at the 2012 BISA/ISA Conference, June, Edinburg, UK, 7.

[54] Nyerges, "How to Negotiate?" 178.

[55] Laatikainen, "Group Politics at the UN," 5.

Table 3.1 *Relational and practical dynamics of permanent representation*

Relational features	Practical logics
Clique structure	
Relatively small size	Esprit de corps (making things work, being a good ally, duty to help, joining the consensus)
High density, propinquity and multiplexity	Discipline (peer pressure, learning the ropes, sanctions), informality
Audience	Forum effects (public reason), chain reactions, constructive ambiguity
Partial seclusion	
Relatively closed	Specific temporality
Exclusive ties with capitals (information asymmetry)	Leash slipping, translation games, information gathering (gossip)
Clustering	
Unequal strength of ties	Shifting coalition landscape
Brokers	Local distribution of roles

The practical logics of permanent representation

The relational features of permanent representation produce a distinctive set of practical logics and rules of the game (see Table 3.1).[56] In fact, the generative force of relational features becomes particularly visible in times of organizational change, which is often followed with intersubjective transformation. For example, in her study of the implications of regional integration for national diplomacy, Angers documents a number of practical changes in the everyday practices of

[56] Of course, multilateral diplomacy is also characterized by a set of formal procedures. For example, the rule of consensus (or weighted voting, etc.) introduces key dynamics in the negotiation process: in fact, Thuysbaert (in *L'art de la diplomatie multilatérale*, 24) goes as far as to write that in multilateral diplomacy, "issues of procedure often prejudge substantive problems." Working methods have a huge influence over outcomes, and their establishment is usually front and center in multilateral negotiations. Generally speaking, formal rules get more complex as the number of participants increases. As a result of space constraints, in this chapter I focus exclusively on practice-bound rules of the game.

Austrian practitioners.[57] First, the repositioning of the Ministry of Foreign Affairs vis-à-vis other national ministries implies not only the loss of its monopoly over diplomacy but also increasing diplomatic interaction with domestic policy makers, turning diplomats into bureaucrats. Second, the repositioning of national diplomats vis-à-vis their regional counterparts leads to a socialization process in the community game, a new stake in making regional businesses work (largely thanks to compromises), and adaptation to a new temporal logic dictated by regional politics. Third, a series of organizational adjustments creates bloc diplomacy outside the region, new consultative and deliberative processes on the regional scale, and a diplomatic practice that is characterized by self-restraint and constructiveness. Conducting national diplomacy as an EU member, Angers concludes, involves a number of distinct practical logics.

It is by now well established that diplomacy in general relies on a set of skills and dispositions generally learned in and through practice. Nicolson contends that "common sense" is the essence of diplomacy;[58] Satow equates the practice with "the application of intelligence and tact to the conduct of official relations between the governments of independent states";[59] Kissinger asserts that diplomacy is "an art, not a science";[60] and Acheson contends that it involves a "mysterious wisdom, too arcane for the layman."[61] In what may be the first in-depth ethnography of diplomacy, Neumann similarly brings to the fore its practical and mundane dimensions.[62] What these various studies point out is that the practice of diplomacy rests on some forms of inarticulate knowledge from which strategic, reflexive, and intentional action becomes possible.[63]

57 Kathleen Angers, "Intégration européenne et pratique diplomatique. L'expérience autrichienne (1987–2009)" (M.A. Thesis, Université de Montréal, 2010).
58 Harold Nicolson, *Diplomacy*, 3rd edn (New York: Oxford University Press, 1963 [1939]), 43.
59 Ernest Mason Satow, *Satow's Guide to Diplomatic Practice*, ed. Lord Gore-Booth (London: Longman, 1979), 3.
60 Henry A. Kissinger, *A World Restored: Metternich, Castlereagh, and the Problems of Peace, 1812–22* (Boston: Houghton Mifflin, 1973), 2.
61 Quoted in Paul Sharp, *Diplomatic Theory of International Relations* (New York: Cambridge University Press, 2009), 3.
62 Neumann, *At Home with the Diplomats*.
63 Vincent Pouliot, "The Logic of Practicality: A Theory of Practice of Security Communities," *International Organization*, 62(2), 2008; Emanuel Adler and

The rules of the clique

In the preceding section, I argued that permanent representation forms a clique-like, relatively secluded and clustering configuration of national delegates. From a political sociology perspective, diplomacy is conceived as a particular form of social intercourse involving human beings who act as representatives of larger corporate actors. As Walker writes in his manual for delegates: "An international conference is an interaction between states . . . but that interaction takes place between delegates as representatives of states. The principal ways in which the delegates interact is by communicating with each other and most of that communication takes the form of face-to-face conversations."[64]

As a form of group diplomacy, permanent representation rests on a set of communitarian rules of the game, which are more or less prevalent depending on the size of the group. One such rule, which is particularly strong in tightly knit settings such as NATO, is esprit de corps, that is, in-group identification and solidarity.[65] As clique members, multilateral diplomats have a stake in making things work out. Permanent representatives must achieve some kind of accord with partners: that the multilateral group has to come up with a joint policy is an unspoken, and generally unquestioned, departure point. Given the repeated and multidimensional negotiations involved, everybody – weak or strong, directly concerned or not – begins with a vested stake in achieving some kind of agreement. In a multilateral setting, the first goal has to be to make the community move forward, to make it work – even, sometimes, at the expense of substance.

Permanent representation also rests on a "tradition of helping"; as one permanent representative to NATO put it: "we have a longstanding tradition in this house . . . that those who have a particular problem, we all try to walk the proverbial extra mile to help them out, and that we don't want to ride roughshod over their issues before we really have to." He continued:

Vincent Pouliot, eds., *International Practices* (Cambridge: Cambridge University Press, 2011).

64 Ronald A. Walker, *Manual for UN Delegates: Conference Process, Procedure and Negotiation* (Geneva: United Nations Institute for Training and Research, 2011), 43.

65 See also Paul Sharp and Geoffrey Wiseman, eds., *The Diplomatic Corps as an Institution of International Society* (Basingstoke: Palgrave MacMillan, 2007).

If it's really a heartfelt issue with that particular colleague, if I could, I would try to say, "Well this is not exactly what I would want if I could have my unadulterated way. But maybe would it help you if we did it like this?" Such and such and such and such, put the emphasis at a certain point which is different from where we started, that sort of thing. That happens routinely, I think. And it's only on an exceptional basis that we don't. That is really what negotiations are about. So I think that is part of being, if you will not react to my being slightly pretentious, of being a good ally to try to help out when others have issues that are important to them.

This key practice of "being a good ally" is, of course, much more than a moral imperative. As is always the case in social life, it is also a matter of positioning oneself in an advantageous way: "the next time, you could be the one in need of a certain largess, a certain generosity on the part of your partner, and usually it works like that." One of Angers's interviewees provides another telling illustration of how multilateral diplomacy creates a requirement for ever-constructive participation:

The danger is that you say something only when you have to defend your position. And this you have to avoid. You have also to come in with helpful positions, compromises even if it doesn't concern your own country ... it is seen as positive ... the Irish, the Dutch and the Luxembourgers are good at it ... And if they want something for themselves, it's much easier to get it.[66]

The multilateral practice of reaching out combines a moral or identity-based imperative with an instrumental incentive in producing a functional good.

Because perm reps espouse not only their country's point of view but also the success of negotiations, they value the process of negotiation (and, where applicable, of consensus building) in and of itself. In a multilateral setting, negotiations cannot and should not be rushed. As one NATO representative put it:

Sometimes it takes a longer time that the most impatient members would want it to ... you have to accept that the price of that is that sometimes it takes time to sort of get to the point where everybody is at least equally unhappy with the position that we are adopting but everybody is at the same time willing to live with it.

[66] Quoted in Angers, "Intégration européenne et pratique diplomatique," 65.

In this perspective, what the negotiation process entails is a search not for a solution that pleases participants but rather for an outcome that sidesteps potential pitfalls. Despite this lowest-common-denominator dimension, the at times fastidious process of reaching a negotiated outcome strengthens its legitimacy. In the words of one NATO permanent representative:

> The consensus building, of course, takes quite a long time, but the process, as such, is not a bad one and you can also say, when you then finally got the consensus, then it's rock solid. I mean, although, of course, we can have discussions afterward, what was exactly decided, but at least the process means that the decision has a stronger status.

A second key practical logic of permanent representation that stems from its clique structure has to do with discipline. Indeed, the possibility of sanction is a fundamental condition for any community to hold together. In multilateral diplomacy, this dynamic takes a number of forms. First, new perm reps must learn the ropes, meaning that there is a well-known socialization period when entering a new organization.[67] In fact, new delegates must learn not only what the local rules of the game are but also how to use these rules. For example, Angers explains how, for Austrian diplomats entering the EU in the mid-1990s, there was a long way from "knowing the rules" to "actually using all these procedures in a skillful way."[68]

Interestingly, beyond the social sanction per se, which can obviously be quite painful in terms of standing, it is also the very credibility and efficiency of diplomatic practices that is at stake in following family rules. For this reason, the clique tends to be self-disciplining and seldom requires the application of an external form of authority. For example, as a diplomacy of groups, permanent representation may generate tensions and even create sparks between coalition leaders. One perm rep admitted that within the community, "you cannot avoid [cliques]. It's like school class." But he rushed to add, "the nature of ambassadors, they are people with a strong experience this way or the other and seasoned operators, so it's really not a problem." In other words, it is considered to be part of the diplomatic role to domesticate impulses

[67] Cf. Jeffrey Lewis, "The Janus Face of Brussels: Socialization and Everyday Decision Making in the European Union," *International Organization*, 59(4), 2005.

[68] Angers, "Intégration européenne et pratique diplomatique," 59.

and put interpersonal rifts aside. In actual practice, of course, the urge to get an agreement cannot suppress the struggles of corridor negotiations, which are all about cornering others, preempting objections, undermining arguments, gossiping, sapping authority, devising winning strategies, and so on. Multilateral diplomacy is a social struggle like others, in which agents vie for positions, compete over resources, and seek to foster clashing interests. What is distinct about multilateral diplomacy is that ultimately these tensions usually remain confined to the negotiations process; down the road, reconciliation is always in sight.

Another central strategy in massaging group dynamics consists of involving the secretary-general (or whatever external chair the multilateral forum may have). In the words of a seasoned NATO diplomat:

> There is, and should also be, quite a lot of work in the back rooms of the Alliance, in order for the secretary general, also for the Council, to be aware of the sensitivities which may exist on a specific subject and how you can meet these sensitivities . . . the sec gen can test the waters and see what are the possibilities, where is the flexibility with ones in difficulty, etc. So, it's become very much a part of the decision-making process.

At the end of the day, multilateral diplomats know of various strategies to keep the family together, such as joining with unusual partners to move a given file forward. Walking the fine line between getting the upper hand while preserving esprit de corps is a key practical logic of permanent representation.

A third practical implication of the clique structure of permanent representation is that it often entails the presence of an audience, that is, the direct presence of fellow counterparts around the negotiations table. During formal meetings with all members around the table, a permanent representative must be able to state her position in such a way that resonates with the contrasting views held by her various counterparts. The public dimension of multilateralism, thanks to which reasons must be given in a way that echoes the group's own culture, is a rather distinctive feature. Of course, diplomatic signaling is always and by necessity a profoundly ambiguous act, whose dynamics are targeted at multiple audiences and negotiated by the different parties according to local practical logics. Cables and media reports generally take care of transmitting these messages. But the distinctive feature of permanent representation is that some of the most important recipients are physically present in the room, with an immediate opportunity to gesture, frown, or grimace live in the diplomat's face. As a result, the multilateral diplomat must be skillful to not only signal ambiguously enough to please different publics but also to craft a position that will not disrupt actual negotiations that are taking place right before her eyes, typically with some shoulder rubbing.

More generally, the presence of an audience sparks what Mitzen calls "forum effects of talk," including procedural reciprocity and public reason (see also Chapter 4 in this volume).[69] Although evidence is lacking to judge whether these dynamics lead to genuine persuasion and changes of mind,[70] it certainly does create a shared intersubjective background of interaction that transpires in discursive practices. Put differently, the question of whether diplomats really believe in shared norms, that is, whether they have "transformative effects on basic actors properties," is not empirically tractable, and probably of lesser analytical import anyway.[71] What matters is that permanent representatives have to work within that intersubjective background, making use of its discursive resources. Appropriateness does not necessarily involve internalization: rules are being put in use, in and through practice, and that is something we can readily observe.[72]

The bubble and the world outside

The peculiar, star-shaped and double-layered relational structure of permanent representation also generates interesting practical logics on the ground. First, as a partly secluded social configuration, multilateral diplomacy develops its own temporality. Put differently, the negotiations conducted by perm reps have their own specific tempo, which often does not match the pace of negotiations in capitals or other forums. This is due to various institutional procedures and bureaucratic practices, on the one hand, and also to other local rules of the game. For instance, the practical feeling that NATO perm reps usually have that allows them to identify the ripe moment to join the consensus is based on the particular pace of negotiations with colleagues, the give-and-take tango, the crafting of compromises, and the application of pressure. Of course, all of these dynamics are partly determined in

[69] Mitzen, "Reading Habermas in Anarchy," 411. [70] Cf. Ibid., 401.
[71] Lewis, "The Janus Face of Brussels," 938.
[72] See also Ian Hurd, Chapter 1, this volume.

capitals, and regular summits of heads of state or ministers ensure that overall multilateral diplomacy remains in synch with the larger evolution of world politics. But in the everyday world, permanent representation remains quite isolated and it advances at its own pace. In a striking example, Schia shows how Norwegian diplomats at the Security Council agree on a text in New York even before getting Oslo's approval, because of local dynamics and the rapid pace of negotiations.[73]

The nearly exclusive ties that perm reps enjoy with their capital is also the source of complex intersubjective dynamics, which are largely the result, as I argued earlier, of information asymmetry. Diplomats have an insider feeling for the unfolding of negotiations that civil servants at home do not. Likewise, government officials are often aware of the larger picture, based on their extensive bilateral contacts with other capitals, and possess information that may escape perm reps. As a result, perm reps have to carve as much room for maneuvering as they can within the framework of their instructions.

Practices vary across countries when it comes to the nature of instructions sent to PRs. For instance, at the Security Council, the British and French delegations are known to benefit from much more leeway than others.[74] They make daily usage of this flexibility to take time-sensitive initiatives, craft local compromises, or coordinate positions. As Blair notes:

> Instructions are not always clear and can hinder the ability of the staff in the permanent representation to adequately negotiate on behalf of government, with a concurrent reduction in that nation's influence in particular debates ... The trick is for the government to provide its negotiators with a suitable balance of clarity and room to adapt the national position depending on the course of the discussions.[75]

In fact, flexible instructions can even augment one's influence around the table, according to Walker:

[73] Niels Nagelhus Schia, "Being Part of the Parade – 'Going Native' in the United Nations Security Council," *Political and Legal Anthropology Review*, 36(1), 2013.

[74] For an illustration, see Rebecca Adler-Nissen and Vincent Pouliot, "Power in Practice: Negotiating the International Intervention in Libya," *European Journal of International Relations* 20(4), 2014.

[75] Blair, "Permanent Representations to the European Union," 146.

Most governments which operate successfully at international conferences find that they get better results if they refrain from giving explicit directives to their delegations.

The reason for this is that explicit directives can tie a delegation's hands. They can make it much more difficult for the delegation to react appropriately to situations that headquarters has not fully anticipated. In real life, headquarters will never be aware of all the information held by its delegation at any given moment, nor of all the subtleties of tactical situations as they arise.[76]

There exist, broadly speaking, three types of instructions: "everything deal with in detail," "general position outlined," and "position related to that of other countries."[77] In tighter communities, we should add a fourth type – that of "joining the consensus." In a setting such as NATO, this practice is a fundamental requirement and competent diplomats should be able to figure at what specific point in time it applies. There is, in the words of a NATO permanent representative, "some sort of understanding that those who feel less strongly about an issue might find it in their hearts not to raise whatever trivial or non-trivial objections they have." Permanent representation comes with a responsibility, explained one delegate:

The compunction for every member of this organization to do as much as they can to avoid coming into that sort of situation [blocking a consensus] there is a very strong expectation on the part of all of us in regard to all of our colleagues that they should do as much as they can to avoid coming in a situation where they need to use their weapon of last resort, which is saying, "We don't go along with this." And that is a day-to-day issue for us.

For instance, Angers tells the story of an Austrian permanent representative who, shortly after joining the EU, was abruptly put back in place for requiring too many derogations and for raising repeated objections.[78] Joining the consensus is an imperative of multilateral diplomacy. One perm rep mentioned the "heroic instruction" that he would sometimes receive from his capital: "You can join the consensus." This very loose set of instructions, he explained, is made possible when "we don't have a secure stake in [the discussions]. Of course, we follow them, but

[76] Walker, *Manual for UN Delegates*, 22.

[77] Kaufmann, "Some Practical Aspects of United Nations Decision-Making, Tactics and Interaction between Delegates," 237–238.

[78] Angers, "Intégration européenne et pratique diplomatique," 63.

we would be very consensus-minded and that would be in most cases our general attitude ... you fight for the views which you have, but in the end, if you have to limit your front a bit, then you join the consensus."

In this endeavor, tracking the positions of other delegations becomes critical. Because of the number of partners involved and the dense, repeated pattern of negotiations, a number of multilateral practices become salient. One is the development of a political role for a small unit of international civil servants, as described by one ambassador:

> The secretary-general and the assistants, the private office, the international staff – I mean, they have an obligation. They are the ones who should oil the machinery here and try to find the ... and so it's very important, as is the case and has been the case, that the secretary, you know, is actively involved ... either in an informal or a formal setting.

Another key practice is the multiplication and cultivation of informal venues to conduct negotiations in parallel with committee meetings. As one NATO perm rep explained: "we meet informally, the ambassadors, more than we used to do. There used to be this Tuesday – famous Tuesday lunch ... and that is combined very frequently with a so-called coffee, which is also an informal setting; and the difference between lunch and the coffee, apart from what you eat and drink, is that at lunch, it's ambassadors only." These informal gatherings help defuse tension and soften entrenched policy cleavages.

Gangs and brokers

As a diplomacy of groups or clusters, permanent representation significantly compounds negotiation dynamics around the multilateral table. The relational geometry of the setting rapidly shifts as some social ties strengthen or weaken and a coalition forms. As Zartman puts it:

> Negotiators in a multilateral encounter enter with such questions as, What is going on here? How can we find our way through this scene? How can we give some direction to these proceedings? How can we make something happen? Negotiators need to orient themselves both to the other parties and to the issues, and at the same time to an array of roles, particularly of competing leaders and contributing followers.[79]

[79] I. William Zartman, "Introduction: Two's Company and More's a Crowd: The Complexities of Multilateral Negotiation," in Zartman, ed. *International Multilateral Negotiation*, 1.

From a network perspective, higher numbers breed social complexity. For that reason, the multiparty structure of permanent representation renders the waters through which diplomats navigate particularly challenging.

From a practical point of view, variations in the strength of relational ties determine the distribution of roles and status around the multilateral table. Most clearly, the diplomacy of groups generates endogenous hierarchies between those who lead clubs and the rest. It also elevates brokers above the fray by providing them with more social resources.[80] Thus, the multiparty structure of permanent representation generates diplomatic resources for the delegations that lead or coordinate coalitions. This role obviously augments the amount of work for leading countries, but it is also a significant source of influence, as many smaller affiliates rely entirely on the group to get information and formulate a position.[81] What is more, group leaders are likely to be the preferred interlocutors of other partners, including chairpersons and other dominant nations.

Conclusion: permanent representation as a rising form of governance

This chapter advances four key arguments. First, permanent representation is an increasingly prevalent practice in world politics. Second, its relational features include a clique structure, a star-shaped set of outside ties, and internal clustering. Third, a number of practical logics flow from this structure, including esprit de corps, discipline, forum effects, distinct temporality, leash slipping, translation games, and local pecking orders. To conclude, I want to argue that these practical logics are far from innocuous when it comes to the constitutive effects of diplomacy on world politics. The logic of practicality of permanent representation pushes diplomatic representation – which is the original function – into new territories of governance.

In their everyday practices, perm reps do much more than simply represent the views of their national governments. They also develop a stake in the success of multilateralism itself, they seek to help their

[80] E.g., Stacie E. Goddard, "Brokering Peace: Networks, Legitimacy, and the Northern Ireland Peace Process," *International Studies Quarterly*, 56(3), 2012.
[81] Walker, *Manual for UN Delegates*, 51.

partners in trouble, and they contribute to the collective effort at compromise. National delegates also come to frame their positions in a language that echoes local norms and rules, they maneuver amid chain reactions, and they strive for constructive ambiguity in addressing multiple audiences. In their relationship with capitals, PRs advance at their own pace, they play with their instructions so as to create wiggle room, and they report back in a way that reinforces their hand at the table. Finally, in navigating the coalitions within the group, they tag onto some partners, assume leadership, or broker compromises, all of which foster a local pecking order with real effects on the distribution of ranks and roles around the table. In fact, far from being passive conveyor belts, national missions can even become involved in "policy formulation," argues Blair. Directly present on the ground, they "adjust to policy as the negotiating situation develops. Permanent representations also assess or predict the actual (as well as the potential reactions of other member states." In the end, Blair contends, the mission is "often acting in an independent manner." [82]

This finding is echoed in the dozens of interviews I have conducted over the years, as well in other independent studies. In the case of the EU, Cross argues that "European security integration is occurring largely through the diplomatic dialogue and agency of key transnational knowledge-based networks, known as epistemic communities."[83] Mérand presents similar findings about security and defense officials.[84] To be sure, other IOs constitute harder cases because the level of political integration is much more shallow. However, as this chapter showed, it is also the relational structure of multilateral diplomacy as a general social form that produces peculiar practical logics, taking it progressively deeper into governing functions. This relatively autonomous dynamic, which stems from organizational logic, works in mutually reinforcing ways with other dynamics, including the institutionalization of the IO, the tightness of its membership, and its scope of

[82] Blair, "Permanent Representations to the European Union," 149.

[83] Cross, *Security Integration in Europe*, 3. See also Christian Lequesne, "EU Foreign Policy Through the Lens of Practice Theory: A Different Approach to the European External Action Service," *Cooperation and Conflict* 50(2), 2015; and Merje Kuus, "Symbolic Power in Diplomatic Practice: Matters of Style in Brussels," *Cooperation and Conflict* 50(2), 2015.

[84] Frédéric Mérand, "Pierre Bourdieu and the Birth of European Defense," *Security Studies*, 19(2), 2010.

competence. This is, perhaps, the most important lesson to be drawn from this chapter: to the extent that perm reps partake in governing, they cannot be discarded as epiphenomenal of deeper forces or systemic dynamics. Their everyday practices are constitutive of world politics and, as such, they often have autonomous causal effects on policy outcomes.[85]

[85] Vincent Pouliot, International Pecking Orders: The Politics and Practice of Multilateral Diplomacy (Cambridge: Cambridge University Press, forthcoming); For an illustration, see Adler-Nissen and Pouliot, "Power in Practice." For a broader discussion, see Vincent Pouliot and Jérémie Cornut, "Practice Theory and the Study of Diplomacy: A Research Agenda," *Cooperation and Conflict* 50(2), 2015.

PART II

Making international cooperation

4 *From representation to governing: diplomacy and the constitution of international public power*

JENNIFER MITZEN

A goal of this volume is to gain analytic traction on what seem to be great changes in the character and effects of diplomacy by bringing international relations (IR) and social theory to bear on the question. Toward this end, the Introduction proposes that while diplomacy has long been understood as a practice of representation, it is now "about much more" in that it also is about governance (Introduction, 17). Several scholars have offered interpretations of diplomacy as representation – for example, James Der Derian,[1] Iver Neumann,[2] Paul Sharp,[3] Saffron Sofer,[4] and Rebecca Adler Nissen.[5] But that work does not consider how representation relates to governance. Representing and governing are distinct, and the distinction matters, because the practice of diplomatic representation is constitutive of the international society of states and its members,[6] while the practice of global governing is potentially transformative of it. To assess the provocative proposition that the international system is moving beyond diplomatic representation, therefore, we need to have in mind what a practice of governing might entail, and along which dimensions it differs from versus overlaps with representation. That is the goal of this chapter.

[1] James Der Derian, "Mediating Estrangement," *Review of International Studies*, 13(2), 1987: 91–110.

[2] Iver Neumann, "Returning Practice to the Linguistic Turn: The Case of Diplomacy," *Millennium*, 31(3), 2002: 627–651.

[3] Paul Sharp, "For Diplomacy: Representation and the Study of International Relations," *International Studies Review*, 1(1), 1999: 33–57; Paul Sharp, "Who Needs Diplomats? The Problem of Diplomatic Representation," *International Journal*, 52(4), 1997: 609–634.

[4] Saffron Sofer, "The Diplomat as Stranger," *Diplomacy and Statecraft*, 8(3), 1997: 179–186.

[5] Rebecca Adler-Nissen, "Diplomacy as Impression Management: Strategic Face-Work and Post-Colonial Embarassment," Working Paper #38, Center for International Peace and Security Studies, McGill University, 2012.

[6] Hedley Bull, *The Anarchical Society* (New York: Columbia University Press, 1977).

The chapter has three parts. I first summarize how IR scholarship has treated diplomacy as a practice of representation and suggest a variation that is broadly consistent, that diplomacy functions as a system of social virtue. Second, building on previous work,[7] I propose that governing is a form of what philosophers of action call collective intentionality – more specifically it is a case of "joint action" or "concerting."[8] Governing is associated with acting together and its goal is to steer a social order, self-consciously, toward the pursuit of some shared ends. Governing takes on a particular importance when it is done by states. In domestic political theory, the state's public power is valued when it is understood as the capacity and responsibility to pursue its population's common good. I propose that if states can sustain joint action on common problems, they can act as an international public power. In the third, concluding section, I bring the two together and defend the continuing relevance of diplomacy's representational practices.

Diplomacy as representation

Diplomacy as a practice of representation has two possible meanings. First, it can mean that the diplomat represents her state's interests in the sense of conveying a set of beliefs and preferences to other states. Second, diplomacy as representation can refer to how diplomatic practices embody the state on the world stage, making it possible for the state to appear to others as a social actor pursuing interests and

[7] Jennifer Mitzen, *Power in Concert: The 19th Century Origins of Global Governance* (Chicago: University of Chicago Press, 2013).

[8] The literature on collective intentionality is extensive. Contributions include Michael Bratman, *Intention, Plans, and Practical Reason* (Stanford, CA: CSLI Publications, 1999); Margaret Gilbert, *On Social Facts* (Princeton, NJ: Princeton University Press, 1992); John Searle, *The Construction of Social Reality* (New York: The Free Press, 1995); Hans Bernhard Schmid, "Plural Action," *Philosophy of the Social Sciences*, 38(1), 2008: 25–54; Deborah Tollefson, "Collective Intentionality and the Social Sciences," *Philosophy of the Social Sciences*, 32(1), 2002: 25–50; Raimo Tuomela, "We-Intentions Revisited," *Philosophical Studies*, 125, 2005: 327–369; J. David Velleman, "How to Share an Intention," *Philosophy and Phenomenological Research*, 57(1), 1997: 29–50. Joint action is one particular form of collective intentionality, but here I use the terms synonymously. On concerting as a form of joint action, see Maksymilian Del Mar, "Concerted Practices and the Presence of Obligations: Joint Action in Competition Law and Social Philosophy," *Law and Philosophy*, 30, 2011: 105–140.

capable of negotiating. While both strands of thinking can be found in the IR literature, only the latter has been able to make visible the distinctiveness of diplomacy as a practice.

Mainstream IR scholarship (realist and rational choice institutionalist) treats diplomacy implicitly or explicitly in the first sense of representation, as an instrument of foreign policy. As Paul Sharp points out, for the IR mainstream, diplomacy is virtually synonymous with negotiation.[9] It is a tool states use to pursue their interests, and it is not a particularly effective tool compared to others in the state's arsenal. What truly drives outcomes in world politics, from this perspective, is the distribution of interests and material power. Generally speaking, diplomatic negotiation processes are treated as epiphenomenal, reducible to "cheap talk" or, at best, a form of information exchange that might reveal underlying preferences. The diplomat's world of embassies and ambassadors, ceremony and protocol, makes no appearance at all, and world politics could function without it. This way of thinking about diplomacy treats the states system and anarchy as given and analytically prior to interaction. State interests are domestically derived, constituted prior to interaction, and pursued strategically in the competitive environment of anarchy.

Not all work beginning from these premises dismisses the impact of diplomacy, however. For example, a large body of scholarship, particularly since the work of Harald Muller[10] and Thomas Risse,[11] draws on Habermasian insights to bring analytic attention to communicative processes among states in world politics.[12] Much of this scholarship acknowledges that true Habermasian communicative action is a "theoretical paradise" that is "empirically lost."[13] That is, scholars see the

[9] Sharp, "For Diplomacy," 49.

[10] Harald Muller, "International Relations as Communicative Action," in Karin M. Fierke and Knud Erik Jorgensen, eds., *Constructing International Relations: The Next Generation* (New York: M. E. Sharpe, 2001), 160–178; Harald Muller, "Arguing, Bargaining, and All That: Communicative Action, Rationalist Theory and the Logic of Appropriateness in International Relations," *European Journal of International Relations*, 10(3), 2004: 395–435.

[11] Thomas Risse, "'Let's Argue!' Communicative Action and World Politics." *International Organization*, 54(1), 2001: 1–39.

[12] A recent example is Corneliu Bjola and Markus Kronprobst, eds., *Arguing Global Governance: Agency, Lifeworld, and Shared Reasoning* (Oxford: Routledge, 2011).

[13] Nicole Deitelhoff and Harald Müller, "Theoretical Paradise – Empirically Lost? Arguing with Habermas," *Review of International Studies*, 31(1), 2005:

difficulty of treating the ideal speech situation as a counterfactual ideal among states, and few simply assume the existence of a shared life-world in anarchy. Nonetheless, what is attractive to IR theorists about the Habermasian communicative action framework is that it shows how a pluralistic society might settle the terms of its common life by negotiating its common norms rather than succumbing to the outputs of a clash of interests or processes of homogenization.[14] As such, it is tempting to scale up to international society. Despite the imperfect discursive environment of world politics, this scholarship sees the potential for communicative processes among states to transform identity and interests and to produce consensual outcomes. As long as states recognize one another as deliberative partners and enter the discourse with an orientation to listen and possibly change their minds, many scholars argue that there can be an exchange of reasons orientated to mutual understanding among transnational and international actors. International institutions are often analyzed as sites for argumentative legitimation[15] and persuasion,[16] while diplomatic negotiations are

167–179. Also see Thomas Dietz and Thomas and Jill Steans, "A Useful Dialogue? Habermas and International Relations," *Review of International Studies*, 31(1), 2005: 127–140; Müller, "International Relations as Communicative Action," and "Arguing, Bargaining, and All That."

14 Lars Lose, "Communicative Action and the World of Diplomacy," in Fierke and Jorgensen, eds., *Constructing International Relations*, 179–200, at 187.

15 For example, Corneliu Bjola, *Legitimising the Use of Force in World Politics: Kosovo, Iraq, and the Ethics of Intervention* (London: Routledge, 2009); Neta Crawford, *Argument and Change in World Politics: Ethics, Decolonization, and Humanitarian Intervention* (Cambridge: Cambridge University Press, 2002); Ian Hurd, *After Anarchy: Legitimacy and Power in the UN Security Council* (Princeton, NJ: Princeton University Press, 2008); Ian Johnstone, "Security Council Deliberations: The Power of the Better Argument," *European Journal of International Law*, 14(3), 2003: 437–480; Ian Johnstone, "US-UN Relations after Iraq: The End of the World (Order) as We Know It?" *European Journal of International Law*, 15(4), 2004: 813–838; Markus Kornprobst, *Irredentism in European Politics: Argumentation, Compromise, and Norms* (Cambridge: Cambridge University Press, 2008); Jens Steffek, "The Legitimation of International Governance: A Discourse Approach," *European Journal of International Relations*, 9(2), 2003: 249–275.

16 For example, Jeffrey Checkel, "Why Comply? Social Learning and European Identity Change," *International Organization*, 55(3), 2001, 553–588; Nicole Deitelhoff, "The Discursive Process of Legalization: Charting Islands of Persuasion in the ICC Case," *International Organization*, 63(1), 2009: 33–65; Alastair Iain Johnston, "Treating International Institutions as Social Environments," *International Studies Quarterly*, 45(4), 2001, 487–515; Rodger

linked to processes whereby talking the talk leads to walking the walk and the state's behavior and preferences change.[17]

In that work, diplomacy is seen as necessary, but like with the realist and rationalist work discussed earlier, the term is used basically as synonymous with negotiation and dialogue, and the world of the diplomat remains invisible. What is going on in the negotiations is representation of the state's interests, which are conveyed through the diplomat's starting position and instructions. Diplomacy per se is not generally treated as a distinct, much less constitutive social practice.[18] Diplomatic negotiators exchange information, bargain, and sometimes argue, but the analytic focus is on how these practices communicate and secure the state's self-interest. In other words, while individuals certainly are the mouthpieces of states, what's bracketed in that work is awareness of the fact that to successfully represent the state's interests, that diplomat must be seen as if she is the state. The state must appear to fellow states as the type of social actor that can be represented in the first place.

That is the work of diplomacy and the diplomat. So, while most IR theorists treat the international world as given, the diplomat knows, says Sharp, that the international is "built on sand."[19] That "sand" is a set of practices, ceremonies, and rituals, which on a day-to-day basis "secure the social distance"[20] among states. Scholars of diplomacy such as Sharp treat diplomacy differently from mainstream IR, as constitutive of the states system and not an epiphenomenon within it. Diplomacy's representational practices create a world in which state

Payne, "Persuasion, Frames and Norm Construction," *European Journal of International Relations*, 7(1), 37–61; Risse, "Let's Talk."

17 For example, Deitelhoff, "The Discursive Process of Legalization"; Thomas Risse, Stephen Ropp, and Kathryn Sikkink, eds., *The Power of Human Rights: International Norms and Domestic Change* (Cambridge: Cambridge University Press, 1999). For an argument about the distinctiveness of diplomatic persuasion, see Pauline L. Kerr, "Diplomatic Persuasion: An Under-Investigated Process," *The Hague Journal of Diplomacy*, 5, 2010: 235–261. On the Nordic approach, characterized as "deliberative diplomacy," see Norbert Gotz, *Deliberative Diplomacy: The Nordic Approach to Global Governance and Societal Representation at the United Nations* (St. Louis, MO: Republic of Letters Publishing, 2011).

18 An exception is Lose, "Communicative Action and the World of Diplomacy," who productively juxtaposes Habermasian communicative action to diplomacy as understood by English School scholars.

19 Sharp, "For Diplomacy," 53.

20 Sofer, "The Diplomat as Stranger," 183.

difference is (re)produced as non-threatening, or, at least, it is produced as less threatening than facing undifferentiated chaos. Hedley Bull famously argued that society exists when actors, conscious of common interests, set up rules to facilitate ongoing interaction. In international society, diplomacy is a core institution for states in which they regularly perform their basic rules of mutually recognizing sovereign equality, granting the right of nonintervention, and keeping their agreements.[21] As such, diplomacy is, as Sharp puts it, a "response to the common problem of living separately and wanting to do so, while having to conduct relations with others."[22] Similarly, Der Derian theorized diplomacy as "the mediation of estrangement."[23] Finally, Sofer calls diplomacy a system wherein presence is separate from (personal) identity; the diplomat estranges herself from the local to uphold the ceremonies and rules of this formalized world, even as that formalized world elevates "strangeness" and detachment.[24]

A premise of diplomacy as representation in this sense is that international society is a "sparse or thin"[25] social context. Sending develops this point in this volume and elsewhere,[26] drawing out the sense in which diplomatic practices are procedural more than substantive and privilege form over content. He argues that this culture, while thin, provides a "noncontingent infrastructure" for interaction. I would like to suggest another dimension of the thin culture created by diplomacy, which is that the practices seem to function analogously to a system of manners for a modern democratic society, producing the social virtue of civility.[27] Among practices that produce civility in a democratic society are those oriented around what Iris Young calls "greeting" – "those moments in everyday communication where people acknowledge one another in their particularity." We say hello and goodbye to others and often "lubricate discussion with mild forms of flattery, stroking of egos, deference, and politeness."[28] Such gestures are

[21] Bull, *The Anarchical Society*. The other four institutions are the balance of power, international law, war, and great power management.

[22] Sharp, "For Diplomacy," 51. [23] Der Derian, "Mediating Estrangement."

[24] Sofer, "The Diplomat as Stranger." [25] Sharp, "For Diplomacy," 34.

[26] Ole Jacob Sending, "United by Difference: Diplomacy as a Thin Culture," *International Journal*, Summer 2011: 643–659.

[27] Cheshire Calhoun, "The Virtue of Civility," *Philosophy and Public Affairs*, 29 (3), 2000: 251–275.

[28] Iris Marion Young, *Inclusion and Democracy* (New York: Oxford University Press, 2000), at 57–58.

superficial and often ritualized, but Young argues that without greetings no one would bother to listen to what others had to say, and communicative interactions "would feel like the science fiction speech of an alien, some sort of heartless being for whom speech is only for getting things said, interrogating their truth or rightness, and getting things done."[29] Deliberative democracy needs greetings.

Young is building on a distinction drawn by Emanuel Levinas, between the "said" and the "saying." The former refers to the information to be communicated; the latter is simply about announcing one's presence "as ready to listen and take responsibility for her relationship to her interlocutors," while also "announc[ing] her distance from the others, their irreducible particularity."[30] Greeting is a moment of saying, that is, it is an ethical moment that occurs "without the mediation of content." Taking Levinas's insights to the political realm, Young argues that such practices have the important democratic function of "assert[ing] discursive equality and establish[ing] or re-establish[ing] the trust necessary for discussion to proceed in good faith." Practices of saying are particularly important in environments where contentious issues are discussed.[31]

Mark Warren[32] develops these ideas further in his discussion of the treatment of sensitive issues in democratic deliberation. He argues that even "basic, seemingly superficial habits" such as "the habits of greeting, of saying please and thank you, of seeking not to offend, and to apologize if offense is inadvertently given" are ethically equalizing in that their purpose is to "interfere with expression for the sake of responsiveness to others."[33] That is, manners prevent us from expressing our innermost thoughts when those might cause offense to or humiliate others. In political situations where conflict is likely, "good manners are more likely to exist than good intentions." In potentially conflictual situations, then, insincerity can have a higher social worth than sincerity, in that it creates a greater possibility that interlocutors can continue their conversation. Where good will is lacking, good manners can have the "peacekeeping function" of "inhibiting behavior likely to cause offense, deflecting reaction

[29] Young, *Inclusion and Democracy*, 59. [30] Ibid., 58. [31] Ibid., 60.
[32] Mark E. Warren, "What Should and Should Not Be Said: Deliberating Sensitive Issues," *Journal of Social Philosophy*, 37(2), 2006: 163–181.
[33] Ibid., 174.

through apologies and reparations, and providing methods of settling conflicts without rancor."[34]

Young and Warren each suggest that greetings and manners might serve a similar function in international diplomacy. As Warren puts it, "[the] lack of shared backgrounds, the histories of power imbalances, the memories of past invasions, the resentments of differential power, or the suspicions that injuries inflicted in the past will be avenged in the future, all function to bias politics against deliberation. Diplomacy – which draws most carefully on manners – holds open the possibility of talk."[35] In diplomacy, a host of seemingly superficial practices take place among all states, from friends to foes, from the arranging of state dinners and leaders' handshakes; to the ritualized statements by states of their interests, values, and priorities opening annual General Assembly meetings; to the elaborate face-work of international negotiations, whereby participants go to great pains to preserve one another's sense of equal status.[36] Through all of these, diplomats display respect and consideration to one another, regardless of whether they are in agreement on substantive issues or even approve of one another's actions.[37]

The idea is that diplomacy's representational practices are ways of affirming and attesting to the good faith of one's opponent. They say, "I see you" as a fellow sovereign equal who is capable of good faith negotiation, even when everyone knows there is no good faith at all. Warren argues that such displays remind those present that their discussion has a higher standard. A ritual of representation cannot produce true good faith, but it "makes space for the possibility that over the course of deliberations, a hidden strategic motive may be silently retracted in favor of a cooperative one."[38] Thus, it keeps open the possibility of agreement. In contrast, demanding sincerity and truth telling or calling out lies "can undermine the transformative possibilities of recognition embedded in manners."[39] One can imagine such practices at work among the permanent representatives Pouliot

34 Ibid., 178–179. 35 Ibid., 175. See Young *Inclusion and Democracy*, 60, 62.

36 Adler Nissen, "Diplomacy as Impression Management"; Neumann "Returning Practice to the Linguistic Turn." For a critique of the diplomatic habit of speaking as if the state, see Carne Ross, *Independent Diplomat: Dispatches from an Unaccountable Elite* (Ithaca, NY: Cornell University Press, 2007), esp. 85–86, 99.

37 For example, see the discussion of "going too far" in Ross, *Independent Diplomat*, 140–141.

38 Warren, "What Should and Should Not Be Said," 177. 39 Ibid., 178.

discusses in this volume (Chapter 3), for example, and in the conversations states have in the course of complying with international law, discussed by Hurd (Chapter 1).

Importantly, diplomatic practices themselves are not animated by a social purpose beyond that of constituting and recognizing state separateness, and the capacity and right to be part of the conversation. They affirm the thin social space between states. The diplomatic order is one in which states have permission to remain "strangers," that is, not to conform to any extra-political standards or form an extra-political community of values. Consider, for example, the diplomatic "we." Each time an ambassador or diplomat uses the pronoun "we" or "our," the term is assumed to refer to the interests of the state she represents. Each time other states recognize or accept without question that pronoun as attached to the interests that follow, this (re)constitutes international society as a plural society of states. "We" does not refer to the group of states with whom the diplomat negotiates, much less to the universal community of humankind. For Sharp, this is as it should be.[40] In the post–Cold War world, as diplomats began to speak in large abstractions such as global peace and human security or to suggest that "we" should refer to our common status as humans, the universal we, Sharp argued that diplomats ought not act as if they are representatives of such abstractions but to remember that they actually represent political groups and that the international society they produce through those representations is valuable in itself. By trying for more, he cautioned, they will accomplish less.

Pulling this section together, the two ways of characterizing representation found in the IR literature are complementary. The practices of the diplomat that mediate estrangement readily can be seen to construct the world that is given in rationalist and realist accounts: a competitive anarchy populated by self-interested corporate actors acting strategically and worrying about the security dilemma, while sometimes building on their mutual recognition and sustaining deliberative processes.[41] To the extent that this is the anarchy that exists, though, it is because diplomatic practices continue to produce anarchy this way. States' instrumentally rational behavior both assumes the diplomatic world

40 Sharp, "For Diplomacy." Cf Ross, *Independent Diplomat.*

41 Alexander Wendt, "Anarchy Is What States Make of It: The Social Construction of Power Politics," *International Organization*, 46(2), 1992: 391–425.

and reproduces it in day-to-day performances. Without diplomacy, international society would not be possible. While the international society produced has tended to be compatible with realist and rational choice assumptions, what is important for us is that if such practices reconfigure, then the state system and international society as we know it will disappear or morph into something wholly different. One place to look for such changes is diplomacy, since it is there that actors, drawing on a shared stock of seemingly superficial practices, present themselves and recognize others as ready to see and be seen, hear and be heard.

Diplomacy as governing

Nowadays, diplomacy's representational practices can seem old fashioned. Although states certainly represent their own interests, since the end of World War II and especially the end of the Cold War, what diplomats mainly do is work together to solve problems. Representatives of states in their negotiations often take a first person plural perspective in which the "we" is not each diplomat's respective state but the group of states acting together; they make commitments not solely to end wars but to address common problems and work toward common goals into the future. In other words, some of the commitments states make and some of the practices that ensue look like governing together more than representing individual states. To govern is to make authoritative decisions that steer power toward what is understood to be the public interest (cf. Introduction, 22). It is intentional and collective, and when states work together in this way, it is possible that their estrangement is not so much mediated as to some extent transcended. In this section I conceptualize governing as a case of joint action. After painting a picture of the phenomenon of collective intentions, I define the terms *intention* and *collective intention* and then discuss what makes global governing a distinct case, illustrating it with reference to the nineteenth-century Concert of Europe.[42]

Collective intentionality

The idea behind collective intentionality is that some group actions are neither reducible to the intentions of individual members nor

[42] This section draws on Mitzen, *Power in Concert*, especially chap. 2.

necessarily collected into a unitary corporate agent. Actions are not reducible in that, in John Searle's words, "the crucial element in collective intentionality is a sense of doing something together, and the individual intentionality that each person has is derived from the collective intentionality that they share."[43] This purposiveness is common in everyday life and is something we all know how to do – we go on walks with friends or on family bike rides, we play basketball and tennis. In each case, there is a single commitment to do something together. Accomplishing that goal requires many individual choices, each of which is certainly comprehensible in individualistic terms. But the choices need to be understood in the context of the overall collective goal, which is something all participants desire and intend but none can accomplish alone.

Scholars of collective intentionality argue that the fact that there is a single commitment to act creates a single locus of agency even as each maintains the capacity to make her own choices. That is, the actors create a new agency, for a particular purpose. Because more than one agent is necessary to produce the goal, they must act "hand in hand," sharing authority over and taking responsibility for actions relevant to it. Forming a collective intention therefore creates what Margaret Gilbert calls a "plural subject." The term *subject* conveys that a collective intention creates an agency separate from the agency of the actors participating in it; the term *plural* suggests that the intentionality of those actors is not thereby erased or subsumed. It is a larger, "macro" purposiveness that does not necessarily coalesce into unitary actorhood. A useful way to think about plural subjecthood is as an emergent phenomenon, one that arises from interaction among a set of actors but is not reducible to them. To be part of a plural subject is to take a first person plural, or "we," perspective for the purpose of pursuing some specific goal or project. "We" is an identity term, and there is a sense in which plural subjects share a collective identity. However, the "we"ness of collective intentions is circumscribed by the specific intention toward which action is directed, and as such it can be relatively thin and potentially quite transient. Intentions can be shared purely behaviorally or in silence. But in many cases collective intentions are produced and maintained by talking and particularly so in the case of governing together.

43 Searle, *Construction of Social Reality*, 24–25.

Intending alone and together

IR scholarship uses the term *intention* rather loosely, but for some philosophers of action,[44] intentions refer to something precise: they are commitments, that is, action-oriented resolutions of issues. Going beyond the rational model where choices are understood to result from a combination of an actor's desires and beliefs, the idea is that actor's intentions intervene between those desires (or preferences) and beliefs on the one hand and her actions on the other. Specifically, after we consider our preferences and calculate expected utility, but before we actually do anything, we commit. That is, we go beyond our calculations and aim ourselves into the future.

Commitment is a normative concept, and placing intention between desires/beliefs on the one hand and action on the other has two distinct normative aspects. The first is the assertion of sovereignty over our desires. We may have many preferences that conflict or do not yield a clear message for what to do; so we commit. There is something normatively desirable about this decision to commit, since without commitment, we cannot realize a sense of agency and without a sense of agency it is difficult to "be" oneself or maintain an identity. It is difficult to feel ontologically secure.[45]

The second normative aspect of a commitment concerns the relationship between our commitment and our future action. We obligate ourselves to follow through, even if our preferences change. There is normative value in following through on our commitments, all else equal. Follow through is important for ourselves, in that if we do not do so, we do not fully realize a sense of agency. Our follow through also is normatively good for society. Social stability rests on the assumption that people will follow through on their commitments. In other words, part of the meaning of the word *commitment* entails an obligation to follow through. Because commitments are so important for individual and social life, committing to do something gives an actor a special kind

[44] Bratman, *Intention, Plans and Practical Reason*; Velleman, "How to Share an Intention," 32–33; Richard Holton, "Intention and Weakness of Will," *Journal of Philosophy*, 96(5), 1999: 241–262; Abraham Sesshu Roth, "Shared Agency and Contralateral Commitments," *The Philosophical Review*, 113(3), 2004: 359–410, at 375.

[45] Jennifer Mitzen, "Ontological Security in World Politics: State Identity and the Security Dilemma," *European Journal of International Relations*, 12(3), 2006: 341–370.

of reason, that is, a sufficient reason, for doing something. Having made a commitment is sufficient reason to act consistently with it.[46]

At the same time, the normativity of commitments, simply as commitments, is thin. Their obligatory force is independent of the content or normative value of the actions one has committed to. The commitment to rob a bank obligates in the same way as the commitment to rescue a cat from a tree. A commitment to bomb civilian targets obligates in the same way that a commitment to rescue civilians from harm does. If we do not follow through on our commitments, regardless of their content, we can be criticized for dithering or being weak willed. The concept of *intention* thus foregrounds aspects of action that can be overlooked or obscured in the baseline rationalist model: its intrinsic future orientation and normative quality, and our authorship of our choices.

While IR scholarship tends to treat intentions as synonyms for preferences, an intentions framework actually shifts the analytic focus away from preferences and brings attention closer to action. While it is normatively desirable to commit to things we desire, and irrational to commit to things we do not want at all, a commitment is not the same thing as a preference. It is closer to, and better accounts for, behavior. At the same time, our commitments imperfectly predict our behavior: we might be weak willed and give up. Still, the important thing is that we know we ought to follow through. The obligatory pull of an intention, rooted as it is in identity needs, helps account for how social actors override their in-the-moment whims or inner desires.

Now consider collective intentions. With collective intentions, we commit to ourselves, but we also commit with others to a common purpose: let's keep the peace; let's manage proliferation.[47] Intentions are commitments; collective intentions are *joint* commitments. Anchoring collective intentions in the concept of commitment suggests that collective intentions are inherently normative, that is, they constitute obligations.[48] Just like individual intentions, collective intentions

46 Bertram Malle and Joshua Knobe, "The Distinction between Desire and Intention: A Folk-Conceptual Analysis," in Bertram Malle, Louis Moses, and Dare Baldwin, eds., *Intentions and Intentionality: Foundations of Social Cognition* (Cambridge, MA: MIT Press, 2001), 45–67, at 47.

47 There is disagreement in the literature on how explicit the initial agreement must be.

48 Not all philosophers of collective intentions agree that they are inherently normative. I am thus siding with normativists such as Gilbert and Pettit, as opposed to those such as Schmid and Tuomela for whom collective intentions

constitute obligations to ourselves. But the fact that a joint commitment is to other people gives rise to a distinct normativity or obligation that has to do with togetherness. When we commit to doing something together together, as a body, we are committing to keep together for the purposes of that goal. There is what Gilbert calls a "relationship of owing." None of us can accomplish the goal alone; the actions of each have become essential to the agency of the other.[49] As Gilbert puts it, when we are parties to a joint commitment, our right to expect actions from one another that satisfy that intention gives us a special "standing to demand explanations" if some members of the group choose not to conform.[50] In the sphere of behavior covered by the commitment, participants have authority over or partially "own" each other's actions, because reneging by one potentially undermines the capacity for every one of the participants to successfully execute the intention.

As with individual intentions, collective intentions draw the analytic attention away from preferences. For collective intentions to guide behavior does not require that actors fully align their preferences, put aside strategic modes of interaction, or develop high levels of collective identity. What matters is how the behavior aligns (or not) with their commitments. If a group of states commits to manage a conflict together by, for example, asserting that sovereigns must be supported, then any member state of that group that arms the rebels undermines the collective intention. The other states have standing to criticize and demand an account of the behavior, and the unilateral actor owes the others an explanation. The shared goal of ending the conflict together means all relevant practices in a sense belong to the group.

Because they involve committing with others, collective intentions have a key feature that individual intentions do not. They must be "fully out in the open," or public, for all participants to see.[51] Sharing authority over one another's actions is possible only if each knows that the

are interpersonal but not normative. Even some who accept obligation as part of individual intending reject it at the collective level. See Tollefson, "Collective Intentionality and the Social Sciences," 5–9.

49 Margaret Gilbert, "The Structure of the Social Atom," in Frederick, Schmitt, ed., *Socializing Metaphysics: The Nature of Social Reality* (Lanham, MD: Rowman and Littlefield, 2003), 39–64; Roth, "Shared Agency and Contralateral Commitments," 380.

50 Margaret Gilbert, "Rationality in Collective Action," *Philosophy of the Social Sciences*, 36(1), 2006: 3–17, at 11.

51 Gilbert, *On Social Facts*, 191.

others have committed and what they then do to fulfill their part of the commitment. Such visibility, which I call "publicity," among those who have committed is what allows them to share authority over their actions. If a joint commitment is not out in the open, that is, if each does not know the other is party to it, then even if all individuals are committed to the same end, they are not acting together and the commitment may not have any effect on their subsequent behavior. The need for publicity among participants is explicit in most accounts of collective intentions.[52] Raimo Tuomela usefully unpacks its role in his "bulletin board view"[53] of collective intentions, distinguishing between two necessary dimensions of openness – epistemic and ontic (material).

Epistemically, intending together has a common knowledge requirement. All participants must know, and know that they know, what they have committed to and whether and how each participant is following through. Tuomela proposes that a collective intention is "epistemically strong" when each participant can see, on a metaphorical bulletin board, that a group plan exists, who is party to it, and what the plan entails. With this information, each potential participant can then make up her mind about whether to join. The epistemic requirement of collective intentions parallels the role of transparency in rationalist IR scholarship. The transparency literature is concerned with how "the acquisition, analysis, and dissemination of regular, prompt, and accurate regime-relevant information" affects a state's compliance behavior in international agreements.[54] Insofar as transparency arrangements reduce uncertainty about one another's intentions, each state can make better choices about what to do. But while information certainly is important, it is not the same as action; actors might respond to the same information differently.

This brings us to what Tuomela calls the ontic or material requirement for collective intentions. Collective intentions must exist in the world; there must be some actual, empirical referent. For Tuomela, the fact that the bulletin board is a "board" matters, because it is a tangible object that all participants can orient themselves around and talk

[52] Cf. Searle, *The Construction of Social Reality*. See Tollefson, "Collective Intentionality and the Social Sciences."
[53] Tuomela, "We-Intentions Revisited," 336–340.
[54] Ronald B. Mitchell, "Sources of Transparency: Information Systems in International Regimes," *International Studies Quarterly*, 42 (1), 1998: 109–130, at 109.

about, and therefore it can anchor the commitment. A material anchor can help individuals interpret the information about the commitment in a similar way. It also serves as a reminder that the joint commitment exists. This material requirement of a collective intention might be a physical object such as a board, but most collective intentions are instantiated less through objects than through practices, that is, behaviors with the same meanings for all participants.[55] Several types of practices can serve the function of materializing a collective intention. For example, consider the intentionality of a tennis match or of pianists playing a duet. But at least in some instances of collectively intending, and global governance is one, sharing authority over action is a verbal, communicative process. Governing together implies an ongoing conversation about the joint commitment(s) and actions that could be relevant to it – criticism, justification, reconciling of actions to intentions, and so on.

In sum, collective intentions have two conceptual components, joint commitments and publicity; they also have a normative core – it is good for us to make commitments and to follow through on them, especially when we commit with others. Collective intentions are macro- not micro-level phenomena, which means that the pull they exert on behavior is from the top down more than the bottom up. The upshot is that individual behavior can be pulled by commitments and not merely pushed by individual interests and intentions.

Thinking about commitments among states as obligations moves beyond how practitioners and IR scholars in the past have understood them. Consider the principle of *pacta sunt servanda*, which has been a long-standing principle of international society. The idea is that successors are bound by predecessors' agreements, that is, the state's commitments remain in force unless explicitly revoked. This generally has been interpreted in conservative terms, as a principle that facilitates social order, insofar as it means that royal successions and even revolutions are potentially less (internationally) disruptive.

How would the principle facilitate order in anarchy? From the perspective of IR theory, it is baffling. As Hurd points out in Chapter 1 and elsewhere,[56] conventional IR theory cannot make sense of the fact that diplomacy is full of claims by states that they are

[55] Emanuel Adler and Vincent Pouliot, "International Practices," *International Theory*, 3(1), 2011: 1–36.

[56] Ian Hurd, "Law and the Practice of Diplomacy," *International Journal*, Summer 2011: 581–596.

keeping their agreements and complying with international law – IR scholarship assumes that the commitment problem prevents states from following through on commitments.[57] Without a central enforcer to hold states to their agreements, it is difficult for states to know whether others will follow through. Leaders cannot credibly commit to actions in the future, because both leaders and contexts of action may change; in a changed context, it might be more rational for a new leader to renege on the commitment than to follow through. States therefore cannot trust that others will follow through, and they cannot credibly commit to following through themselves. As a result of the commitment problem, many argue that any commitments among states must be – in rationalist terminology – already incentive compatible, so that the commitment serves merely as a focal point.[58] If incentives are not compatible with commitments, or not reliably so over time, then external mechanisms such as sanctions and transparency arrangements must be created to reliably channel behavior. From this perspective, *pacta sunt servanda* cannot actually reliably *produce* order on a day-to-day basis; it has no capacity to obligate. The diplomacy Hurd points to would then be merely "cheap talk." The concept of collective intentions applied to interstate agreements helps us make sense of the pervasiveness of compliance talk. It provides a framework for thinking about how interstate obligations are constituted and how state behavior might manifest the pull of an obligation to act together, which is by talking together. In other words, this conceptualization of governing provides a way to talk in positive terms about the obligations created by international commitments.

Governing

Collective intentionality is a general notion.[59] Governing is a hard case, and governing in anarchy is an even harder one.[60] Like all collective

57 James Fearon, "Rationalist Explanations for War," *International Organization* 49(3), 1995: 379–414. Also Robert Powell, "War as a Commitment Problem," *International Organization*, 60, 2006: 169–204.

58 For example, Jack Goldsmith and Eric Posner, *The Limits of International Law* (Oxford: Oxford University Press, 2005).

59 For example, Schmid, "Plural Action," 36ff develops three models of collective intentions: corporate, influence, and team.

60 For applications of collective intentionality to, respectively, the state and the post–World War II order, see Alexander Wendt, "The State as Person in

intentions to act together, governing presumes an orderly social environment. But in the collective intentionality literature, this presumption remains unstated. Paradigmatic cases of joint action include going for a walk together or cleaning up the public parks. What many of the paradigmatic cases of joint action have in common is that they are relatively small groups in which the actors are generally friendly (or at least indifferent) toward one another and interaction is optional. The stakes of acting together are relatively low. These joint actions also take place in a rule of law setting where violence is generally not on the table.

Governing differs from each of these in that social order cannot be taken for granted. When it comes to governing, we cannot assume low stakes, or that those who govern together see their governing as optional and voluntary; and we cannot assume that they are friendly or even indifferent to one another. Generally speaking, modern governing is an activity made necessary when individuals who are interdependent and who expect their relationship to extend into the foreseeable future recognize that they face problems they cannot address alone. In such situations, decisions must be made about how to live together and what to do. They might disagree about a whole range of issues: the definition and scope of the problems they face, their role as a group in solving them, and even the most basic questions of how to disagree and discuss problems.[61] And in political discussions, the stakes are high, because the resulting decisions can have enduring impact, and there are always winners and losers. A political group engaged in governing together might share extra-political ties of community and friendship, but it might not. The political relationship itself is a relatively thin bond that does not require that actors share such ties. Indeed, even as individuals come to share institutions, rules, and norms, they may choose to remain "strangers," that is, to permit one another to maintain a sphere of privacy about extra-political values. This might facilitate social order, but it does not ensure that these strangers can sustain governing together. Governing is inherently contentious; as strangers,

International Theory," *Review of International Studies*, 30(2), 2004: 289–316; John G. Ruggie, "What Makes the World Hang Together? Neo-Utilitarianism and the Social Constructivist Challenge," *International Organization*, 52(4), 1998: 855–886.

[61] This definition of governing is drawn loosely from William Galston, "Realism in Political Theory," *European Journal of Political Theory*, 9(4), 2010: 385–411.

when they disagree they cannot fall back on their extra-political ties to hold them together.

Violence, in short, is a live empirical possibility when it comes to governing. At the domestic level, the state's monopoly on force solves, or is supposed to solve, this problem. States are set up to make it possible for political groups to pursue collective goals. Their claim to be responsible for society's general interests is what makes states unique and valuable. Private actors pursue private, particularistic interests; states pursue the public good. And the state's positive law backstops the political processes and keeps the group from coming undone.

In an anarchic context such as international society, life is different. Diplomatic culture might have "the power of normalization in a Leviathan-less world,"[62] but states still face the security dilemma. States cannot be sure of one another's intentions, and because they are armed and outside the cocoon of positive law, we might expect collective intentions among states to be rare and brittle. It is difficult enough for states to produce social order, much less to pursue positive goals together. Governing – a practice that entails a relationship of obligation, shared authorship of action, and shared responsibility for outcomes – on a global scale would seem out of reach.

Governing in anarchy

For states to govern together requires that they are capable of committing and holding one another to obligations. States must be able to perform a relationship of obligation, acting out the practice of owing. They do this by talking to one another. As it turns out, talking in a particular setting – public, in front of each other – can have a causal power. It has been found in the lab and supported in historical work that people talk differently when in front of others, and that giving reasons for action can result in people acting differently than they otherwise would.[63] So, recalling the normative link developed earlier between intention and action, if the forums in which states talk produce

62 Bull, *The Anarchical Society*; Der Derian, "Mediating Estrangement," 92, points this out.

63 For a review of this literature, see Marcus Holmes, "The Force of Face-to-Face Diplomacy in International Politics" (Ph.D. dissertation, Ohio State University, 2011).

the ways of talking and norms of speech that mimic a relation of owing, then intentions can become in part causal, and follow-through would be causally produced.

I propose that this can indeed happen among states. Of course, there are preconditions for states to be able to talk to one another in this way. They must, for example, recognize one another as capable of speaking as the state, and they must share a political language and a practice of committing. But with these preconditions in mind, the argument is that when states commit to do something together as a body and when there are forums linked to their commitments, talk in public can pull them to engage in behavior that is consistent with the commitment.

This is a two-part claim. First, the forum setting changes how states talk. Talking in front of others leads to speaking in general terms and making impartial arguments, and repeatedly appearing also can lead to a behavioral norm of giving reasons. Second, forum-induced ways of talking can affect state behavior outside the forum. Once shared rationales for behavior exist, that is, once there are agreed-upon principles for action relevant to the commitment, invoking this "public reason" in public, to one another, helps actors stay on track. The mechanisms that form the basis of those claims are drawn especially from the work of Jon Elster[64] as well as that of several IR scholars, rationalist and constructivist, who have extended Elster's insights and/or engaged with Habermas's work on communicative action.[65] What's distinctive in my framework is linking the forum mechanisms to the idea of collective intentionality, which in my approach is an agency beyond the state aimed at acting in the public interest, and to propose that states' commitments to one another thereby can pull behavior.

The claim rests on specific definitions of its key terms: forum and discussion. A *forum* is any locale where more than two actors who have entered into a commitment meet face to face to discuss issues of common concern. These days when we refer to public forums, even among states, we tend to mean forums that are visible and accessible to non-state actors. I want to bracket that meaning for the purposes of

[64] Jon Elster, "Strategic Uses of Argument," in Kenneth Arrow et al., eds., *Barriers to Conflict Resolution* (New York: W. W. Norton, 1995), 236–257; Jon Elster, "Deliberation and Constitution-Making," in Elster, ed., *Deliberative Democracy* (Cambridge: Cambridge University Press, 1998), 97–122.

[65] See authors cited in notes 10–17.

conveying the analytic core of global governing, because my concern is the ability of states to act together. The framework for acting together articulated here does not presume an audience beyond those in the room. It conceptualizes the pull of the commitment among those who have committed, which is a discrete problem that should be understood on its own terms before adding the problem of audience effects.

What happens in a forum is a general form of group talk that can be called *discussion*. The deliberative democracy literature defines discussion as talk among actors who believe they face some need for coordinated or regulated action. Importantly, unlike deliberation, which can take place in silence, discussion requires the presence of others; it is fundamentally dialogic.[66] Such talk can include reason giving, justification, rhetorical posturing, the verbal exchange of offers, and so on. If all talk can be pictured along a continuum, ranging from a cooperative pole where we would find the ideal of Habermasian communicative action to a conflictual pole where we would find (verbal) bargaining and strategic interaction, then *discussion* is the term for group talk that encompasses the full range of this spectrum. It requires the presence of others but does not have the demanding precondition of Habermasian communicative action, that participants are oriented to listen and prepared to change their minds.[67] In discussion, parties may come to agreement, but they may not. And if they do, their agreement will not necessarily be a reasoned consensus; it could be a compromise, a case of losing an argument or finding a lowest common denominator or being rhetorically trapped. Of course, talking the talk does not always lead to walking the walk, but it does so more reliably than silence. Invoking commitments increases the likelihood that they will be kept.

My argument is that discussion in the forum dampens the effects of states' individual and varying preferences as they pursue goals they have jointly committed to. At the micro level of interaction among units, through talking the talk of commitment in the forum, negotiating the meanings of actions by putting forward interpretations and

66 For a definition of discussion, see James Fearon, "Deliberation as Discussion," in Elster, ed., *Deliberative Democracy*, 44–68.

67 Jurgen Habermas, *Theory of Communicative Action*, Vol. 2 (Boston, MA: Beacon Press, 1984). In appealing to a general, empirical phenomenon, my approach is similar to that of Ronald Krebs and Patrick Jackson, "Twisting Tongues and Twisting Arms: The Power of Political Rhetoric," *European Journal of International Relations*, 13(1), 2007: 35–66.

scrutinizing the behaviors and interpretations of others, states translate their own plans into joint action and give meaning to one another's actions as part of (or not) their collective intention, which helps them stay on track. In addition, and at the macro or structural level, forum talk can help sustain collective intentions into the future, thereby making it more likely that actors can keep their commitments over time. Once a collective intention is supported by a structure of public reason, public reason can condition social outcomes somewhat independently of the motives and interests of the actors involved. Of course, some actors must be talking in the forum, but the point is that different constellations of actor preferences at the micro level are consistent with the macro-level state of maintaining a collective intention.[68]

To illustrate states governing together, consider the long peace of the nineteenth century among the European great powers.[69] The Vienna Settlement of 1815 ending the Napoleonic Wars contained a separate treaty referring back to it, which stated that if anything happened that could threaten the Vienna Settlement, "we" the signatories would meet to consult. The states that constituted that "we" were the self-proclaimed great powers: Great Britain, Austria, Russia, and Prussia, later joined by France. Nothing like the consultation provision had been attempted in Europe before. Paul Schroeder has written about this moment as a transformation of international politics.[70] It can also be seen as the origins of what we know today as global governance. The combination of a settlement plus the expectation to meet to keep the settlement together gave the great powers a new capacity to define and act on public interests.

Because of the consultation provision, suddenly every crisis in Europe was potentially a shared problem. If a great power decision maker called for a meeting, invoking a problem as European, the others had to respond, yes or no. A relationship of owing, created by the commitment, was activated by the provision to consult. Other treaties before the Vienna Settlement had talked in the name of European

[68] For a discussion of the relationship between micro and macro social structure, see Alexander Wendt, *Social Theory of International Politics* (Cambridge: Cambridge University Press, 1999), chap. 4.
[69] See Mitzen, *Power in Concert*, chaps. 4–6.
[70] Paul Schroeder, *The Transformation of European Politics, 1763–1848* (Oxford: Oxford University Press, 1994).

peace, but none had provided any mechanisms for preserving it. And it worked. From 1815 on, the great powers faced several crises, such as instability, revolution, and the imploding Ottoman Empire. In response, something we could call governing together occurred – they talked together about their joint commitment, and they acted differently than they otherwise might have. Any unilateral action was restrained and non-expansionist, which was a big change from the eighteenth century.

For example, in 1821 the Greeks revolted against the Ottoman Empire. Despite strong temptations to intervene for the Greeks, Russia decided not to, thereby preventing the revolt from escalating into great power war. As I have argued elsewhere, Russia's choice not to intervene was due to the great powers' collective intention to keep the peace together.[71] Specifically, Russian restraint was possible because the great powers created, through talking, a shared definition of the Greek revolt that kept it within the public reason of the Vienna Settlement. In 1826–27, still facing that same revolt, three suspicious parties, Britain, France, and Russia, signed the Treaty of London, which made the Greek revolt a European problem and hived off other Russo-Turkish grievances as bilateral and beyond their purview. That treaty also established the London Conference on Grecian Affairs at the ambassadorial level for continuing discussion. References to the treaty and conference were a key part of great power diplomacy in 1828–29 as Russia and the Ottoman Empire went to war. The 1828 Russo-Turkish War did not widen, and together the great powers even devised a novel, joint solution to the problem posed by the Greek revolt – an independent, national state.

Of course, their governing did not last forever. But the ability of these states to maintain a long peace in the first half of the nineteenth century supports the claim that when state interests are sufficiently overlapping and states commit to do something together, that commitment and the public talk surrounding it make it possible to realize their shared goals. That governing was made possible through practices of representation: these states did not share regime type and had a long history of hot rivalry. But the diplomatic practices that had evolved in Europe constituted these states as the kind of social actors

[71] Mitzen, *Power in Concert*, 123–140.

capable of entering into commitments with one another and taking responsibility for shared problems. As such, diplomacy, the mediating of estrangement, was the necessary platform for the emergence of governing among European states.

Pulling this section together, I have proposed that states govern in international society by engaging in joint commitments and linking those commitments to forums. Commitments create obligations, and forums can produce obligations talk, so the combination can result in commitment-consistent behavior and enable states to achieve outcomes together that they could not alone. Two points need to be made. First, this model of global governing is not inconsistent with the realist-rationalist premise of a competitive anarchy populated by states acting strategically and facing security dilemmas between them. But it is not limited to that hard case either. Second, the preconditions for joint action mentioned earlier – recognition, shared political language, shared practices of commitment – all are met through diplomatic practices.

Beyond representation?

Diplomacy seems to be changing. By bringing social theory to bear on diplomatic practices, this volume seeks to further our understanding of those changes and help us think about their implications for world politics. Toward that end, in this chapter I have juxtaposed received understandings of diplomacy as representation to a conceptualization of global governing rooted in the concept of collective intentionality. The centrality of interstate forums and talk to this understanding of global governing immediately suggests that diplomacy plays a central role. Indeed, if diplomacy is equated with negotiation, as it is in most mainstream IR scholarship, then forum talk simply *is* diplomacy and diplomacy and governing bleed into each other. The specificity of diplomacy only comes into focus when thinking about what it means for a state to represent and be represented. Interestingly, however, as diplomacy comes into analytic focus, its continued empirical existence becomes a question. In this final section, I consider the relationship between the two practices, representation and governing, and ask whether the deepening of global governance implies that estrangement is no longer mediated but in the process of becoming transcended.

Because contemporary global governance especially involves practices associated with cosmopolitan or human-centered norms and values, diplomacy as we have known it, that is, as one of the institutions constituting the international society of states, seems increasingly to be a relic. That diplomacy is associated with a world in which states are the rights-bearing subjects (the diplomatic "we" refers to the diplomat's own state), and they engage in representational practices to manage their interdependence in a competitive anarchy. Contemporary cosmopolitan global governance, in contrast, points toward the existence of a world community in which individuals are the rights-bearing subjects (the cosmopolitan "we" refers to our common status as humans), and today's system of sovereign states stands in the way of realizing a world where those rights can be universally recognized. The rise of cosmopolitan global governance thus suggests the world might face a zero-sum relationship between diplomacy and governing: diplomacy declines as governing expands. This is because the end state or *telos* of global governing from a cosmopolitan perspective is a fully domesticated politics on a global scale, and domestic politics is not a realm in which we are accustomed to talk about diplomacy. States' representational practices may have made their governing possible in the first place, but once states habitually govern together, continued estrangement only complicates effective global governing.

The simplicity and the progressive feel of a zero-sum approach make it appealing, but the analytics suggest a more complicated relationship between representation and governing. Once global governing is seen as a collective intention, what could be called a diplomatic moment comes into focus that is inherent to all joint action, including governing from the local to the global and suggesting that even a world state would need diplomacy's representational practices, as do the crowded global governing forums we see today.

To convey a sense of the universality of the diplomatic moment, consider, first, that in all joint action, from taking a walk to governing among states, the act of commitment is a moment when actors represent themselves as ready to do something together. In this moment of commitment to their collective intention, actors bracket – or, one could say, estrange themselves from – a fair bit of their individual preferences and other commitments. At least, they open up the possibility that as they act together, the particular choices they make and actions they accept from others will not be precisely consistent with what each would have wanted or sought out alone. In the course of pursuing their shared goal, each might be tempted to give in to a whim or idiosyncratic preference. But maintaining the joint commitment requires that they do not.

Second, for joint action to succeed, its participants must also represent those with whom they have committed as if these others, too, are willing to do something together, even if their preferences dictate otherwise. Acting together requires a mutual recognition that each of us is somewhat estranged from our personal preferences. Of course, we might not respect all of the preferences and commitments of our action partners. It can be tempting to demand that they share our value commitments and difficult to sustain action with those who hold values we do not respect. But insofar as we share an action commitment, each has the obligation, rooted in the normative value of action, to follow through in that particular sphere of action. By committing to pursue our goals together, we took on the responsibility for one another's agency.

These two aspects of acting together, self-estrangement and the mutual recognition of it, highlight the fundamental role of diplomacy for joint action. When acting together, each actor must keep in mind that the others are making the very same estranging move, or at least that the collective intention cannot be sustained unless they do. It is not always easy to keep up that public face of being ready to continue to follow through. Diplomatic practices mitigate the difficulty, helping participants temporarily leave aside personal, idiosyncratic beliefs and preferences. In this sense, we could say that diplomatic representational practices function as a protective belt surrounding action commitments.

Recalling Warren's argument discussed earlier, the simple, day-to-day habits and routines of representing ourselves and greeting others through our good manners sustain an ethos of mutual respect that can help support our collective intentions. In international politics, the routines, ceremonies, and rituals of diplomacy do the same. To be sure, these practices do not create the conditions for Habermasian communicative action. But they allow actors to display respect where real respect might be lacking. In such situations, if actors ignore diplomacy, if they choose instead to display disrespect, for example, by rhetorically undermining or snubbing partners, joint action breaks down. With this in mind, Warren argues that such superficial, "as if" displays are not so superficial after all but link up to actual respect by signaling to participants that the speaker will treat them the way that society tells them they ought to treat people, that is, as deserving recognition. Engaging in diplomatic practices does not guarantee problems will be solved or conflicts will be avoided. But it leaves open that possibility in a way that diplomacy-free interaction does not.[72]

It is hard to imagine sustaining joint action on any scale without some measure of diplomacy. Even among friends, diplomacy in the form of manners is helpful when acting together, since situations change, opportunities arise, and people change their minds. It is particularly difficult to sustain joint action when actors have different cultural backgrounds and values. This is famously the case in international society, which can be productively interpreted as a case of collective intentionality. European sovereigns jointly committed to act together to preserve their rights to be independent political units and not be absorbed by one another, and diplomatic practices produce and maintain estrangement. But the point also holds for contemporary liberal societies, which are characterized by complexity and deep cultural differences. Indeed, the impact on democratic deliberation in a liberal society of expressing sensitive views is what motivated Warren to theorize the social virtue of manners in the first place.

With this in mind, diplomacy would seem to be essential even in two hard cases. First, diplomacy remains necessary in a cosmopolitan world where political relations are domesticated. Unlike the international society of the Concert period, or even today's international society where many illiberal states are legitimate members, in a cosmopolitan governed world, participants would be liberal friends more than strangers. Nonetheless, to continue to address joint problems across long distances and on a large scale over time, the task of maintaining readiness for joint action among political units would remain. Only when readiness is reliably present could authority over action be shared. Diplomacy's representational practices provide an infrastructure and stock of socially shared, recognizable routines that allow actors to continue to seem as if ready. This is not to suggest that acting together is the highest value and objective in all cases, but to

[72] Warren, "What Should and Should Not Be Said," 175.

distinguish the practice of global governing from other practices in world politics such as socialization and persuasion. Diplomacy is associated with governing but not necessarily with the other two, since as a protective belt it cautions actors against a rush to persuade and socialize.

The second hard case is today's world of changing configurations of actors and authority claims. As the editors point out in their Introduction, today's diplomatic stage is not monopolized by sovereigns but is populated by an "intriguing combination of the diplomacy inherited from a state-centric world with various heterodox forms of political intercourse made possible by globalization" (Introduction, 11). Nontraditional actors engage in diplomacy alongside states, claiming other sorts of authority – expertise, values, and so on – that are valid for the task. Diplomacy remains necessary here as well, although we are witnessing a change in its center of gravity. State representation today is in the service of public problem solving, but problems other than those that prompted international society (outright conquest/absorption) are recognized as important ones for states to address. With international society, diplomacy's protective belt has surrounded the capacity for sovereigns to remain independent. With global governance, it surrounds a range of different problems, from state implosion to climate change to mitigating humanitarian harm, and many others. Whatever the particular problem, states' global governance commitments differ from their societal commitment, in that many of these problems admit the relevance of non-state authority claims. The shift in focus suggests a direct link between treating global governing as collective intentionality and incorporating the changing configurations of actors and authority claims. To the extent that we see global governing, sustaining joint problem solving spawns relations and cooperation with non-state actors that are useful and necessary for governing tasks. Global governance as collective intention thus contains within itself the mechanisms for its own transformation.

In sum, the relationship between diplomacy and governing ought not be seen as zero sum. The rise of global governance is not moving world politics beyond representation and transcending estrangement, at least if we think of estrangement not in Der Derian's strong sense but in a weaker sense of needing to remain estranged from one's personal or private desires to govern in a complex, plural environment. Without diplomacy, that is, without attention to the saying and not just the said, talk would break down and global governance would be impossible. Insofar as global governing is about acting together, diplomatic practices of representation capture an essential moment. Whatever the scale and whoever the actors, where we see governing we always will see diplomacy.

5 *Institutionalizing peace and reconciliation diplomacy: third-party reconciliation as systems maintenance*

IVER B. NEUMANN

Introduction

Recent changes in diplomatic practice include a marked increase in peace and reconciliation efforts by third parties aimed not at interstate, but at intrastate, conflict. One immediate observation is that as war itself has shifted from being less of an interstate and more of an intrastate phenomenon, efforts to mediate have followed suit. A general one is that the shift from interstate to intrastate peace and reconciliation efforts also dovetails with a wider change in global politics, which has seen interaction change from being state-to-state (international) to being multi-actor and multiaxial (global).

This chapter treats third-party mediation of civic conflict as what, with Andrew Abbot, we refer to in the Introduction as a "thing of boundary," that is, as a phenomenon over which a new profession, in this case diplomats, tries to claim authority, so that the profession's turf may expand. Where such practices come from will vary empirically. The case at hand in this chapter is the pioneer in institutionalizing this new set of diplomatic practices, namely Norway. Norwegian diplomacy seems first and foremost to be propelled by an interest in systems maintenance. Systems maintenance is of the essence for an agent such as Norway that, as a small state with an open economy, stands to gain a lot from upholding the system and has little or nothing to gain from its transformation.

A much shorter and empirical version of this chapter was published in *International Journal*. Subsequent versions were presented as the Henrich Steffens lecture at Humboldt University, Berlin, July 3, 2012 and at the book workshop in New York, September 25, 2012. I should like to thank participants as well as Morten Andersen, Tina Blohm, Cedric de Conig, Øyvind Eggen, Sophie Haspelagh, John Karlsrud, Halvard Leira, Heidi Mogstad, and Indra Øverland for comments.

The Introduction's emphasis on the need to see change in diplomatic practice not only in functional but also in constitutive terms invites us to pin down the nature of this change in diplomatic practice. A functional reading would note that the mentioned change in the system has thrown up new sand for diplomacy to grind. The set of agents in global politics has grown into something more manifold, and diplomats have followed suit. The intensity with which established great powers such as the United States but also Great Britain and France engage with third-party roles is increasing.[1] So is the number of engaged actors.[2] A constitutive reading would see this change in diplomatic practice not as a task-solving response to wider change, but as a constitutive part of that change. A constitutive reading has the advantage that it focuses on how the change has actually come about, and so a constitutive focus may help us specify the changes in diplomatic practice that follow.

The major change highlighted by a constitutive reading of change in peace and reconciliation is that contrary to prevalent expectations in international relations (IR) theory, the most conspicuous agents are not great powers, but small states, typically Western and rich. Specifically, systems maintenance, in the form of going to war against rising hegemons and containing other kinds of war, has traditionally been seen as a great power preserve. Ongoing changes in peace and reconciliation efforts, therefore, invite another look at this expectation. My response is to set up the investigation in this chapter as follows.

Part one examines the expectation that great powers will dominate systems maintenance under anarchy. By systems maintenance, I mean conscious action and unconscious behavior that results in upholding the present international system, be that by upholding discourse and practices or by strengthening its institutions and organizations. When

1 This is the key theme of the state-building literature; see Michael Doyle and Nicholas Sambanis, *Making War and Building Peace: United Nations Peace Operations* (Princeton, NJ: Princeton University Press, 2006); Michael Barnett, "Building a Republican Peace: Stabilizing States After War," *International Security*, 30(4), 2006: 87–112; Roland Paris and Timothy D. Zisk, eds., *The Dilemmas of Statebuilding: Confronting the Contradictions of Postwar Peace Operations* (London: Routledge, 2009); Séverine Autessere, *The Trouble with the Congo: Local Violence and the Failure of International Peacebuilding* (Cambridge: Cambridge University Press, 2010).

2 Chester Crocker, Fen Osler Hampson, and Pamela Aall, eds., *Herding Cats: Multiparty Mediation in a Complex World* (Washington, DC: United States Institute of Peace, 1999).

this is done consciously by states, we may follow Adam Watson and talk of the rationality in question as a *raison de système*, "the belief that it pays to make the system work."[3]

The point made here is that such a way of thinking and acting may be observed in parts of Norwegian diplomacy. I start by bracketing systems-oriented realist scholarship, for it simply exogenizes the issue by looking at systems maintenance as a by-product of the balance of power, and so it bars the question of who is actually maintaining the system from empirical analysis. Such an approach has value in other regards, but it cannot be used to address the subject matter in question. In part two, I turn to theorists, exemplified by Henry Kissinger and Adam Watson, who address the question in terms of agency. *Contra* Kissinger and Watson, and following Weber, I argue that we cannot think of actions as *either* interest oriented or altruistic. Action always has many sources, and agents are not necessarily in touch with them all on a permanent basis. Constitutive social analysis should bracket psychological factors such as intentions and look at which practices are actually in play.

Having traced the expectation that great powers will dominate systems maintenance, and having located its roots to lie either in a theory of the contemporary states system that is insulated from wider historical concerns or in a theory of action that is way too muscular, in part three I turn to the historical record. Is it really the case that anarchic systems have tended to be maintained by their major agents? The answer is no. I muster a comparative case of systems maintenance under anarchy, namely that of the interwar Nilotic Nuer, to demonstrate how systems maintenance may fall exclusively to a minor unit. Historically, then, we have examples not only of systems wherein systems maintenance is overwhelmingly in the hands of major units (the European Concert system of the first half of the nineteenth century) but also of how it may be exclusively in the hands of a minor unit (the Nuer). The Nuer example is not an isolated case. On the contrary, according to archaeological scholarship, minor-unit systems maintenance was the rule in Neolithic Europe.

Having thus changed the question from being axiomatic to becoming the object of empirical analysis, in part four, I substantiate the claim that small powers spend increasing resources by presenting a case study

[3] Adam Watson, *The Evolution of International Society* (London: Routledge, 1992), 14.

of how Norwegian peace and reconciliation efforts have been institutionalized over the past 20 years. The means has been the kind of networked, multi-stakeholder diplomacy noted in the Introduction. The means suits the end, which is to maintain the system and, if possible, further institutionalize it exactly by strengthening networks and tying in new stakeholders. This part ends with an interview-based discussion of how diplomats themselves think of what they do.

In the Conclusion, I argue that small and medium powers that are reasonably happy with a system will have a strong vested interest in maintaining it, since they are by definition less well equipped than are great powers to deal with other and violent kinds of conflict resolution. In a world of new emerging great powers that are increasingly engaged in systems-changing practices, increased systems maintenance by small and medium powers may be read as a countermove. The result of such systems-maintaining diplomacy may be a diplomacy that deals increasingly not only with peace and reconciliation but also with global social issues. Peace and reconciliation diplomacy is, I would argue, one of the key examples of how present-day diplomacy is in the throes of that move from representation to governance that we discuss in the Introduction to this volume.

Diplomacy, national interest, systems maintenance

Among the many virtues of classical realists is their preoccupation with prudence. Long before anyone talked about two-level games, Henry Kissinger saw the task of what he referred to as "statesmen's diplomacy" to be the reconciliation of particular state interests with the general need for a working international order. The statesman should aim to create "the representation of a ground of action which reconciles [a state's] particular aspirations with a general consensus [in the states system]," according to Kissinger. Kissinger's statesman is not free to "represent" the state. On the contrary, since state administration and "the character of the people and the nature of its historical experience" may be dysfunctional and out of synch with systems demands, it often goes with the job to attempt a change of the state.[4] IR scholar and

[4] Henry Kissinger, *A World Restored. Metternich, Castlereagh and the Problem of Peace, 1815–22* (Boston: Houghton Mifflin, 1975), 324–326, also 213. See also Ole Wæver, "Resisting the Temptation of Post Foreign Policy Analysis," in Walter Carlsnaes and Steve Smith, eds., *European Foreign Policy: The EC and Changing Perspectives in Europe* (London: Sage, 1994), 238–277.

sometime diplomat Adam Watson defines diplomacy as "*negotiation between political entities which acknowledge each other's independence.*" The dialogue may turn on compatible demands or on incompatible ones, in which case its function is "either the search for a compromise, or else is designed to transcend the dispute and to bring in a new element that makes a wider agreement palatable to both sides."[5] To Watson, it is in preparation for and in the performance of this dialogue that diplomats formulate the national interest:

> In the nineteenth century we begin to see statesmen like Talleyrand consciously serving what they conceived to be the long-term interests of the state. In Talleyrand's view, the welfare of France required the removal of his master Napoleon, and he remained in office to protect the same French interests after the Bourbon restoration ... The formulation of the national interest, and especially of the available ways to promote it, is made by diplomats who in the exercise of their profession are brought into continual contact with the similar purposes of other states, and study in great detail how they converge or conflict, and what inducements could bring about greater convergence. So the national interest emerges in practice from these diplomatic deliberations as a many-faceted affair, tempered by the art of the internationally possible, the art of the negotiable, rather than as simply the determined assertion of the national will.[6]

Kissinger and Watson diverge on how the national interest emerges. To Kissinger, the budding statesman, it is the statesman who formulates it; to Watson, the former ambassador, that task is a social one, performed by a state's diplomats. Kissinger the American and Watson the Brit agree, however, that responsibility for the system falls to the large states. The great powers are the great responsibles. To Kissinger, this is so obvious that it need not be stated, but Watson does acknowledge the importance of small states. He is particularly complimentary of small and medium powers that perform so-called third-party roles, that is, act as go-betweens for states that have fallen out. Drawing on his own experience as British representative to Havana, Watson recounts how Switzerland and certain others such as Sweden maintain foreign services that in size and especially in caliber are in excess of their strict national requirements, and how Switzerland has acted as a

5 Adam Watson, *Diplomacy: The Dialogue between States* (London: Methuen, 1984), 33, 69, respectively.
6 Watson, "Diplomacy," 148.

representative of other states such as the United States to, among others, Castro's Cuba. He also notes the importance of the Netherlands to international law, the contributions of small and medium powers to peacekeeping efforts, and the not inconsiderable role played by groups of small and medium states, such as OPEC. Still, he concludes that

> It is the larger powers that determine the effectiveness of diplomacy. This mechanical fact goes far to explain why in many systems of states special responsibilities for the functioning of international relations, the management of order and the leadership of the diplomatic dialogue have been entrusted by a general consensus to great powers.[7]

On the face of it, there is little to take issue with here. The realist tradition often claims a distant predecessor in Thucydides, who famously, and in Hobbes's translation, argued that the strong do what they do, and the weak suffer what they must. Little Melos became collateral damage as great Athens and great Sparta fought it out. To realists, that is often the end of the story. Hegemonic stability theory, arguably the leading contemporary realist theory of systems maintenance, is predicated on the idea that the leading great power will be the principal provider.[8] Many systems-oriented realists, such as offensive realists and neo-realists, see diplomacy as an epiphenomenon of the balance of power. To them, systems maintenance equals the emergence of like units and the clarification of relative capabilities between states. Kissinger and Watson should be commended for focusing on how the system is actually working socially, instead of simply assuming that it works in this and that manner. By that token, diplomatic practices are opened to empirical scrutiny.

On closer inspection, however, Kissinger and Watson seem to be guilty of a sleight of hand. While I see little reason to quarrel with the basic assumption that a comparative advantage in resources generally translates into a comparative advantage over outcome, it does not follow that great powers have the same kind of comparative advantage over systems maintenance. While Gilpin and other hegemonic stability

[7] Ibid., 198.

[8] See Robert Gilpin, *War and Change in International Politics* (Cambridge: Cambridge University Press, 1981); for a pedestrian version of the argument, see Paul Kennedy, *The Rise and Fall of Great Powers. Economic Change and Military Conflict from 1500 to 2000* (New York: Vintage, 1987).

theorists have a good functional point regarding leading great power interest in systems maintenance, there are also sound functional reasons why small and medium powers would take a special interest in this. First, while a great power can by definition fall back on the use of force should other ways of ordering conflict fail, other powers cannot. Small powers therefore have a general interest in institutionalization. Second, the more ordered and predictable the principles of conflict resolution are, the harder it is to convert military resources into influence over outcome. In other words, small and medium powers have a relatively larger interest in cutting down on backroom deals and going for rules and transparency. Hence, also the enthusiasm for multilateralism, which in addition to giving them a place at the table will also tend to work as a force for more institutionalization of decision making. Third, and this is of immediate salience particularly but not exclusively in Africa, should states break down, small states in the vicinity are open to destabilization from the fallout. The horn of Africa provides a recent example. Note that under conditions of globalization, "vicinity" may no longer be an exclusively geographical term. For example, in Norway, there are sizeable immigrant communities of Somalis generally arrived in the 1990s as well as Eritreans who arrived in the 1980s.[9] As seen from small states, a whole range of social issues may be relevant to maintaining international order. Consequently, efforts to do so must be equally wide ranging, from preventing social preconditions that are deemed to be conducive to conflict via good offices to reconstruction after conflict and natural disasters. A realist great power perspective that limits systems maintenance stands against a wider perspective that takes in the entire international social order.

In light of these points, I would argue that the entire focus on motivation and intention in state action might be misleading.[10] First,

[9] Cf. Axel Borchgrevink, "Aiding Rights? Dilemmas in Norwegian and Swedish Development Cooperation with Ethiopia," *Nordisk tidsskrift for menneskerettigheter*, 27(4), 2009, 452–466. Norway has had a diplomatic break in relations with both Eritrea and Kenya.

[10] The national Norwegian debate is dominated by psychological approaches ("why do we do it"), either in an idealistic variant ("trying to help is reason enough") or a realist one ("why do we do it when it does not work, we do not get any tangible dividends, etc."); for an overview, see Kristian Berg Harpviken and Inger Skjelsbæk, *Nytt norsk tidsskrift*, 27(4), 2010, 379–388. For the official line, see Jonas Gahr Støre, "Norway's Conflict Resolution Efforts – Are They of Any Avail?" Speech at the House of Literature, Oslo, June 11, 2010,

while psychological issues are no doubt important for understanding action, they are not open to immediate scrutiny. Second, as first pointed out by Max Weber, and as most if not all of us know from personal experience, there is no such thing as a strictly instrumentally motivated action or a strictly emotionally motivated action.[11] To draw on Weber's examples, a business transaction has an emotional dimension, and a wedding proposal has an instrumental dimension. By weak analogy, to talk about state motivations and state intentions, and to divide such motivations into the two types of "interest maximization" and "systems maintenance," may simply be mistaken. Having worked in the Norwegian Ministry of Foreign Affairs in four capacities for a total of six years, at least in the case of that institution, I can attest that internal discussions do not proceed in this manner. Routine diplomacy may, at least in the case of Norway, rather be understood as a result of a rationality of government that spells both maximization of the national interest and systems maintenance to be imperative.[12] Kissinger and Watson should be radicalized at this point. If the national interest is shaped by ongoing systems maintenance concerns, it may actually be misleading to try to keep the two apart. To sum up so far, both great powers and small and medium powers have systems maintenance concerns, and, for various reasons, it seems to be a futile exercise to keep such concerns apart from the national interest.

To continue the debate on preferred realist turf, consider not Melos, but another Greek polis, Corinth, which was a key trading hub,[13] or consider the hosts of the Amphychtrionic Leagues, which were both great and small in size. These *poleis* were key providers of systems

www.regjeringen.no/en/dep/ud/aktuelt/taler_artikler/utenriksministeren/2010/konflikt_hjelperhtml?id=608187, retrieved May 15, 2014. For a recent outside perspective, see Anna Louise Strachan, "Interests, Identity and Nordicity. Explaining Norwegian Mediation Efforts" (Ph.D. dissertation, S. Rajaratnam School of International Studies, Singapore, 2013).

11 When Zeev Maoz and Lesley Terris, "Credibility and Strategy in International Mediation," *International Interactions*, 32(4), 2006, 409–440, state that mediation always happens out of self-interest, they are stating the obvious; the question is what self-interest and which (if any) other interests.

12 Iver B. Neumann, *At Home with the Diplomats: Inside a European Foreign Ministry* (Ithaca, NY: Cornell University Press, 2012).

13 A rare mention of this is made in Christopher Mitchell, "Mediation and the Ending of Conflicts," in John Darby and Roger MacGinty, eds., *Contemporary Peacemaking: Conflict, Violence and Peace Process* (Houndmills: PalgraveMacmillan, 2003), 77–86, on 78.

maintenance in the ancient Greek world. Given the state of our knowledge, the ancient Greek world may not be the optimal case for demonstrating how systems maintenance is not necessarily a great power task, however. We should look to cases where we find systems logics in their barest outlines. Watson himself does as much when he argues that

> In a civilized community, which is not a mere tyranny, the power to judge and the power to enforce judgements must rest mainly on consent. This is true of a society of individual states, as it is of a society of individual men. In the days of the Vikings and other wild peoples, when the king was little more than the leader of a band of warriors and did not have the authority to dispense justice according to his judgement, two other ways of tackling the problem were evolved. The first was trial by combat, or by ordeal; and the second was the judgement of a man by his peers. Both are still highly relevant to an international society of independent states where by definition there is no overall authority.[14]

Actually, genealogically we are in an optimal situation here, for we happen to have a case based on observation of a system that was more differentiated than trial by combat or judgment by peers and yet was not a diplomatic system. Among the three founding texts of political anthropology, we find Evans-Pritchard's study of the Nilotic Nuer.[15] Among the Nuer, we find a proto-diplomatic institution, the Leopard-Skin Chief.

[14] Watson, "Diplomacy," 1984.

[15] E. E. Evans-Pritchard, *The Nuer: A Description of the Modes of Livelihood and Political Institutions of a Nilotic People* (Oxford: Clarendon, 1949). Adam Kuper, *Anthropologists and Anthropology. The British School 1922–1972* (Harmondsworth: Penguin, 1985), 84; states that "the brief partnership of Radcliffe-Brown, Evans-Pritchard and Fortes at Oxford produced a series of studies, dealing mainly with politics and kinship, which established a new paradigm. After the war British social anthropology picked up where they had left off. In 1940 three major works in political anthropology appeared from this group. These were *African Political Systems*, edited by Fortes and Evans-Pritchard, and with a preface by Radcliffe-Brown, and two monographs by Evans-Pritchard, *The Nuer*, and *The Political System of the Anuak*." While Evans-Pritchard's work is definitely functionalist, as is most work on diplomacy, the oft-waged accusation of evolutionism is not necessarily warranted. What is at issue here is not claims about genealogy, but claims about degrees of differentiation of systems, which is something quite different. Most present-day study of evolution is multilinear, meaning that there are different routes to complexity and that there is no teleology; see Timothy Earle, *How Chiefs Come to Power: The Political Economy in Prehistory* (Stanford, CA: Stanford University Press, 1997), 13, 208.

Systems-maintaining proto-diplomacy: the Nuer Leopard-Skin Chief

In his general picture of the Nuer in the 1930s, Evans-Pritchard highlights the lack of governmental organs, the absence of legal institutions, of developed leadership and of most organized political life. He calls them "an acephalous kinship state" and argues that they live in an "ordered anarchy"; it is, he writes, "impossible to live among the Nuer and conceive of rulers ruling over them. Each male Nuer is structurally defined by his position within a clan and, more specifically, within a "tribal segment," and then by his immediate agnatic relations. Conflicts are structured according to an alliance formula that he calls segmentary opposition: it is I against my brother, I and my brother against our cousin, I, my brother, and my cousin against our second cousin and so on, up to my clan segment against the other clan segments and my clan against the other clans and the Nuer against the Dinka: "the structure of the dominant clan is to the political system like the anatomical structure to the system of an organism."[16]

Evans-Prichard's work on the Nuer is well known among students of international relations and of politics both. In a minor classic, Roger D. Masters built on observations by the likes of Hans Morgenthau, George Modelski, Klaus Knorr, Sidney Verba, and David Easton to demonstrate the structural similarities between the Nuer system and systems of states.[17] This notwithstanding, the fact that the Leopard-Skin Chief was a minor player, whereas the great powers that Morgenthau and others hailed as major systems maintainers were by definition big players, was lost on them all. This is a point that needs unpacking.

Social life among the interwar Nuer is but one example of a mode of social organization that is quite widespread throughout human history. Given this chapter's choice of case study, it seems apposite to note that where Northern Europe is concerned, Kristian Kristiansen has drawn an explicit parallel to the Nuer when analyzing mid-Neolithic (around 2500 BC) societies as segmentary and warrior based. Acephalous political organization only gave way to fully fledged chiefdoms that waxed

[16] Evans-Pritchard, "Nuer," 181, 228, respectively.

[17] Roger D. Masters, "World Politics as a Primitive Political System," *World Politics*, 16(4), 1964, 595–619, www.sharework.net/www/cuny-gc/intl-politics/World-Politics-Primitive.pdf, retrieved August 2, 2012.

and waned with the coming of the Bronze Age around 1700 BC. The mode of social organization in question here is familiar to the student of international relations. Nuer acephalous society and what has been called the anarchical society are comparable systems. I evoke the Leopard Skin chief not for exotic effect but to draw on a mode of political organization that is widespread throughout human history and which demonstrates unequivocally that relatively powerless units may be key to political systems maintenance.[18]

The Nuer Leopard-Skin Chief (*kuaar twac*) or the chief of the soil (*kuaar muon*) of the 1930s took up the task of mediation when conflicts arose, typically over the stealing of cows or the killing of other Nuer. In the latter case, the killer is safe in his tent, which is treated as holy. In the former, when some cow has been stolen,

> The chief goes first, with several of the elders of his village, to the plaintiff's homestead, where he is given beer to drink ... the visiting elders sit with elders of the defendant's village and the chief in one of the byres and talk about the matter in dispute ... No discussion can be held unless both parties want the dispute settled and are prepared to compromise and submit to arbitration, the chief's role being that of mediator between persons who wish other people to get them out of a difficulty which may lead to violence.[19]

Evans-Pritchard recounts how the Leopard-Skin Chief is the only person to have been assigned a political function, and so he alone is the agentic systems-maintaining force. His negotiation techniques amount to a game in which everybody knows the rules and the stages of development: when one is expected to give way, when to be firm, when to yield at the last moment, and so on.

The key point for us is that the Leopard-Skin Chief is not a powerful man. On the contrary, he does not even belong to the stratum that, by dint of its position in the kinship system, owns land. Neither does he act

18 Kristian Kristiansen, "Ideology and Material Culture: An Archaeological Perspective," in Matthew Spriggs, ed., *Marxist Perspectives in Archaeology* (Cambridge: Cambridge University Press, 1984), 72–100; Leopold Pospisil, *Kapauku Papuans and Their Law* (New Haven, CT: Yale University Press, 1958). Hedley Bull *The Anarchical Society. A Study of Order in World Politics* (London: Macmillan, 1977). For a critique of how Evans-Pritchard and followers have drawn on the institution of the Leopard-Skin Chief for a variety of purposes, see Sharon E. Hutchinson, *Nuer Dilemmas: Coping with Money, War, and the State* (Berkeley: University of California Press, 1996).

19 Evans-Pritchard, "Nuer," 163–164.

as the representative of someone who does (which was the case of mediaeval European diplomats, of whose practices the chief's are often reminiscent). When, in the heat of negotiations, nobody wants to listen to him, all he can do is to wave his spear. He is shown no particular respect and his judgments are not authoritative. Evans-Pritchard notes a saying about Leopard-Skin Chiefs to the effect that "we took hold of them and gave them leopard skins and made them our chiefs to do the talking at sacrifices for homicide."[20] The reward for the Leopard-Skin Chief is to be fed by the village and to gain a status that was not there before, namely that of facilitator. What we have here is a clear-cut case of systems maintenance by a unit of the system that is definitely minor in power resources.

Present-day small and medium power systems maintenance: a case study

Historically, it is an empirical question, rather than an analytical given, whether or not great powers of a system are also in charge of systems maintenance. We have examples of systems where this is overwhelmingly in the hands of a minor unit (the Nuer), and where it is overwhelmingly in the hands of major units (the European Concert system of the first half of the nineteenth century). Historically, we also have a number of different roles in which small and medium powers have maintained international systems. Medium states can take the role of regional great power, as aspired to by, inter alia, South Africa, and perhaps Canada in the Caribbean. Corinth's experience is one example of a role that is today played by small states such as Singapore and the Emirates, namely the trading entrepôt that wants to maintain trade routes and communication pertaining thereto. Then there is the buffer state; Andorra, Belgium, Nepal, and Jordan may serve as present-day examples. Good ideas may have a greater chance of being realized if they emanate from great powers, but small states certainly have a role to play here.[21]

[20] Ibid., 173.

[21] For examples from the peacekeeping, the environmental, and the arms control areas, respectively, see Christine Ingebritsen, "Norm Entrepreneurs: Scandinavia's Role in World Politics," *Cooperation and Conflict*, 37(1), 2002, 11–12; Peter Viggo Jakobsen, "Small States, Big Influence: The Overlooked Nordic Influence on the Civilian ESDP," *Journal of Common Market Studies*, 47(1), 2009, 81–102; and Iver B. Neumann, "Harnessing Social Power: State Diplomacy and the Land-Mines Issue," in Andrew F. Cooper, John English, and

Certain states have specialized in institutionalization of the system. The Netherlands has already been noted as an early example from the European states system. Today's examples would still include the Netherlands, as well as Switzerland and the Scandinavian countries, which have consistently spent sizeable resources on systems maintenance in diverse areas such as institution building (the League of Nations, the UN), peacekeeping, development aid, disaster aid, and third-party roles. For example, the annual sum earmarked for development aid by Norway alone is about 4 billion Euros.

The road is now clear for me to present my thesis, which is that resourceful small and medium powers in today's states system, typically Western and rich states, are spending more resources on systems maintenance. One of the professions in charge of this is that of diplomats. To back up that thesis, I turn to the case study, which is one particular third-party role, or, more specifically, one particular facilitation role, played by one particular state, namely Norway and its increasing institutionalization of peace and reconciliation efforts after the end of the Cold War.[22]

By definition, and as noted by Watson, all known diplomatic systems offer examples of third-party activity toward conflicts. Brokerage – active participation in crisis management and/or long-term trust building, would be one form of third-party activity.[23] Another and weaker

Ramesh Thakur, eds., *Enhancing Global Governance: Towards a New Diplomacy?* (Tokyo: United Nations University Press, 2002), 106–132, respectively. See also Peter Lawler, "The Good State in World Politics: In Praise of Classical Internationalism," *Review of International Studies*, 31(3), 2005, 427–449.

22 While diplomacy has a role to play around the conflict cycle, it comes particularly to the fore in the phase where it is all about getting the parties to the table, and third parties "typically help the conflicting parties by putting them in contact with one another, gaining their trust and confidence, setting agendas, clarifying issues and formulating agreements," see Oliver Ramsbotham, Tom Woodhouse, and Hugh Miall, eds., *Contemporary Conflict Resolution*, 2nd edn (Cambridge: Polity, 2005), 168. For an incisive discussion of how proscription lists hamper work by third parties, see Sophie Haspeslagh, "'Listing Terrorists': The Impact of Proscription on Third-Party Efforts to Engage Armed Groups in Peace Processes – a Practitioner's Perspective," *Critical Studies on Terrorism*, 6(1), 2013.

23 There is a well-established debate within peace and conflict studies regarding appositeness and temporality of use of force by mediators, see, inter alia, I. William Zartman and Saadia Touval, "International Mediation: Conflict Resolution and Power Politics," *Journal of Social Issues*, 44(2), 1985, 27–45; I. William Zartman, *Ripe for Resolution: Conflict and Intervention in Africa*

form is facilitation, whereby a state offers its services not as an active broker but as a discreet presence with certain human and material resources to offer. Facilitation and brokerage cannot readily be disentangled, either. Suffice it to say that, as is the case with the distinction between military operations and peace operations, the difference hangs on structural factors such as the military capability of the polity in question, with centrally placed polities being more associated with brokerage than with facilitation. It is also path dependent, in the sense that a previous history of conflict, conquest, colonialization, and so on with one or more of the parties would suggest that the role in question is that of broker rather than facilitator.

A sizeable community of organizations in Geneva and elsewhere specializes in facilitation, converging on organizations such as the International Committee of the Red Cross (ICRC) and the Centre for Human Development. States were late to this networked, multi-stakeholder ball, with one interesting feature of post–Cold War politics being how a number of polities have increased the resources allocated to facilitation. The first state to do so was Norway, where there was a distinct move in this direction in the early 1990s.[24] The Norwegian Ministry of Foreign Affairs (MFA) established a separate section to deal with peace and reconciliation in 2000. Other states now regularly seek out Norway to discuss doing something similar, but to date, Ireland and Switzerland are the only other states to actually institutionalize facilitation as part of their diplomacy.[25] A number of other

(New York: Oxford University Press, 1989); and John Paul Lederach, "Cultivating Peace: A Practitioner's View of Deadly Conflict and Negotiation," in Darby and MacGinty, *Contemporary Peacemaking*, 30–37. Against Zartman's metaphor of the mediator gauging when a metaphor is ripe for mediation, Lederach stakes the metaphor of cultivating peace. But what is cultivation other than speeding up ripening?

24 Of course, a number of states had previously sponsored Governmental Non-Governmental Organizations (GONGOs) in this area, such as the International Peace Research Institute, Oslo (PRIO, est. 1959) and the United States Institute for Peace (USIP, est. 1984).

25 Interview with head of the Section for Peace and Reconciliation, April 23, 2010. The Irish MFA founded a peace and reconciliation unit in 2006. The Section for Multilateral Peace Policy is one of the eight sections of the Swiss MFA's Human Security Division. Recent interest takers include Australia; cf. John Langmore and Jan Egeland, "Distinctive Features of Norwegian Foreign Policy: Possible Lessons for Australia," ms., 2011. For Britain, see www.gov.uk/government/uploads/system/uploads/attachment_data/file/67475/Building-stability-overseas-strategy.pdf, retrieved March 12, 2015.

MFAs are now stepping up their efforts on peace and reconciliation, though. Recent examples include Finland and Sweden's joint proposal to establish a European Union Institute for Peace, the joint Finnish-Turkish announcement that they will work to strengthen the UN's work in this area, and British strategic planning. Reflecting on these cases, the acting head of section summed it up as follows in an interview:

> We are probably leading in this field. We can raise money at a moment's notice, and we are not risk averse. Over the last two years, we have visitors from the MFAs of Turkey, Switzerland, Belgium and Finland. We have been invited to a Saudi think tank that was part of their MFA to talk about the Norwegian model, and to the Quatari MFA to talk about how to organize peace and reconciliation work. Switzerland held a meeting earlier this year in Oberhoff within the framework of The Friends of Mediation Group within the UN; [initiated by Turkey and Finland, resolution no 65/283 passed a few months back] 17 countries were present, Middle Eastern countries, and they had an excellent man from Burkino Faso, who had been active in Mali and Chad. In meetings like this, people are very interested in hearing about how we had institutionalized the field and how we had organized the work. Our major partners the last couple of years [have been] Turkey, Quatar, and Brazil.[26]

As seen from Norway, nothing would be better than an institutional lock-in, whereby more and more states seconded the good offices of the secretary-general of the UN in this respect, and as seen by Norwegian diplomats, nothing would be better than their profession taking over as much of this action as possible.

Norway became a state in 1814. The central milieu of Norwegian state builders at the end of the nineteenth century were also involved in the international peace movement, and Norwegian nation building had what was referred to in Norwegian discourse at the time as "European warrior states" as one of its central others. There was also a strong missionary tradition as well as a strong internationalist workers' movement. To this day, two of the five key NGOs in this field are directly rooted in these traditions (Norwegian Church Aid and Norwegian People's Aid). Norway was a key player in the humanitarian work of the League of Nations, a founding member of the UN, and also one of the very few states to answer the call by the UN General Assembly in the 1970s to allocate 1 percent of its gross national product (later gross national income) to international development work. In the 1970s,

[26] Interview, head of section, June 4, 2012.

both within the context of the debate about a new economic world order and where overall foreign policy was concerned, it became an explicit axiom of Norwegian foreign policy to work for a better organized and more institutionalized international social order.[27] These were all preconditions for the emerging Norwegian peace and reconciliation discourse. In particular, the earmarking of money was important. The money available for development in 2005 was about $30 billion and has risen steadily since then. We are talking about a separate post on the state budget here, earmarked for cooperation with the countries listed by the Development Assistance Committee (DAC) of the OECD. In practice, it takes hard work to spend all this money in any given year, which means that any worthy project that comes the MFA's way and can be filed under development is fairly easy to fund.

Although Norway was involved in a small way in third-party reconciliation during the Cold War, it was only in the late 1980s that possibilities opened up for extending work on development and humanitarian aid into the area of peace and reconciliation.[28] From day one, the main fount for all this work was the interface Geneva/Oslo, with the ICRC playing a focal role. In 1989, former Foreign Minister Thorvald Stoltenberg was appointed as UN High Commissioner for Refugees and, wanting to bring in an activist, he contacted the key Norwegian presence at the ICRC in Geneva, Jan Egeland, to work with him. Here is Egeland's version of how and why he was recruited:

Stoltenberg contacted me during his stint as High Commissioner for Refugees in 1989–1990. I think he had seen me on TV; I was the head of

[27] Cf. e.g. the analysis in Knut Frydenlund, *Lille land – hva nå?* (Oslo: Universitetsforlaget, 1982), in which a three-time foreign minister gives an overall sketch along these lines. See also Halvard Leira, "'Hele vort folk er naturlige og fødte Fredsvenner' – Norsk fredstenkning fram til 1906," *Historisk Tidsskrift*, 83(2), 2004, 153–180; and Øyvind H. Skånland, "Norway Is a Peace Nation: A Discourse Analytic Reading of the Norwegian Peace Engagement," *Cooperation and Conflict*, 45(1), 2010, 34–54.

[28] For example, in 1971 Norway received a feeler from the Thai Foreign Minister Khoman to be a go-between vis-à-vis China. The MFA acquiesced but stressed that Norway should be a facilitator, not a negotiator (*formidler ikke megler*; telegram from Beijing, March 31, 1971, Norwegian National Archives, MFA, ad-doss 25 4/33, II). The basic approach, to wait for initiatives and to limit the work to facilitation, has long roots. For a discussion of another case of early Norwegian mediation, see Christine Smith-Simonsen, "Eritrea-initiativene – En forløper for Den norske modellen innen fred og forsoning," *Internasjonal politikk*, 72(2), 2014, 175–197.

international relief and the media face of the Red Cross at the time. I did not know him personally, and he did not know me. Later I found out that he had had me in mind already when he became foreign minister before that, he had discussed it with [his junior minister] Helga Hernes, and she had been positive. I quit my job at the Red Cross and started to pack my bags, but before I had a chance to go, Thorvald was called back to Oslo to become Norwegian foreign minister once again. So he turned to me and said, there has been a change of plans, would you like to be my personal advisor at the Foreign Ministry instead? In the beginning, junior ministers were recruited from the ranks of the diplomats. Then it was a woman, and then it was an activist – me. From the very beginning, he gave me wide reins, and I more or less continued to do what I had been doing before [*jeg fortsatte omtrent med å gjøre det jeg gjorde i Røde kors, jeg*], and that was to work with what I see as the greatest challenges of our time – conflicts, humanitarian aid, societal crises – and of course, at the Foreign Ministry there was money for this, around a billion [approximately 125 million Euro], much of it being non-earmarked cash.[29]

One notes from this account that the media crops up here as an aid for new diplomacy in a rather unexpected way – as a showcase for politicians not only from which to learn about what is being presented as going concerns, who is authorized by the media to say what about what, but also as source of prospective aides. Aides are being picked not only for their telegenic potential but actually also because they are active in areas that the incoming foreign minister deems to be politically salient. Looking back on this recruitment from his position as president of Red Cross Norway, Stoltenberg himself told the story a bit differently:

I had met him [Egeland] a couple of times and wanted him because he was capable, and because he came from the voluntary sector. The very day he came to Geneva, I had to tell him that I was to become foreign minister for the second time. So he came back with me, first as my personal advisor, because I wanted to retain ... my secretary of state, then, when I had established the second post, he too became secretary of state.

[29] This quote and the succeeding one from Stoltenberg are taken from interviews I did in the year 2000 and are previously published in Iver B. Neumann, "Harnessing Social Power: State Diplomacy and the Land-Mines Issue," in Andrew F. Cooper, John English, and and Ramesh Thakur (eds.), *Enhancing Global Governance: Towards a New Diplomacy?* (Tokyo: United Nations University Press, 2002), 106–132.

Drawing mainly on his ICRC network and the information that flowed from it, Egeland proceeded to involve Norway in a number of peace and reconciliation initiatives, with the Oslo Process being the most conspicuous one. A diplomat who has been key to this work since its inception (having been recruited to do work on the Sudan in the early 1990s and staying with peace and reconciliation work in this region of the world ever since, summed it up as follows:

> A key actor at the DPA [the UN's Department of Political Affairs] once observed that the Norwegian MFA and the DPA seem to cooperate so well because they are both dysfunctional organizations, which need informal networks of doers to crank into action. When these doers meet, things tend to happen. The main doer, the one who kicked off what is now Norway's peace and reconciliation portfolio, was Jan Egeland ... Egeland's strengths were broad expertise in the area of humanitarian assistance, a strong network from his time with the Red Cross nationally and in Geneva, and an opportunistic approach to conflict, in the sense that he worked with what seemed pliable and left other business alone. Time and again, he delivered results that served to adorn the administration's cap with new feathers, so received more money, which translated into even broader networks, which made for more successes and new feathers for the administration's cap, which meant yet more money. A positive feedback loop was created which began to feed adjacent issue areas as well.[30]

Egeland preferred to work with ad hoc setups, drawing in Norwegians who had networks in the relevant areas and fearing that codification of the peace efforts he initiated would hamper their development within the MFA. Egeland's name for this was "the Norwegian model." To him, institutionalization within the MFA would not be worthwhile. Another concern was that formalization on the part of the MFA would signal an investment of prestige on the part of Norway that could be used against it; parties to a conflict could threaten to withdraw if Norway did not concur in doing this or that, and the threat would be credible because Norway had been seen by all the world to have invested heavily in the process. As a result, during Egeland's stint in the MFA, there was little or no institutionalization of this portfolio. When the Labor government of which Egeland was part lost the election in 1997, a professional diplomat who was also a member of the Christian People's Party took over as foreign minister. The

[30] Interview with Hans Jacob Frydenlund, June 22, 2010.

Christian People's Party was traditionally one of the mainstays of Norwegian policy on peace and reconciliation. The years 1997 to 2000 turned out to be caretaker years. The processes that were already initiated continued more or less by dint of their own momentum, but there was little by way of new initiatives. A short Labor hiatus in 2000 created new momentum, as State Secretary Raymond Johansen took steps to formalize the work on peace and reconciliation. Four people – three career diplomats and one former politician recruited from outside the MFA – were placed one in each regional section of the Bilateral Department of the MFA with a mandate to work specifically on peace and reconciliation and report directly to the foreign minister (in practice, to Johansen himself, in his role as state secretary).

These four MFA employees, who were lodged within different desk sections of the Bilateral Department, initially tried to have meetings among themselves, but they quickly found that their conversations amounted to little more than a swap of "strangely named people we had talked to in strangely named places,"[31] While this lack of further institutionalization did little to hamper work, a more serious challenge came from two of the senior diplomats within the Bilateral Department within which these four worked. Not surprisingly, given the importance of the line principle of organization within the MFA, they disliked having underlings who had direct access to the political leadership, and so not only could but were actually meant to bypass them. The kind of expected resilience from old diplomats to new practices that we discussed in the Introduction is on ample display. Still, the new practices took hold in the wake of the Cold War. Formal institutionalization dates from the year 2000, when a unit was formed within the MFA. The unit was upgraded to a section in 2004. Some of the employees have been working as special envoys to specific conflicts such as the ones in Nepal and the Philippines. From the very beginning, the work evolved in close cooperation with non-governmental organizations, and the MFA would draw on and even hire non-diplomats to perform this work (a recent example is the special envoy to Timor Leste). As the head of section summed it up in the summer of 2012:

[31] The formulation was that of the second head of the section, reported by Frydenlund in a June 22, 2010, interview and since confirmed by the horse's mouth in an interview with the author (the "horse" was promised anonymity).

We have around 12 to 14 people in the section and are involved in around 20 conflicts, plus a number of minor dialogue projects. We have a budget of NOK 750 mill, which gives us flexibility and enables us to react quickly on requests from parties in different conflicts.[32] Some conflicts, notably the Israeli-Palestinian and the Sudanese ones, are still lodged elsewhere in the organization [i.e. the MFA]. The relationship to other sections within the division is very good, but we have some turf battles with the other divisions. Nothing special, and I understand full well that it is not all that thrilling to be the desk officer for a country but not have responsibility for the peace process.[33]

The centerpiece of the work is facilitation. As it happens, one of the places in which Norway facilitates is South Sudan. Leopard-Skin Chiefs and Norwegian conciliators are no longer just concurrent, but also co-present.

As seen from the point of view of NGOs and activists, the story of how peace and reconciliation diplomacy was institutionalized is the story of how they themselves changed diplomacy (see also Sending's Chapter 9). As seen by the optics outlined in the Introduction to this volume, however, a profession such as the diplomatic one is defined by efforts to establish and maintain jurisdictional control over certain tasks. In this optic, Foreign Minister Stoltenberg, himself a diplomat, as well as an important cadre of younger diplomats enrolled NGOs and activists in their campaign to widen the jurisdiction of diplomats. The interesting institutionalizing battle did not play out between these two groups, but between this alliance and conservative senior diplomats who feared that the new tasks in question would contaminate the extant diplomatic portfolio.

Peace and reconciliation as seen by diplomats: four steps

The Sri Lanka experience was definitely formative for the work of the section in one specific regard, namely, the need to separate the state-to-state work done by embassies abroad and desks at home from peace and reconciliation work. As one former head of section pointed out, if

[32] Note that this is only a fraction of the resources spent by other sections within the Department for the UN, Peace and Humanitarian Questions. By comparison, the Section for Humanitarian Questions had 16 employees and a budget almost five times as large.

[33] Interview with head of section, June 4, 2012.

the job is to find out where different parties to a conflict stand and bring those two parties to the table, then a neutral approach is called for. Since one of those parties would be the state, such an approach is diametrically opposite to the state-focused approach of bilateral diplomacy, which has as its main job to work with the host government.[34] The practices involved – and by practices I simply mean "socially recognized forms of activity, done on the basis of what members learn from others, and capable of being done well or badly, correctly or incorrectly"– are very different and cluster around four logically consecutive (but not easily disentangled) situations or steps.[35] These are mapping the parties to a conflict, clearing their path to the table, assisting in their deliberations going across that table, and, finally, being indirectly involved in the monitoring of any agreement being struck.

Step one of peace and reconciliation work is to develop contacts with all parties involved, indeed with as wide a group of societal agents as possible. In the early 1990s, the MFA would draw on the contacts of Norwegian NGOs. In the Oslo Process, they came through a trade union think tank doing humanitarian work in the region.[36] In Guatemala and Ethiopia, and also in Mali, they came through Norwegian Church Aid.[37] In the Sudan, a number of Norwegian

[34] Interview with former head of section, July 9, 2010.

[35] Baeer Barnes, "Practice as Collective Action" in Theodore R. Schatzky, Karin Knorr Cetina, and Eike von Savigny, eds., *The Practice Turn in Contemporary Theory* (London: Routledge), 17–28.

[36] Jan Egeland, "The Oslo Accords: Multiparty Facilitation through the Norwegian Channel," in Crocker, Hampson, and Aall, eds., *Herding the Cats*, 527–546.

[37] Kåre Loder, "The Peace Process in Mali," *Security Dialogue*, 28(4), 1997, 409–424. Particularly in Guatemala, Norwegian state action was crucial. As noted by the Canadian ambassador to Guatemala at the time, "[the first Norwegian ambassador] Arthur opened the office, [his successor] Arne Aasland came down, and that was it. The Norwegian NGOs were good; we had a lot of informal contacts with them, and they had contacts with the military. The Canadians [NGOs] didn't have that; they were of the Vietnam generation, and ideological purity was more important to them than getting the thing moving. Norwegian NGOs were not like that. I remember Asbjørn Eide came to a seminar in Canada and we [DFAIT] were clashing with the Human Rights activists from the NGOs. It was really bad, and Eide said [to the Canadian NGOs] you are 10 years behind the Norwegian NGOs. By that, he meant that the Norwegians were keeping their eyes on the job. They [Norwegian diplomats] would invite people from the military, and then the guerrillas over to chat, soften them up, with a view to making them sit down together. The first meetings are not usually very productive in such cases. Arne would have them over to his own

NGOs that were involved in development furnished the contacts, whereas in Sri Lanka, it was basically one former politician's network that got the ball rolling.[38]

These projects, which, as we have seen, gave the impulse to institutionalization within the Norwegian MFA, also had a certain path dependence on the international level. As already noted, besides the UN in New York, the main focal point for peace and reconciliation work internationally is Geneva, and the most important actor based in Geneva is the ICRC. It was therefore anything but surprising that when Norwegian Foreign Minister Stoltenberg recruited a Norwegian to develop the peace and reconciliation portfolio at the MFA, he handpicked a person who was working at the ICRSC's headquarters in Geneva. As Marilyn Strathern has pointed out regarding knowledge workers in general,

> The knowledge that is attached to them goes with individuals when they leave one job for another, moving locations; insofar as their knowledge was originally created in the company of others, then it is the community from which they take. It is visible in being left behind. But in what sense can a person ever leave a previous community (so to speak) completely behind? To the extent that knowledge is embedded in what they do, it will in turn show traces of their training, occupation and the contexts in which they have used it.[39]

The institutionalization of peace and conflict work at the international level means that once a certain agent is involved, it becomes privy to information on a whole plethora of different conflicts that is more or less freely shared. The symbiotic relations that ensue between a state such as Norway and the ICRC and other agents in Geneva means not only that information on new conflicts and overtures to Norway about playing a facilitating role in them will ensue but also that Norway

home in Oslo. Colombia was the same. One problem would be that that they would be suspicious of Norway's motives. Arne told me they would ask 'do you have a petroleum thing coming or something.'" Interview with Dan Livermore, DFAIT, former Canadian ambassador to Guatemala, Waterloo, September 29, 1999.

[38] Since the Oslo Accords were signed in 1993, Norway has been officially facilitating in Guatemala, Sri Lanka, the Sudan, the Middle East, Colombia, the Philippines, Timor-Leste, Haiti, Burundi, Eritrea, Mali, Nepal, Cyprus and the West Balkans, and unofficially in Spain (the Basque country).

[39] Marilyn Strathern, Commons and Borderland: Working Paper on Disciplinarity, Accountability and the Flow of Knowledge (Wantage, UK: Sean Kingston), 23.

becomes involved in a gift economy where certain services will at some time have to be set against certain others. Note also that this kind of symbiosis means that the diplomacy pursued by Norway must necessarily involve non-state agents and so be transformative of diplomacy itself. In the succinct analysis of one former head of section:

> Our [i.e., Norway's] contacts with the ICRC and the cooperation we have developed with the Centre for International Dialogue in Geneva are parts of a greater whole ... Operating together with a private actor makes so many things so much easier. They have easier access to all parties involved. Once states are seen to enter the fray, it all becomes more serious; stakes increase and deniability decreases. As the process matures, however, there usually comes a time when you [i.e. the parties to the process] need services that only a state can provide in order to clinch the process. For example, a state is a much more credible witness; it offers much better security services and it can bring stuff to the table that others often cannot, such as territory. I think we have a school for new diplomacy here, in the sense that this is a new way of working. When we talk to states, we often cannot penetrate beyond their presentations of the general line. We get more of the static [*vi får mye mer av støyen*]. By working with a whole gamut of actors and not only states, we come closer to the gist of the political. It is interesting to see how the private actors we work with used to be Norwegians only, but now we use whoever is handy.[40]

When a conflict is diplomatized, it changes the conflict, but it also changes diplomacy, in two principal ways. The object of state diplomacy goes from being another state to being all the agents that are relevant to a certain conflict, state or otherwise. Furthermore, instead of drawing only on the society that an MFA ostensibly represents, the MFA draws on a whole plethora of different agents in its work:

> We work a lot with C[entre for] H[umanitarian] D[dialogue], for they have tailor-made expertise on mediation, but also with Jonathan Powell, Interpeace, Conciliation Resources, International Peace Institute, Centre for International Cooperation at the N[ew] Y[ork] U[niversity] and so on. In addition to building up our own expertise and consolidate the section, I think of us as a kind of administrative hub on managing different peace processes.[41]

This amounts to no less than a decentering of diplomacy, whereby traditional bilateral and multilateral state-oriented diplomacy gives

[40] Interview with former head of section, July 9, 2010.
[41] Interview with head of section, June 4, 2012.

way to networking. It turned out that the subject matter engaged in – desecuritization – changed the face of diplomacy by changing the way it had to be conducted – less state-to-state, more networked.

If step one of a facilitator's work is mapping the parties in terms of political structure and political views, step two is to nudge the parties in the direction of dialogue. This may be done by indirect means, by initiating or bending already existing frameworks in the margins of which the parties may meet. One example of such a framework would be a religious dialogue. Such efforts will have to be preceded by direct contacts, however. Whereas the state side to a conflict usually controls territory and has the accompanying freedom to maneuver that comes with such control, for other parties the physical security aspects of surfacing may loom large. The non-state parties take a risk by surfacing. Even if a number of intermediaries are used, they incur a substantial risk simply by talking to facilitators, meaning that facilitators have to be utterly discreet. One former head of section made a comment in this regard that strikes to the heart of diplomats' self-understanding. Highlighting the covert aspect of operations, the following point was made: "This is why peace and reconciliation work is found at the interstice of diplomacy and intelligence. It is imperative, however, that diplomats take care of this, since the intelligence people always have a double agenda. They also want to know who they might have to kill."[42] It is the understanding of this diplomat, and, I would add, of diplomats generally, that they have a firm commitment to the diplomatization of conflict. This is in keeping with how professions are defined by efforts to establish and maintain jurisdictional control over certain tasks. Other professions involved, and particularly the military, are seen by diplomats as having a double agenda, always asking themselves whether diplomatization or acts of violence would bring about what they at any one given time hold to be the optimal course of action. It must also be said, however, that the diplomatic self-understanding differs from what one learns from the historical record on this point, for, as discussed in the Introduction to this chapter, diplomats themselves were, and still are, also prone to consider moves other than desecuritizing ones.

Once the parties have agreed to talk, a third facilitating step would be to bring them physically to the table. This involves finding, and often

[42] Interview with former head of section, July 9, 2010. See also note 2 in this regard.

paying for, spaces where the parties may meet in a secure and relaxed atmosphere conducive to work and trust building. This is delicate stuff, for if the setting is too reclusive, the ties between negotiators and their constituencies become weaker, and a lot of time-consuming shuttling between negotiators and (the rest of) the leadership will tend to ensue. The facilitator needs a light touch at this point, for on the one hand, there will always be incentives to speed up the process, whereas on the other hand, too much rushing may bring the dialogue tumbling down.

The facilitator's work may end at this stage, but it may also involve a fourth step, namely, monitoring the agreements reached. Again, this is risky business, for as pointed out by a former head of the section, "facilitators of a certain deal should not become the umpires of that deal. Facilitation and monitoring should be treated as two discreet functions."[43]

There are, of course, qualitative and quantitative differences between the peace and reconciliation work performed by the Leopard-Skin Chief and Norwegian diplomats. It also transpires, however, that they share an understanding of their role as being an important but frequently ineffective one. Most important to the argument here is that they both emphasize their own powerlessness in the face of the combatants, and that the frequent ineffectiveness of their actions bears out the accuracy of this self-understanding. These systems maintainers experience themselves as minor players. Logically, that has no bearing whatsoever on the question of whether they are actually systems maintainers. They are, and rightly understand themselves as such, but as with all human actions, theirs sometimes prove ineffective.[44]

Conclusion

Diplomacy is about the formulation and pursuit of national interests, and it is about systems maintenance. Great powers may by definition

[43] Interview with former head of section, July 9, 2010.

[44] Note, also, that Norwegian peace and reconciliation are unashamedly systems maintaining in another sense. As discussed by Oliver P. Richmond, *The Transformation of Peace* (Houndmills: Palgrave, 2005), 89–101, third-party work tends to happen within a wider frame that he names "the liberal peace." He further identifies two generations of peace activities in this field, with the first being problem solving, and the second being more attuned to structural issues. While Norwegian diplomats are definitely not blind to such issues, their peace and reconciliation work is explicitly set up as an exercise in problem solving.

draw on more resources than other units in the system, and so they are better placed to fulfill their interest. Received wisdom, as formulated, for example, by hegemonic stability theorists, has it that great powers are also the great responsibles, that is, they are the important systems maintainers as well. Drawing on a contrasting case of mediation under anarchy to the one we find in the case of the states system, namely, the situation among the Nilotic Nuer in the interwar period, I noted that in some cases, systems maintenance is in the hands of lesser units in the system. I also noted that the kind and number of third parties that aspire to solve conflicts are increasing. Having thus opened the question to empirical scrutiny, I discussed how one small to medium state in the system, namely Norway, is allocating an increasing amount of resources to systems maintenance. Neither the Leopard-Skin Chief nor Norway possesses the kind of power resources that are often seen as key to mediation.[45] Still, they play an important role.

The allocation by Norway and other small and medium powers of more resources to systems maintenance changes the face of diplomacy. As discussed in the Introduction to this book, we see the unfolding of networked, multi-stakeholder diplomacy. We also see a fully fledged example of how, in the words of the Introduction, "new tasks emerge to become more or less recognized as constituting 'diplomacy.'"

One consequence of the institutionalization of peace and conflict that works at the international level is that diplomats who are involved in one sequence get wind of information about other cases. The result is a gift economy wherein one good turn deserves another. This system includes non-state agents, and this very fact will transform diplomacy itself by making it less state centric. The ongoing networked third-party mediation by a group headed by Malaysia and including both state actors such as Norway and non-state actors makes for a good example.[46] A number of indications in extant literature support the claim that we are looking at a major shift in diplomatic practices here. For example, already in 1986, John Vincent

45 See, for example, the discussion of different kinds of power resources in Jeffrey Z. Rubin, "International Mediation in Context," in Jacob Bercovitch and Jeffrey Z. Rubin, eds., *Mediation in International Relations* (New York: St. Martin's Press, 1992), 249–272.

46 See www.c-r.org/featured-work/international-contact-group-mindanao, retrieved June 15, 2013. I thank Sophie Haspeslagh for directing me to this source.

discussed the issue of human rights and found a systems-transforming potential.[47] Thinking on human rights starts from the individual, not the state, but human rights are handled by states and so make up a potentially disruptive subject of international relations. Vincent advanced the argument that attempts to resolve the clash between an inherent rights logic and the logic that dominated the working of the states system seemed to focus crucially on the institution of international law, whereby a body of what is called *ius gentium intra se* (law of peoples within themselves) is being worked out. This body of law regulates the boundary and working of a bundle of human rights defined as a common concern to states, the violation of which may lead to a humanitarian intervention being launched. Diplomats, Vincent argued, had to find ways of dealing with this new subject matter. He also argued that to the extent that they succeed, this would boost systems maintenance (or, in his terms, international society).

Vincent's highlighting of international law also holds the clue, I would argue, to why small and medium powers allocate more resources to systems maintenance. Realist small state people and diplomats cannot fall back on overwhelming gun power. If peaceful systems maintenance breaks down, and other forms of conflict resolution such as forceful coercion, military intervention, and war take over, they are stumped. It may or may not be the case that the strongest power in the system will allocate resources to systems maintenance, as argued by hegemonic stability theorists. If they do, it may indeed give small and medium powers a free ride. A complementary thesis would be that these powers have a clear self-interest in systems maintenance, and particularly in peaceful reconciliation of conflicts. To small and medium powers that are doing well out of a system, interest and systems maintenance merge into a diplomacy of systems commitment. For the Nuer Leopard-Skin Chiefs, the commitment to systems maintenance held, regardless of how many times they had to throw down their spears in frustration over a lack of results. The same seems to hold for Norwegian diplomats. The commitment holds, even when Norway is pointed up as a sheep in leopard's clothing, such as it was in Sri Lanka, where Norwegian facilitation had few positive results and ended up being seen as counterproductive by both parties to the

[47] John Vincent, *Human Rights and International Relations* (Cambridge: Cambridge University Press, 1986).

conflict. Like the Leopard-Skin Chief, Norway certainly does not belong to the major units of the system, and it certainly gains recognition from the status, but that does not imply that Norway dons the leopard skin simply as a branding exercise. The recognition earned is a by-product of following a particular rationality of government. In the lingo of the Introduction, a state's diplomatic representation to the world is increasingly couched within a rationality of government, whereby the best way to be represented is as a force for global social change. The analysis suggests an additional point. In today's world, where new great powers are emerging, the increasing facilitation work by rich small and medium powers documented here may be read as a systems-stabilizing counter tendency.

Further work on systems maintenance in today's system should take three principal directions. First, we need to know how and to what degree other small and medium powers contribute. Second, we need to know to what degree the practices of great powers mimic those of small and medium powers. One place to look in this regard would be the new US strategy for leadership in the areas of diplomacy and development by mustering "civilian power," which signals that the United States may copy diplomatic practices pioneered by small and medium powers in areas such as development.[48] A third locus that seems particularly apposite is the new United Nations Mediation Support Unit, whose very existence demonstrates how networked multi-stakeholder diplomacy is now being institutionalized at such a pace that it is changing diplomacy overall in the direction of more systems maintenance by governance.

[48] Hillary Rodham Clinton, "Leading through Civilian Power," *Foreign Affairs*, 89(6), 2010.

6 *Christian ethics, actors, and diplomacy: mediating universalist pretentions*

CECELIA LYNCH

Introduction

This volume explores questions regarding diplomacy's social configurations, authority structures, and modes of governance to conceptualize more clearly many of the central practices that are constitutive of international politics and provide analytical tools for examining them. As the editors point out, the idea that civil society actors have infiltrated interstate diplomacy, transforming it into something new, is important, but it does not tell the whole story of diplomatic interactions and their complexity in the present day (see Introduction). As a result, a relational approach is needed, one that does not eliminate conventional state representatives in diplomatic stories but rather understands them as embedded in new forms of interaction with other, non-state actors and both territorial and de-territorialized spaces of governance.

My previous work addressed this conundrum (*Beyond Appeasement*, 1999), although it did not use all of these terms. Looking at the role of peace movements in a time (the 1920s and 1930s) when conventional diplomats openly disdained attempts by civil society actors to influence both bilateral and multilateral arms control and arbitration agreements, I argued, was critical for understanding important normative changes in global governance and the delegitimization of traditional forms of diplomatic practice. The relationality among conventional diplomats and social forces (who were frequently not united in their demands), against a background in which the knowledge of the state and the expertise of diplomats as well as other officials were widely and publicly questioned, resulted in significant changes in authority structures and modes of governance. These changes resulted in legitimizing and institutionalizing global international organization, from the League of Nations to the United Nations, not as a space in which negotiations and treaties occurred in settled or technocratic fashion, but rather as a space of contestation and debate for the relations between "new" and "old" actors, representing a wide range of ideas and interpretations of what was necessary in global politics.

In this chapter, I elucidate the strong religious components of the social forces that promoted these and other changes during the twentieth century. During the interwar period, Christian groups, especially, formed a significant component of peace movements in both the United States and Britain, although secular and Jewish groups and individuals were also active. Each of these social forces brought particular ethical challenges to the fore regarding how relations among states, peoples, and non-state actors ought to be conducted. Church leaders, theologians, and Christian activists did not all advocate the same interpretations of Christian ethics, which ranged from pacifism to "just war" theorizing, but they agreed that Christian ethics offered important resources for conceptualizing relationality and authority.

Probing this period further reveals a constitutive relationship between Christian ethics and diplomacy, with multiple manifestations. During the interwar and post–World War II periods, Christian ethics shaped the assumptions and worldviews of influential Western diplomats, influenced how diplomatic practices navigated the fraught terrain between sovereign and universalist claims, and underlay components of the justification for resulting institutions such as the League and the UN. The constitutive relationship between Christian ethics and diplomacy, of course, can be traced much further historically, shaping much of what has been seen as conventional diplomatic practice in Western modernity. Peeling back the secularist assumptions of international politics, in other words, demonstrates the degree to which religious and in particular Christian actors, ignored by international relations theory for much of the twentieth century, have always been and continue to be part and parcel of Western diplomacy, conceived as both a profession and a set of practices that are conducted through specific, though evolving, institutions.[1] Christianity's legacy forms a prominent,

[1] See, in particular, Erin K. Wilson, *After Secularism: Rethinking Religion* (New York: Palgrave Macmillan, 2012); José Casanova, *Public Religions in the Modern World* (Chicago: University of Chicago Press, 1994); Talal Asad, *Formations of the Secular* (Stanford, CA: Stanford University Press, 2003); Scott M. Thomas, "Taking Religious and Cultural Pluralism Seriously: The Global Resurgence of Religion and the Transformation of International Society," *Millenium: Journal of International Studies*, 29(3), 2000, 815–841; Cecelia Lynch, "Dogma, Praxis, and Religious Perspectives on

though relatively unexamined, component of the history of Western diplomacy; it also has a historically complicated relationship with state sovereignty, the foundational international institution that makes modern diplomacy possible. Christian guidelines have long helped construct the foundation for Western understandings of the goals to be achieved in diplomatic practice, including the legitimate use of violence and forms of international intervention, and hence they have shaped the profession of diplomacy itself. Christian ethics derived from Augustinian formulations underlie the institutionalization and codification of modern warfare, shaping modern definitions of *jus ad bellum* and *jus in bello*, the laws of war and laws in war, respectively, and it is diplomats who must help interpret as well as represent and communicate state intentions and policies on warfare. Christian ethical debates, divisions, and actions shaped the creation of the nation-state system and the ideas of the US Founding Fathers as well as supranational and international forms of governance.[2] In other words, Christian debates about the nature of sovereignty versus universalist projects address the essence of relational concerns about traditional diplomacy: the question of how estrangement – or the inside/outside problem of world politics – is mediated.[3]

In this chapter, I examine the ethical tensions of Christian actors during two periods: the 1930s and 1940s (from the end of the interwar years to just after World War II) and the post–Cold War era (the 1990s to the present). These two periods are interesting in that the configuration of state versus non-state actors influencing the production of

Multiculturalism," *Millenium: Journal of International Studies*, 29(3), 2000, 741–759; Elizabeth Shakman Hurd, *The Politics of Secularism in International Relations* (Princeton, NJ: Princeton University Press, 2007).

[2] On religious ethics and just war theory, see Terry Nardin, ed., *The Ethics of War and Peace: Religious and Secular Perspective* (Princeton, NJ: Princeton University Press, 1996); on Christianity vis-à-vis the creation of the nation-state, see Christian Reus-Smit, *The Moral Purpose of the State: Culture, Identity, and Institutional Rationality in International Relations* (Princeton, NJ: Princeton University Press, 1999); and Daniel Nexon, *The Struggle for Power in Early Modern Europe: Religious Conflict, Dynastic Empires, and International Change* (Princeton, NJ: Princeton University Press, 2009); on the relationship between Protestantism and the foundations of the United States, see Daniel Philpott, *Revolutions in Sovereignty: How Ideas Shaped Modern International Relations* (Princeton, NJ: Princeton University Press, 2001).

[3] James Der Derian, *On Diplomacy: A Genealogy of Western Estrangement* (Oxford: Basil Blackwell, 1987); R. B. J. Walker, *Inside/Outside: International Relations as Political Theory* (Cambridge: Cambridge University Press, 1992).

diplomatic practice changed enormously during each. In the first period, officials and scholars of international relations who were also Christian assumed that the narrative that moved from Christian spiritual and temporal universalism in the medieval period to statist foreign policy based on secularized (but still essentially Christian) natural law precepts in the modern era was part of the normal progression of history. At the same time, other types of Christian non-state actors (including people of different denominations, newly developing voluntary organizations, and individual activists) were demanding a new chapter in the narrative, one that allowed for their inclusion in foreign policy and transnational decision making, often to protest what they believed to be the unscrupulous growth of state military power that resulted in the carnage of World War I. In the second, contemporary period, the role of non-state actors has become much more taken for granted in assisting state and transnational organizations in newly articulated tasks of "preventive warning," "emergency relief," "peace building," and "sustainable development." The intertwined story of Christianity and the institutionalization of state sovereignty has been largely forgotten by these actors and their state and transnational counterparts; instead, navigating multiculturalisms of all kinds, including religious and ethnic pluralisms, has become articulated as a significant problem for the contemporary configuration of diplomatic actors. Despite these configurational differences, I argue that both periods demonstrate that universalist pretensions are a recurring feature of Christian diplomatic interventions. Yet, despite continuities, these pretensions take somewhat different forms in each period, producing ethical tensions over the specifically Christian and global character of authority and governance, as well as over the legitimacy of identifiably Christian forms of diplomatic representation. Underlying issues of legitimacy and morality, then, accord Christian ethics much of their power in both representation and governance, yet they also require additional justification in analytical frameworks and institutional practices deemed secular in orientation.

Working through these concepts demonstrates that during the 1930s and 1940s, influential Christians attempted to carve a space for what we might call a secularized form of Christian universalism, even while they justified the use of force by sovereign states. This form of universalism also supported the consolidation of global governance from the League of Nations to the United Nations but privileged the US role in the UN's leadership. The next (second) section, therefore, proceeds by examining the theological and political thought of influential religious actors alongside developing diplomatic practices of the 1930s and 1940s, focusing on the universalist aspirations of Christian diplomats such as John Foster Dulles against the backdrop of differential moral obligations for individuals and states put forward by theologian Reinhold Niebuhr. Christian justifications for the use of force against aggressors, as well as for US-led universalist practices through global forms of governance, helped shape the structures of state and multilateral diplomacy that continue to the present (see Pouliot's Chapter 3, this volume). However, the end of the Cold War also brought to the fore pluralist and syncretic questions of national, ethnic, and religious identity that shaped debates about the proper role of Christian forms of authority in global governance. In the United States, these debates in the 1990s centered on the free expression of religious identity, including but not limited to the right to proselytize. The third part of this chapter, therefore, moves to the post–Cold War era, in which an exponential increase in Christian humanitarians in areas of the Global South (as well as the Global North) work out questions of proselytism, religious freedom, and representation "on the ground." Christian humanitarians disagree about what religious freedom means and whether it should be universalized. But how they work through these debates influences the issues that diplomacy has to contend with; it also influences ideas about who has the right to represent religious populations. The fact that Christian actors have moved back and forth from non-governmental to governmental positions, including diplomatic posts, and that in each instance they interact with the international organizations created earlier in the twentieth century, is indicative of the ongoing importance of diplomacy as a profession as well as a practice, and of its infiltration into the NGO world. It is also indicative of the recurring tension between institutions of sovereignty and universalism, a tension that displays both echoes of and differences with the Niebuhrian accommodation articulated in the 1930s. In the conclusion, I bring together the implications of the universalist pretensions of Christian religious actors for diplomatic practices that reinforce and/or challenge contemporary social configurations and modes of representation, authority, and governance.

The interwar period: moral pessimism and liberal universalism

International relations theorists are now returning to "classical realism" to discuss the Christian roots of founders and precursors of the contemporary English School in international relations, including Herbert Butterfield, Martin Wight, Alfred Zimmern, David Davies, Norman Angel, and Arnold Toynbee.[4] Scholars are also reexamining the foundational role of prominent Christian Democrats such as Jean Monnet and Konrad Adenaur in the creation of the European Union.[5]

Asking how Christian ethics informed the worldviews of these diplomats and scholars brings to the fore one of the major questions about institutional forms of governance in the contemporary world: whether they should reside at the level of the state or whether they should be invested in multilateral or global organization or some sort of supranational order. Christian influences and ethics have informed the way diplomats, theologians, and international relations theorists answered these questions on the American as well as the European side of the Atlantic. Conversely, the temporal and geographic experiences of interwar professional diplomats have also influenced their interpretations of Christian ethics. As a result, this is a story of mutual constitution and of popular casuistry rather than one of fixed Christian influences on diplomacy and global order.[6] Yet, while much attention has been given to the Christian bases of influential English School diplomats and scholars, less has been paid to the religious worldviews of US diplomats and scholars of the same period. A prominent exception is the Christian realism of theologian Reinhold Niebuhr, which arguably had the greatest recognized impact on how professional diplomats navigated the sovereign/universalist conundrum during and after the interwar period. The universalist worldviews of John Foster Dulles and the Federal Council of Churches' Commission for a

[4] Studies of the Christian roots of these authors and diplomats are complemented by studies of the Jewish influences on Hans Morgenthau's classical realism. Murielle Cozette, "What Lies Ahead: Classical Realism on the Future of International Relations," *International Studies Review*, 10(4), 2008, 667–679.

[5] Iver Neumann, "Euro-Centrism in Diplomacy: Challenging but Manageable," *European Journal of International Relations*, 18(2), 2011; Timothy A. Byrnes and Peter J. Katzenstein, eds., *Religion in an Expanding Europe* (Cambridge: Cambridge University Press, 2006).

[6] On the concept of popular casuistry as a way of analyzing the ethics and actions of religious actors, see Cecelia Lynch, "A Neo-Weberian Approach to Religion in International Politics," *International Theory*, 1(3), 2009), 381–408.

Just and Durable Peace also had theoretical and policy repercussions far beyond US boundaries. I examine the "international theology" of Niebuhr and Dulles here, focusing on their deployment of particular Christian ethics to found their conceptualizations of authority and governance in diplomatic practice.

For students of international relations theory, Reinhold Niebuhr's impact on twentieth-century moral justifications for state-based sovereignty and the use of force is well known. He has long been heralded as one of the founding fathers of international relations theory, and his ethical construct became foundational for generations of US diplomats who spanned the interwar and Cold War eras: "A whole generation of distinguished American politicians, including such people as Adlai Stevenson, Arthur Schlesinger Jr., McGeorge Bundy and Hubert Humphrey acknowledged him not only as a prime influence on their own lives but on the whole American approach to politics. 'Niebuhr is the father of us all' said George Kennan."[7] Niebuhr began with a pessimistic stance informed by liberal-left insights. Formerly a Social Gospel pacifist, Niebuhr in the 1930s became increasingly disillusioned by the liberal optimism of Christian (and secular) temporal forms of universalism, particularly League of Nations diplomacy and its Christian internationalist supporters. As a result, in a famous debate with his equally famous theologian brother H. Richard Niebuhr, Reinhold articulated the beginnings of a new political theology.[8] The brothers' debate, over what, if anything, should be done after Japan's invasion of Manchuria in September 1931, provides significant insight into the early 1930s mind-sets and limitations of one influential type of religious pacifism as well as into the foundations of the ethical and institutionalist bases of incipient Christian realism.

This is not the place to explicate in full the pacifist position of Reinhold's brother H. Richard, who represented merely one of many prominent (Christian and secular) justifications of pacifism during the period. What is important for the present is Reinhold's response and the political theology that developed from it. The brothers both agreed that "sin" was a social as well as individual construct, permeating political institutions themselves; they also agreed that the West was

[7] Richard Harries, ed., *Reinhold Niebuhr and the Issues of Our Time* (London and Oxford: Mowbray, 1986), 1.

[8] The debate took place in 1932 in the pages of *The Christian Century*.

culpable in fostering aggression, which made its intervention in other parts of the world problematic. As a result, using language and justifications shot through with both theological and political terminologies, Reinhold acknowledged the pervasiveness of sin in the form of political/economic normative and institutional power, stating both that "we have helped to create the Japan which expresses itself in terms of materialistic imperialism" and "the insult we offered her in our immigration laws was a sin of spiritual aggression." Yet, he strongly refuted his brother's argument in favor of "doing nothing" to counteract Japanese aggression, which, he argued, accorded with the naïve, progressivist "assumption that the world will be saved by a little more adequate educational technique." The technique in question is what Reinhold calls a "pure love ethic," which he countered by questioning the idea that God will intervene in history. Reinhold then outlined the basis of his Christian realism, which incorporated the "appreciation of the tragic character of life" that he criticized modern Christianity for lacking. Christian realism, unlike Christian progressivism, for Niebuhr, portrayed human nature as a mixture of the ability to reason and an incurable selfishness: "I find it impossible to envisage a society of pure love as long as man remains man." Regarding the relationship between faith and theology, Reinhold admitted, "I realize quite well that my brother's position both in its ethical perfectionism and in its apocalyptic note is closer to the gospel than mine." But he argued that such ethical perfectionism was in the end irresponsible: while he could not completely "abandon the pure love ideal . . . I cannot use it fully if I want to assume a responsible attitude towards the problems of society."

These arguments demonstrate the critical nature of Reinhold Niebuhr's work for understanding the constitutive relationship between Christianity and diplomacy in the modern West. By articulating his temporal and ethical distinction between governance in "this world" versus that of "the absolute," Niebuhr made perhaps the strongest contribution since Augustine in working through temporal/spiritual relationships and justifying modern sovereign and diplomatic institutional practices, as well as the role of diplomats themselves in carrying them out. For Niebuhr, the "religious imagination" was necessary but could not be used to justify worldly forms of representation or governance:

> Perhaps that is why it is inevitable that religious imagination should set goals beyond history . . . Man cannot live without a sense of the absolute, but

neither can he achieve the absolute. He may resolve the tragic character of that fact by religious faith, by the experience of grace in which the unattainable is experienced in anticipatory terms, but he can never resolve in purely ethical terms the conflict between what is and what ought to be.[9]

Using the language of mediating estrangement, "man's" estrangement from the eternal could not be mediated by humans at all. Humans' estrangement from each other, however, through sin or evil, required the use of multiple forms of mediation, including reliance on the institution of state sovereignty and, at times, the use of force as a component of prudent governance.

Reinhold Niebuhr's concurrent treatise *Moral Man and Immoral Society* (1932) explored many of these arguments in more detail.[10] In this book, Niebuhr appealed to both Augustine and Freud, incorporating modern thought into his interpretation of Christian tradition. He developed his understanding of human nature as a combination of God-given reason and prehuman impulses. Humans must use their reason to transcend natural selfishness and the will to power. This is because, for Niebuhr, the will to power was a primary manifestation of sin on both individual and group levels. Yet, selfishness and the consequent motives of self-interest were natural for nation-states, and for Reinhold, they neither could nor should be overcome. International relations was formed from, and thus could not escape, its inherent sinfulness in the form of struggles over power and self-interest.

Given this foundation, Reinhold Niebuhr then took up the problem of absolute versus relative and individual versus group moral possibility, arguing that Christian morality could not be reconciled with the imperfections of the world. Augustine's City of God and City of Man were two spheres of moral action and ethical possibility that could not be fused into one.

Niebuhr's political theology legitimized the use of force when diplomacy failed. Yet, what is perhaps most interesting is that his doctrine of dual moralities was constructed vis-à-vis a related diplomatic ethic that was also articulated in the West by Christian diplomats: the universalist worldview that promoted global international organization as the

[9] These quotes are from Reinhold Niebhur's response to his brother, in "Must We Do Nothing," March 23, 1932, *The Christian Century*, posted online at www.ucc.org/beliefs_theology_must-we-do-nothing.

[10] Niebuhr's later works continued to develop these themes. See, for example, *Christian Realism and Political Problems* (New York: Scribner, 1953).

primary forum for diplomatic practice, and hence the primary site for mediating estrangement and thereby creating authoritative forms of transnational governance. Global international organization required professional diplomats who worked through new institutionalized forms and developed new practices that mediated sovereign interests and universalist goals.

This universalist worldview merged Christian language regarding equality with ideas about international cooperation in a new world order. Yet, Christian diplomats did not agree on whether it was possible to transcend the statist boundaries justified by Niebuhr. Alfred Zimmern and John Foster Dulles, for example, were each strong Christian proponents of universalism, although with different beliefs regarding the degree to which interstate differences could be not only mediated but also transcended. Zimmern in the 1920s wanted to transcend national interests by strengthening global governance through the League of Nations, while other diplomats, including Dulles, wanted to inscribe US national interests into global moral purpose in a reconstituted United Nations. Here I focus on Dulles, both because his thought was representative of the US mainstream and because it became foundational for post–World War II US universalist claims.

John Foster Dulles was both a leader in Christian church circles and a diplomat who became one of the primary designers of the post–World War II international order, also devoting considerable time and intellectual effort to endowing this order with ethical legitimacy. As a sympathetic observer noted about him, "It is not difficult to identify the structure of Christian conviction that determined his own attitude towards public affairs, which though Christian in origin he felt to be of universal authority, which he believed to be of the essence of the American tradition, and which he sought to have laid as the foundation principles of world order."[11] Like Niebuhr's appeal to Augustine's two cities, Dulles's Christian universalism was not new, going back at least to the Christian universalism of the medieval era. Both types of mediating constructs exemplified intersecting models for diplomatic practice; yet, each also embodied tensions for who was to be represented in diplomacy, and what forms of authority and governance would result.

[11] Henry P. Van Dusen, ed., *The Spiritual Legacy of John Foster Dulles: Selections from His Articles and Addresses* (Philadelphia: The Westminster Press, 1960), xviii.

Dulles articulated many of his views about the role of Christian ethics in world order after his participation in the Oxford Conference of 1937.[12] These included the conviction that "the churches are peculiarly qualified to promote a solution of the kind of problems which today vex mankind." The churches could promote universalism, truth, and equality: "in the eyes of God, all men are equal and their welfare is of equal moment. This is distinctively the Christian approach, and it is only through an approach of such universality that there is any promise of a solution." In other words, "problems which otherwise seem unsolvable become susceptible of solution if approached from the standpoint of the universal brotherhood of man." Nevertheless, in a prescient statement, Dulles insisted that he was not trying to universalize Christianity: "I do not mean to suggest that organized Christianity is the only instrument through which our problems may be solved, or, as a corollary, that it is futile to seek to eliminate wars and social unrest and injustice until the whole world has become Christianized." Dulles, in other words, promoted putting a particular version of Christian ethics in the service of cosmopolitan forms of mediation. His understanding of Christian responsibility was to instill in individuals the proper spiritual qualities, which they would use to foster a world order of universal goodwill. Germany provided a negative lesson: "The German churches had failed to make the people Christian in the sense that, as citizens, they would reject leadership which exemplified qualities which Christ most strongly condemned."

Dulles also contrasted "secular" diplomacy with "Christian" discussions, reflecting on his own role in the diplomatic history of the interwar period, from the Paris Peace Conference to the Ruhr crisis, German debt negotiations and the rise of Hitler, negotiations at the League of Nations, and the worsening situation in East Asia in the late 1930s: "What was the explanation of the amazing contrast between discussions which occurred in a Christian atmosphere and those which occurred in the conventional atmosphere of diplomacy?" Dulles found the difference in secular diplomacy's "idolatry": personifying the state as a "quasi-god" while subordinating "the true welfare of the human beings who composed the nation," as well as "hypocrisy,"

[12] This conference brought together 400 delegates from around the world and represented a broad range of Christianity, with the exception of the Roman Catholic Church. Dulles, "The Faith of a Statesman," in Van Dusen, *The Spiritual Legacy of John Foster Dulles*, 15.

"blindness," and "evil emotion," in the form of unjustified allegiance to one's own state, and one's own short-term interest, over those of others.[13] Here, he attempted to reclassify and even transcend estrangement. States were false constructions and false gods; moving to liberal individualism could transcend estrangement and simplify mediation if not make it unnecessary. The proper form of authority, for Dulles, was in the first instance de-territorialized and transnationalized, representing a significant move from state centered to a universalized liberal form of governance.

Despite this critique of the state, Dulles did not forsake US national interests or US authoritative governance in the interest of universalism. Instead, much of his diplomatic work resided in trying to reconcile the latter in favor of the former. This became evident in his leadership of the US Federal Council of Churches in postwar planning, and later in his role as US secretary of state in the 1950s. Writing in 1942, he stated his faith in US-led universalism: "As our national faith is made manifest by works, and grows under that stimulus, its influence will be contagious throughout the world. As the evil faiths that combat us collapse, leaving death and ruin as their fruit, the faith that makes us strong will encompass the earth."[14] Dulles did not condemn the use of force by the state, but he believed that such use would become less prevalent with US leadership in global international governance. In turn, he assumed that US moral leadership was founded on particular interpretations of Christian values.

The relationship between representation and governance, then, became critically important in Dulles's conception of diplomatic practice. US diplomats could and should represent the moral interests of the United States, which was endowed with special ethical status to lead the world to new forms of institutional universalism. The peculiarly Christian character of this form of representation, for Dulles, provided a moral compass for leadership, even though it need not result in the Christianization of the entire world. Diplomats would mediate the resulting institutions deriving from both state (especially the United States) and transnational forms of governance, moving the world ever closer to American Christian models of liberal democracy.

[13] Ibid., 18–20, 28, 26.

[14] Dulles, "The American Heritage," *Life Magazine* (December 28, 1942), in ibid., 55.

In the post–World War II era, this kind of optimistic Christian universalism merged with Niebuhrian pessimism into the diplomatic ethics of the Cold War. Christian universalism could never transcend the estrangement between West and East, or North and South, because it predicated global governance on the superiority of the West over the Eastern bloc and the Third World. This sense of superiority and resulting paternalism, of course, formed the basis of Dulles's Christian universalism; it also underlay the aspirations of Christian Democrats such as Konrad Adenaur and Jean Monnet to move beyond statist ethics by fostering Franco-German cooperation on a regional level. Adenaur's and Monnet's efforts led to the formation of the European Coal and Steel Community (ECSC), which then grew to become the Common Market and eventually the European Union. Here again, however, universalism could not transcend estrangement, since European unity was fostered as a cushion against the communist "other."[15] Nevertheless, the ECSC and EU became prominent examples of Christian diplomatic overtures in favor of universalist aspirations. Although the resulting institutional frameworks transcended the West European nation-state, they also produced social configurations that reinforced divisions between East and West.[16]

Carl Schmitt, writing in the interwar period, famously argued that all political concepts come from secularized theology. The argument here is different: it is that Christian actors and ethics cannot be separated from the trajectory of Western diplomatic goals and practices. In the early twentieth century, ideas about the ethics of governance and the use of force intersected with universalist understandings of authority based on mid-twentieth-century social and political configurations. These both reaffirmed and called into question traditional territorial boundaries, settling on instantiations of US dominance (diplomatic and material) in schemes of global governance. Modern analytical concepts drawn from purportedly secular categories and distinctions conceal the interpretations of Christian ethics that actors such as Niebuhr articulated in justifying statist morality, and diplomats such as Dulles

[15] Iver Neumann, "Uses of the Other: The 'East,'" *in European Identity Formation* (Minneapolis: University of Minnesota Press, 1998).

[16] J. Bryan Hehir, "The Old Church and the New Europe: Charting the Changes," in Byrnes and Katzenstein, eds., *Religion in an Expanding Europe*, 93–116; Iver Neumann, "Uses of the Other."

(as well as Adenaur and Monnet) employed in promoting modern, transnational, and universalist political institutions. These projects, in turn, form the backdrop for contemporary trends and tensions in Christian humanitarian diplomacy.

Post–Cold War reconstitutions of Christian universalism

Humanitarianism, as Sending points out in Chapter 9, represents increasingly significant interventions into diplomatic practice, and it is worth noting that many Christian humanitarian non-governmental representatives move in and out of official diplomatic posts.[17] Yet, it would be a mistake to consider the relationship between Christianity and humanitarianism as a completely new phenomenon, given that it goes back at least to successive periods of mission that overlapped with, and sometimes served, colonization projects by Europeans in the "New World," Asia, and Africa.[18] The Vatican, of course, was an early practitioner of official Christian diplomacy in the Americas and around the globe. Because of its dual institutional legitimacy – as a microstate and the site of governance of a globalized population of Catholics – the Vatican possesses a long history of navigating sovereign/universal ethical conundrums. Vatican diplomacy along with new interpretations of Church teachings from the 1960s through the 1990s, however, tied together universalist ethics with emerging forms of humanitarian diplomacy in extremely influential ways, from the challenges to statist military and economic power by Church leaders emboldened by Vatican II under Pope John XXIII, to the anti-communist universalism

[17] Two prominent examples include Andrew Natsios, who has served as vice president of the Christian Evangelical NGO, World Vision, as well as US special envoy to Sudan and other diplomatic postings, and Douglas Johnston, founder of the International Center of Religion and Diplomacy and former official in the Navy and Defense Departments.

[18] Assertions that modern humanitarianism traces its roots to secularist assumptions and frameworks of the mid-nineteenth century run into at least two problems, in my view. First is the evidence supporting the Christian motivations of humanitarians such as Henri Dunant, founder of the Red Cross, and second is the fact that the humanitarian endeavors that formed integral components of Christian missionizing, while masked by the development of putatively secular humanitarian organizations, never went away from at least the sixteenth century to the present. On the first, see Daniel Warner, "Henri Dunant's Imagined Community," *Alternatives*, 38(1), 2013, 3–28.

espoused by Pope John Paul II.[19] The explosive spread of Evangelical and Pentecostal forms of Christianity around the world during the 1980s and 1990s also contributed to expanding the institutional scope of Christian diplomatic practice, at the same time increasing tensions over the content of humanitarian goals.

These factors have all shaped the context of Christian religious diplomacy in the post–Cold War period. Scholars increasingly note the increased influence of Christian organizations, both transnational and locally based, on the content and practice of humanitarian governance (on the question of whether governance functions are increasingly taken over by humanitarian NGOs, see Sending's contribution to this volume, Chapter 9). Christian non-governmental organizations form a significant section of the broader constellation of faith-based organizations (FBOs) that operate in virtually all parts of the world, providing emergency relief as well as longer-term aid in education, health, and other areas. For example, figures from several sources indicate that between 30 percent and 70 percent of health care in parts of Africa is provided by (predominantly Christian) faith-based NGOs; major Christian organizations such as World Vision and Caritas and networks of Christian agencies through the World Council of Churches run multimillion and even billion-dollar budgets, and Evangelical organizations, in particular, are growing at a fast rate.[20] Humanitarian diplomacy, including by Christian groups, also includes advocacy at multilateral forums such as those sponsored by the UN High Commissioner for Refugees (UNHCR) as well as daily activities in

[19] See, for example, David Ryall, "The Catholic Church as Transnational Actor," in Daphne Josselin and William Wallace, eds., *Non-State Actors in World Politics* (Houndsmills, Basingstoke: Palgrave, 2002), 41–58.

[20] Africanpress, "Faith-based Organisations Provide up to 70 percent of Healthcare in Some African Communities," Nairobi: 31 July (2010); cited in Cecelia Lynch, "Local and Global Influences on Islamic NGOs in Kenya," *Journal of Peacebuilding & Development*, 6(1), 2011, 22; Elizabeth Ferris, "Faith-based and Secular Humanitarian Organizations," *International Review of the Red Cross*, 87(858), 2005, 313; Stephen Hopgood and Leslie Vinjamuri, "Faith in Markets," 43, and Michael Barnett and Janice Gross Stein, "Introduction: The Secularization and Sanctification of Humanitarianism," 5, both in Michael Barnett and Janice Gross Stein, eds., *Sacred Aid: Faith and Humanitarianism* (New York: Oxford University Press, 2012). I include both emergency relief and long-term aid in my definition of humanitarianism, because non-governmental groups increasingly engage in both types of assistance.

localities on the ground. While some denominations clearly distinguish between their humanitarian work and their "mission" functions (tending to religious adherents and/or increasing the numbers of religious adherents), others tend to blend these tasks.

The multiple functions and levels on which Christian humanitarians work throughout the world have significant implications for the relationships between sovereign rights and universalist pretensions, and hence for conceptions of legitimate authority and governance. More specifically, the actions of Christian humanitarians frequently represent and/or require diplomatic interventions. In the midst of their on-the-ground work on everything from emergency relief and humanitarian intervention to health care and education, some Christian activists engage in advocacy campaigns to pressure governments to enact specific policies on issues from sexuality to economic justice to religious freedom. Post–Cold War examples range from the bill stipulating the death penalty for homosexuality introduced and then dropped in the Ugandan parliament, to the ABC (abstinence, be faithful, use condoms only if necessary) policy of the Bush administration on international HIV/AIDS prevention policy, to the Jubilee Campaign for international financial institutions and governments in the Global North to forgive Third World countries' debt. Christian groups' pressure on governments on each of these issues frequently provokes or requires additional diplomatic actions, such as negotiations among governments and donor agencies to agree on levels of debt forgiveness. Christian groups might assist in carrying out government policies (or reinterpret or challenge them): different Christian organizations, for example, have both implemented and disagreed with Bush administration ABC policies. Still other Christian groups, most notably the Sant'Egidio Community based in Rome, engage regularly with conventional diplomats to act as mediators and interlocutors in bringing adversaries into diplomatic negotiations to end civil wars. Sant'Egidio's work in bringing a resolution to the civil war in Mozambique has been widely noted and used as a model for similar interventions elsewhere.[21]

The diplomatic interventions of these Christian groups occur within a terrain of social configurations marked by two characteristics that

21 See e.g. R. Scott Appleby, *The Ambivalence of the Sacred: Religion, Violence and Reconciliation* (Lanham, MD: Rowman & Littlefield), 2000.

differ from the 1930s and 1940s. First, the role of nongovernmental organizations in assisting government agencies in carrying out tasks of development and relief has become much more regularized than in the early twentieth century, even if NGOs still complain that they are not treated as full partners in decision making regarding these tasks. The "humanitarian international"[22] that consists of transnational as well as local, and faith-based as well as secular NGOs, donors, foundations, and multilateral agencies, and that expands diplomatic practice to include all of these actors, continues to grow. Second, however, the Christian nature of their role is debated both among Christian NGOs and between them and governments with whom they act. Christianity is, in contemporary social configurations, one among many religions practiced by populations on the ground in a religiously plural world. While many Christian denominations and NGOs see this as natural and even good, others either incorporate evangelism in their humanitarian work or direct significant parts of their activism toward saving religiously persecuted populations, especially Christians, in different parts of the world. Given the spread of new forms of Christianity, including nondenominational Evangelicalism and Pentecostalism as well as new forms of religious syncretism, locally as well as transnationally, a vast range of positions are currently taken by Christian groups on whether it is ethically justifiable to attempt to proselytize and convert others. These new features reflect the fact that after the end of the Cold War, foreign aid in most countries in the West has been increasingly channeled through the non-governmental sector, including faith-based NGOs. Moreover, they produce conflicting diplomatic initiatives on proselytism and church/state relationships.

These include, most prominently, initiatives by Christians (along with other religious groups) in the United States to promote religious freedom, both to protect religious minorities of all faith traditions in societies where they are threatened or prohibited from openly practicing their religious beliefs and to open borders and identities to contemporary Christian evangelists. This trend, of course, is also not new, as it recalls and frequently replicates the missionary activity of the fifteenth to nineteenth centuries, when mainline Christian denominations worked in tandem with European officials to shape diplomatic

[22] The term is from Alex de Waal, *Famine Crimes: Politics & the Disaster Relief Industry in Africa* (Bloomington: Indiana University Press), 2009.

interactions and governance to facilitate the conversion of colonial subjects. The line between Christian missionizing and imperial functions then was often thin, as is the line between Christian humanitarianism, missionizing, and state and UN diplomatic functions today.[23]

Christian humanitarians, given these debates, mediate at least two major types of estrangement: that between the "sufferer" and the aid giver, and that between the Christian and the (potential) religious other. The Christian humanitarian diplomat provides assistance out of a desire to mediate both of these types of estrangement, although in different ways. While all Christian humanitarians attempt to reduce the suffering and improve the well-being of aid recipients, they disagree on how to mediate the boundaries between Christian and non-Christian. Christian humanitarians in some cases also mediate a third type of estrangement: that between the (Christian) aid giver of one nationality, and the (Christian) recipient of another. When the US Agency for International Development (USAID), the British Department for International Development (DFID), or other foreign aid offices provide development and emergency assistance through NGOs, those that are Christian aid organizations become unofficial extensions of official diplomatic channels. Under the Bush administration, for example, local and transnational Christian subjectivities, such as the socially conservative nexus between Vatican and African Catholicism, or between American, Asian, and African Evangelicalism, tended to work in tandem on issues of HIV/AIDS prevention (in downplaying the use of condoms) and on sexuality (in condemning homosexuality), actively carrying out the administration's ABC policy on the ground.

At least two documents represent tensions in the way in which humanitarianism, diplomacy, and religion intersect: the Code of Conduct for Humanitarian Relief and the International Religious Freedom Act. The first was designed in the mid-1990s by a network of transnational NGOs, most prominently by the International Committee of the Red Cross (ICRC) and several Christian groups. The second was passed by the US Congress in 1998 and represents (at least theoretically) an extension of human rights to include the murky area of religious freedom.

[23] It should be noted, however, that the definition of religious freedom is also fluid and has taken on different meanings today than during debates over the Universal Declaration on Human Rights in the 1940s, or during the time of Vatican II in the 1960s.

The Code of Conduct for NGOs in Disaster Relief[24] was developed in part to demonstrate and promote NGOs' sensitivity to and respect for other peoples and cultures. The code was sponsored by Caritas Internationalis, Catholic Relief Services, the International Federation of Red Cross and Red Crescent Societies, the international Save the Children Alliance, the Lutheran World Federation, Oxfam, and the World Council of Churches in Geneva; many of these organizations had worked together on the Steering Committee on Humanitarian Response (SCHR), a Geneva-based network of many of the most influential NGOs in humanitarian relief.[25] The code calls for respect for "the culture, structures, and customs" of the communities and countries assisted, and the sponsoring organizations do not condone religious proselytizing. Since its articulation and publication, the code has been signed by numerous secular and faith-based NGOs, including Doctors without Borders and World Vision, among others.

However, the code is also an elastic and nonbinding document, and some Christian organizations interpret its provisions against proselytizing loosely. Many Christian organizations based in the United States are signatories of the code but also supported the US International Religious Freedom Act (IRFA) and the permanent commission to monitor international religious freedom that was created by its passage. The IRFA and the resulting commission instantiate religious freedom as a "core objective" of US foreign policy: "One of the most sweeping human rights statutes on the books, it created new institutions and processes that insure a permanent presence for the cause of religious liberty in America's foreign policy architecture."[26] According to observers, those who promoted the act included Evangelical, Episcopal, Catholic, Jewish, Tibetan Buddhist, and Bahai faith groups, although the impetus and articulation of subsequent lists of cases needing attention concern primarily Christians.

The IRFA and its commission articulate a very different idea of church/state relations and mediating cultural differences than those

[24] The Sphere Project, www.sphereproject.org; see also Cecelia Lynch, "Acting on Belief: Christian Perspectives on Suffering and Violence," *Ethics & International Affairs*, 14(1), 2000, 83–97.

[25] These include Caritas International, Catholic Relief Services, the Lutheran World Federation, and the World Council of Churches (WCC).

[26] Allen D. Hertzke, "International Religious Freedom Policy: Taking Stock," *The Review of Faith and International Affairs*, Summer 2008, 17.

put forth by the Code of Conduct. In arguing in favor of a "fair religious competition," Brian Grimm of the Pew Foundation reformulates estrangement in market terminology:

> Established religions ... often act to curtail competition from new religious groups by preventing proselytism, restricting conversion, and putting up barriers that make it difficult for new religions to gain a foothold ... Our research on 143 countries finds that when governments and religious groups in society do not erect barriers to religious competition but respect and protect such activities as conversion and proselytism, religious violence is less.[27]

Such an articulation has not gone unchallenged by either scholars or Christian activists. As José Casanova warns,

> The fact that religious freedom is becoming a universal aspiration doesn't mean that religious freedom means necessarily everywhere the same thing. It may mean different things in different countries, and these different meanings may be in conflict with one another. Policies intended to implement international religious freedom may conflict with other cultures' understandings of religious freedom, and will be resisted accordingly.

Specifically, echoing documents from the World Council of Churches, he argues that cultures "have a right to protect themselves from imperialist, or overly aggressive, attempts to change them."[28] Some Christian humanitarians, especially those from mainline and Anabaptist traditions, agree, arguing that proselytism hinders and even endangers their humanitarian efforts to relieve suffering and redress conditions breeding poverty and inequality.

Thus, Christian humanitarians disagree on how to mediate relationships between the Christian aid giver and the non-Christian other, as well as on the role of the US government in promoting religious freedom, even to the point of possible intervention in societies that do not accord with the IRFA's provisions. What is at stake in these ethical debates is the form and legitimacy of different social configurations and types of authority, as well as decisions about who has the ability to represent the interests of minority communities, whether host governments have the right to place controls on pluralist religious practices

[27] Brian J. Grimm, "Religious Freedom: Good for What Ails Us?" *The Review of Faith and International Affairs*, Summer 2008, 5.

[28] José Casanova, "Balancing Religious Freedom and Cultural Preservation," *The Review of Faith and International Affairs*, Summer 2008, 13.

within their borders, and whether governments have the right to promote the operation of the "religious marketplace" in other countries. For Christians who advocate proselytizing, successful mediation of estrangement (in Der Derian's terms) results in the assimilation of otherness, in terms of religious practice and secular authority.[29] For those who do not (ironically, these generally include the mainline Christians who were the proselytizers of centuries past), successful mediation of estrangement results in overcoming suffering while respecting cultural difference and forms of authority. This can result in either affirming difference or even in developing syncretic cultural and religious practices. Assimilation, in this view, usually represents a form of violence rather than diplomatic mediation.[30]

In recent years, however, Evangelical, Pentecostal, and charismatic Christian groups have become more "indigenous," with local founders and leaders, similar to the inculturation processes that took place among Catholic, Methodist, Presbyterian, Anglican, and Baptist groups in the Global South over the past century.[31] An increasing number of Pentecostal churches in the Global South are not tied to transnational supporters at all, whereas charismatic Catholic and Anglican churches borrow both from transnational sources and localized forms of Pentecostalism. Christian subjectivities and the mediation that results from them have become somewhat less dependent, therefore, on transnational Christian diplomacy from the United States and elsewhere in the Global North and more on appeals from within shared cultural practices.

On-the-ground humanitarian diplomacy reflects these trends and incorporates tensions over how to mediate religious difference. For example, local as well as transnational Evangelical Christians called for external intervention to protect the Christian population in South

[29] See Naeem Inayatullah and David L. Blaney, *International Relations and the Problem of Difference* (London: Routledge, 2004).

[30] Emmanuel Martey, *African Theology: Inculturation and Liberation* (Eugene, OR: Wipf & Stock Publishers, 2009).

[31] Donald Miller and Tetsuano Yamamori, *Global Pentecostalism: The New Face of Christian Social Engagement* (Berkeley: University of California Press, 2007); Paul Gifford, *Christianity, Politics, and Public Life in Kenya* (New York: Columbia University Press, 2009). In fact, in the Roman Catholic Church today there is much debate about the phenomenon of "reverse missionizing," in which the shortage of priests in North America and Europe has led to importing increasing numbers of clergy from Africa and Asia to tend to the faithful.

Sudan. Local and transnational Evangelicals and Catholics supported the Bush administration's ABC policy for HIV/AIDS prevention and opposed measures to decriminalize homosexuality. (It is important to add that other Christians opposed the ABC policy and supported decriminalization.) On economic issues, local and transnational mainline denominations also frequently support initiatives challenging entrenched state and corporate economic power, from labor challenges to the Jubilee program for debt relief.

These actions can challenge statist notions of authority, appealing to religious ethics and identities over national ones. They also appeal to religious rather than global/interstate notions of universalism. Yet, they still require diplomatic action and support on both the national and multilateral/global levels, in part because they frequently target national laws and international conventions. State funding supports many of their actions; in the United States, government policy supports their attempts to spread particular versions of Christianity around the world. As a result, the representational functions of Christian humanitarian actors need to be viewed in conjunction with those of official diplomats in both national and international institutions. Neither appears to be able to carry out the functions of diplomacy alone – each appears to require the other. The concepts of representation, authority, and governance, therefore, remain important when we consider what types of relationships are constructed and what types of social configurations are supported by contemporary Christian humanitarians.

Christians who support expansive policies of religious freedom act in the tradition of Christian interventionist liberal diplomacy spearheaded by John Foster Dulles during and after World War II. They also take Reinhold Niebuhr's justifications of the use of compulsion by states to a new level (ensuring religious freedom in other countries) that Niebuhr would likely deplore. Even Dulles, however, promoted US moral, and purportedly Christian-inspired, leadership of the world while disavowing any move to convert disparate peoples to Christianity. Today's religious freedom advocates proclaim the necessity for diplomats – and US foreign policy – to intervene actively to promote freedom of choice abroad by creating a "fair" religious marketplace, but at the same time the predominance of Christian voices in religious freedom debates and the presumption of the right to proselytize indicate a desire to put diplomacy in the service of expanding the reach of Christianity globally.

Today's Christian humanitarians who do not advocate strong policies of religious freedom promote very different forms of diplomacy. While they retain the liberal Christian ethos of Dulles and acknowledge the existence of evil in the world articulated by Niebuhr, they generally reject combating evil with force or seeing the United States as the manager of the globe. Instead, they promote a kind of internationalist diplomacy that relies on the combination of non-governmental, nonpolitical action that works alongside international agencies to provide relief and assistance. This type of diplomacy inherits some of the cosmopolitan character of peace movements of the interwar period, while exchanging advocacy for action to provide aid to disparate parts of the world.

Conclusions

Articulations of Christian ethics are an essential component of the diplomatic history of the West, and increasingly the Global South. As a result, we need to drop the assumption that Christianity no longer figures in Western diplomatic practice. During the 1930s and 1940s, the ethical bases of diplomacy were informed by Christian arguments about politics and theology to legitimate in powerful ways the normative bases of post–World War II world order. In the post–Cold War era, some figures such as former Pope Benedict XVI have gone further to insist on the explicit recognition of the Christian bases of European supranational order in the constitutional documents of the EU. These Christian universalist ethical pretensions, along with statist justifications for the use of force, shaped diplomatic practice in the West throughout the Cold War. They also continue to exist, still frequently in tension, in the post–Cold War era.

Yet, examining humanitarian diplomacy in the post–Cold War era (see also Sending's contribution to this volume, Chapter 9) offers an opportunity to assess echoes of these ethics and practices as well as new configurations of diplomatic actors and assumptions. The content of Christian ethical struggles regarding the proper forms of authority and governance results from different kinds of universalist pretensions to humanitarianism and human rights. More specifically, some Christian humanitarians today argue that universal rights to religious freedom should be protected through diplomatic practices, and that these rights can allow or possibly require proselytizing, while others promote religious and cultural pluralism. These types of faith-based motivations for universalist forms of governance are also not new, as they have important antecedents in successive periods of Christian missionizing. Contemporary Christian humanitarian groups, however, function in a context of contradictory diplomatic norms regarding proselytism and religious freedom. While the IRFA and the Code of Conduct do not reflect all of the norms and policies promoted by Christian ethics and actors (others e.g. range from Christian nonviolent pacifism to more extremist forms of Christian nationalism), they inform significant tensions in contemporary diplomatic practice.

Contemporary Christian humanitarians conduct their activities against a background in which representatives of NGOs as well as states and multilateral and global organizations practice diplomacy regularly. Today, Christian humanitarians channel state and transnational aid to achieve emergency, educational, and health goals. Universalist pretensions remain embedded in the cosmopolitan nature of contemporary Christian humanitarianism, as they were in Christian ethics of the past. Their local and transnational loyalties, however, do not map neatly onto statist forms of authority, nor do they completely accord with their own universalist pretentions. Christian humanitarians work with and on behalf of governments while trying to maintain their independence; they also engage in projects that sometimes require diplomatic interventions by more traditional state and international actors. Christian humanitarians also increasingly include individuals and groups from the Global South as well as the Global North.

These social configurations produce tensions that remain unresolved, especially given the religiously plural terrain on which Christian humanitarians operate. Christians no longer hold a monopoly on ethical universalism, even while Christian and other NGOs regularly carry out old and new diplomatic tasks. Christian ethics and actors will undoubtedly remain significant in future diplomatic configurations, but future assessments must also take into account complementary and competing sources of authority that are increasingly prevalent in our pluralist and syncretic world. The upshot of understanding the importance of Christianity to diplomacy as a profession and practice is to underscore the importance of viewing diplomacy in relational terms. In this case, its very constitution, in the past but also continuing into the allegedly modern, secular present, must be seen as part and parcel of its evolving, ongoing relations with religious, and specifically Christian, actors, including diplomats, and interpretations of ethics.

PART III

Diplomacy as a contested terrain

7 *Diplomacy as economic consultancy*

LEONARD SEABROOKE

Introduction

Our common picture of formal diplomatic relations between modern states is a historical abnormality. It is derived from a Eurocentric conception of formal and public interstate relations that has been built from the Westphalian myth.[1] The popular imagining of diplomacy centers on negotiations between officials from foreign ministries, secretly discussing conflicts related to questions of sovereignty, the balance of power, and international order.[2] In this chapter, I explore the emergence of diplomacy via economic consultancy. The chapter focuses on professionals who conduct what can be termed "political work" as third parties under an economic consultancy model of working – providing international best practice services for clients in return for fees to the arranging organization for profit and/or the costs of service provision.[3] The emergence of these professionals is a response to the rigidities of the current international order, and how formal diplomacy is conducted within it. The entrepreneurs who have pushed forward diplomacy via economic consultancy both reinforce the current system while also seeking means to subvert it in many ways. Their role can be understood – in keeping with the editors' emphasis on shifting authority claims – as "brokers" who are using their ideas about how to conduct diplomacy through forms of economic consultancies as

1 Benjamin de Carvalho, Halvard Leira, and John M. Hobson, "The Big Bangs of IR: The Myths That Your Teachers Still Tell You about 1648 and 1919," *Millennium*, 39(3), 2011, 735–758.

2 Henry Kissinger, *Diplomacy* (New York: Simon & Schuster, 2004); Martin Wight, *Systems of States* (Leicester: Leicester University Press, 1977).

3 This research is funded by the European Research Council grant "Professions in International Political Economies" (ERC-2010-STG, #263741, 2011.2014) based at the Copenhagen Business School, Denmark.

filling "structural holes" within political networks in the current international order.[4] These non-territorial transnational brokers conduct political work in that they actively seek to redistribute choices for identity formation and resource allocation, including who can make authoritative claims as legitimate territorial units in world politics. This work is also diplomatic in that it obeys the protocols of communication within the international system and relies heavily on tacit rather than known public information.

This chapter discusses how these brokers have emerged and what positions they occupy in formal and informal diplomacy, including public diplomacy. I contend that these professionals matter for the evolution of diplomacy because their claims to authority are chiefly non-territorial and embedded in norms associated with humanitarian values and/or professional services firms. The mix of humanitarian values and professional services firms will strike many as odd, but it is the combination of different forms of professional knowledge that permits these brokers to provide diplomacy as economic consultancy and occupy unique positions within political networks. This brokering role is often between established states and populations seeking recognition from the interstate system or mobility. I suggest that humanitarian and professional service firm norms take prominence over specific states or official organizational bodies and integrate market logics into diplomatic and humanitarian work, be they through the front door or the back door.

The professionals engaging in diplomacy as economic consultancy engage in what I refer to as "epistemic arbitrage," whereby they generate symbolic and economic gains by exploiting and combining forms of knowledge from different professional arenas.[5] Following this notion of epistemic arbitrage, the brokers occupying structural holes in political networks can eventually be understood as "epistemic arbiters," who, if successful in their acts of arbitrage, become the referees of what is appropriate professional knowledge to tackle particular problems. I

[4] See Introduction, this volume. On structural holes, see Ronald Burt, "Structural Holes and Good Ideas," *American Journal of Sociology*, 110(2), 2004, 349–399; Stacie E. Goddard, "Brokering Change: Networks and Entrepreneurs in International Politics," *International Theory*, 1, 2009, 249–281.

[5] Leonard Seabrooke, "Epistemic Arbitrage: Transnational Professional Knowledge in Action," *Journal of Professions and Organization*, 1(1), 2014, 49–64.

detail how brokers engaging in diplomacy via economic consultancy use epistemic arbitrage to combine "diplomatic-tacit," "economic-systematic," and "programming-managerial" forms of knowledge from different professional and organizational arenas. These forms of knowledge include informal knowledge to be used in negotiations, formal abstract knowledge about how economic systems work, and pragmatic applications of general principles to operations and tasks. These forms of knowledge are not exclusive to any particular professional domain but are dominant within professional ecologies occupied by, respectively, diplomats, economists, and management consultants.

In combining these forms of professional knowledge, the professionals engaging in diplomacy as economic consultancy also create a style that induces deference in others and draws on powerful symbols strongly associated with humanitarian norms and professional service firm norms. I follow Harrison White's view that "professionalism is a style recognized in deference relations onto provision of service valued for existence, not by test. So it is the syntax of deference rather than the content of its lexicon that singles out professionalism."[6] Professional services valued for their existence as a form of representation are crucial to the story here about diplomacy as economic consultancy, just as is what White refers to as the "syntax of deference." A focus on professionalism as style allows us to identify an important source of change to diplomatic practice, especially what can be understood as professional mobilization[7] rather than established professions competing to control a jurisdiction within a national or transnational context.[8] This is important because the use of style within these symbolic frameworks of humanitarianism and management consultancy informs the conditions of possibility for how to govern, including the prominence of market logics in formal and informal diplomatic relationships.

6 Harrison C. White, *Identity & Control: How Social Formations Emerge*, 2nd edn (Princeton, NJ: Princeton University Press, 2008), 137.

7 Ibid., 257.

8 Andrew Abbott, *The System of Professions* (Chicago: University of Chicago Press, 1988); Marion Fourcade, *Economists and Societies: Discipline and Profession in the United States, Britain, and France, 1890s to 1990s* (Princeton, NJ: Princeton University Press, 2009). See also the discussion in the Introduction to this volume.

Competing norms in the conduct of political work can also raise ethical questions between serving to provide clients' national interest or principles associated with professionalism. International work practices matter because if the practice of diplomacy is delegated to parties who are not located in ministries but in economic consultancies, then there are also potential effects on how professionals in ministries behave, including changing notions of what skill sets are required, and what qualifies a "competent performance" to be effective as a modern diplomat.[9]

Changing conceptions of appropriate international practices in diplomacy are also informed by trends in the demand for transparency from states, international organizations (IOs), non-governmental organizations (NGOs), and firms. This drive comes primarily from dominance of economic-systematic knowledge and the view that all problems can be handled best when information asymmetries are lowest. This logic can also be found in programming-managerial knowledge following markets trends introduced by the corporate sector[10] and New Public Management in the public sector,[11] with a shift from management for control or vocation to profit and performance. Despite not being formally recognized as a profession, management consultancies pay a particularly important role here in transforming knowledge through "the quality and other standards applied by consulting firms and individual consultants, who can demonstrate their professional values and behaviour."[12] This general shift also implies a change from viewing professionalism as an occupational value, based on an allegiance to occupation trained in a particular way, to an organizational value whereby common practices across different environments are favored by the employing organization.[13] A shift from

9 Emanuel Adler and Vincent Pouliot, "International Practices," *International Theory*, 3(1), 2011, 1–36.

10 Dick Zorn, "Here a Chief, There a Chief: The Rise of the CFO in the American Firm," *American Sociological Review*, 69(3), 2004, 345–364.

11 Kevin T. Leicht, Tony Walter, Ivan Sainsaulieu, and Scott Davies, "New Public Management and New Professionalism across Nations and Contexts," *Current Sociology*, 57(4), 2009, 581–605.

12 Milian Kubr, ed., *Management Consulting: A Guide to the Profession*, 4th edn (Geneva: International Labor Office, 2003), 131.

13 James R. Faulconbridge and Daniel Muzio, "Organizational Professionalism in Globalizing Law Firms," *Work, Employment and Society*, 22(1), 2008, 7–25; Julia Evetts, "Professionalism: Value and Ideology," *Current Sociology*, 61(5–6), 2013, 778–796.

occupational to organizational forms of professional value has been ushered in by rise of "vague experts" – those who know how to organize well and can provide general solutions to complex problems – through management consultancies and global professional service firms.[14] A range of international organizations have introduced ever greater numbers of consultants into their ranks, including those such as the International Monetary Fund that are commonly considered to be rigid institutions that only use formally trained PhDs.[15] The rise of consultancy as an accountable yet guarded way of working has important implications for how knowledge is managed and valued, and diplomacy is not immune to these changes. In policy making, the zest for transparency has empowered technocrats and raised conflicts with the traditional role of the diplomat, who is responsible for guarding secrets and using tacit knowledge.[16]

Iver B. Neumann[17] has described the common roles in diplomacy as a mix of "bureaucrats," "heroes," and "mediators," and certainly these styles can be found in formal diplomacy. When considering changes in configurations of social relations beyond the state, we need to add actors whose claims to authority are non-territorial and who contribute to the range of actors actively engaged in diplomatic work. The brokers identified in this chapter are such characters and I detail how they combined different forms of professional knowledge.

In what follows, I discuss the role of diplomatic practices and private authority and note the importance of style in professional mobilization. This is followed by a discussion of the different forms of professional knowledge are being combined and how they are linked to occupational and organizational forms of professionalism in the field of diplomacy. I then delve into two examples of organizations that provide diplomatic services via economic consultancies and display

14 Seabrooke, "Epistemic Arbitrage," 58–59.

15 Leonard Seabrooke and Emelie Rebecca Nilsson, "Professional Skills in International Financial Surveillance: Assessing Change in IMF Policy Teams," *Governance: An International Journal of Policy, Administration and Institutions*, 28(2), 2015, 237–254.

16 Paul Keal, *Unspoken Rules and Superpower Dominance* (London: Macmillan, 1983); Vincent Pouliot, "The Logic of Practicality: A Theory of Practice of Security Communities," *International Organization*, 62(2), 2008, 257–288.

17 Iver B. Neumann, "To Be a Diplomat," *International Studies Perspectives*, 6(1), 2005, 72–93.

different kinds of epistemic arbitrage and where brokers are seeking to carve out a position on diplomatic work that both challenges and reaffirms the existing international order. The conclusion reflects on the prominence of the phenomena and how professional mobilization and styles are not linked to organizational types, since what appear to be professional service firms can behave like NGOs, while what appear to be NGOs may actually operate like a professional service firm. Rather, professionals use epistemic arbitrage to gain positions in political networks that combine different styles, professional knowledge, and elements of different organizational types. This phenomenon is important to understand for the making of world politics because it signals greater uncertainty around formal diplomacy and the heightened prominence of market-based logics in professional diplomatic work.

Diplomatic brokers and professional mobilization

In *The Anarchical Society*, Hedley Bull suggests that economic activity is becoming more important, and that greater strength to the private sector and the growth of international cooperation through such organizations as the Organization for Economic Co-Operation and Development (OECD), the World Bank, and the International Monetary Fund (IMF) forces a "change in the character of the professional diplomat's work rather than a decline in his role."[18] The relationship between diplomats and the market place is certainly one that has evolved. Some of this evolution has been recognized in work on the "new diplomacy," which raises questions of who holds authority as well as the nature of the evolution of diplomatic practices. The editors of this book suggest that authority claims can be separated by territorial versus non-territorial representation, and that diplomatic functions can be broadly separated by representation and governance functions. An important issue here is to understand the practices of diplomacy and if they conform to our assumptions of private and public forms of authority. For example, James Muldoon,[19] among others, has pointed

[18] Hedley Bull, *The Anarchical Society. A Study of Order in World Politics* (London: Macmillan, 1977), 168.

[19] James P. Muldoon, "The Diplomacy of Business," *Diplomacy & Statecraft*, 16(2), 2005, 341–359.

to the role of corporate elites in providing a form of diplomacy, and this is to be expected in areas of high cost/ high profit and associated with issues such as energy security. Donna Lee and David Hudson have insightfully commented that "governments are reorganising their diplomatic systems so that commercial activities are far more centralised and the commercial activities of diplomats are extended."[20] The notion that we can study public authority as a separate sphere with regard to diplomatic practices is particularly problematic if one considers how actors commonly move between public and private spheres of activity.[21] This is equally true for the notion of private authority as something separate from the influence of public institutions. To ascribe public or private identities to actors and then seek to link those identities to forms of authority that are understood as absolutes distorts how we understand how international practices are formed. Ascribing public or private labels provides a pre-social determination that inhibits us from identifying new practices and may exclude other logics behind decision making.[22] Ole Jacob Sending and Iver Neumann, for example, have asserted how concepts such as "global governance" replicate a public versus private dichotomy and assume a logic of command, while staff on the ground have to learn from policy as practice if programs such as population control are to be successful.[23] As this chapter describes, we can clearly identify new practices from brokers who are bringing together different forms of professional knowledge to carve out new markets for political work.

Opportunities for brokers to conduct political work via economic diplomacy have emerged from greater diversity in who is actually engaged in diplomacy. As Iver B. Neumann has recently commented,

[20] Donna Lee and David Hudson, "The Old and New Significance of Political Economy in Diplomacy," *Review of International Studies*, 30(3), 2004, 344.

[21] Leonard Seabrooke and Eleni Tsingou, "Revolving Doors and Linked Ecologies in the World Economy: Policy Locations and the Practice of International Financial Reform," Centre for the Study of Globalisation and Regionalisation, working paper 260, no. 9, University of Warwick (2009).

[22] Ole Jacob Sending, "Constitution, Choice and Change: Problems with the 'Logic of Appropriateness' and Its Use in Constructivist Theory," *European Journal of International Relations*, 8(4), 2002, 443–470.

[23] Ole Jacob Sending and Iver B. Neumann, "Governance to Governmentality: Analyzing NGOs, States, and Power," *International Studies Quarterly*, 50(3), 2006, 651–672.

One consequence of the exponential growth in international, transnational, and nongovernmental organization is the number of people who, though not diplomats traditionally understood, are nonetheless engaged in practices akin to diplomatic ones. Such people are producing knowledge that is in direct competition with the kind of knowledge that diplomats traditionally attempted to monopolize. "Globalization" describes what we are talking about.[24]

Neumann is pointing to the expansion of the range of actors doing diplomatic work, one of the concerns of this volume, and stresses how the diplomatic monopoly on knowledge has weakened. I suggest that this has occurred precisely from emerging brokers who combine different forms of professional knowledge to mobilize and create new markets that can also have an effect on how those engaged in traditional diplomacy understand professional standards.

The literature in international relations typically identifies these people as "issue entrepreneurs," "norm entrepreneurs," and "political entrepreneurs,"[25] which correctly describes the role of the person and the drive to create. In this work, entrepreneurs engage in tactics and information politics to campaign on issues of bodily harm and injustice, and with the organizations they engage in selecting, vetoing, and vetting particular issues that do not suit their interests. In this conception, the entrepreneur is responsible for pushing forward the issue, taking it to NGOs and to IOs and to states, and seeking to create a norm cascade or to give the issue "political salience."[26] Entrepreneurs engage different organizations to place pressure on them to adopt an external value system, not to be convinced by a superior way of working or by different forms of knowledge. In my view, the idea of the entrepreneur describes who is in charge of organizing and the likely source of drive and passion on the issue being promoted. But the term "entrepreneur" does not permit us to locate how the person is able to get control of the

24 Iver B. Neumann, *At Home with the Diplomats: Inside a European Foreign Ministry* (Ithaca, NY: Cornell University Press, 2012), 171–172.

25 Margaret Keck and Kathryn Sikkink, *Activists Beyond Borders: Advocacy Networks in International Politics* (Ithaca, NY: Cornell University Press, 1998); Charli R. Carpenter, "Vetting the Advocacy Agenda: Networks, Centrality and the Paradox of Weapons Norms," *International Organization*, 65(1), 2011, 69–102.

26 Wendy A. Wong, *Internal Affairs: How the Structure of NGOs Transforms Human Rights* (Ithaca, NY: Cornell University Press, 2012).

activities he or she wishes. To put this differently, entrepreneurs have particular attributes but what we are really interested in is how the actors are related to others within a network and how they are able to carve out their own autonomy and gain control within the network.[27] As such "brokers" and "epistemic arbiters" provide more fitting terms for discussing diplomacy as economic consultancy. Acts of epistemic arbitrage occur when brokers seek to play off different pools of professional knowledge within different networks, exploiting informational asymmetries and using identity switching and styles to be persuasive and induce deference in others.[28]

Professional mobilization occurs when actors produce a style that is able to link up to other higher-level actors in networks and follow particular story sets on why their mobilization impact on professional arenas.[29] For example, Carne Ross's intervention to form the group Independent Diplomat, which is described in greater depth later, is built around the narrative that there is a "democratic deficit" in international politics and how formal diplomacy is conducted.[30] As such, new actors can emerge to fill this gap and present diplomatic practice in a different way. Professionalism as style can also be seen in organizations that seek to sustain themselves in highly uncertain environments. One could posit that such cases of epistemic arbitrage are more likely in policy areas where there is greater uncertainty about the world.[31] This is certainly the case in the examples provided that primarily address established sovereign states dealing with displaced peoples, non-state peoples seeking representation, and would-be asylum seekers. In such cases, brokers are able to bring together different kinds of professional knowledge to carve out their own space in political networks and promote their particular way of conducting diplomacy via economic consultancy.

27 Leonard Seabrooke and Duncan Wigan, "Emergent Entrepreneurs in Transnational Advocacy Networks: Professional Mobilization in the Fight for Global Tax Justice," GREEN Working Paper No. 42, Centre for the Study of Globalisation and Regionalisation, University of Warwick (2013).
28 Seabrooke, "Epistemic Arbitrage."
29 White, *Identity & Control*, 123, 222.
30 Carne Ross, *Independent Diplomat: Dispatches from an Unaccountable Elite* (Ithaca NY: Cornell University Press, 2007), 10–12.
31 Barbara Koremenos, Charles Lipson, and Duncan Snidal, "The Rational Design of International Institutions," *International Organization*, 55(4), 2001, 761–799.

Professional knowledge in diplomatic work

I suggest that brokers who are carving out new markets for political work and who are occupying positions in political networks are engaging in epistemic arbitrage by drawing on different types of professional knowledge. Three forms of knowledge are particularly relevant here. I refer to them as diplomatic-tacit, economic-systematic, and programming-managerial forms of knowledge and practices. These forms are action oriented and represent skill sets more than representational knowledge in the form of norms and ideas. They also represent different ways of organizing professional activities rather than reflecting particular formal occupational training. While diplomatic-tacit knowledge has affinities with the legal profession, economic-systematic knowledge with the economics profession, and programming-managerial with the quasi-profession of management consultancy, these forms of knowledge are more styles of organizing than abstract specialized skills acquired through formal training and specialism. They reflect professionalism as an organizational value more than an occupational value.

As a practice and skill set, diplomatic-tacit knowledge is related to what we can understand as how to guard secrets, mediate, and call on precedents from law and how to maneuver with national foreign ministries, NGOs, and IOs. For example, knowledge of how to interpret and push forward humanitarian issues within complex bodies such as the UN is included here.[32] Iver Neumann has documented the skill of diplomats in being able to "keep a bracket" during negotiations, meaning the capacity to hold on and insist on a minority position during negotiations even when issues have been bracketed from the main discussion.[33] Similarly, Rebecca Adler-Nissen has discussed how diplomats call on specific knowledge of treaties, embassies, and institutions, such as diplomatic immunity, to codify and protect themselves in professional settings with journalists and scholars.[34] Tacit knowledge is not only concerned with the keeping of secrets but also with learning to read others and provide selected information accordingly, in pursuit

[32] Nicholas J. Wheeler, *Saving Strangers: Humanitarian Intervention in International Society* (Oxford: Oxford University Press, 2001).
[33] Neumann, *At Home with the Diplomats*, 114.
[34] Rebecca Adler-Nissen, *Opting Out of the European Union: Diplomacy, Sovereignty and European Integration* (Cambridge: Cambridge University Press, 2014).

of defined strategic objectives.[35] Diplomatic-tacit knowledge is also strongly related to style and self-presentation, including networks of esteem and regard and knowledge of correct habits in public and private settings. This form of knowledge is much more associated with art than science, with interpretation rather than the application of formal theories.[36]

In contrast to diplomatic-tacit knowledge, economic-systematic knowledge represents more science than art and is strongly associated with practices of benchmarking, seeking to reduce information asymmetries through the adoption of common templates, and by focusing on the efficient use of information and resources. Rather than holding secrets, economic-systematic knowledge is concerned with locating incentive structures for action and pricing them via a "good science" understanding of the relevant and applicable theories. This is, of course, closely related to market-based logics of resource allocation and profit generation, including the notion that information is not only important to selectively share, but that the information is also worth something that can be priced within a market.[37]

Programming-managerial knowledge is linked to both diplomatic-tactic and economic-systematic forms of knowledge, with a key distinction being an emphasis on how to organize relationships within networks to achieve strategic tasks. This form of knowledge and the practices from it are strongly linked to management consultancy, wherein discretion is valuable both for organizing and for generating profit. Here, the distribution of information follows the logic that information should be used to achieve clearly defined established goals, and that information should be parceled and distributed not according to a market model of highest price wins, but to enhance organizational control. Such control is essential as management consultants seek to guide innovation processes through standardization of service provision to clients, seeking to create international or global best practices.[38] As

35 Keal, *Unspoken Rules and Superpower Dominance.*

36 As conveyed to me during an interview with the director of the Brussels Office of Independent Diplomat, August 2012.

37 Leonard Seabrooke, "Economists and Diplomacy: Professions and the Practice of Economic Policy," *International Journal*, 66, Summer 2011, 629–642.

38 Christopher Wright, Andrew Sturdy, and Nick Wylie, "Management Innovation through Standardization: Consultants as Standardizers of Organizational Practice," *Research Policy*, 41(3), 2012, 652–662.

work by Mehdi Boussebaa and colleagues has demonstrated, the flows of programming-managerial knowledge follow former colonial ties and can be viewed as neocolonial and represent a new form of dependency, with information transferred via knowledge management systems from management consultants being mainly a one-way affair from, for example, London to the Middle East.[39] Programming-managerial knowledge also contains strong ethics about how to conduct operations and obligations to clients, including norms of confidentiality. While the ethics involved in diplomatic-tacit knowledge are often derived from international laws that have a special place for individual and human rights,[40] ethical considerations within programming-managerial knowledge are primarily related to corporate notions of responsibility, primarily those to clients and shareholders.

These different forms of knowledge also have their own internal prestige systems that provide professional incentives for conformity rather than risking a loss of credibility and recognition through unfamiliar pursuits or exploring new territory.[41] Brokers create connections in political networks through acts of epistemic arbitrage that is not about making connections between different nodes in a network, but about how particular actors can draw on particular forms of knowledge to heighten their position in specific networks while also reinforcing their prestige across the networks they engage.

I refer to them as brokers rather than mediators, as is common in work on diplomacy, because there is a clear market logic in their activity and because they are not only involved in lowering information asymmetries between parties and creating consensus, but they also actively create new information problems at the national and international levels. One obvious example here is ADRg Ambassadors, which draws explicitly on those who have experience in diplomatic service to provide "corporate diplomacy" to public and private clients.[42] These brokers gain credibility from their ties to policy communities as much

[39] Mehdi Boussebaa, Glenn Morgan, and Andrew Sturdy, "Constructing Global Firms? National, Transnational and Neocolonial Effects in International Management Consultancies," *Organization Studies*, 33(4), 2012, 465–486.

[40] Christian Reus-Smit, *Individual Rights and the Making of the International System* (Cambridge: Cambridge University Press, 2013).

[41] Leonard Seabrooke and Eleni Tsingou, "Distinctions, Affiliations, and Professional Knowledge in Financial Reform Expert Groups," *Journal of European Public Policy*, 21(3), 2014, 389–407.

[42] See www.adrgambassadors.com

as to wealth-generating communities in the private sector, and they combine the diplomatic-tacit, economic-systematic, and programming-managerial forms of professional knowledge. The use of former ambassadors to establish investment routes is largely about hiring those able to use discretion and obtain secret information for a fee, while also being recognized as a pillar of the international community with significant managerial experience in handling information. While this business is significant, it does not represent a real break with normal behavior in the international system, in which various forms of emissaries bring together state and corporate interests.[43]

The business of doing political work can take a variety of forms through an economic consultancy model that seeks to offer best practice services to clients in return for fees to cover costs and/or make profits.[44] In the following two sections, I provide examples of diplomacy as economic consultancy. The two organizations, Independent Diplomat and STATT, differ in many respects, including how brokers within them function, how and who they charge for their services, and how they combine diplomatic-tacit, economic-systematic, and programming-managerial forms of knowledge.

Independent diplomat

A particularly important example of diplomacy via economic consultancy, and professional mobilization through style, can be found in the group Independent Diplomat, which can be described as a humanitarian NGO that works to address the democratic deficit between nations that are cash and diplomacy rich and those that are not. Independent Diplomat (ID) occupies a unique position in political networks within the international order. This position is unique because it does not directly challenge the established system of sovereign states but subverts it in addressing power asymmetries and promoting particular conceptions of norms within the international

43 Yves Dezalay and Bryant G. Garth, *Dealing in Virtue: International Commercial Arbitration and the Construction of a Transnational Legal Order* (Chicago: University of Chicago Press, 1996).

44 Matthias Kipping and Christopher Wright, "Consultants in Context: Global Dominance, Societal Effect, and the Capitalist System," in Matthias Kipping and Timothy Clark, eds., *The Oxford Handbook of Management Consulting* (Oxford: Oxford University Press, 2012), 165–185.

system, including human rights, rule of law, anti-corruption, and transparency. ID promotes itself as an advisor to clients seeking to address democratic deficit problems and is based on a fusion between diplomatic-tacit, programming-managerial, and economic-systematic forms of knowledge, especially the first two.

ID is formally registered as a not-for-profit organization in New York and refers to itself as a "diplomatic advisory group" in the letterhead on its contracts. ID has fewer than 20 employees based in offices in New York, London, Brussels, Juba in South Sudan, and Hargeisa in Somaliland. The group uses the term "diplomatic advisory group" to distinguish itself from advocacy groups and typical NGOs, with ID's executive director and founder Carne Ross suggesting that ID's staffers do not consider themselves as working for a charity and "don't regard ourselves as table-banging advocates for our clients ... We're former diplomats."[45] From its annual filing for 2011 to the New York State Charities Bureau, the total expenditure from the New York office was $2,075,389, and assets, including grant contributions, $853,531. During that year, ID spent $130,100 in providing services to European clients; otherwise, it appears that operations occurred in the offices named earlier.[46] To provide a comparison here, the advocacy NGO Global Witness, which concentrates on economic networks behind corruption, conflict, and environmental harm, has 60 staff with offices in Washington and London and expenditure in 2011 of $8 million.[47] As such, ID is a small operation in financial terms and has sought to acquire stable funding from foundations rather than targeted funding for particular projects from various states and donors.[48]

The staffers at ID in the various offices act as brokers in various political networks, with the London director commenting to me that ID often acts as a "network enabler."[49] Of these brokers, Carne Ross is the

45 "How Carne Ross Created a New Kind Of Diplomacy," BuzzFeed Politics, 07–09-2013, www.buzzfeed.com/rosiegray/how-carne-ross-created-a-new-kind-of-diplomacy.

46 Information available from New York State Department of Law, Office of the Attorney General, Charities Bureau, Annual Filing for Charitable Organizations, 2011, #41-01-83, www.charitiesnys.com.

47 Global Witness, *Seeing the Strings: Global Witness Annual Review 2011* (London: Global Witness Ltd, 2012).

48 Interview with the director of the London Office of Independent Diplomat, September 2012.

49 Ibid.

most prominent in the international press and noted as a "cosmopolitan anarchist" and author of two works that provide the intellectual backbone behind ID and other initiatives.[50] A diplomat who worked for the British Foreign Office and the UN, including his role as strategy coordinator for the UN in Kosovo (UNMIK) and establishing UNMOVIC, the weapons inspection body in Iraq, Ross formed Independent Diplomat shortly after giving evidence that the British government had exaggerated the case for the war with Iraqi. Professionally, Ross is identified as a diplomat and an economist.[51] The directors of the London and Brussels offices identified themselves professionally as, respectively, a former diplomat with experience with management consultancy, and a former political strategist with experience in law.[52] These backgrounds are useful in permitting epistemic arbitrage by combining the forms of knowledge noted earlier and provide the unique style of those engaged in ID, particularly in the combination of styles associated with diplomacy and management consultancy.

ID's main work has been in assisting governments to declare independence and to be recognized by IOs and the European Union. Earlier work by ID included advising Kosovo on its independence process, including key considerations for its negotiations with the informal "Contact Group," including the United States, the UK, France, Germany, Italy, and Russia. Kosovo declared independence in 2008 and, following a challenge from Serbia to the International Court of Justice, was recognized as independent according to international law in 2010. From its 2011 annual filing, the range of clients ID does diplomatic work for include the government of the Republic of South Sudan in its engagement with the UN Security Council and with diplomatic matters in relation to the UN membership process. It also assisted the US Tamil Political Action Council in seeking accountability for

[50] Ross, *Independent Diplomat*; Carne Ross, *The Leaderless Revolution* (London: Simon & Schuster, 2010).

[51] As noted on his ID website: 'www.independentdiplomat.org/about-us/our-staff/carne-ross and also by Stephen Colbert during Ross's appearance on the Colbert Report: Carne Ross – *The Colbert Report* – May 2, 2012, www.colbertnation.com/the-colbert-report-videos/413500/may-01–2012/carne-ross.

[52] Interview with the director of the Brussels Office of Independent Diplomat, August 2012; interview with the director of the London Office of Independent Diplomat, September 2012.

serious crimes during the civil war, and to draw attention to human rights abuses in the north and east of Sri Lanka. It also advised the Republic of the Marshall Islands and the Alliance of Small Island States (AOSIS) on climate change politics and engagement with the UN Framework Convention on Climate Change (UNFCCC).

Importantly, ID worked with the POLISARIO Front in the Western Sahara on human rights abuses in what POLISARIO considers to be occupied territory, and to counter illegal exploitation of fishing and phosphate resources by Morocco and other foreign entities. ID notes that the European Parliament's decision to block the renewal of the EU-Morocco Fisheries Partnership Agreement is a consequence of ID's engagement on the issue.[53] The UK Foreign Office considered ID's work on Somaliland as "transformative," consisting mainly of ID conducting briefings with Somaliland representatives prior to meeting the Foreign Office to be updated on international affairs.[54] Such work has also been supported with direct funding from foundations such as the National Endowment for Democracy.[55] In general ID's clients include foundations such as the Open Society Foundation and the Joseph Rowntree Foundation, and from governments including Norway, Finland, Liechtenstein, and Switzerland, as well as the UK's Department for International Development.

How ID works with its clients is of interest because it follows a model strongly associated with consultancies rather than the typical NGOs. ID staffers are "relationship managers" in dealing with clients and their relationships to other governments provide a source of institutional memory for clients. As such, they maintain an information management system like a consultancy but do not rely on a knowledge-management system like the big corporate consultancies. Rather, the teams in different offices speak regularly to update one another on the common treatment of problems to "hunt as a pack."[56] This

[53] Information available from New York State Department of Law, Office of the Attorney General, Charities Bureau, Annual Filing for Charitable Organizations, 2011, #41–01-83, www.charitiesnys.com.

[54] Interview with the director of the London Office of Independent Diplomat, September 2012.

[55] "National Endowment for Democracy: Somaliland," www.ned.org/where-we-work/africa/somaliland.

[56] Interview with the director of the London Office of Independent Diplomat, September 2012.

information sharing is critical to ID's work and to avoiding conflicts with governments and NGOs working on similar issues.[57]

Importantly, ID charges fees for its services, a decision based on the logic that clients will only trust advice that is valuable and costly, and that charging fees is linked to neutral and impartial advice.[58] This view of advice from consultants as neutral and superior to in-house bureaucratic expertise is pervasive within the management consultancy community,[59] and ID has identified this desire from both the client and donor sides of its work. For ID, fees are structured according to an ability-to-pay model and as a nonprofit organization, most fees are simply to support the costs of the work. For example, a 2009 contract with the government of Southern Sudan established a fee of US$294,000 plus expenses under US$50,000 for 100 consulting days,[60] whereas ID's earlier contract with the Sahrawi Arab Democratic Republic notes that no fees were charged but that travel and reimbursements could sum up to US$10,000.[61] The use of fees is a demonstration of the combination of diplomatic-tacit, economic-systematic, and programming-managerial forms of knowledge. Confidential advice to clients is in part legitimated by the fact that it costs money, and that ID has operating practices that are aligned with management consultancies rather than typical NGOs. This style of engagement signals to the clients and donors that ID is professional.

A further glimpse into ID's contracts reveals how ID's brokers combine their normative standpoint with providing political work for their clients. In a 2013 contract with the US Office of the National Coalition of Syrian Revolution and Opposition Forces, greater detail is provided

[57] Cf. Alexander Cooley and James Ron, "The NGO Scramble: Organizational Insecurity and the Political Economy of Transnational Action," *International Security*, 27(1), 2002, 5–39.

[58] Interview with the director of the Brussels Office of Independent Diplomat, August 2012; interview with the director of the London Office of Independent Diplomat, September 2012.

[59] Bessma Momani, "Management Consultants and the United States' Public Sector," *Business and Politics*, 15(3), 2013, 381–399.

[60] US Department of Justice, Registration Statement, Pursuant to the Foreign Registration Act of 1938, registration no. 5860-Exhibit-AB-20090720-5, registered on 07-09-2009, www.fara.gov/.

[61] US Department of Justice, Registration Statement, Pursuant to the Foreign Registration Act of 1938, registration no. 5860-Exhibit-AB-20080403-1, registered on 0325-2008, www.fara.gov/.

on ID's criteria for working with its clients. To quote from the agreement:

1. All of ID's clients must have been assessed positively against ID's ethical criteria, which are commitment to democratic, accountable, transparent and corruption-free government; protection of human rights; and respect for international law. Independent Diplomat's advice will always be in the framework of international law and accepted human rights norms and ID will not condone or advocate the use of violence or abuse of human rights.
2. ID's purpose is to assist in the prevention and resolution of conflict. It does not in any way seek to get involved in political activity or to produce specific political outcomes but assists its clients in seeking peaceful resolution to their needs. ID does not wish to be party-political in the countries in which it operates and seeks to serve the best interests of the country as a whole.
3. ID does not act as an advocate for individuals or organizations or their programmes or for any political or ideological point of view, and is a politically neutral facilitator.[62]

This contract, which specifies the covering of costs and seeking external donor funding, was to provide the client with an analysis of Syria's diplomatic situation and to provide diplomatic advice, including the drafting of Aide Memoires and letters to the UN Security Council. The criteria for considering clients are important for noting how ID operates within the established international order while providing consultancy-like services to governments seeking representation within it.

An important element for ID is professional style, and this is apparent from interviews and conversations with ID's directors. A contrast here can be drawn with work on transnational advocacy groups, which choose to campaign on issues of injustice and bodily harm, and where passion for the issue is important in the mobilization of a campaign.[63] For example, Stephen Hopgood notes that the "proliferation of management speak" in Amnesty International was leading to a loss of

[62] US Department of Justice, Registration Statement, Pursuant to the Foreign Registration Act of 1938, registration no. 5860-Exhibit-AB- 20130408–12, registered on 04-08-2013, www.fara.gov/.
[63] Keck and Sikkink, *Activists Beyond Borders*.

passion and demoralizing the staff.[64] Legitimacy problems felt by human rights campaigners resulting from management speak or practices associated with the private sector are not apparent in ID. Indeed, ID provides a contrast with NGOs that draw on practices from diplomatic-tacit and programming-managerial forms of knowledge that directly informs its style. Superficially, this can be seen in the crisp pink, blue, or white shirts and appropriately chosen ties that are important for the self-presentation of ID staffers, just as is speaking calmly about issues of great political sensitivity. Carefully chosen offices also reflect this, with ID's modest London office located strategically close to the Foreign Office in a grand building, Hamilton House. More substantively, however, it is the combining of different forms of knowledge and identities that provides the brokers in ID with a particular style. This permits ID to do work that some of its government and NGO clients are not able to. For example, it was commented in an interview that often a woman in her 30s or 40s represents the funding body and that clients from Africa prefer to speak with someone with grey hair.[65] The capacity to call on different identities from diplomacy and consultancy is a strong part of ID's profile and success.

STATT Consulting

ID is an example of a nonprofit organization providing political work via a form of organization that has many similar traits to consultancies. A different example of diplomacy via economic consultancy can be found in STATT Consulting, a Hong Kong–based for-profit organization providing political work to a range of governments. STATT provides strategic advice, education and training, public relations, and operational support to a number of governments and NGOs. Its clients include the governments of Afghanistan, Australia, Canada, Denmark, Thailand; NGOs such as ActionAid; IOs such as various UN agencies and the World Bank; and a range of think tanks. To quote directly from its website, STATT describes itself as follows:

64 Stephen Hopgood, *Keepers of the Flame: Inside Amnesty International* (Ithaca, NY: Cornell University Press, 2006), 133–134.

65 Interview with the director of the London Office of Independent Diplomat, September 2012.

> STATT is a network of practitioners dedicated to mitigating transnational threats and expanding transnational opportunities. We bring together those driving globalisation and those who are vulnerable to it. Our approach emphasises the need to secure strong evidence and community engagement to guide innovative responses that combine transnational forces with local knowledge and needs. We work for communities, countries and companies seeking targeted services that shape transnational connections and leverage their benefits.[66]

Although based in Hong Kong, STATT's operational hubs are in Afghanistan, Australia, Austria, Indonesia, Iraq, and Pakistan, drawing on networks linked to NGOs and IOs, particularly UN agencies in those locations. STATT operates five programs that target different areas of political work: Neutrino (migration), Prescience (natural hazards and climate change), White Hat (security risks), Resonance (aid effectiveness), and Collateral (illicit finance). The programs combine different elements of diplomatic-tacit, programming-managerial, and economic-systematic forms of knowledge, with all three in play across the programs from the emphasis on efficiency in the mitigation of threat and also the specialism in illicit financial markets.

STATT has 60 full-time staff but operates most programs through local NGOs that coordinate closely with country managers. For 2012, STATT's revenue was estimated at approximately $6.5 million, with strong growth from new and renewed contract arrangements with their clients.[67] Clearly this annual revenue differs from the comparably small amounts of money involved in ID, and a key source of revenue is from government contracts. STATT relies on interaction with other networks and NGOs and particularly on the identification of risks to clients by conducting surveys and fact-finding missions. The managing director of STATT from 2010 to 2013, Jacob Townsend, previously worked for the UN Office on Drugs and Crime in Central Asia, Afghanistan, and Pakistan. Now director of capacity development, Townsend's background is in international relations and international law, with education and actual in-field work coinciding. STATT's other directors have government and some UN experience; others are from an information management background tied to the corporate sector rather than to NGOs or IOs. As such, STATT talks explicitly

66 www.statt.net.
67 Confidential interview with STATT staff member, December 2012.

about the development of its business model and the processes for the handling of people and operations necessary to take its business to the next stage.

The key move in the formation of STATT has been the identification of client demand for particular information related to diplomatic issues. Townsend identified this prior to forming the consultancy. Testimony to an Australian Senate standing committee in 2007 on directions in public diplomacy make this clear:

> A major reason ... we cannot operationalise a comprehensive public diplomacy component of our counter-terrorism strategy is that we have so little information about our audience. In counter-terrorism and counter-radicalisation, differentiating the opponent and the audience can be quite difficult. For example, you might have someone who hates Australia but preaches nonviolence. On the other hand, you might have someone who takes up a gun against an Australian organisation or interest but has very little knowledge or attachment to any kind of opposing ideology in a concrete sense.[68]

Townsend suggested that survey-based research would be a way to address this problem and to understand credible threats, that "if you are measuring them, you have a chance of seeing where the problem lies." This insight is the basis for STATT's operations as a consultancy engaged in diplomatic work, with the organization spending most of its resources in research to identify problems and then make contracts with governments and other organizations to further the research, address particular policy problems for clients, and develop advisory products.[69] STATT's ongoing revenue relies on project performance like other consultancies, and it recognizes that it cannot solely engage in fund-raising activities based on advancing humanitarian principles but seeks to achieve these goals through private contracts and ongoing brand recognition of the kinds of service STATT provides. Assisting this recognition is STATT's placement within NGO and IO networks in operations and also in securing funding. For example, in 2011 the

[68] Australian Government, Senate Standing Committees on Foreign Affairs, Defence and Trade, Inquiry into the Nature and Conduct of Australia's Public Diplomacy: Building Our Image, chap. 6 – "The Coherence and Consistency of Australia's Public Diplomacy Message," Committee Hansard, 04–11-2007, 15, www.aph.gov.au/Parliamentary_Business/Committees/Senate_Committees?url=fadt_ctte/completed_inquiries/2004–07/public_diplomacy/report/c06.htm.

[69] Confidential interview with STATT staff member, December 2012.

UK-based NGO ActionAid hired STATT to conduct surveys of women in Afghanistan.[70] STATT's directors and staff act as brokers within these political networks, drawing on different forms of professional knowledge to customize services to their clientele.

In recent years, some of the major clients for STATT have been the Australian government and its agencies, including the Australian Customs and Border Protection Service (hereafter Customs), the Australian aid agency AusAid, the Department of Immigration and Citizenship, and the Department of Foreign Affairs and Trade. While STATT is not required to disclose its operations as is ID, because of ID's charitable status, the character of awarded contracts can be gleaned from the government tenders databases and departmental and ministerial annual reports, as well as information released under the Australian Freedom of Information Act. For example, in 2011 Customs hired STATT for strategic planning consultation services for $1,739,245 based on the need for "skills currently unavailable within agency." Customs also hired STATT for public relations for $570,890 because of a "Need for specialised or professional skills."[71] AusAid hired STATT in 2012 for "management advisory services" for $158,968 to conduct a review of Indonesian NGOs.[72] In 2013, Customs hired STATT again for education and training services for $1,412,698, again citing professional expertise as the reason.[73] These numbers indicate the size of contracts but tell us little about the work being conducted and why it is a form of diplomacy via economic consultancy.

Delving into the kind of work done a little further, STATT has been engaged in market testing of government policies in areas of significant political sensitivity, where tacit information and confidentiality are

[70] ActionAid, *A Just Peace? The Legacy of War for the Women of Afghanistan* (ActionAid: London, 2012).

[71] Australian Customs and Border Protection Service, Strategic Planning Consultation Services, 2011, A $1,885,014.50, contract number CN470088, www.tenders.gov.au; Australian Customs and Border Protection Service, Education and Training Services, 2011, A $617,854.00 Public Relation Services, contract number CN451388-A1, https://www.tenders.gov.au.

[72] AusAid, 2012, A $174,919 Management Advisory Services, contract number CN722181-A, www.tenders.gov.au.

[73] Australian Customs and Border Protection Service, 2013, A $1,529,027 Education and Training Services, contract number CN1281531, www.tenders.gov.au.

crucial diplomatic skills. Customs had a contract in 2010 for $985,487 with STATT to conduct "Public Relations and Advertising"[74] based on three projects: Joya, Intrepid, and Whisper. A 2011 internal report from Customs outlines that in 2010 STATT conducted three projects for them in Afghanistan and Pakistan to "assess the impact of the Australian Government's policy announcement on the suspension of processing asylum claims."[75] Work in Project Joya included advertising on television, radio, websites, and bus and taxi stops, including messages such as "Australia closed: Australia may send you back and you will lose your money then who will care for your family?" and "Say NO to people smugglers; protect your family, money and self-respect."[76] Project Whisper found that half of those interviewed (mainly Afghans) were aware of changes in Australian government policy and nearly half had specific information on policy changes related to the processing of Afghan arrivals, leading most to delay any plans to migrate.[77]

Prior to 2010, Customs had a number of contracts for the same purpose with public relations firms, such as Porter Novelli and the International Organization for Migration (with a contract of $802,430).[78] One can assume fairly that the change to STATT was for a specialized professional skill set that a firm or IO could not provide, particularly the blending of diplomatic-tacit, economic-systematic, and programming-managerial knowledge from one organization. A further contract was made in 2011 for $1,380,159 for STATT to conduct surveys under its "advertising and market research" budget.[79] Research from the Australian Parliament that points to increasing asylum flows from Afghanistan relies on STATT's input,[80] suggesting ongoing demand for the consultancy's

[74] See Australian Customs and Border Protection Service (ACBPS), "Strategic Assessment of Counter People Smuggling Communications Activities, November 2011," www.customs.gov.au/webdata/resources/files/2012-018673_Document04_Released.pdf, p. 12.

[75] Ibid. [76] Ibid. [77] Ibid., p. 18.

[78] Australian Customs and Border Protection Service, *Annual Report 2009–10* (Canberra: Australian Customs and Border Protection Service, 2010), 219.

[79] Australian Customs and Border Protection Service, *Annual Report 2011–12* (Canberra: Australian Customs and Border Protection Service, 2012), 302.

[80] Janet Phillips and Harriet Spinks, "Boat Arrivals in Australia since 1976," Department of Parliamentary Services, Social Policy Section, Parliament of Australia (2013).

political work and the importance of the knowledge STATT generates for policy considerations.[81] The ongoing sensitivity of asylum claims as a political issue can be seen in the shift to the right in Australian asylum seeker policy. The hardening of Australia's policy on asylum seekers has occurred despite UN criticisms of Australia's earlier detention policies for asylum seekers as not following the spirit of international refugee law.

As with ID, an important element for STATT is professional style, with the consultancy integrating itself among NGOs and IOs with little trouble. The choice of organizational form as a private consultancy is, in part, tied to the ease of access to difficult countries where STATT's research and operations are conducted. The administrative scrutiny placed on NGOs and IOs is greater than that placed on private businesses, which are permitted with greater flexibility.[82] In general, it is STATT's capacity to combine different forms of professional knowledge and to engage in epistemic arbitrage that lands it with select and valued information that permits the brokers within the organization to traverse NGO, IO, governmental, and consultancy networks.

Conclusion

Brokers engage in political work by acting on behalf of their clients to provide diplomatic services. They specialize in providing information to parties on how a problem can be addressed by offering confidential advice to their clients on politically sensitive topics, and by briefing and preparing clients for meetings with powerful institutions. They play an important part in mediation between different interests in the determination of policies, primarily by combining diplomatic-tacit, economic-systematic, and programming-managerial forms of professional knowledge that compensate for absences or deficiencies in

[81] Asylum flow information is attributed to STATT (2013) "Afghan Migration in Flux," *Synapse*, January 2013, Issue 10, www.unodc.org/cld/bibliography/2013/afghan_migration_in_flux.html. See also Khalid Koser and Peter Marsden, "Migration and Displacement Impacts of Afghan Transitions in 2014: Implications for Australia," Department of Immigration and Border Protection Irregular Migration Research Program, Occasional Paper Series 03.2013, Belconnen, Australia, 14, www.immi.gov.au/media/research/irregular-migration-research/_doc/migration-displacement-impacts-afghan-transitions-2014.pdf.

[82] Confidential interview with STATT staff member, December 2012.

NGOs, IOs, governments, and firms. By engaging in epistemic arbitrage to move around networks in which this professional knowledge can be found, brokers doing political work have a great deal of information at their discretion to inform policy choices and use selectively within the networks they operate in. This chapter has outlined how brokers doing political work are organized as economic consultancies, be they for-profit or not-for-profit, and how they are engaged in diplomatic practices. The implications of this activity for the international order are significant: if foreign ministries and other government departments are outsourcing their international political work to consultancies, this reflects a rigid international system in which the need to find information and keep secrets is not simply in the hands of states. In part, this is due to discussions of transparency within NGOs, IOs, and governments – that when all is documented and all are heard, the executive answer is to nod and then outsource the task to those who can keep their mouths shut.[83] As discussed in this chapter, the inadequacies of the international order, including the democratic deficit addressed by ID and the political need for the market-testing operations conducted by STATT, have led to the emergence of brokers who specialize in doing political work and operate across different networks. We should not expect this emergent professional form to disappear but for the heterogeneity of those doing diplomatic work to increase as the demand for keeping secrets on politically sensitive topics increases.

[83] Neumann, *At Home with the Diplomats*, 89–91.

8 *US military diplomacy in practice*

CAPTAIN MIRIAM KRIEGER, LIEUTENANT COMMANDER SHANNON L. C. SOUMA, AND DANIEL H. NEXON

Airmen understand Airmen, and that's where the partnership begins.

General Mark A. Welsh, Chief of Staff of the US Air Force, speech to the Air Force Association Air Power Working Group, Washington DC, May 20, 2013. Quoted with his permission.

In their Introduction to this volume, Sending, Pouliot, and Neumann argue that "if we want to account for changes in diplomatic practices by virtue of the proliferation of actors involved in diplomatic work, the question of how and why different actors do diplomacy must be central."[1] In this chapter, we discuss US defense diplomacy with the aim of providing answers, however partial, to this question.

The significance of studying US military diplomacy should require little elaboration. The United States is currently the dominant military power in the world. Its power projection capabilities are unprecedented in human history. As Barry Posen argues, for the past few decades the US military has possessed "command of the global commons," that is, it "gets vastly more military use out of the sea, space, and air than do others . . . it can credibly threaten to deny their use to others . . . and . . . others would lose a military confrontation for the commons if they attempted to deny them to the United States."[2]

This condition rests on raw US military might, but "two important Cold War legacies contribute to U.S. command of the commons – bases and command structure." Indeed, US primacy "is further secured by the world-wide U.S. base structure and the ability of U.S. diplomacy

The views expressed in this publication are entirely those of the authors and do not necessarily reflect the views, policy, or position of the US government, US Department of Defense, US Navy, or US Air Force.

1 Introduction, p. 14.

2 Barry Posen, "Command of the Commons: The Military Foundation of US Hegemony," *International Security*, 28(1), Summer 2003, 8.

to ... secure additional bases and overflight rights."[3] Bases and overflight rights, though, reflect simply one dimension of the extensive system of alliances and partnerships built by the United States. Indeed, a significant degree of contemporary global security governance operates within and through this US-centered network.[4]

Our analysis draws on a variety of sources, including interviews and the personal experiences of the authors.[5] It builds on two basic wagers: first, "routine diplomacy is a matter of network construction and maintenance"[6] and second, the content of those networks – the meanings actors attach to or impose on them – reflects and shapes the conduct of diplomacy. In this sense, an analysis of the meanings that US military and civilian officials attach to their diplomacy provides insight into the practice of US primacy.

We begin with a brief theoretical elaboration of the previous points before turning to an illustrative survey of various dimensions of US defense diplomacy. In general, US defense diplomacy stresses the creation and nurturing of partnerships at the institutional and individual levels. Participants describe the development of interpersonal trust – augmented with the development of contextual knowledge about the culture and practice of foreign interlocutors – as critical to the pursuit of national security objectives. US defense diplomacy mirrors the ethos of the US military as primarily concerned with problem solving, the dissemination of best practices, and the importance of "the uniform" as a basis for transnational community. In practice, this orientation helps maintain an extensive network of security governance that extends from interstate cooperation to socializing foreign interlocutors into US military norms, procedures, practices, and forms of communication.

3 Ibid., 16, 21. On the structure and politics of the US overseas basing network, see Alexander Cooley and Daniel Nexon, "'The Empire Will Compensate You': The Structural Dynamics of the U.S. Overseas Basing Network," *Perspectives on Politics*, 11(4), 2013, 1034–1050.

4 For discussions of the importance of alliances in this architecture, see Daniel Byman, "Remaking Alliances for the War on Terrorism," *Journal of Strategic Studies*, 29(5), 2006, 767–811; Cooley and Nexon, "The Empire Will Compensate You"; and David Lake, *Hierarchy in International Relations* (Ithaca, NY: Cornell University Press, 2009).

5 Particularly Krieger and Souma.

6 Robin Brown, "Diplomacy, Public Diplomacy and Social Networks," paper presented at the 2010 Annual Convention of the International Studies Association, New Orleans, Louisiana, 6.

Although we only provide illustrative sketches of these claims, we think they have important implications for the study of diplomacy, governance, and power politics. As Tarak Barkawi argues in Chapter 2, "the web of international relations that makes war possible" plays a fundamental role in constituting international order. His analysis showcases how marginalizing military activities and relations skews our understanding of "traditional" diplomacy. Military diplomacy in general, and US defense diplomacy in particular, impacts the entire contemporary international diplomatic field.

Indeed, all the talk of "new" diplomats and "new" diplomacy risks obscuring the ways in which military power – and its unequal distribution – suffuses contemporary diplomacy. This suggests that the study of diplomacy must pay careful attention not only to the security arena but also the politics of hegemony. Hegemonic socialization, management, and influence rest on – and create – an infrastructure of diplomatic activity – much of which takes place within the realm of defense diplomacy.

At the same time, hegemonic-order theories would benefit from more attention to not only diplomacy but also military diplomacy. For example, Ikenberry and Kupchan argue that US authority and leadership rest on the socialization of elites into US values and vision.[7] But they pay little attention to the comprehensive mechanisms of socialization – including the production of structurally similar defense institutions among US partners – at work in defense diplomacy. In this respect, cognate theories replicate many of the patterns criticized by Barkawi, insofar as they treat military power as analytically distinctive from the social and cultural dimensions of hegemony. After all, are military capabilities not the most important component of "hard power," whereas "soft power" resides in its cultural and social capital? This leads us to neglect the soft power of US military prestige – as well as the ways in which defense diplomacy builds transnational cultural and social capital among military personnel, institutions, and states. Seen in this light, the deliberate attempt by the US military to cultivate soft power reinforces this problematic distinction. At the same time, it should come as no surprise. In a sense, it involves military practitioners giving fashionable names to long-standing practices and orientations.

[7] G. John Ikenberry and Charles A. Kupchan, "Socialization and Hegemonic Power," *International Organization*, 44(3), 1990, 283–315.

Diplomacy, relations, meanings

Diplomatic activity creates, sustains, and alters ties among states, institutions, and individuals. This is an intrinsic feature of modern diplomacy, which operates through both routine and irregular interactions among individuals operating on behalf of, and within, organizations of various kinds. In traditional interstate diplomacy, agents of the state form interpersonal connections with counterparts. Such relationships may be limited to official functions or involve social transactions. They may be friendly, indifferent, or downright hostile. In other words, diplomacy, just like other forms of human interaction, produces social networks among its participants.

Indeed, traditional diplomatic practice stresses the kind of information and influence associated with interpersonal relationships. As Neumann notes, the collection of information about the doings and nature of other communities amounts to one of the most long-standing purposes of diplomatic activity. Diplomats collect this information by developing cross-boundary relations with members of the relevant "other." It should not be surprising, then, that diplomats often specialize in the collection of information "about the views and policies of a country's political leadership, now and in the future. It is knowledge of personalities rather than of forces and conditions which shape a country's policy over the long term."[8]

In the era of professionalized diplomats, these interactions often attach to bureaucratic positions and roles. For example, representatives of states at international organizations develop interpersonal ties with their colleagues. When new diplomats replace them, the interpersonal ties they form will have a different quality. But the persistence of someone in that role ensures routine interactions among individuals as representatives of their states. A well-developed state apparatus works in other ways to maintain some degree of continuity. Bureaucracies accumulate and produce stores of knowledge that they deploy to allow newcomers to take up diplomatic roles from their predecessors. These include diplomatic cables, intelligence dossiers, and after-action reports. Such parts of the archive of knowledge are

[8] Hedly Bull, quoted in Iver B. Neumann, *At Home with the Diplomats: Inside a European Foreign Ministry* (Ithaca, NY: Cornell University Press, 2012), 35.

themselves sometimes collected and deployed in briefing materials and trip books.[9]

Thus, we adopt the formulation "individuals, institutions, and states" to discuss defense diplomacy in the context of interstate relations. Relations at each of these levels overlay and penetrate one another, but they do not perfectly mirror one another. The friction and mismatch among them can prove consequential. Consider the period before the 2008 Russia-Georgia conflict. For a number of years, the US foreign policy apparatus developed extensive ties with the Georgian state, its institutions, and specific officials. Georgia was awash with US contractors providing security assistance, a major recipient of aid and arms sales, a common destination for US officials, and a contributor to the US-led coalition in Iraq.

As tensions between Tbilisi and Moscow escalated, various high-ranking US officials attempted to communicate to the Georgian government that the United States would not risk war with Russia over Georgia. These messages were undermined, however, by the existence of close personal friendships between Georgian officials and US politicians, political operatives, and national security officials – including a group of Russia skeptics who occupied important foreign policy positions at the end of President George W. Bush's second term. These interpersonal trust networks helped deflect earlier concerns within Washington about possible entrapment while enhancing Tbilisi's misplaced confidence that Washington would support it in a military confrontation with Moscow.[10]

Once, as the editors of this volume urge us, we adopt a more expansive understanding of diplomacy – and particularly the institutions and actors that engage in it – then we can think of diplomatic relations as producing a topography of networks that link together individuals,

[9] See, for example, Neumann, *At Home;* and Neumann, "'A Speech That the Entire Ministry May Stand for,' or Why Diplomats Never Produce Anything New," *International Political Sociology*, 1(2), 2007, 183–200; and Vincent Pouliot, *International Security in Practice: The Politics of Nato-Russian Diplomacy* (Cambridge: Cambridge University Press, 2012). Trip books are produced for officials by their subordinates and include biographies of interlocutors, background information, and talking points.

[10] See Alexander Cooley and Daniel H. Nexon, "'We Are all Georgians Now': Symbolic Capital, Trust, and Authority under Hierarchy," ms. presented at the 2011 Annual Convention of the International Studies Association, Montreal, Canada.

institutions, and states. Some of these relations are ephemeral; others endure for long periods of time. Insofar as they not only create vectors for information, influence, and leverage but also embed content – such as identities, repertoires, and practical knowledge – these networks structure much of the processes and behaviors that comprise international politics.[11]

One implication is that we should concern ourselves with mapping this topography – of charting its formal organizational properties. Much of this is underway via the importation of social-network analysis into international relations scholarship, although too little of that work has focused on diplomatic networks of various kinds.[12] Another is that we should study the meanings that participants attach to these networks and how they understand those interactions. It is not simply the *form* of diplomatic networks that matter, but their *content*.[13] In the case of US-Georgian relations, for example, ties between the two countries revolved around stories of friendship, a commitment to democracy, and Georgia's "westernizing" outlook. This content, in turn, shaped the form of ties by creating the disposition in the United States to further increase the strength and density of cooperative linkages.[14]

The US-Georgia example highlights another feature of the US defense-diplomatic network: much of its structure is asymmetrical. The United States, and by extension its institutions and officials, enjoys a superordinate position in international politics that is conferred on it by its military strength, economic power, and attendant prestige.[15] This

[11] On the cultural dimensions of ties and networks, see, for example, Charles Tilly, *Stories, Identities, and Political Change* (Lanham, MD: Rowman & Littlefield, 2002).

[12] See Emilie M. Hafner-Burton, Miles Kahler, and Alexander H. Montgomery, "Network Analysis for International Relations," *International Organization*, 60(3), 2009, 559–992.

[13] This is, obviously, an important wager of the entire volume and its "relational" approach to diplomacy. On the importance of integrating formal and cultural analysis of networks in the study of international politics, see Daniel H. Nexon, *The Struggle for Power in Early Modern Europe: Religious Conflict, Dynastic Empires, and International Change* (Princeton, NJ: Princeton University Press, 2009), chap. 2; and Nexon, "Relationalism and New Systems Theory," in Matthias Albert, Lars-Erik Cederman, and Alexander Wendt, eds., *New Systems Theory and International Relations* (London: Palgrave, 2010), 99–126.

[14] Cooley and Nexon, "We Are All Georgians," 27–34.

[15] On the United States and international hierarchy, see Cooley and Nexon, "The Empire Will Compensate You"; and Lake, *Hierarchy in International Relations*.

is particularly true in the context of its security relationships. Although the United States has long been in relative economic decline, in the post–Cold War period, the military gap between the United States and other countries has, with a few notable exceptions, expanded.[16] Despite setbacks in Afghanistan and Iraq, officials in other countries generally see the US military as the most competent military power in the world. At the very least, the US military understands itself this way. Such power and prestige inevitably, as we shall see, inflect how US defense officials understand their diplomatic relationships.

Although this chapter focuses on conveying the empirical details of the configuration of US military diplomacy, we also note some implications of the expanding authority of civilian defense officials and military personnel on the wider practice of diplomacy. The Introduction to this volume reminds us that, in some periods, a rigid distinction between war and diplomacy meant that diplomats accompanied militaries for the purpose of negotiating terms at the conclusion of battle. The modern US military – through its extensive transnational networks and competencies – has acquired de facto and de jure jurisdiction over putatively diplomatic territory. Moreover, the pragmatic and utilitarian discourse of military diplomacy – in both its narrow and broad senses – effaces the distinction between what Mitzen calls "diplomacy as representation" and "diplomacy of governance." But to the extent that it, to borrow her terminology, mediates or even transcends estrangement,[17] it does so in the context of US military superiority and the pursuit of, at heart, US interests.

US military diplomacy: an overview

War and the shadow of war stand at the center of interstate diplomacy; common understandings of diplomacy treat it as an alternative to the use of force.[18] It should therefore come as no surprise that military officials

[16] See Keir A. Lieber and Gerard Alexander, "Waiting for Balancing: Why the World Is Not Pushing Back," *International Security*, 30(1), 2005, 109–139. For more recent data, see the International Institute for Strategic Studies, The Military Balance 2013, www.iiss.org/en/publications/military%20balance/issues/the-military-balance-2013–2003

[17] Mitzen here comments on James Der Derian, *On Diplomacy* (Oxford: Basil Blackwell, 1987).

[18] See, for example, Angelo M. Codevilla, "Tools of Statecraft: Diplomacy and War," Foreign Policy Research Institute, www.fpri.org/footnotes/1301.200801.codevilla.statecraftdiplomacywar.html, accessed June 3, 2013. Tarak Barkawi

are deeply implicated in diplomatic activity. The US Department of State maintains a Bureau of Political-Military Affairs, whose mission is to integrate diplomacy and defense and forge "strong international partnerships to meet shared security challenges."[19] However, US military and civilian defense officials routinely engage not only in political-to-military(pol-mil), but also military-to-military (mil-mil) activities with foreign counterparts – in most cases outside the formal auspices of the State Department.

Military diplomacy includes "creating bilateral and multilateral contacts between senior military and civilian defense officials, ... appointment of defense attachés, ... bilateral defense cooperation agreements, ... training activities for foreign military and defense personnel, ... exchanges between military personnel, [and] providing military support and aid with material and equipment."[20] The United States has also traditionally provided instruction to foreign military personnel on its views concerning the proper role of the armed forces in democracies, such that some sources go so far as to describe such socialization as a key element of US military diplomacy.[21]

As we alluded to at the outset of this chapter, it would be difficult to understate the importance of pol-mil and mil-mil activities in the web of diplomatic relations. Members of the Department of Defense – soldiers, sailors, air force personnel, and civilians – form the largest, most pervasive, and best-financed component of the US diplomatic network. In 2013, the United States has almost 1.5 million active duty personnel, maintains a military presence in approximately 150 foreign countries – with something in the vicinity of 600 overseas military installations – and budgets more than $500 billion to defense.[22] In regions where US

provides an extensive discussion, and demolition of, the diplomacy/war dichotomy in Chapter 2 of this volume.

19 www.state.gov/t/pm/, accessed June 2, 2013.

20 Göran Swistek, "The Nexus between Public Diplomacy and Military Diplomacy in Foreign Affairs and Defense Policy," *Connections: The Quarterly Journal*, 11(2), Spring 2012, 82.

21 Ibid., 82; and Carol Atkinson, "Constructivist Implications of Material Power: Military Engagement and the Socialization of States," *International Studies Quarterly*, 50(3), 2006, 509–510.

22 US Defense Manpower Data Center, www.dmdc.osd.mil/appj/dwp/dwp_reports.jsp; "Active Duty Military Personnel Strengths by Regional Area and by Country," US Department of Defense, 2012, accessed May 30, 2013. Budget figures retrieved from www.defense.gov/news/2014budget.pdf, accessed May 16, 2013.

military relationships – in the form of arms sales, training, basing, and so forth – are particularly extensive, these relationships often emerge as critical vectors for influence, communication, and negotiations.[23] Indeed, Washington may maintain strong mil-mil relations with foreign counterparts even in the absence of robust civilian diplomacy.[24]

We cannot possibly address the full scope of US military diplomacy. Thus, we focus on a number of specific roles, practices, and settings that help elucidate how it operates. It includes a number of official diplomatic roles and specializations, such as the defense attaché and the foreign area officer. Among the most important high-level US military diplomats are the regional combatant commanders (COCOMs) and their subordinates. In some regions of the world, COCOMs number among the most influential and prestigious representatives of the US government. Indeed, some observers have dubbed COCOMs "viceroys" or "proconsuls" for their role in US-centered security governance.[25]

Although we focus on the "military" side of military diplomacy, a significant number of civilian officials play diplomatic roles in that part of their job that involves forming relationships with, interacting with, and negotiating with foreign counterparts. Some officials are embedded in international security institutions, such as NATO. In regional offices of the Office of the Secretary of Defense for Policy – OSD(P) – for example, most low-level civilian employees have a portfolio that covers a single country – or a handful of countries. A not insignificant part of their job involves engaging with relevant foreign officials. Each office has a deputy assistant secretary of defense (DASD) who may spend a significant amount of time traveling to the region under her jurisdiction or engaging with foreign counterparts in Washington, DC. As we travel up the food chain to assistant secretaries of defense (ASDs) and even to

[23] Interview with Colin Kahl, former deputy assistant secretary of defense (DASD) for the Middle East (2009–2011).

[24] See e.g. Kevin Baron, "Pentagon's China Guru David Helvey: Friction Is 'Inevitable' but Mil-Mil Relations Are 'As Good as It's Been,'" *Foreign Policy*, May 8, 2013, http://foreignpolicy.com/2013/05/09/pentagons-china-guru-david-helvey-friction-is-inevitable-but-mil-mil-relations-are-as-good-as-its-been/, accessed June 15, 2013; and "Friendly Foes: US-Russia Military Relations Soaring," *Foreign Policy*, October 16, 2012, http://foreignpolicy.com/2012/10/16/friendly-foes-u-s-russia-military-relations-soaring/, accessed August 4, 2013.

[25] See e.g. Derek S. Reveron, *American Viceroys: The Military and US Foreign Policy* (New York: Palgrave Macmillan, 2004) and Dana Priest, "The 'Proconsuls: A Four Star Foreign Policy.'" *Washington Post*, September 28, 2000, A1.

the secretary of defense (SECDEF), the geographical scope of their diplomatic activity increases. Although functional offices cover specific policy areas rather than regions, their personnel may be extensively involved in diplomatic activity, such as negotiating and implementing interstate agreements.[26]

At the same time, defense diplomacy is often a by-product of other routine mil-mil and pol-mil activities. The Bush administration's war on terror brought increased attention, from both policy makers and analysts, to the degree that US military personnel mediate US relations with the rest of the world.[27] But the extent that unofficial diplomatic activity embeds in routine US military practices goes far beyond special operations and counterinsurgency warfare. US security assistance, partnerships, and activities create an extensive web of unofficial diplomatic interactions among US defense personnel and their foreign counterparts. These activities not only amount to de facto diplomatic interactions in and of themselves, but they also build relationships that structure opportunities for further conduct of diplomacy. They provide the day-to-day infrastructure for negotiation and coordination in security affairs and create vectors for socialization and influence among militaries and military personnel.

We provide a number of examples of such military diplomacy in action: the training of foreign aviators in US flight schools, professional military education, overseas military exercises, and processes surrounding US arm sales. Participants may or may not see their role as primarily diplomatic in character, but, as we note, specific dimensions of operational training constitute military personnel as "warrior-diplomats."

Our illustrative examples highlight variation in the magnitude and scope of US military diplomacy. The intensity of unofficial and official military diplomacy differs across time and space. It generates different degrees of interpersonal and institutional interdependence, with possible downstream consequences for influence and socialization. In fact, some states have even sought to generate such interdependence to

[26] For a good "users guide" to the complicated bureaucracy that is the Pentagon, see Perry M. Smith and Daniel M. Gerstein, *Assignment Pentagon: How to Excel in a Bureaucracy*, 4th edn (Washington, DC: Potomac Books, 2007).

[27] See e.g. Robert D. Kaplan, *Imperial Grunts: On the Ground with the American Military, from Mongolia to the Philippines to Iraq and Beyond* (New York: Vintage, 2006).

advance their strategic goals.[28] The scope and substance of military diplomacy also vary significantly – from being largely concerned with security issues to becoming the driving force of almost all diplomatic activity.

Military diplomacy and the sinews of US primacy

The US military stations representatives in nearly every country in the world to support and coordinate with ambassadorial diplomatic missions. The defense attaché (DATT), an officer holding full diplomatic status, serves as the designated chief military liaison to a host nation and usually leads a military component within the US embassy consisting of foreign area officers (discussed later in this section) and others. Traditionally, the attaché has also played an intelligence role, acting as the US's eyes and ears. This role was particularly vital for the United States prior to the advent of high-tech reconnaissance, although thousands of reports sent by attachés in interwar Germany, Italy, and Japan "languished forgotten in the files."[29] The intelligence role of attachés now focuses more on the day-to-day acquisition of knowledge that enables diplomatic relations and foreign policy.

Indeed, "the term *military diplomacy* … was and is still very closely linked to the role of the military attaché." Although it has very old antecedents, the modern position "emerged as part of nineteenth-century European diplomacy" with the duty "to observe and assess military developments in a foreign country, as well as to maintain a close relationship with the foreign military elite."[30] As Timothy C. Shea notes, "from the beginning, the military attaché was something of a hybrid in the world of international relations. He was part diplomat, part soldier, part scout, and perhaps, as Lord George Curzon suggested, not entirely welcome."[31] The tasks assigned to defense attachés are now complicated and varied. They might range from developing the itinerary for a visiting

[28] See e.g. Cooley and Nexon, "We Are All Georgians."

[29] See Scott A. Koch, "The Role of US Army Attachés Between the World Wars: Selection and Training," *Studies in Intelligence*, 38(5), 1995, www.cia.gov/library/center-for-the-study-of-intelligence/csi-publications/csi-studies/studies/95unclass/Koch.html, accessed June 5, 2013.

[30] Swistek, "The Nexus between Public Diplomacy and Military Diplomacy," 81.

[31] Timothy C. Shea, "Transforming Military Diplomacy," *Joint Forces Quarterly*, 38, 2005, 50.

US defense official to meeting with the host country's defense minister to discuss ongoing security disagreements.[32] In consequence, the US normally maintains Defense Attaché Offices (DAOs) that house multiple attachés from different branches of the armed forces. As the senior military attaché, the defense attaché must navigate a variety of institutional responsibilities and equities:

The DAO is the permanent [Department of Defense] office assigned to U.S. diplomatic missions. Headed by the Defense Attaché (DATT), it has complex command relationships with the ambassador, the combatant commander, Office of the Secretary of Defense, the Joint Staff, and the Defense Intelligence Agency. The ambassador's country team is a microcosm of the interagency with representation by most Federal agencies, all under the umbrella of the U.S. Embassy. The DATT represents all DOD organizations on the country team and manages complex command relationships with all these elements inside and outside the Embassy.[33]

Defense attaché positions are often filled from traditional stakeholder services or specific communities within services, such as aviation. Attachés receive tailored training that focuses primarily on diplomatic issues, such as diplomatic immunity and protocol. In countries where the US military presence is small, one or two officers may perform both attaché and security cooperation duties. Many projects and events involve a mix of military-diplomatic players.[34] Considerable overlap can exist among the military-diplomatic categories and roles.[35]

The officers who fill the role of defense attaché may or may not be trained foreign area officers (FAOs). The defense attaché is a historic military diplomatic position; the advent of foreign area officers is a relatively new development, reflecting the military's desideratum for greater specialization in diplomatic functions. As the Cold War saw an increased emphasis on US security assistance to aid allies and further US security objectives, the armed forces required more officers with the necessary special expertise to manage programs such as Foreign Military Sales and International Military Education and Training. Over time, the security

[32] See e.g. Robert Bridge, "Tough Talking: Russia and US Discuss European Missile Defense," *RT 31*, August 2011, http://rt.com/politics/russia-us-missile-defense-embassy-moscow-519/, accessed June 5, 2013.

[33] Shea, "Transforming Military Diplomacy," 49.

[34] Souma, Skype interview with mid-level US Marine Corps Foreign Area Officer, May 19, 2013.

[35] Ibid.

cooperation community has grown to thousands of defense personnel and contractors. Additionally, each military service independently – and with differing degrees of enthusiasm – cultivated a cadre of foreign area officers.[36]

Members of the foreign area officer corps serve as experts in the culture, politics, and strategic affairs of other countries and regions. These officers generally hold advanced degrees and receive extensive language training. Most also boast significant operational experience, having been selected mid-career from war-fighting communities. Such officers often handle US security assistance implementation overseas. They may serve as senior defense official/defense attaché, security assistance officer, military liaison officer, or intelligence analyst, among many other international roles.[37] Interestingly, a number of the active-duty and retired personnel serving in positions within the regional offices of the OSD(P) are foreign area officers by training.[38] Each of the military corps has its own organization, specific missions, and officer career paths. Some officers return to war-fighting communities or alternate between formal diplomatic and operational tours. For navy and army foreign area officers, transition to the community is permanent.[39]

The recent wars in Afghanistan and Iraq led many decision makers to conclude that US military effectiveness suffered from an inadequate number of personnel with local cultural knowledge. As a result, the foreign area officer program has received increased attention and resources. In fact, despite current fiscal constraints, the military is expanding the program. As a percentage of US military personnel, the total number of FAOs remains quite small, with numbers ranging from around a thousand in the army to less than 300 in the navy. But the number of active-duty FAOs – already over two thousand in 2012 – is

[36] The US Air Force has adopted the titles "international affairs specialist" (IAS) and "regional affairs strategist," (RAS) but these officers are still commonly referred to as foreign area officers (FAOs). See www.safia.hq.af.mil/internationalaffairsspecialist. From author Souma's experience, US Air Force IASs, RAS, and political affairs strategists (PAS) are still often grouped and generically called FAOs, especially in a joint environment.

[37] Author Souma's personal knowledge and discussions with multiple experienced FAOs.

[38] OSD(P) is part of the civilian division of the Department of the Defense.

[39] Author Souma's personal knowledge. See Oliver Stuenkel, "How Many Diplomats Does an Emerging Power Need?" *Post-Western World*, October 14, 2012, www.postwesternworld.com/2012/10/14/how-many-diplomats-does-an-emerging-power-need/, accessed September 10, 2013.

more than triple that of the total number of diplomats currently employed by countries such as Belgium, India, and the Netherlands.[40]

In practice, attachés and FAOs develop military-to-military contacts and work to build trust between the local armed forces and the US military. These US officers live in the host country and are expected to become familiar with local military concerns and operations. Thus, the Pentagon and the US combatant commands may turn to attachés and FAOs for intelligence about "ground-truth" conditions. Attachés and their teams may also coordinate combined military exercises and assist visiting US dignitaries and legislators. In high-level meetings, such as between the US secretary of defense and host nation minister of defense, attachés and FAOs will often attend to provide local knowledge and advice concerning issues specific to their host nation.[41]

An important component of this work involves connecting US military expertise to the particular needs of the host nation military. FAOs link their host nation counterparts to subject matter experts or may spearhead exchanges of subject matter experts. For example, if a host nation is transitioning to an all-volunteer force, such officers might organize visits to recruiting commands in the United States and arrange for consultations with US experts on the workings of all-volunteer forces. If the host nation is developing its anti-pirate capabilities, an FAO might arrange for training in boarding and search and seizure operations.[42]

FAOs also serve as liaisons during the planning stages of exercises or when designing assistance programs. The assumption is that these officers are best positioned to understand the military intentions of the host nation, as well as to explain their needs to other US defense officials. FAOs are expected to understand the host nation's logistical, cultural, political, economic, and operational constraints. They may provide an explanation, in the form of what is sometimes called the "back story," for otherwise puzzling requests or objections. Knowing both US objectives and host nation objectives for any project, the FAO

[40] For FAO numbers, see DOD 2012 Annual Foreign Area Officer Report, https://fao.nps.edu/documents/10249/2373fa8b-4446-46d7-baac-954c67554250, accessed September 10, 2013. For the number of diplomats employed by India, Belgium, and the Netherlands, see Stuenkel, "How Many Diplomats Does an Emerging Power Need?"

[41] Souma interview, May 19, 2013.

[42] Ibid., examples from conversations with multiple FAOs.

works to find the common ground and to align goals. Indeed, these officers aim to demonstrate their value added by enabling more efficient and productive military exercises, effective and appropriate arms sales, and improvement in the training of partners' militaries. In other words, the value of cultural and linguistic knowledge resides in facilitating various forms of problem solving when it comes to enhancing US security partnerships.

However, many formal military diplomats establish lasting friendships and may even find a spouse in the host country. Foreign area officers move from country to country with each tour but typically stay within a certain geographic region, primarily because of the investment in foreign language proficiency.[43] Regardless of their specific career trajectories, military-diplomats see themselves – and are often treated as – the face of the US military in international settings. Host nations may come to see US military members as the "trusted brokers," tending toward the apolitical, and keeping a long-term perspective that remains steady through changes in political fortunes.[44] The same can be said of the role of foreign attachés in the United States. Colin Kahl, the deputy assistant secretary of defense for the Middle East from 2009 to 2011 recalls that "within hours" of the Israeli military raid on the Gaza Freedom Flotilla in May 2010, he was "on the phone with the Israeli DATT [defense attaché] to find out their perspective and to express US concern."[45]

The formal mechanisms for the practice of diplomacy do not end with military defense cooperation and embassy personnel. Rather, they extend to the highly visible and comparatively political positions of geographical combatant commanders, the regional diplomatic face of US military operations, and service chiefs, the highest-ranking officers in each service. Combatant commanders are assigned responsibility for

[43] Author Souma's personal knowledge. Note that throughout the US military, service members change location as standard practice, usually with each tour. Thus, it is difficult to impute a purely Machiavellian purpose for preventing FAOs from "going native."

[44] This perception derives from the consistency of the military presence through both warm and cold bilateral political relations and associated rhetoric; see Cooley and Nexon, "We're All Georgians Now." Also, ambassadors are often political appointees and thus strongly associated with the policies of the US president. See Dmitri Trenin, "Rice and the Russians," *Foreign Policy*, June 7, 2013.

[45] Interview with Colin Kahl.

a geographical region such as Europe or Africa. These senior officers have peacetime and wartime responsibility for all air, sea, and ground forces assigned to the region. The primary task is to plan and prepare for a variety of conflicts and contingencies within their theater of influence, but in their peacetime role they maintain an extensive travel schedule, liaising with ministers of defense and armed forces commanders of the countries in their "backyard." Their interactions are supplemented by those of the service commanders in region. For example, the commander of Pacific Air Forces makes similar rounds visiting the air chiefs of Singapore, Thailand, Indonesia, the Philippines, and so on.[46]

The topics of discussion in these visits range from weapons procurement to exercise coordination to doctrinal compatibility. However, many officials view the topics as less important than the practice of interaction itself. Lieutenant General Francis Wiercinski, commander of US Army Pacific, comments that the "emphasis on engagement and open communication, and partnering with allied friends and partners" is the material gain, that "in this business, ... relationship building is building trust."[47]

This sentiment is echoed by both military and civilian officials. In regions where the US military is particularly active, such as the Middle East, the combatant commanders and their staffs tend to become more central to US diplomacy. As Kahl observes, the assistant secretary of state for the Middle East is based in Washington, DC, "but CENTCOM[48] basically lives in the region." Because the combatant commander is "traveling so often," he "is treated as a super-ambassador." There, "security relationships" are essentially "the bedrock" of all other US relations. The combatant commander not only enjoys critical "gravitas" but is "also the senior official on what countries care about." This is especially true in the Persian Gulf; for example, the combatant commander "meets with the king and crown prince" of Saudi Arabia.[49]

46 See materials at "Unified Command Plan," .www.defense.gov/home/features/2009/0109_unifiedcommand/, accessed June 15, 2013
47 Kevin Baron, "US Army 'Fences Off' Military Diplomacy from Sequester," *Foreign Policy*, Tuesday, May 14, 2013, http://foreignpolicy.com/2013/05/14/u-s-army-fences-off-military-diplomacy-from-sequester/, accessed May 26, 2013.
48 CENTCOM is the combatant commander of all US military forces in the Middle East.
49 Interview with Colin Kahl.

High-level diplomatic practices extend to the service chiefs and staffs in Washington, DC. Not only do the chiefs of staff of the army and air force and the chief of naval operations routinely host their foreign counterparts, but staff-level interactions continue to build relationships and alter doctrine in foreign forces. For example, Operator Engagement Talks bring in foreign officers to discuss tactics, techniques, and procedures on a variety of topics between the US Air Force and a select group of nations.[50]

These structures and mechanisms for engagement involve developing the personal relationships between military members. Lieutenant General David L. Goldfein, the commander of all US Air Force units in the Middle East (2011–13), was known to comment that he knew his counterparts on a callsign (aviator nickname) basis, which reflects a significant level of familiarity bred through frequent and repetitive interaction in exercises and meetings.[51] US officials see these relationships as critical mechanisms for exerting influence.[52] While Egypt was undergoing its revolutionary political transition during the 2011 Arab Spring, the combatant commander for the Middle East and other US military officials called their counterparts in the Egyptian military and inquired about their intentions. They could ask directly if the Egyptian Army would permit the transition to occur without violence or repression: "It was all about making sure they sat it out while the political process ran its course."[53] US officials believe that these connections played a crucial role in at least moderating the Egyptian Army's response to ongoing protests and quite likely influenced the Egyptian Army's decision to (initially) support the transition.[54] A senior international strategy officer notes that "before a war or crisis ever starts, I think the relationship between air chiefs is critical, absolutely fundamental."[55]

Such leverage may cut both ways. When the Egyptian military eventually overthrew the Muslim Brotherhood government in July 2013, the extensive US-Egyptian military partnership contributed to Washington's

50 Author Krieger's personal knowledge.
51 Krieger interview with Colonel Michael Fleck, chief, Strategy and Plans Division, Deputy Under Secretary of the Air Force for International Affairs, Washington, DC, May 19, 2013.
52 Ibid.; authors Krieger's and Souma's observations.
53 Souma interview, May 13, 2013.
54 Interview with Colin Kahl.
55 Krieger interview with a senior ranking international strategy official within the Department of Defense, Washington DC, May 21, 2013.

unwillingness to condemn the coup. With the outcome of Egypt's latest crisis uncertain, observers generally view the US-Egyptian security relationship as profoundly inflecting both sides' decision making.[56]

US military officials fully appreciate these dynamics. Speaking on his ability to protect engagement funds from sequestration in the Pacific theater, Gen. Wiercinski said, "I believe [engagement is] one of our primary missions, and literally my primary mission in the theater."[57] A senior US Air Force international strategy official commented, "at the star level, it is their J-O-B to know their international counterparts and to have access [to them]" to facilitate basing during deployments, defuse crisis situations caused by accidents or misperceptions, and leverage high-level contacts in the event of war.[58] It is no secret that the ultimate goal of these relationships is often access to territory and partner capability in pursuit of US interests.

As we noted earlier, civilian officials carry out a great deal of defense diplomacy. This ranges from low-level interactions between US civil servants and their counterparts to high-level meetings among political appointees and foreign interlocutors.[59] Civilian defense officials generally engage in diplomatic activity focused on security affairs, such as those involving transit agreements, security institutions, arms sales, and cooperative activities. But high-ranking civilian officials also engage in a broader array of diplomatic activity.

One reason is that security affairs seldom operate in complete isolation from other diplomatic considerations. Another reason is the centralization of foreign policy decision making in the US National Security Council staff. This staff tends to be opportunistic in the communication of important messages to foreign officials. For example, it may choose to relay those messages through a Department of State, Defense, or other official already traveling to a particular country or region on other

[56] Thom Shanker and Eric Schmitt, "Ties with Egypt Army Constrain Washington." *New York Times*, August 16, 2013, www.nytimes.com/2013/08/17/world/middleeast/us-officials-fear-losing-an-eager-ally-in-the-egyptian-military.html, accessed September 10, 2013.

[57] See Baron, "US Army 'Fences Off' Military Diplomacy from Sequester."

[58] Interview with Colin Kahl.

[59] The relationship between the civilian and military sides of the Department of Defense is complicated and deserves treatment in its own right. As already noted, active-duty and former military personnel occupy a number of posts within the Office of the Secretary of Defense.

business. Defense officials themselves often are expected to reiterate standing policy on important concerns.[60] In this respect, the lines between security, economic, and military channels are increasingly blurred in high-level US diplomatic activity.

Military sales and assistance

Observers and participants have long recognized that US arms sales to foreign nations amount to a form of diplomacy. With these sales – which often consists of a package of training, replacement parts, and upgrades and signify a sustained commitment between the United States and its customer – the United States aims to extend its influence and strengthen relationships abroad.[61]

One of the oft-stated goals of arms sales to allies and friends is "interoperability." The term, usually applied to technology, equipment, procedures, and doctrine, refers to the ability of different military organizations to conduct combined operations. It is commonly recognized that interoperability between allies increases war-fighting efficiency, reduces errors, and cuts down planning time.[62] Confidence in interoperability lessens the risk and uncertainty of deploying with multinational services and systems.

Government-to-government military sales are brokered through the Defense Security Cooperation Agency. The stated purposes of this agency are to build relationships that promote US security interests, build allied and friendly nations' military capabilities, and in this way help ensure global access.[63] Equipment may be purchased from the United States via Foreign Military Sales (a Security Assistance program) or Direct Commercial Sales. US arms transfers are governed by two congressionally formulated laws – the Arms Export and Control Act and the Foreign Assistance Act – that are administered by the US

[60] Interview with Colin Kahl and author's personal observations.

[61] Indeed, Kinsella argues that arms transfers are a powerful predictor of compliance with US foreign policy priorities. See David Kinsella, "Arms Transfer Dependence and Foreign Policy Conflict," *Journal of Peace Research*, 35(1), 1989.

[62] Authors Krieger's and Souma's observations. Souma notes that interoperability played an important role in airborne coordination between coalition partners during Operations Iraqi Freedom and Enduring Freedom (Afghanistan).

[63] See www.dsca.mil/, accessed August 5, 2013.

Department of State.[64] It falls to the Department of Defense – and various military members – to implement and execute these provisions, making them particularly useful in reflecting the logic of practice.

Military and defense civilian personnel at many levels assist in the implementation of these arms deals. In the US Navy, Program Management-Aviation offices, commonly called "program offices" act as the procurement agencies that oversee the technical side of aviation purchases.[65] Headed by program managers, who are either senior aviators or defense civilians, often having extensive engineering or test flight experience, or both, the program offices may substantially influence the execution of arms agreements.[66]

The program offices, staffed with military engineers, test pilots, and technicians, execute foreign military sales through the same processes as domestic funds. The program offices are accountable for cost schedule and performance and work to ensure that interoperability requirements are met (when applicable). The offices also advise security cooperation agencies as to what is available for purchase, on what timeline, and with what options, effectively defining constraints of the deal. Furthermore, the program offices may offer feedback regarding the deal as brokered. The program manager and his or her staff, having expertise in both operational aviation and aerospace engineering, may offer better options for fulfilling the customer's military needs. For example, the manager could suggest a platform more suited to the customer's requirements or ask the operational questions that force a rethinking – and redesign – of the deal.[67]

Some program offices take an aggressive role in "marketing" US aviation platforms and related equipment. Incentives exist to increase production runs in many cases; as more of any one item is ordered and manufactured, the greater the economies of scale. The production cost of each unit decreases, to the benefit to the US taxpayer. Thus, program offices may arrange familiarization flights and demonstrations with

64 Security Assistance Management Manual, updated July 18, 2013, www.samm.dsca.mil/.

65 The US Navy's Program Management-Ships (PMS) offices are the equivalent for ship acquisitions.

66 Author Souma's phone interview with a senior naval officer with 15 years of experience in acquisitions, May 20, 2013.

67 Ibid.

perspective customers or send representatives to help sell the product at international air shows.[68]

According to Colonel Michael Fleck, the chief of the strategy division in the International Affairs office of the Secretary of the Air Force, it is the act of negotiating a complex purchasing process that matters, not necessarily the finished product. Cases take years to develop and execute and require teams of civilian and military specialists on both sides to work out the details: "No system ever works perfectly – this relationship is built through creative struggling through tough problems." The desk officers, technicians, and the buyer nation must work together to overcome supply line breakdowns, capability adjustments, or unexpected cost increases: "What it comes down to, is their nation and our airmen working out those problems together. That develops this relationship and this trust."[69] The long, and sometimes painful, process builds the relationship.

This US approach contrasts with that of other nations that simply deliver the promised goods. Moreover, the United States takes a holistic approach to the design of arms deals themselves. In addition to the long-term practice of establishing relationships and trust via contract negotiations, further opportunities to build relationships and trust are built into the sales contracts. Col. Fleck concludes, "We do the 'total package approach' and include other forums for connection such as [military education], pilot training, doctrinal development, maintenance schools, exercises, and exchange officers that accompany the shiny object."[70]

Overseas staffs and exercises

Military members often find themselves abroad in operational or staff tours. Many of the various regional service components, task forces, and combatant commands are headquartered in foreign countries. Military members, and often their families, thus live among the host nation population and conduct an informal kind of diplomacy through everyday interactions. One count places the total number of US military members abroad at more than 186,400, distributed in 144 countries.[71]

[68] Ibid. [69] Ibid. [70] Ibid.

[71] Edward F. Bruner, "CRS Report for Congress: US Military Dispositions: Fact Sheet," 2007, www.fas.org/sgp/crs/natsec/RS20649.pdf, accessed May 16, 2013.

At many levels, military members at foreign bases coordinate with host nation counterparts in the course of normal activities and processes. Perhaps the coordination of international exercises best highlights the intensity of some "unofficial" diplomacy, and how consequential the interpersonal skills of a mid-level officer may be. According to one officer who worked extensively with foreign navies while stationed at US 5th Fleet Headquarters in Bahrain, understanding the culture of regional militaries proved critical to planning and executing combined operations. However, officers tasked with this coordination often receive little or no formal language or cultural training.[72]

Having some knowledge of Arabic, this officer was chosen to liaise between US and Qatari, Bahraini, Kuwaiti, and other militaries. "Trial and error does not work," he emphasizes, "If you make a mistake, they will not trust you; you will be shut down." Interpretation of statements and preferences can be tricky; subtleties of language convey a lot in Arabic. Fortunately, the US military's multiculturalism yielded an Arabic speaker on staff, quite by chance. More typically, officers must improvise.

As with flight school and other extended international training, coalition exercises provide a way to build habits of communication and predictability. Annually, the US Air Force alone conducts nearly 100 ally or partner exercises, both large and small.[73] At times, the exercise is limited to a few small units. For example, in a 2010 deployment to Romania, a US fighter squadron based in Lakenheath, England, conducted training with a Romanian fighter squadron. In addition to flying mock missions together, the airmen briefed and debriefed together, sharing lessons learned and working to improve flying techniques on both sides. The pilots even took turns flying in one another's aircraft simulator and traded backseat rides so both sets of aviators might experience the employment of the other's aircraft.[74]

In these small-squadron exercises, the practice extends to social interactions, reinforcing perceived military-cultural and historic ties.

72 Author Souma phone interview with mid-level naval officer with experience in the Middle East and Caribbean, May 19, 2013.

73 International Institute of Strategic Studies, *The Military Balance 2012–2013* (London: IISS, 2013).

74 Author Krieger interview with Captain Kevin Kenney, USAF pilot at Lakenheath AB, England, and Red Flag Team Chief for Operation 12-2, Washington DC, May 21, 2013.

Both squadrons hosted each other in traditional "heritage parties" to eat, drink, tell stories, and sing flying songs. In addition, the US squadron collected toys and school supplies to distribute at a local orphanage. This public diplomacy was not formally directed but rather was initiated at the micro level by junior ranking officers seeking to connect with their counterparts. In seeking approval for the endeavor from US embassy staff, the organizer depicted it as a bridge-building opportunity, suggesting the children would forever remember the US pilots in flight suits handing out toys.[75]

The explicit goals of small-unit exercises include enhancing cooperation and building cross-national relationships. The same is true of large operations, such as "Red Flag," an aerial combat exercise that unites members from all US armed services and more than 32 nations in missions that simulate the first five days of war. The missions are fully integrated. International pilots assume leadership roles alongside their US counterparts. In general, US aviators walk away with a sense of greater confidence in their allies' capabilities; an experienced pilot and exercise planner commented on the Singapore squadron, "I was impressed with them – they operated to standards, as well as I would expect any US unit would do."[76] Another suggested, "Young US airmen think we're the best of the best, [and then] see the Brits, Aussies, and others come in and hold their own."[77] Such anecdotes illustrate the reciprocal respect built through traditional military interactions that, by their nature, result in incidental diplomacy.

Critically, a recent Red Flag organizer indicated that he has seen improvement in both performance and cooperation over the years: "when nations show up again, we already know them, and it helps. It greases the skids, and makes it easier to interact."[78] These relationships are built over time and in the intense simulated combat environment of exercises such as Red Flag.

Tactical operations

Military officials recognize the pervasiveness of military diplomatic practice at the tactical level. So much interaction occurs between

[75] Ibid. [76] Ibid.

[77] Author Krieger phone interview with a senior pilot and officer executing a Red Flag exercise, May 23, 2013.

[78] Ibid.

ordinary soldiers and members of the local population, particularly in counterinsurgency warfare, that each operator becomes an ad hoc diplomat for the United States. This recognition is evinced by a number of recent military adaptations associated with the war in Afghanistan. The evolution of counterinsurgency doctrine, which stresses the importance of dismounted patrols – even forgoing sunglasses – to project an aura of approachability, recognizes the impact of daily positive interaction on both security and wider political aims. Changes in military education curricula that emphasize cultural sensitivity and reading context clues from foreign interactions reflect this shift in focus. So does the development of units such as the Marine Corps Lioness units, which were entirely female units that performed their own village-by-village interaction to build trust and relationships with the 50 percent of Afghan and Iraqi society unreachable by male soldiers.

Iraq provides a complementary case study in the evolution of the military's diplomatic practices. The conventional wisdom within the US military holds that its counterinsurgency operations in Iraq ultimately succeeded, and that they did so, in part, because the "Surge" allowed units to leave their strongholds and engage with the local population. They provided a visible and familiar reassurance to an insecure civilian society.

Similarly, US military planners believe that a military presence at the tactical level also facilitates confidence building and trust between third-party factions. They point to examples such as the disputed internal boundaries between Kurdistan and the rest of Iraqi territory. To secure these boundaries from exploitation by terrorists and insurgents, US, Kurd, and Iraqi army units established 27 checkpoints manned by both Iraqis and Kurds. US soldiers acted as the "process police" – forcing both sides to abide by the terms of the agreement: "The [US] military was able to make that deal stick . . . it was confidence-building steps that allowed discussion to occur without acrimony."[79]

Many other examples of tactical-level diplomacy exist in the world of Special Operations. Some Special Forces operators such as Army Green Berets identify themselves with the catchphrase "warrior-diplomats" because their primary role involves evaluating and training internal security forces in partner nations. These operators integrate

[79] Author Krieger confidential interview with military staff officer with extensive combat experience in Iraq, Washington, DC, May 19, 2013.

into local cultures to best assess the strengths and weaknesses of resident armed groups, and to marry the appropriate practices and technology of the US military culture with the foreign one. Prerequisite training stresses cultural practices – such as always eating food the locals offer – to build the necessary credibility to perform tactical diplomacy. Informal diplomacy is so central to this mission that tensions arise in maintaining a balance between following US military doctrine and integrating deeply into local cultures. The iconic Special Forces operator on horseback calling in air strikes with a satellite phone straddles two cultures and must maintain sufficient authenticity in each to be credible.[80]

Military diplomacy as transnational identity

Official defense diplomacy, as well as the direct implication of defense officials in diplomatic activity, constitutes only a small part of the practice of military diplomacy. As some of our earlier examples make clear, military diplomacy often rests on, leverages, and cultivates relationships generated through routine interactions with foreign military personnel. At the same time, self-conscious diplomacy has become integrated into many traditional military activities.[81] Even in the absence of an explicit commitment to diplomacy, a variety of military activities embed de facto micro-level diplomacy in their routines and practices.

US officials stress how these activities socialize their foreign counterparts – how they teach them to understand US values, ways of seeing the world, proper military conduct, and so on. It would be more accurate to characterize the process as bidirectional socialization.[82] US military personnel generally believe that the uniform itself symbolically connects officers of different militaries; it stands for a common martial background and suggests common perspectives.[83] The trust US personnel develop in foreign counterparts provides advantages to both sides of the relationship.[84] As examples in this section suggest, the

80 Author Krieger's multiple conversations with operators in the Special Forces community with extensive intercultural experience in combat settings, Washington, DC, 2012–13.

81 Sending makes a similar point about humanitarian actors in Chapter 9, this volume.

82 Interview with Colin Kahl and all authors' personal observations.

83 Discussion with multiple FAOs; Krieger's and Souma's personal observations.

84 On the importance of trust in alliances, see Mark J. C. Crescenzi, Jacob D. Kathman, Katja B. Kleinberg, and Reed M. Wood, "Reliability, Reputation,

networks created through professional military education, flight school, and other military interactions have important downstream implications for security cooperation.

Flight school

Naval Air Station Pensacola, Florida, nicknamed "the cradle of naval aviation," is the center of all US Naval and Air Force tactical aircrew training. These aviators, the "back-seaters" who specialize in tactical navigation and who operate the aircraft weapons systems, earn their wings through a course of training that includes formal classes, simulator time, and training flights. For several decades now, the United States has trained German, Italian, Singaporean, and Saudi officers side-by-side with US flight students. The training squadrons have also welcomed international flight instructors representing these nations into their ranks.[85]

The US Air Force has also invested in combined international flight training in the form of the Euro-NATO Joint Jet Pilot Training program at Sheppard AFB in Texas. This school is the primary flight-training school for top US Air Force and NATO talent; while all classes have some international presence, many reflect a more equitable 50/50 ratio of US pilots to international ones. Five nations – Germany, Italy, the Netherlands, Norway, and the United States – assign instructor pilots based on their number of students. Other NATO nations, including Canada, Greece, Portugal, Spain, and Turkey provide at least one instructor pilot. The program fact sheet provides an example of the level of integration in this structure: "an American student pilot may have a Belgian instructor pilot, a Dutch flight commander, a Turkish section commander, an Italian operations officer, and a German squadron commander."[86] These programs at Pensacola and Sheppard

and Alliance Formation," *International Studies Quarterly*, 55(2), 2012, 259–274. On trust and cooperation, see Bill McEvily, Vincenzo Perrone, and Akbar Zaheer, "Trust as an Organizing Principle," *Organizational Science*, 14(1), 2003, 91–103. On affective interpersonal ties and cooperation, see Ranjay Gulati, Nitin Nohria, and Akbar Zaheer, "Strategic Networks," *Strategic Management Journal*, 21(3), 2000, 203–215.

85 Author Souma's personal knowledge.

86 ENJJPT, www.sheppard.af.mil/library/factsheetspage/factsheet.asp?fsID=5168, accessed May 27, 2013.

provide just a sample of the international presence in a variety of aviation and other military training units across the armed forces.

In both programs, there is virtually no difference in the training received by US and international flight students. All students and instructors are pooled for scheduling purposes, so US students may be paired with an international instructor, and international students may receive training from an instructor from the United States or any of the several foreign countries. The prerequisite qualifications required to instruct is the same regardless of nationality. Moreover, the students' syllabi are primarily determined by which aircraft each is likely to fly, not their nationality.

For these students and instructors, the international aspect of their training seems normal. US and international flight students meet in class the first day of flight school and work (and socialize) together until graduation day. As most of the instructors were once students in the programs, working with international instructors is a natural extension of what they have experienced from the beginning. Integration with international aviators seems expected and is considered standard practice, normalized through institutions. As an example, the German presence is especially enduring and established, with several *Luftwaffe* Squadrons permanently located in the United States.

The training at Pensacola, Sheppard, and other military flight school locations is designed to provide a foundation for these aviators to work together later, in more advanced settings. Standardization allows for combined exercises and operations without in-depth procedural preparation. The students learn the same standardized communications and aerial administrative procedures, best practices, and basic tactics. Aviators from each nation learn what to expect from the others in the air. They literally speak the same language.

All instruction is conducted in English. All in-flight communication is in English, which conforms to International Civil Aviation Organization standards. Additionally, inter-cockpit communication must be in English. Procedures are adapted to the difficulties this raises for training foreign nationals. For example, as a result of linguistic dissimilarity, students from Saudi Arabia often face the greatest challenge when it comes to clear and concise communications, a required skill for graduation. Saudi students are usually afforded extra preparation through classes that emphasize aviation-related words and phrases. However, grading standards for communications during flights do not vary by student's nationality. "I am always impressed they [Saudi students] can do this in a second language," a US instructor reflects, "They really earn my respect."[87]

Such expressions of "respect" are part and parcel of the development of attitudes about the other that, as other contributors to this volume argue, plays an important role in diplomacy as the management of intersocietal relations. These kinds of institutional incentives, of course, also ensure a large pool of foreign aviators conversant in the language and syntax of US military activity. Ensuring competency in both formal English and the conventions of US communication is an important component of US education of foreign military and defense officials. For example, the Defense Language Institute maintains programs to teach English to foreign military personnel.[88] Some defense officials note that the "true" purpose of the Regional Centers for Security Studies, which provide various classes and seminars to US defense partners, is to teach foreign military and civilian officials "to understand how we talk to them."[89]

Indeed, the daily interaction between students in US military training programs amounts to ongoing micro diplomacy. Because they are embedded in US squadrons, international students experience the US military way of doing things. In the view of US military personnel, this involves firsthand knowledge of the US emphasis on teamwork, attention to detail, candor, and the "US work ethic." US participants note that the amount of individual responsibility placed on students for their own training surprises and challenges many foreign students. For military personnel from autocratic states, the combination of US-style training and greater personal freedom can be particularly challenging.[90]

For US students, these settings provide a sense of understanding of their foreign interlocutors. "I've learned to think about how to work in an international setting," says one US instructor, "I've learned a lot about other nations' air forces, what their missions are, and what constraints they face. I've also asked myself many times, 'How do they

[87] Author Souma interview with experienced US Navy flight instructor, Falls Church, VA, May 17, 2013.

[88] See "About DLIFIC," www.dliflc.edu/about.html, accessed June 13, 2013.

[89] Author Krieger interview with US Defense Department official, Washington DC, May 3, 2013.

[90] Author Krieger interview with Captain Kenney, May 21, 2013; authors Krieger's and Souma's observations.

perceive us?'" This instructor, like most, was a student at NAS Pensacola a few years prior to becoming an instructor: "We bonded as students, because the challenge united us, and because we relied on each other to get through. We shared a goal: to get our wings. It didn't matter what country anyone was from. We worked together, and flew together."[91]

These relationships often survive the flight-training classroom as pilots progress in rank and authority. Students stay in contact via social media and travel and greet each other at exercises as self-identified "brothers and sisters in arms." An explicit goal of the Sheppard program is that "the student pilots and staff instructors of today will be the leaders of NATO's air forces of tomorrow. Having trained together, they will be much better prepared to fight and win together, when the need ever arises."[92] As a case in point, the April 2013 combat fatality of a flight school graduate garnered international expressions of regret via social media and email from his fellow students now serving as officers and aviators in the Italian, German, and Dutch air forces.[93]

Professional Military Education

Flight training is not the only forum for integration in the practice of diplomacy. Professional Military Education is a formal requirement for all members of the US armed forces, designed to educate and train officers and enlisted personnel to move up to higher levels of authority. Focused on a spectrum of issues from civil-military relations to strategy, every such school maintains a number of international slots open to allies and partners. Both US and foreign militaries consider this academic interaction – learning together the complexities and nuances associated with a professionalized military cadre – to be fundamental to professional development. The US Air Force alone educates and trains nearly 12,000 members of partner air forces annually.[94] In fact, as of May 2013, of the world's sitting air chiefs, 24 are graduates

91 Author Souma interview, May 17, 2013 (sentiments shared by authors Krieger and Souma).
92 ENJJPT website.
93 Author Krieger's personal knowledge as garnered from Facebook, email, and other social media correspondence.
94 General Nordy Schwartz, chief of staff of the Air Force, in a speech delivered to The Atlantic Council, April 9, 2012, www.atlanticcouncil.org/events/past-events/the-future-of-the-united-states-air-force-prospects-for-partnerships-and-international-cooperation.

of US Professional Military Education programs, connected to the US system via the students and professors with whom they interacted, and via the educational elements they learned.[95]

Military personnel see these outcomes as an important benefit associated with Professional Military Education.[96] In a speech entitled "The Future of the United States Air Force," then-Chief of Staff of the Air Force General Nordy Schwartz discussed the ease with which the NATO Strategic Airlift Capability was established as a result of four partner nations' air chiefs having been classmates at the US Air War College years prior:

> When airmen, say from Bulgaria and Hungary and Sweden and Poland, during a period of several years each attend the Air War College and formed lasting relationships with each other and with their US counterparts, and then went on to become heads of their respective services, we gained a distinct advantage in efforts such as forming the 12-nation C-17 consortium in Europe known as the Strategic Airlift Capability.[97]

He noted that "many of these interactions, in fact, begin even earlier in a career timeframe, with lieutenants and captains who train and operate together today, and thereby will be better prepared to lead broader multinational efforts as the colonels and generals of tomorrow."[98] He continued, "it should be very clear, therefore, that we place a high premium on individual relationships, which are often just as important as aircraft, spacecraft, and weapon system interoperability and high-tech effects." His message – that the root of cooperation lies in the practice of working together in peacetime, training together in exercises, and learning together in schools – facilitates larger diplomatic efforts in international institutions and beyond.

Embedded diplomacy and the politics of primacy

It should have come as little surprise that official US military diplomacy centers on US-led security governance. Relevant defense officials focus

95 Author Krieger interview with Colonel Michael Fleck.
96 Authors Krieger's and Souma's observations. Souma notes that both international and US students at the Air Command and Staff College valued relationships built during that course of study and sought to maintain contact through social media.
97 General Nordy Schwartz, Atlantic Council Speech, April 9, 2012. 98 Ibid.

much of their activity on managing political-military and military-military relationships. They aim to, among other things, avert crises, maintain and expand US military access, gather intelligence, enhance US diplomatic leverage, and facilitate cognate diplomatic efforts. This is pretty much the stuff of traditional interstate diplomacy, albeit with both a "defense skew" and the specific opportunities created by institutional affiliation with the world's most powerful military force.

The meanings that US military personnel attach to what we have called "unofficial" diplomacy are, in some ways, more interesting. Consider the widespread understanding of these settings and practices as diplomatic in character. This reflects not only a view of diplomacy congruent with the broad approach adopted in this volume but also the kind of attitude one would expect from a military engaged in global security governance. Here, cross-national and inter-temporal comparison would be helpful. To what degree, for example, is the colonization of routine military practices and relationships by the framework of "diplomacy" specific to the United States or a function of broader changes in international politics?

Regardless, two features of unofficial defense diplomacy deserve elaboration. First is the way that what we might term "background hierarchy" inflects it. The importance of the US role reflects its superordinate position in the hierarchy of military capabilities, as does the attractiveness of its training, weaponry, and educational programs. This privileges US knowledge, techniques, and ways of doing. At the same time, US officials see much of what they do in light of equality of opportunity: anyone can prove that he or she is worthy of respect by stepping up and exceling.

But they also stress the importance of gaining knowledge of the other – of understanding the culture of partners and allies – as a means of achieving political and military objectives. Assumptions about the commonality created by wearing the uniform also undergird many spheres of unofficial diplomacy. Here, we have claims about transnational commonality of a kind that implicitly separates military personnel from other foreign interlocutors. Somewhat paradoxically, however, the inclusion of foreign military personnel in US training and education programs seeks to create both that sense of sameness and to socialize foreign militaries to look more like that of the United States. This is a form of governance via replication of similar norms, rules, and procedures.

Second, the rhetoric and practice surrounding a lot of unofficial military diplomacy has interesting implications for Geoffrey Wiseman's insights into US diplomacy. Wiseman argues that one aspect of US "distinctive" diplomacy is a "cultural disposition towards a direct, low-context negotiation style" that has been "accentuated" by its "hegemonic status over the past half century." While a high-context negotiating style "is characterized by an emphasis on process and relationship-building and on indirect, implicit, and non-verbal forms of communication," a low-context style "focuses on results rather than relationships" and is direct and explicit in communication preferences."[99] Much of what military personnel laud about their unofficial diplomacy resonates with low-context styles of interaction; it builds relationships with other military personnel on the common ground of solving problems, mission-oriented activity, and making coordination more efficient. At the same time, the embrace of high-context skills – through, for example, cultural awareness – is resolutely for instrumental purposes.

This, of course, makes a lot of sense in the context of military strategy and operations. But it may make defense diplomacy more congruent with US cultural proclivities than traditional diplomacy. It certainly contributes to a sense that military micro diplomacy and security partnerships are more effective in creating enduring institutional and interstate relationships than traditional diplomatic activity.

Indeed, a core wager of this volume holds that changes in the agents and modalities of diplomacy connect to transformations in international affairs and global order. US defense diplomacy relates to that proposition in ambiguous ways. After all, many of its features long predate the contemporary period. Ship captains in the US Navy have exercised a jurisdictional claim over diplomatic territory as floating ambassadors in every port of call since the founding of the country. Security alliances in the twentieth century demanded that US generals negotiate force agreements and operational details with foreign officials. For example, General Dwight Eisenhower described his role as Supreme Allied Commander thus: "In a place like this the Commanding General must be a bit of a diplomat, lawyer, promoter, salesman, social hound, liar (at least to get out of social affairs), mountebank, actor, Simon Legree, humanitarian, orator and incidentally (and sometimes I

[99] Geoffrey Wiseman, "Distinctive Characteristics of US Diplomacy," *The Hague Journal of Diplomacy*, 6, 2011, 255.

think most damnably incidentally) a soldier."[100] Further, the military's self-awareness and enthusiasm for diplomatic interactions ebbs and flows with historical events and mental models: pre-1963 Vietnam was flooded with US political-military officers embedded in Vietnamese units to educate and professionalize their forces, but internal backlash after the Vietnam War led the army to eschew anything that sounded like foreign military partnership building.

There is, however, a basic trajectory: the breadth and depth of US military diplomacy has expanded in concert with US primacy. US military diplomacy focuses on maintaining a vast network of installations and access, but the existence of this network also endows defense officials with quasi-diplomatic powers and roles. After more than a decade of deep diplomatic involvement in Afghanistan and Iraq, where even low-level soldiers assumed the roles of interlocutor, negotiator, and relationship builder, the army is moving further in the direction of diplomatic jurisdiction. Current Army Chief of Staff General Raymond Odierno envisions the army organized into "regionally aligned forces" or RAFs, which have a permanent relationship with specific geographical regions and the education and training to support them. These RAFs would engage in efforts including "influencing local populations, establishing friendly relations with local leaders, [and] strengthening military-to-military cooperation."[101] The fact that the military views this interaction as "shaping" across the "spectrum of conflict" is indicative of the growing ownership of the diplomatic space as part of a core war-making responsibility.

Such expansion may disempower traditional diplomatic actors. As we have seen, when a single military commander assumes responsibility for an entire region, the resulting centralization of processes facilitates a rapid and coherent analysis of changing dynamics. In comparison, other actors face coordination problems created by the need for different diplomatic agencies and bureaus – divided by country, region, and subject matter – to agree on a consolidated message. Derek Reveron identifies three broad advantages the US military holds

100 Quoted in James C. Humes, *Eisenhower and Churchill: The Partnership That Saved the World* (Roseville, CA: Prima Publishing, 2001), 165.

101 Rosa Brooks, "Portrait of the Army as a Work in Progress," *Foreign Policy*, www.foreignpolicy.com/articles/2014/05/08/portrait_army_work_in_progress_regionally_aligned_forces_raymond_odierno, accessed July 14, 2014.

over traditional diplomatic actors. First, military actors are simply better funded than their traditional diplomatic counterparts. Second, the military is embedded in congressional offices and committees, forming an "impressive infrastructure designed to cultivate relationships on Capitol Hill."[102] The Department of State's reach suffers in comparison. Third, the military formulates diplomatic authority in the authoritative language of national security. These factors disadvantage traditional diplomatic officials in the US government at a time when military actors expand to encompass greater bureaucratic space.

The transfer of diplomatic authority extends beyond bureaucratic power sharing. As we have seen, military actors enjoy access to an expansive network of international relationships independent of traditional diplomatic ties. The authority the military wields over security-related matters provides it with an advantage to the extent that previously diplomatic topics fall under the umbrella of security – such as refugees, climate change, commerce, and telecommunications.

Conclusions

Attitudes within the military concerning its own diplomatic practices vary considerably. Both rank and branch of service shape opinions and awareness of defense diplomacy. For example, while the navy thinks highly of its attachés and foreign area officers, air force culture generally considers attachés and ad hoc military diplomats to be nonessential; indeed, air force officers who take those posts reduce their chances of promotion to high-ranking commands. One Air Force International Affairs officer suggests that in the air force, formal diplomacy is largely ignored because "that's not the tool that butters your bread." In other words, diplomacy is not the military's main task; war fighting is.[103] A common view within the US military holds that diplomacy is little more than a niche capability of little importance compared to expertise in core functions, namely the use of military force. Thus, despite an increasing recognition of the potential impact (not always positive) of foreign interactions, in this view, diplomacy does and should occur primarily as a by-product of war-fighting activities. Still other

102 Reveron, *American Viceroys*.
103 Author Krieger interview, May 21, 2013.

practitioners remain unaware that they are, in fact, regularly engaging in diplomatic activity.

There are indications that the US military is growing increasingly self-reflective with regard to diplomatic activity as a result of recent lessons learned in combat zones. In Iraq and Afghanistan, and other hostile environments, soldiers found themselves conducting micro diplomacy and in many cases taking the lead in nation building. Veterans of these conflicts who have worked alongside official diplomats saw themselves as more effective at conducting diplomacy, in part because of a greater focus on mission accomplishment and a longer-range perspective, perhaps as a function of longer tours of duty.[104]

Some of this perception may derive from the growing multiplicity of roles assigned to military members in combat zones. There, insecurity precludes or complicates engagement by unarmed diplomats, and discussion of military tasks such as security-sector reform occupies the bulk of diplomatic bandwidth.[105] In combat arenas, the military possesses more personnel, more money, and the time to develop relationships, and so it tends to overpower other diplomatic efforts at every level, outpacing and out-engaging the formal civilian diplomatic organizations. The former director of strategy and plans for the US Office of Security Cooperation in Iraq describes his dealings with formal diplomats: "They just didn't roll up their sleeves, put their body armor on and go out of the Green Zone every day and drink three cups of tea; we [the military] had people running all over and doing that engagement."[106]

Regardless of the truth of these perceptions, they highlight the degree that defense diplomacy is an important factor for the US military. It might be an explicit or implicit part of the mission. It may be highly valued or seen as a distraction from core competencies. Yet, defense diplomacy runs through a significant percentage of military activity. Indeed, the fact that standard diplomatic relationships involve an important role for defense diplomacy should come as little surprise.

104 State Department rotations averaged 90 days; see Joshua Hammer, "Uncivil Military," *New Republic*, March 1, 2004. Military tours typically lasted at least one year.

105 Author Krieger interview with former director of strategy and plans for the US Office of Security Cooperation Iraq, Washington, DC, May 19, 2013.

106 Ibid.

More significant is the degree to which the US Department of Defense – which, by definition, is a military institution – has acquired sometimes enormous slices of the totality of US diplomatic interaction.

Military personnel, such as two of the authors of this chapter, often take this role as a natural extension of military affairs. Although the degree and scope to which the US military assumes a diplomatic position remains controversial both within and outside of the Pentagon, it is a significant part of the fabric of US primacy and contemporary international order. In particular note, the global reach of US military power positions the US military as both a source of, and vector for, security governance. At the institutional, state, and micro levels, it creates transnational connections, socializes participants, and disseminates military practices.

In fact, scholarship on international order would benefit from taking more seriously the constitutive role of official and unofficial defense diplomacy, whether in the context of debates over global governance, the infrastructure and architecture of security cooperation, hegemonic stability, or other arenas. US defense diplomacy is deeply implicated in what Tarak Barkawi calls, in Chapter 2, the "contemporary modalities by which states constitute force internationally." Deliberate and inadvertent military diplomacy at the micro level scales up to help structure international politics, while high-level defense diplomacy is often – at least in the US context – difficult to distinguish from traditional diplomatic activity.

9 Diplomats and humanitarians in crisis governance

OLE JACOB SENDING

Introduction

The past two decades of research on globalization is replete with claims about the power of non-state actors and the implied demise or transformation of diplomacy.[1] Claims about the transformation of diplomacy are not new, however. In 1908, for example, a press officer at the German Foreign Office opined that times were gone when "the fates of nations were decided in small, closed circles of courtly and diplomatic individuals ... the public opinion of the nations has acquired a degree of influence on political decisions previously unimaginable."[2] This serves as a useful reminder that the question of the transformation of diplomacy or of diplomats' loss of core tasks is not only an old one but one that begets a set of more fundamental questions: What characterizes diplomacy as a social practice? How does diplomacy relate to and possibly

I would like to thank the participants at the workshops in March 2011 at McGill University and at the New School in New York in September 2012, the reviewers as well as Morten Skumsrud Andersen, Stein S. Eriksen, Halvard Leira, Bjørn Skogmo, and Andreas Øien Stensland for comments on different versions of this chapter.

1 Jessica Matthews, "Power Shift," *Foreign Affairs*, 76(1), 1997, 50–66; David Held and Anthony McGrew, eds., *Governing Globalization: Power, Authority, and Global Governance* (Cambridge: Polity Press, 2002); Margareth Keck and Kathryn Sikkink, *Activists Beyond Borders* (Ithaca, NY: Cornell University Press, 1998); Paul Sharp, "Who Needs Diplomats? The Problems of Diplomatic Representation," *International Journal*, 52(4), 1997, 609–632; Andrew F. Cooper, "Beyond Representation," *International Journal*, 53(1), 1978, 173–178.

2 Quoted in Dominik Geppert, "German and British Ways with the Press," in Markus Mösslang and Torsten Riotte, eds., *The Diplomats' World: A Cultural History of Diplomacy 1815–1904* (Oxford: Oxford University Press), 133–164, 134. For a comprehensive analysis of the role of the press and parliament in the formation of foreign policy as a separate realm of political action, see Halvard Leira, *The Emergence of Foreign Policy: Knowledge, Discourse, History* (Oslo: University of Oslo, Unipub, 2011).

shape the operations of non-diplomatic actors? What is at stake in bringing some event or phenomenon within the remit of diplomacy?

I seek to answer these questions by analyzing the relationship between diplomacy and humanitarian action. My answer is that it is not really possible to understand the character of humanitarian action – and the ideology of humanitarianism – without analyzing how diplomacy defines the conditions of possibility for its particular form and its mode of operation. As such, diplomatic practices reproduce the system within which humanitarian action operates and therefore structure world politics in fundamental yet often unacknowledged ways.

I focus on the relationship between humanitarian action and diplomacy for three principal reasons. First, humanitarian action has expanded considerably during the past two decades, and diplomats and humanitarian actors engage one another on a range of issues that are high on the international agenda.[3] Examples include the unfolding conflict in Syria, debates about "humanitarian space" in Afghanistan, and the invocation of the humanitarian principle of "protection of civilians" in the intervention in Libya and Cote D'Ivoire. Second, whereas humanitarians invoke claims to universality – "humanity" – and thus seek to transcend territoriality, diplomats represent territorial units. This makes the exploration of their relationship important as a tool to unearth the distinctive features of both. Third, because of the importance of humanitarian actors in global efforts to respond to emergencies, it is important to ask whether and how humanitarian actors take on diplomatic functions as they (claim to) represent victims of humanitarian crises and speak on their behalf.

I conduct a double reading of the relationship between humanitarian action and diplomacy.[4] I first define diplomacy and humanitarianism, respectively, in terms of distinct cultures and offer a stylized account of diplomacy as being organized around a "thin" culture, and humanitarianism organized around a "thick" culture. These respective cultures and modes of operation are constructed in no small part through boundary-drawing vis-à-vis one another.

3 Michael N. Barnett, *The International Humanitarian Order* (London: Routledge, 2010).

4 This is inspired by Richard K. Ashley, "Untying the Sovereign State: A Double Reading of the Anarchy Problematique," *Millennium – Journal of International Studies*, 17, 1988, 227–262.

I highlight the attention to form and process among diplomats, and to proximity to those in need among humanitarian actors. On this reading, I stay close to diplomats' and humanitarian actors' practice categories, exploring how they claim authority and describe their differentiation from one another.

While it is important to understand the meaning that actors attribute or draw from the particular practices they engage in, it is crucially important to situate and account for these practices using analytical categories that can shed critical light on them. I therefore shift gear to a more structural reading, analyzing how the social form of diplomacy structures humanitarian action. I argue that diplomacy makes up an infrastructure through which both diplomats and humanitarian actors operate, and that diplomacy has a doxic feature, as can be seen in how the boundary drawn by both humanitarians and by diplomats is principally drawn from within the remit of diplomacy. Diplomacy is, on this reading, a specific way of organizing political processes – geared toward reproducing the state as the naturalized venue for political mobilization and agency, thereby foreclosing debates about how states, and diplomacy, are implicated in the suffering of those who are not their citizens. At the same time, humanitarian actors typically step in to mobilize resources and demand agency to save distant strangers from a claim of standing outside of politics and thus also as operating partly outside formal diplomatic channels, thereby also displacing, albeit in a different way, debates about political responsibility for the causes and consequences of humanitarian crises.

Culture and constituencies

The identification of core elements of diplomacy is less straightforward than one might expect. We may, for example, draw up a list of tasks performed by diplomats and see if others, too, are performing such tasks. And if we can tick a given number of boxes – representation, communication, negotiation, for example – then that constitutes diplomatic work. Or we can differentiate diplomats from other actors by adding prefixes (celebrity diplomacy, NGO diplomacy, etc.). But none of this tells us much about the structures through which diplomats operate, or how diplomats – and others – attribute meaning to what they do.

To move beyond an analysis of actors' attributes, I draw on the analytical framework presented in the Introduction – types of authority claims and the relationship between representation and governance – and do so on the basis of an ideal-typical specification of the culture that can be said to define diplomacy and humanitarianism, respectively. Hedley Bull defined diplomatic culture as "the common stock of ideas and values possessed by the official representatives of states."[5] Neumann has noted that this is an overly ideational reading of culture and as such misses out on central aspects of diplomacy.[6] I use "culture" here in a specific way – to refer to ideal-typical features of a set of tasks that we typically group together as making up a distinct way of doing things and over which some actors' claims of a level of jurisdictional control.[7] I therefore conceptualize culture in terms of the relationship between the diplomat and that which the diplomat represents (and conversely for humanitarians). The tasks that these actors perform and the skills that are judged as important by relevant others flow from the character of the relationship between the actor and that which he or she claims to represent.[8] Moreover, culture is here seen in generic terms as that which enables communication and evaluation. It is a view of culture that does not presume that actors have internalized certain norms or dispositions. Rather, culture is a set of criteria that others use in granting or withholding recognition.[9] In short, I locate the driver of both stability and change not in omnipotent discourses, nor in internalized norms, but

5 Hedley Bull, *The Anarchical Society: A Study of Order in World Politics* (London: Macmillan, 1977), 316.

6 Iver B. Neumann, "Returning Practice to the Linguistic Turn: The Case of Diplomacy," *Millennium: Journal of International Studies*, 32(3), 2002, 627–652; Vincent Pouliot, *International Security in Practice: The Politics of NATO-Russia Diplomacy* (Cambridge: Cambridge University Press, 2010).

7 See the discussion in the Introduction about professions and their tasks.

8 This emphasis is inspired by the work of Andrew Abbott, "Linked Ecologies: States and Universities as Environments for Professions," *Sociological Theory*, 23(2), 2005, 245–274, 248. See also Leonard Seabrooke, Chapter 7, this volume.

9 Note that I do not use "recognition" here in the formal or legal sense of "diplomatic recognition." Rather, I use it to refer to the social dynamics by which actors evaluate self and other in particular contexts, which is typically structured in hierarchical ways. For a discussion and application along these lines – inspired by Bourdieu – see George Steinmetz, "The Colonial State as a Social Field: Ethnographic Capital and Native Policy in the German Overseas Empire before 1914," *American Review of Sociology*, 73, 2008: 589–612. See also Ole Jacob Sending, *The Politics of Expertise: Competing for Authority in Global Governance* (Ann Arbor: University of Michigan Press, 2015).

in the shared registers for communication and evaluation that actors in a given social space use.[10] Thus, culture is a descriptive term for the raw material from which actors draw when acting, and the criteria of evaluation that others use to assess such actions. Without a minimum of shared criteria of what is appropriate, effective, and so on, there is no basis from which to seek or be accorded recognition. In diplomatic circles, recognition may be accorded to those who can "hold a bracket" in negotiations vis-à-vis other states,[11] or to those who can subtly signal different meanings to various audiences when delivering a speech. Diplomats recognize and value certain skills in other diplomats even when these represent and advance different interests than they do themselves. Seen in this way, diplomacy is reproduced and may change over time in and through how different actors search for and are granted recognition. It changes when the criteria of evaluation change, and these criteria are themselves very much at stake in the interaction between diplomats and other actors. As I explore later, however, diplomats often prevail because diplomatic practices of how to engage others are already institutionalized.

Friends and strangers

What unites diplomats is at the same time what separates them, namely, the representation of distinct polities. For this reason, diplomacy is characterized by a thin culture in that it places a premium on communication and the management of friction in the absence of shared values.[12] Humanitarian actors, by contrast, share a thick culture in that what constitutes humanitarian action is defined by a set of substantive values that underwrites their claim to both represent and act on others.[13] Underlying this difference in the constitution of

[10] On this, see Ian Hurd, Chapter 1, this volume. See also Ole Jacob Sending and Iver B. Neumann, "Banking on Power: How Some Practices in an International Organization Anchor Others," in Emmanuel Adler and Vincent Pouliot, eds., *International Practices* (Cambridge: Cambridge University Press, 2011), 231–254.

[11] On this, see Iver B. Neumann, *At Home with the Diplomats* (Ithaca, NY: Cornell University Press, 2012), 113–115.

[12] Paul Sharp, "For Diplomacy: Representation and the Study of International Relations," *International Studies Review*, 1(1), 1999, 33–57.

[13] The distinction between "thick" and "thin" and between "friends" and "strangers" is arguably somewhat stark. Humanitarian actors are every bit as instrumental and strategic as other actors, as, for example, Clifford Bob has

diplomatic and humanitarian work is a more general mechanism: the characteristics of diplomatic work and humanitarian work, respectively, flow from the character of the relation that is established and continually reproduced between the actor and the object that the actor seeks to represent and/or govern.[14] Diplomats represent territorial units whose existence is at one level institutionally given. Or rather, diplomacy organizes political relations in such a way that the image of the state as a distinct actor with agency to control outcomes is continually reproduced through diplomatic practice.[15] Humanitarian actors similarly reproduce the governance object (i.e., suffering individuals) that is the rationale for their existence, but there is a significant difference insofar as humanitarians operate within the parameters set by diplomacy as a way of organizing politics between polities.

Strangers in a thin culture

Diplomatic culture places a premium on consulting others, of taking note of others' concerns, as Pouliot's contribution to this volume (Chapter 3) also demonstrates. Bourdieu notes, as a more general observation on the search for recognition, that an actor is "continuously led to take the point of view of others on himself, to adopt their point of view so as to discover and evaluate in advance how he will be seen and defined by them."[16] This description fits diplomatic culture well and helps explain how and why diplomats are so attentive to form and why "diplomatic" is associated with having tact and being

shown in his *The Marketing of Rebellion: Insurgents, Media, and International Activism* (Cambridge: Cambridge University Press, 2005). Conversely, diplomatic culture can, as Pouliot demonstrates in Chapter 3, this volume, be quite "thick" and be characterized by distinct substantive orientations. See also Geoffrey Wiseman, "Pax Americana: Bumping into Diplomatic Culture," *International Studies Perspectives*, 6(4), 2005, 409–430. See also Cecelia Lynch's Chapter 6 in this book on the Christian roots of modern-day diplomacy. Cf Iver Neumann, "Euro-centric Diplomacy: Challenging but Manageable," *European Journal of International Relations*, 18, 2012, 299–321.

14 I explore in more detail the character and effects of the relationship between those that govern and the objects being governed in Sending, *The Politics of Expertise*.

15 For a discussion of the role of the concept of representation, adopted from Roman law, in Hobbes's writings on sovereignty, see Ben Holland, "Sovereignty as Dominium?" *International Studies Quarterly*, 54, 2010, 449–480. See also Benno Teschke, *The Myth of 1648: Class, Geopolitics, and the Making of Modern International Relations* (London: Verso, 2003).

16 Pierre Bourdieu, *Pascalian Mediations* (Cambridge: Polity Press, 2000), 166.

sympathetic to others' views in ordinary language. In that sense, diplomacy is about maintaining and reproducing a set of tools for making communication between distinct units possible. For example, the speeches of state representatives during the opening of the UN General Assembly are a testament to the ritualized – and highly scripted – character of diplomacy: all speeches start by praising others for their efforts, of thanking the chair, of duly noting past achievements, and for generally couching criticisms of others in language that appears trivial to outsiders but carries a specific meaning for diplomats.[17] This feature of diplomacy is inherently linked to its thinness: ritualizing and regularizing the representation of and interaction between polities not only reinforces, or recognizes, states' differences but also provides a substitute for the lack of shared substantive values and political outlook.

Diplomats are in this sense usefully treated as "professional strangers." Building on Sasson Sofer's observation about diplomats as "strangers," Sharp argues the following:

> Diplomats ... are examples of a particular kind of stranger. Like other strangers, they seek to become familiar with and to those with whom they have relations. Unlike them, however, they also work to maintain a distance. This is not just the distance that all professionals – doctors, lawyers, teachers – need to prevent personal relations getting in the way of what they sometimes must do. It is a distance bound up with their professional identity. They are, as it were, professional strangers and need to remain so to do their job.[18]

Operating within a system that is geared toward the recognition of difference, management of friction, and the perpetuation of lines of communication, diplomats seek to acquaint themselves with the political situation where they are posted and court relations with government and other stakeholders, but they are by definition strangers. The

17 See, for example, the analysis of the importance of the ceremonial in maintaining good relations between France and Germany after the French Revolution by Verena Steller, "The Power of Protocol: On the Mechanisms of Symbolic Action in Diplomacy in Franco-German Relations, 1871–1914," in Markus Mösslang and Torsten Riotte, eds., *The Diplomats' World: A Cultural History of Diplomacy 1815–1904* (Oxford: Oxford University Press, 2008).

18 Paul Sharp, *Diplomatic Theory of International Relations* (Cambridge: Cambridge University Press, 2009), 99–100. Sason Sofer, "The Diplomat as Stranger," *Diplomacy and Statecraft*, 8(3), 1997, 179–186.

reference in diplomatic circles of the dangers of diplomats "going native" and of the practice of having diplomats circulate between different postings abroad is a reflection of this institutionalized ideal of maintaining a professional distance.[19]

This is reflected in diplomats' self-descriptions. When asked about what diplomacy is, diplomats offer a range of different formulations: "representation," "advance national interests," "implement foreign policy," and "negotiate and communicate." But all diplomats interviewed for this project sought to differentiate themselves from other actors – be it line ministries, humanitarian actors, religious actors, corporations – by emphasizing that they are in charge of the totality of national interests and are thus tasked with balancing sectoral interests against one another. One described the difference with line ministries as follows:

> Line ministries will often operate within a national frame of reference ... We offer a global reality check – a filter if you like. I do think that we have – and I know that many refer to us as being arrogant and whatnot – seen different countries and the realities there and thus offer a different frame of reference.[20]

This may seem like a dated or extreme view, given the generally recognized importance of line ministries operating through transgovernmental networks. Nonetheless, the stress on capturing the totality of national interests and of being in charge of coordinating different inputs is a common theme. Another diplomat noted, for example, that issue-specific experts would typically not understand the whole international context.[21] The accent here is placed on being knowledgeable about other actors' (states') concerns, and taking these into account when advancing and formulating national interests. It concerns making the national frame of reference less dominant and inserting the 'reality and concerns of other countries. The same diplomat also pointed out, however, that those representing line ministries were often quite quick to learn how to operate as they were among peers within the same issue area. Similarly, a representative of a humanitarian organization that

19 See, for example, John Leczowski, *Full Spectrum Diplomacy and Grand Strategy* (Lanham, MD: Lexington Books, 2011), 108.

20 Interview, official with the Ministry of Foreign Affairs (MFA), Oslo, Norway, March 8, 2011.

21 Interview, MFA official, Oslo, Norway, May 10, 2011.

was involved in the campaign to ban cluster munitions said that they "learned over time how to deal with states"[22] and to operate as diplomats. Interestingly, tensions emerged within the humanitarian caucus over how far those within the secretariat of the Cluster Munitions Coalition (CMC), who were responsible for negotiating with states, could or should go in terms of accommodating states. The same representative also noted, "I think some diplomats were a bit scared of some of the NGOs that operated in the hallways of the negotiation room. They were important for the CMC as a whole for their advocacy vis-à-vis the general public, but they could also jeopardize our relations with some key states."[23] Perhaps the most clear-cut expression of the distinctiveness of diplomatic culture is found in the following description of the "added value" of diplomats relative to other actors, where the emphasis is very much on the unique skill set of a trained diplomat to gauge others' reactions, to know what are pet issues and so-called "red flags":

> What you say and how you say it is extremely important in these settings. If you say the wrong things, even often just using the wrong words, you've destroyed the whole thing. And you can win over important allies by including key words in the speech or text that you know they care strongly about. You also signal support to others through body language and eye contact so as to make sure that they get that this paragraph here is for you etc. An "expert" will be totally lost in such a setting if he or she does not know how to operate. What are the different states' pet issues? What are the red flags? How far can you push that state? How do you win over other states? Who are the most important actors in this setting? All of this is the purview of the diplomat, and it takes time to perfect this skill and the network required to operate effectively.[24]

The premium placed on the feel for other actors' interests and concerns is an instantiation of a diplomatic culture organized around making communication possible across political units. Diplomats claim a position of superiority to adjudicate between and put into a broader picture the interests and views advanced by actors representing "mere" issue-specific expertise or sectorial interests. They claim to represent the state *tout court*, doing so by subsuming other actors' concerns and views within a register that aims to mediate between the inside and the

[22] Interview, official with Norwegian Peoples Aid, Norway, February 16, 2011.
[23] Ibid. [24] Interview, MFA official Oslo, Norway, March 8, 2011.

outside of the state. Importantly, diplomatic practice also prevails in settings where, for example, representatives from line ministries meet and head delegations such as in some of the UN's specialized agencies. This influence is also found in the professional culture and orientation of staff in international organizations, where issue-specific expertise and bureaucratic norms are put into a diplomatic register as civil servants engage member states. The establishment of the League of Nations, for example, was heavily shaped by diplomatic practice:

> There was in the Secretariat of the League of Nations a diplomatic or rather foreign office atmosphere. The daily routine of the officials necessitated contacts with diplomatic representatives and the permanent delegates accredited to the League. On missions at home or in other countries one of the first steps undertaken by officials was to get in touch with the foreign office. Moreover, a good deal of the social life of the official was diplomatic.[25]

This diplomatic orientation – in terms of who to interact with and how work was organized – was subsequently the template for the UN Secretariat and for the regulations of the international civil service that was institutionalized from the late 1940s onward.[26] As such, also non-diplomatic actors partake in and adapt to diplomatic practices, and the associative evaluative criteria that dominate them. This does not mean that diplomatic actors necessarily remain dominant, but that diplomatic practices proliferate and are being used also by non-diplomatic ones.

Friends in a thick culture

In contrast to diplomats, humanitarians can be said to share a substantive commitment that cuts across territorial units, namely, (the claim to) humanity and universality and offering relief to suffering individuals.[27] Humanitarianism is thus defined by reference not only to international legal treatises, notably international humanitarian law. It is more fundamentally shaped by the idea or claim that there is a

[25] Egon Ferdinand Ranshofen-Wertheimer, *The Position of the Executive and Administrative Heads of the United Nations International Organizations* (Washington, DC: Carnegie Endowment of International Peace, 1945), 403.

[26] See Sending, *The Politics of Expertise*, chap. 2.

[27] Didier Fassin, "Heart of Humanness: The Moral Economy of Humanitarian Intervention," in Didier Fassin and Mariella Pandolfi, *Contemporary States of Emergency* (New York: Zone Books, 2010), 269–293.

common humanity and that suffering individuals should be helped on the principle of needs only.[28] They are also – and most importantly – what defines humanitarian action as nonpolitical. Hugo Slim has observed that the humanitarian tradition has a "strong conviction that an ethic of restraint, kindness and repair in war is universal, a trans-cultural phenomenon that is found in all peoples."[29] The relationship between humanitarian professionals and those that they represent is thus not only non-territorial, it is also infused with a moral ideal of care for distant others.[30]

This amounts to a thick culture in that there is a set of substantive objectives around which humanitarian activity is organized. For humanitarians, there is a premium on "speaking out" and letting the world know about abuse, atrocities, and suffering. Humanitarianism can thus be said to be anchored in a claim to moral authority that is outside and above history, politics, and territorial borders.[31] The difference with diplomacy is striking, as it is organized around the representation of and communication between distinct polities recognized in their independence and potential difference. Humanitarians' professional identity is in this way tied to identification with victims of humanitarian crises: they offer life-saving relief and claim to speak on behalf of victims, and they draw their authority as participants in global governance in large part by their ability to access and convey information and knowledge from their presence in and intimate knowledge of what is going on in conflict zones.

The ideal of *temoignage* – witnessing – is here central, as is the direct interaction, through medical treatment and food delivery, between humanitarians and those to whom relief is offered. As several authors have argued, humanitarian organizations' extensive use of images of suffering can be seen as a technique for producing proximity, of

[28] Michael Barnett and Thomas Weiss, "Humanitarianism: A Brief History of the Present," in Michael Barnett and Thomas Weiss, eds., *Humanitarianism in Question: Politics, Power, Ethics* (Ithaca, NY: Cornell University Press, 2008), 1–48.

[29] Hugo Slim, "Humanitarianism with Borders? NGOs, Belligerent Military Forces and Humanitarian Action," paper for ICVA Conference on NGOs in a Changing World Order: Dilemmas and Challenges, February 14, 2003, 1.

[30] On suffering and the "politics of pity," see Luc Boltanski, *Distant Suffering: Morality, Media, and Politics* (Cambridge: Cambridge University Press, 1999).

[31] Stephen Hoopgood, "Moral Authority, Modernity and the Politics of the Sacred," *European Journal of International Relations*, 15(2), 2009, 229–255.

bridging the distance between the suffering individuals and the constituencies that fund humanitarian work.[32] Thus, if diplomats are professional strangers, humanitarians can be said to be professional "friends" inasmuch as they seek to save, bear witness for, and speak on behalf of civilians in need. Then-president of Médicins Sans Frontières (MSF) James Orbinski expressed this notion of a professional ethic of friendship when he noted that "Proximity for MSF means that we wish to be and remain in solidarity, in actual physical contact with the populations in danger that we serve, and whose suffering we seek to address."[33]

Humanitarian actors perform a range of tasks that are similar to those of diplomats: they negotiate, report, communicate as they are engaged in representing others, speaking on their behalf, and also acting on them in terms of offering relief. But they do not see themselves as diplomats or describe their work as being diplomatic in character. Larry Minear notes that diplomacy is seen as "well beyond – and quite separate from – what [humanitarians] do."[34] This is linked to humanitarians' well-known self-identification as operating outside the political realm.[35] Being asked whether they are engaged in politics, one representative argued, for example, "We defend humanitarian principles and seek to influence decision makers to adhere to them. But this is not politics, it is advocating on behalf of humanitarian principles."[36] This view was reinforced also by MFA officials with the Foreign Ministry in Norway working on humanitarian issues, one noting, "What is distinct about humanitarian work inside the MFA is that it is in principle apolitical."[37] This is a testament to the substantive values that humanitarian actors use to differentiate themselves from others and to seek recognition for their distinctive role and authority to self-regulate what they do.

32 Lisa Malkki, "Speechless Emissaries: Refugees, Humanitarianism, and Dehistoricization," *Cultural Anthropology*, 11(3), 1996, 377–404.
33 James Orbinski, "On the Meaning of SPHERE Standards to States and Other Humanitarian Actors," lecture delivered in London, December 3, 1998, p. 2.
34 Larry Minear, "The Craft of Humanitarian Diplomacy," in Larry Minear and Hazel Smith, eds., *Humanitarian Diplomacy: Practitioners and Their Craft* (Tokyo: United Nations University Press, 2007), 8.
35 David Chandler, "The Road to Military Humanitarianism: How the Human Rights NGOs Shaped a New Humanitarian Agenda," *Human Rights Quarterly*, 23(3), 2001, 678–700; Michael Barnett, *Empire of Humanity: A History of Humanitarianism* (Ithaca, NY: Cornell University Press, 2011).
36 Interview, official at Norwegian Refugee Council, Oslo, Norway, February 10, 2011.
37 Interview, MFA official, Oslo, Norway, January 20, 2011.

The set of humanitarian principles that make up a thick culture is important not only in producing conformity among humanitarian actors in terms of agreement on what is at stake in doing humanitarian work but also in drawing boundaries to other actors outside of the humanitarian realm. Indeed, the maintenance of distance to things political – as in the case of debates about "humanitarian space" – is integral to the constitution of humanitarian objects of governance and thus also to the representation and governance that humanitarian actors engage in. The construction and reproduction of humanitarian relief as a distinct set of tasks and of suffering individuals as a group are therefore central to the representation and governing that humanitarian actors engage in. The insistence on an apolitical stance – as manifest in the principles of independence, impartiality, and not least neutrality – persists despite humanitarians' gradual expansion to act on and be concerned also with the causes of conflicts.[38] The boundary drawing by humanitarian actors between humanitarian work and political work would not succeed were it not for the commitment to – and mutual evaluation of – others with reference to such a set of shared substantive commitments. If an actor that claims to be humanitarian is seen by other humanitarians to violate core humanitarian principles, it is not to be trusted. One humanitarian actor noted, for example, that "I do not listen if I hear USAID talk about humanitarian principles. What they are doing in Afghanistan completely contradicts humanitarian principles."[39]

This type of boundary drawing is intimately related to a claim to jurisdictional control over certain tasks. As one close observer notes about debates about humanitarian space and humanitarians' relations with other actors:

> The main issue seems to be a feeling that humanitarian NGOs want to put *moral boundaries around what can rightfully be considered humanitarian action.* In doing so, they seem to be suggesting that such boundaries to humanitarian action are not about activities (*what* is being done: food, water, shelter etc.) but agents and motives (*who* is doing these activities and for what reason).[40]

[38] See the distinction drawn between "alchemical" and "relief" organizations made by Barnett, *Empire of Humanity.*

[39] Interview, NRC official, Oslo, Norway, February 10, 2011.

[40] Slim, "Humanitarians with Borders," p. 1. Emphasis added.

If the universalism of humanitarian ideals is what shields humanitarian actors from regarding themselves as political, then the practical mechanism through which this is made possible is the insistence that their advocacy flows from their role as bearing witness. Because they are present in conflict areas, and because they give victims of humanitarian crises shelter, food, and medicine – humanitarian actors argue – they not only claim to represent those who cannot speak for themselves, but bearing witness is in itself a key source of humanitarian actors' authority vis-à-vis that of diplomats and others. They are present in conflict zones and can report to others what is going on, and they can thereby fuse an objectified reporting mode based on assessments of lives lost and medicine needed with a personalized, morally charged testimony about suffering. MSF describes how their authority flows:

> Directly from . . . experience in the field, through medical data and eyewitness accounts . . . If we speak of government forces pillaging villages and burning food stocks, we do so because our medical responsibility includes asking caretakers in our feeding centres why their children are malnourished. Conceiving of fieldwork as a filter for advocacy initiatives implies that we are obliged to report what is happening when faced with the consequences. It also implies that we confront political actors with their responsibility. However, we do not propose political solutions.[41]

Such advocacy is either seen to be referencing universal principles, in which case it is a matter of holding states to account for their legal obligations, or it is reporting on or serving as a channel of communication from those in need to the international community. But here, a tension runs through the humanitarian community: the International Committee of the Red Cross (ICRC) is cautious about how it handles information gathered in conflict zones because of concern that were it to publish this information, it might be denied future access. MSF was established – as the official version goes – in opposition to the silence of the ICRC about the behavior of the parties to the conflict over the Biafra secession.[42] MSF thus places a premium on bearing witness relative to others, as it sees other humanitarian organizations' silence about what they observe as morally untenable. Givoni provides a

[41] Marc DuBois, "Civilian Protection and Humanitarian Advocacy: Strategies and (False?) Dilemmas," *Humanitarian Exchange Magazine*, no. 39, 2008, 1.

[42] Rony Baumann, "Médicins Sans Frontieres and the ICRC: Matters of Principle," *International Review of the Red Cross*, 94(888), Winter 2012.

somewhat different interpretation: the MSF was established in no small part because it could help bolster the status of medical experts in humanitarian relief while offering medical doctors the opportunity to act out their professional identity without borders:

At a time when humanitarian expertise was only starting to take shape, MSF was viewed by its founders as a tool for bolstering the role of medical experts in the aid apparatus ... MSF's members, who professed that they were not "secular saints" but "men and women who have chosen a profession whose principal end is to serve humanity, and which they intend to implement so as to realise this purpose."[43]

Both interpretations are valid and together they offer what I take to be a crucially important point: the relationship between humanitarianism and diplomacy cannot be grasped by only exploring ideal typical differences at the level of value systems or claims to authority. It must also rest on an effort to unearth the substantive skills and forms of knowledge that have come to dominate different organizations: for MSF, medical knowledge prevails as the register from which the organization and seeks to differentiate itself and carve out operational space. For the ICRC, by contrast, its status as guardian of international humanitarian law and access to governments (at the price of confidentiality) structures how it construes its relationship with those in need and how it claims authority.[44]

I have focused on the distinct features ("culture") of diplomacy and humanitarianism and have done so by looking at how they construe the relationship to those that they (claim to) represent and the

[43] Michal Givoni, "Humanitarian Governance and Ethical Cultivation: Médicins Sans Frontieres and the Advent of the Expert-Witness," *Millennium – Journal of International Studies*, 40(1), 2011, 43–63, 52.

[44] Note that there are differences between types of humanitarian organizations – between service delivery organizations and advocacy organizations, and between what Barnett calls "alchemical" (Oxfam, CARE) and "emergency" humanitarian organizations (ICRC, MSF). Nonetheless, the proximity to those in need is a crucial ingredient of their claim to representation, and thus authority. How those claims are couched and rendered effective vis-à-vis both state diplomats and other constituencies, however, has changed significantly over time. Humanitarian worker's eyewitness account is increasingly coupled with so-called needs assessments produced through survey methods. See Margie Buchanan-Smith, "How the Sphere Project Came into Being: A Case Study of Policy-Making in the Humanitarian Aid Sector and the Relative Influence of Research," *ODI Working Paper*, 215, 2003. See also Barnett, *Empire of Humanity*.

attendant practices and skills that characterize both humanitarian and diplomatic action. This analysis has stayed rather close to humanitarian and diplomatic actors' practice categories. It is now necessary to shift gears and adopt a different reading, focused on the structural conditions within which these distinct types of activities emerge and evolve. In doing so, a new dimension emerges, where diplomacy is marked by a social form through which one particular actor, the state, is continually reproduced as a sovereign and thus with agency.[45] I discuss two dimensions of this feature of diplomacy: as an infrastructure through which humanitarian actors act as they engage in advocacy, negotiations, and the delivery of relief, and as a grammar of politics, against which humanitarianism defines itself.

Diplomacy as a social form

I noted earlier that diplomacy is organized around the representation of independent or different territorial units. This implies that while diplomacy may very well take place between other types of polities that are not organized in terms of exclusive territorial boundaries, it is nonetheless a *spatial* extension of the territoriality of a polity since it makes possible and organizes relations with other polities. Diplomacy extends the reach of the state (through embassies) and establishes practices for states to meet and act together (through multilateral fora, see Pouliot, Chapter 3). This spatial extension of the state is generally seen to be limited by the nature of the task of representation, as it is not seen to include governing. If, say, a Swedish diplomat sought publicly to persuade the citizens of France to elect a particular candidate in an election or if the German Embassy in Washington, DC, financially supported a particular political party in US elections, there would be strong political (and diplomatic) reactions.[46]

[45] Diplomacy may serve to reproduce other polities as well. The point is that it is fundamentally about reproducing some type of actor with agency vis-à-vis others. The discussion of diplomacy as social form is based on discussions with Iver B. Neumann.

[46] For sure, a central part of what states do through their embassies in other countries is to attempt to govern or shape behavior or decisions in some way. This is particularly the case for powerful states – witness the United States and the USSR during the Cold War. For an account of the role of the Central Intelligence Agency in other countries, often using embassies as cover, see Tim Weiner, *A Legacy of Ashes* (New York: Random House, 2007).

For sure, the system of diplomatic representation aids and legitimizes a host of governing efforts, even coercive ones as the chapters by Barkawi and Krieger, Souma, and Nexon demonstrate. This legitimizing function is effective precisely because diplomacy is generally seen to exclude the meddling in other states' domestic affairs. In diplomatic protocol and practice, a diplomat, qua representative of a state, is not supposed to meddle in the internal political affairs of another state, but to advance particular interests, negotiate agreements, and convey concerns, even threats, through counterparts at the appropriate level who represent another state. Representation therefore implies more than that one actor – the diplomat – represents one particular state. It also implies that diplomacy is about representation rather than governance on the territory of another state. It is no coincidence that the relations (and representation) between donors and so-called partner countries (those that get so-called development assistance) are generally described in terms of development rather than diplomacy.[47] The funding involved and the particular type of governing project in question – acting on and transforming other countries – is categorized as development first and diplomacy second precisely because it has to do with something that is outside of, even possibly opposed to, diplomacy as a form of interaction between formally equal states.[48]

At the most fundamental level, therefore, diplomacy is linked to the reproduction of the state as distinct from its environment and as the naturalized venue for the mobilization of resources to achieve collective, or public, goals. Diplomacy constitutes, I submit, a particular method for the continual drawing of the boundary of the state vis-à-vis its environment at the same time as diplomats draw in and mobilize non-diplomatic and non-state actors in their work. It is in this sense that diplomacy constitutes an infrastructure – one that privileges some practices over others. The practices that make up diplomacy set up some actors as content- and process-independent authorities to determine where, and how, the boundary of the state is to be drawn. For

[47] I base this observation in part on my own experience from working in the Minister of International Development's Policy Analysis Unit at the Norwegian Ministry of Foreign Affairs, where the category of development prevailed over that of diplomacy in discussions about those countries that received aid.

[48] On this, see Costas Constaninou Constantinou, "Between Statecraft and Humanism: Diplomacy and Its Forms of Knowledge," *International Studies Review*, 15(2), 2013, 141–162.

Timothy Mitchell, this boundary "never marks a real exterior . . . It is a line drawn internally, within the network of institutional mechanisms through which a certain social and political order is maintained."[49] Diplomacy helps make this continual process of re-drawing boundaries naturalized and doxic.

In James Der Derian's genealogical account, diplomacy is conceptualized as the "mediation of estrangement."[50] Nonetheless, the very practice of mediation also reinforces or reproduces the distinctiveness and difference between the estranged units. As such, diplomacy is arguably as much about the perpetuation of distinctiveness as it is about the mediation of estrangement since the social form of diplomacy is first and foremost geared toward making every unit or actor (polity) distinct from every other – as being bounded, thus needing representatives posted elsewhere to represent it. At one level, this is trivial, since there should be no need to mediate between units that are not estranged and therefore not distinct. At another level, however, diplomacy here emerges as a most central part of the continual reproduction of the state as the venue par excellence for politics. I discuss two dimensions of this structural aspect of the relationship between humanitarianism and diplomacy, having to do, first, with how humanitarian actors go diplomatic as they seek to do their work, and second, with how the meaning of humanitarianism is defined with reference to the parameters already set by the diplomatic practice through which the state emerges as sovereign.

Humanitarians going diplomatic

Global governance is typically said to be performed by a host of actors who are supplementing, even supplanting, diplomats. These claims have some merit: if regulatory work is increasingly done through transnational networks with participants from domestic regulatory agencies, experts, and staff of international organizations, then diplomats stand to lose their hitherto privileged position of serving as gatekeeper between the inside and the outside.[51] Traditional

[49] Timothy Mitchell, "The Limits of the State: Beyond Statist Approaches and Their Critics," *The American Political Science Review*, 85(1), 1991, 77–96, 90.

[50] James Der Derian, *On Diplomacy: A Genealogy of Western Estrangement* (London: Basil Blackwell, 1987).

[51] Anne-Marie Slaughter, *A New World Order* (Princeton, NJ: Princeton University Press, 2004).

diplomats may be partly replaced by a transnational network of officials representing distinct issue areas or ministries or by epistemic community-like groups that share both substantive knowledge and a policy agenda.[52] And to the extent that global governance involves fragmentation of governance efforts and an increase in importance of arenas outside formal multilateral settings where all states are represented, there is a higher premium on in-depth and technical knowledge, also within diplomatic circles, as witnessed – in the field of humanitarian relief – by the character of the efforts to ban cluster munitions and before that, antipersonnel land mines. This has engendered changes in how diplomats operate to shape policy in multilateral settings.

But the emergence of governance as the matrix for diplomatic representation does not lead to the transformation of the social structure of diplomacy, nor necessarily of the role of diplomats. Diplomatic practice is defined by protocol for how meetings are to be called, how agendas are developed, how preparatory work is organized, and how alliances are sought and texts negotiated. To the extent that humanitarian actors engage diplomats, they typically do so on the turf of diplomatic practice, as when humanitarian organizations are called on to speak before the UN Security Council, or when humanitarian actors push for new policy initiatives to be adopted by states. As a result, diplomats can perpetuate a position of dominance even in settings where diplomats are wholly dependent on non-diplomatic actors' skills and resources. For example, large humanitarian organizations have long had resident representatives and country offices with ex-pats and local staff similar to embassies in the countries where they offer relief. They also have resident representatives at the headquarters of central international and regional organizations who work through diplomatic practice, and with diplomats, to advance humanitarian ideals through advocacy work, lobbying, sharing knowledge from crisis situations, and so on.

Moreover, humanitarian actors have to adopt the style of diplomats to succeed in their advocacy work once the process is brought into the remit of diplomacy. During the process to establish a ban on cluster

[52] For a good discussion of this, see the contributions in Deborah Avant, Martha Finnemore, and Susan Sell, eds., *Who Governs the Globe* (Cambridge: Cambridge University Press, 2010). See also Sending, *The Politics of Expertise*.

munitions, for example, humanitarian actors had detailed technical knowledge about different types of ammunition, and they prepared extensive documentation – using statistics gathered by humanitarian organizations with field presence – about the destructive effects of such ammunition.[53] Their expertise on how to define and address the issue rivaled that of any one state.[54] As such, their operations were similar to those of transnational advocacy networks.[55] But their operations were thoroughly structured by diplomatic practice: a former ambassador in Geneva observed how humanitarian organizations would come to him and ask for help to push a certain issue, which would happen fairly regularly. He then established a monthly lunch meeting between representatives from other (like-minded) missions and representatives from humanitarian organizations, thus establishing a typical diplomatic exchange that included humanitarian actors. These meetings were then used to discuss and coordinate mobilization around certain issues, with humanitarian actors partaking in what was very much a diplomatic practice, with preparatory meetings, lengthy negotiations on texts, and so on.[56] During the process of negotiations, moreover, the humanitarian organizations learned and adapted to the procedures of diplomacy: those in the NGO secretariat that coordinated the humanitarian advocacy assumed diplomatic roles in that they engaged diplomats as diplomats and became well versed in negotiating texts and establishing alliances aimed at marginalizing recalcitrant states from blocking the initiative.[57] At the same time, these humanitarian actors had to defend their positions vis-à-vis more critical humanitarian organizations on their concessions. While some humanitarian actors were busy negotiating with states, others were protesting outside the building where the negotiations took place.

Indeed, there is a historically established pattern for how humanitarian actors become more "diplomatic" in their operations. The ICRC is *primus inter pares* in the humanitarian field, being guardian of the Geneva Convention and formally something between an international

[53] John Borrie, *Unacceptable Harm: A History of How the Treaty to Ban Cluster Munitions Was Won* (Geneva: United Nations Institute for Disarmament Research, 2009).

[54] Interview, MFA official, Oslo, January 26, 2011.

[55] Margaret Keck and Kathryn Sikkink, *Activists Beyond Borders: Advocacy Networks in World Politics* (Ithaca, NY: Cornell University Press, 1998).

[56] Interview, MFA official, Oslo, Norway, September 10, 2012.

[57] Interview, MFA official, Norway, February 7, 2011.

organization and a non-governmental organization. As a cornerstone of its activities, the ICRC grants confidentiality and only in rare circumstances does it go public with criticism of specific states or political leaders. It is this confidentiality – coupled with its insistence on neutrality, impartiality, and independence – that in part explains why, for example, the ICRC has met with President Assad during the ongoing war in Syria, while most state representatives (save for its closest allies) and other humanitarian organizations have not. As such, the ICRC engages heavily in and adopts the same type of rules for confidentiality that diplomats do. The ICRC may very well refer to this as "humanitarian diplomacy" and thus as distinct from what diplomats representing states engage in, but the practice it engages in is similar.

This structuring force of diplomatic practice is also found at the way humanitarian actors solicit information and seek to influence processes at the UN. A former official with the UN's Office of the Coordination of Humanitarian Affairs (OCHA) official observed, for example, "If you look at large humanitarian organizations like Oxfam and others, the way they operate vis-à-vis members of the Security Council is almost identical to that of the Nordic states."[58] His point was not only that small states are as dependent on good relations with members of the Security Council for information about what is said in closed meetings of the Council as are humanitarian organizations. It was also that humanitarian organizations have learned the trade and hired staff who knows how to navigate the corridors of the UN and to engage in diplomatic practices such as swapping information and discussing different policy options. In sum, while non-state actors (advocacy groups, experts groups, international organizations, etc.) have become more prominent in world politics, these actors target states, seek to influence state representatives (diplomats), and adopt diplomatic practices and strategies in their effort to secure policy victories. In this sense, diplomacy facilitates what Richard Ashley once described as the core feature of the practical outlook of diplomats – to engage in the "art of orchestrating the (re)production of the state."[59] Against this backdrop, it is not at all surprising that humanitarian actors find

58 Telephone interview, former OCHA official, September 12, 2012.

59 Richard K. Ashley, "The Poverty of Neorealism," *International Organization*, 38(2), 1984, 225–286, 269. See also Jennifer Mitzen, Chapter 4, this volume.

themselves operating through the same diplomatic practices that they often challenge. Indeed, the very idea of humanitarian action – and of "humanitarian diplomacy" – as distinct from politics and from diplomacy is not really intelligible in the absence of an account of how diplomacy organizes political relations in a particular way.

Humanitarian action as anti-diplomacy

If diplomacy is a set of practices geared toward the reproduction of the boundaries of the state, then humanitarian governance is in one sense a set of practices geared toward the transcendence of the significance of territorial borders – and of the state – in determining whether and how suffering individuals should receive protection and care. As we have seen, humanitarian actors and diplomats share a wide range of features, including the core diplomatic practice of representation, although it is a claim to representation not of citizens of a polity but of individuals and groups deemed to be suffering and in need of help. As such, humanitarian action constitutes a modern version of what Der Derian terms "anti-diplomacy,"[60] informed by a secularized and claimed non-ideological utopia in which concern for suffering strangers is to transcend territorial borders and the attendant lack of global political responsibility that flows from it.[61] Importantly, whereas diplomacy is a horizontal mediation between independent and formally equal polities, anti-diplomacy is vertical, with mediation flowing from the substantive contents of utopian principles.[62]

60 For Der Derian, anti-diplomacy is differentiated from both mytho-diplomacy (mediating the estrangement between humans and God) and from diplomacy (mediating the estrangement between states through *raison d'etat*) by holding up a utopia that can serve as the basis for the mediation of the estrangement between different strata within and between societies. On this, see Jef Huysmans, "James Der Derian: The Unbearable Lightness of Theory," in Iver B. Neumann and Ole Wæver, eds., *The Future of International Relations: Masters in the Making* (London: Routledge, 1997), 360–383, 369–370.

61 See Stein Sundstøl Eriksen and Ole Jacob Sending, "There Is No Global Public: The Idea of the Public and the Legitimation of Governance," *International Theory*, 5(2), 2013, 213–237.

62 Didier Fassin and Mariella Pandolfi, "Introduction: Military Humanitarian Government in the Age of Intervention," in Fassin and Pandolfi, eds., *Contemporary States of Emergency*, 9–25. See also Barnett, *Empire of Humanity*; Chandler, "The Road to Military Humanitarianism."

As many commentators have noted, the concern for suffering individuals in faraway places is an old idea that has evolved into a large system of governing since World War II, and it has become pervasive as the language for how to categorize and act on conflicts and natural disasters, particularly since the end of the Cold War.[63] Only from 1999 to 2009 did humanitarian aid from OECD's Development Assistance Committee (DAC) countries almost double, and the number of humanitarian NGOs operating in conflicts and disasters has similarly grown significantly. Not only have budgets increased dramatically, but humanitarian actors are also present in ever more conflict zones and engage in work that often goes well beyond immediate relief. Indeed, the expansion of UN peace operations since the 1990s and until today has a lot to do with how humanitarian ideals – and in particular the principle of protection of civilians – have become central to international justifications for different ways to intervene in and seek to address violent conflicts.[64]

The upshot of this is that given the presence of an international debate about the need to act, the humanitarian route is often the only one politically available. In Syria, the Democratic Republic of Congo, and in Gaza, no political solutions are on the horizon, and humanitarian relief – by virtue of the insistence on neutrality and impartiality – is often the only thing that external actors can do. A former official at OCHA noted, for example, that the main reason OCHA – as the UN's humanitarian coordinating unit – is now regularly engaged in discussions with members of the UN Security Council is that humanitarian action is often the only action that member states can agree to.[65]

Against this set of developments, we may ask how the relationship between humanitarian and diplomatic actors has changed over time in terms not only of states strategically using humanitarian justifications for action but also of (some) states' adopting the substantive goals of humanitarians as primary for their own foreign policy. The purchase of territorially based authority is reduced because what is to be

[63] Ibid.

[64] Ann Orford, *International Authority and the Responsibility to Protect* (Cambridge: Cambridge University Press, 2011). For an analysis of the operationalization of the concept of "protection of civilians" in UN peace operations, see Benjamin de Carvalho and Ole Jacob Sending, eds., *The Protection of Civilians in UN Peace Operations* (Baden Baden: Nomos Verlag, 2013).

[65] Telephone interview, former OCHA official, September 12, 2012.

governed is defined in universals: states, and their diplomats, invoke universals – and the universals of humanitarianism in particular – to establish themselves with authority to be engaged in governance beyond their borders. In lieu of diplomatic representation and negotiations on behalf of a set of national interests, diplomatic processes are on this reading filled with advocacy in the name of humanity and claimed universals.

But such a reading obscures how humanitarianism is defined as outside of politics – as being apolitical – precisely because it operates within the latter's remit, adjusting its arguments and its mode of operations. It is in this sense that diplomacy and humanitarianism are not on a par, because diplomacy establishes the frame of reference within which humanitarianism is defined and carried out, even though humanitarian ideals do shape diplomatic engagement over how to define and act, say, on violent conflicts. It is with reference to what is considered political that humanitarian action is defined as standing outside out of it as a means to the end of being able to maximize the opportunity to deliver relief. For example, the International Federation of Red Cross and Red Crescent Societies' (IFRC) definition of "humanitarian diplomacy" is that it is "concerned with persuading decision-makers and opinion leaders to act, at all times, in the interests of vulnerable people, and with full respect for our fundamental principles."[66] And the International Committee of the Red Cross (ICRC) – while not an official definition – treats humanitarian diplomacy as being about "making the voices of the victims of armed conflicts and disturbances heard, in negotiating humanitarian agreements with international or national players, in acting as a neutral intermediary between them and in helping to prepare and ensure respect for humanitarian law."[67]

Humanitarianism can thus be said to constitute a particular type of politics, one that steps in to clean up and seeks to alleviate the suffering caused by forces outside of it. Conversely, diplomacy – as the

[66] International Federation of Red Cross and Red Crescent Societies (IFRC), *Strategy 2020: Humanitarian Diplomacy Policy* (Nairobi: ICRF, 2009), 25.

[67] Marion Harroff-Tavel, 'The Humanitarian Diplomacy of the International Committee of the Red Cross" (2006), 5. See also the discussion in Philippe Regnier, "The Emerging Concept of Humanitarian Diplomacy: Identification of a Community of Practice and Prospects for International Recognition," *International Review of the Red Cross*, 93(884), 2011, 1211–1237.

organization of political relations between states – is thereby operating at some distance from the suffering that is ultimately a political responsibility, for while "protection" is arguably – as Ann Orford has shown – the single most important justification for political authority and thus for statehood, this is the key jurisdictional claim of humanitarian actors.[68] It is no coincidence, as Craig Calhoun has observed, that humanitarian action took off as other forms of political engagement seemed to fade in many liberal democratic states from the late 1960s onward:

> The field of humanitarian response to emergencies entered a phase of dramatic growth amid the waning of 1960-era protest politics ... Humanitarianism was in a sense a way to retain the emotional urgency of 1960s politics, but in a form not dependent on any political party, movement, or state.[69]

This is but one way in which humanitarianism operates in the shadows of diplomacy – and thus of international politics – however. Diplomacy can also be said to be ideological in terms of what Slavoj Zizek has called "unknown knowns": disavowed beliefs and doxic practices that shape how political debates are framed and how questions are asked.[70] It concerns how humanitarianism operates in the register of crisis or emergency – as that which is a disruption of the normal and exceptional and thus outside established practices or venues for identifying causes, placing responsibility, and taking action. Because humanitarianism is identified with emergencies, the image of the state as de facto sovereign, as having agency and control and being able to govern to shape outcomes both at home and abroad, is retained. In Pandolfi's analysis,

> On the one hand, humanitarian aid is perceived as action that tends to consolidate state sovereignty, understood as a form of government in its multiple local and global political forms; on the other hand, humanitarian intervention is constructed as a measure of the progressive erosion of state sovereignty – in the name of the principles and practices of its own political organization – that extends over the whole planet ... The entire

68 Ann Orford, *International Authority and the Responsibility to Protect* (Cambridge: Cambridge University Press, 2011).

69 Craig Calhoun, "The Idea of Emergency: Humanitarian Action and Global (Dis)Order," in Fassin and Pandolfi, eds., *Contemporary States of Emergency*, 29–58, 49.

70 *Slavoj Žižek*, "Philosophy, the "Unknown Knowns," and the Public Use of Reason," *Topoi*, 25(1–2), 2006, 137–142.

humanitarian apparatus legitimizes its presence in the name of an ethical and temporal rule that may be defined as the "culture of emergency."[71]

What is at stake here is how diplomacy organizes political processes in particular ways, and how a humanitarian register, with its distinct temporal mode and principles, is made the naturalized discourse for addressing and debating some phenomena (emergencies) as if the fact of such emergencies does not challenge the image of states as being able to act on and control outcomes. In Calhoun's analysis, such a distinction "clearly reflects interests favoured by the existing order and the specific power relations constitutive of that order ... order is the realm of nomothetic generality; exceptions are ideographic particulars. Order is normal, disorder is exceptional, no matter how frequent."[72]

The image of the state as sovereign – as capable of governing and of protecting its citizens – is both strengthened and undermined by the forces of globalization. Invoking the term "crisis" on the part of diplomats serves in part to mobilize humanitarian actors, and humanitarian actors themselves similarly invoke the image of crisis to bring attention, precisely, to neglected and forgotten human suffering. Albeit for different reasons, the boundary drawn between diplomacy and humanitarian relief is here part and parcel of the continual reproduction – through the infrastructure of diplomacy – of the state as capable of governing yet not politically responsible for suffering outside its borders. This reproduction can take place because diplomacy has a social form that allows for tensions and contradictions to coexist. Patchen Markell notes, drawing on Hegel and Marx, that

> A social form ... can be structured in ways that accommodate contradictions, organizing opposed forces in ways that permit them to exist together. The contradiction between universal and particular, for instance, might be given "room to move" if it is plotted onto some other dimension of social space, mapping "universality" onto one concrete group of people and assigning "particularity" to others.[73]

[71] Maria Pandolfi, "Contract of Mutual (In)Difference: Government and the Humanitarian Apparatus in Contemporary Albania and Kosovo," *Indiana Journal of Global Legal Studies*, 10(1), 2003, 369–381, 372–373.

[72] Craig Calhoun, "The Idea of Emergency," in Fassin and Pandolfi, eds., *Contemporary States of Emergency*, 29–58, 47.

[73] Patchen Markell, *Bound by Recognition* (Princeton, NJ: Princeton University Press), 110. The formulation "room to move" is drawn from Marx's analysis of

In much the same way, diplomacy allow tensions "room to move" and thus reproduce the state with agency and the capacity to govern. It does so in no small part through the diffusion – or rather marginalization – of questions of political responsibility for contributions to particular outcomes to actors other than diplomatic ones. In this sense, it is ideological, in that it facilitates the naturalization and/or universalization of the state, making some questions pertinent and others not, and organizing political processes in such a way that state actors have a privileged position even when they have little substantive input. The category of (humanitarian) "crisis" or "emergency" is here instructive because the proclamation of an emergency by humanitarian actors themselves – motivated by humanitarian concerns – displaces the manifest failure of states to control and shape outcomes (sovereign agency) onto a separate system of humanitarian relief that steps in to take over, to take control.

Conclusion

Diplomacy – as a distinct set of practices – is expanding in world politics because it offers an infrastructure for interaction that is at one level misrecognized as procedural and without substantive content. Indeed, the particular form of diplomacy is part of the explanation for why there is an expansion and institutionalization of global governance: governing involves engagement and negotiations over what is to be governed, how, and why, where different actors advance different, and competing, views. Diplomatic practices – centered on representation between polities recognized formally – is here constitutive of the form of engagement over the task of governing because it facilitates and legitimizes not only the fact that diplomats meet one another to commit states to certain courses of action but also a wide range of other practices, including coercive and imperial ones.[74] Diplomats may lose out on some tasks to other actors through the ongoing competition

"Money, or the Circulation of Commodities" in volume 1 of *Capital*. There are other translations that use the formulation "*modus vivendi*, a form in which they can exist side by side." See Karl Marx, *Capital: A Critical Analysis of Capitalist Production*, Vol. 1, translated from the third German edition by Samuel Moore and Edward Aveling. Edited by Frederick Engels (Moscow: Progress Publisher, 1965), 103.

74 See chapters by Barkawi and Mitzen, this volume.

to prevail as competent to define and act on particular objects. But diplomatic practices are used and extended to new areas by both diplomats and non-diplomatic actors. The evaluative criteria of both diplomats and humanitarians may change as they engage one another over what constitutes competent diplomatic and humanitarian action, respectively. In the course of such engagement, however, the social form of diplomacy is reproduced so that it enables the drawing and redrawing of boundaries between what is political and what is not political. In the case of humanitarian action, these boundaries are drawn in such a way that the image of a crisis mobilizes a particular response – humanitarian relief – and generates a political response of a particular type that bypasses the state without undermining the image of the state as responsible and sovereign.

Conclusion: Relationalism or why diplomats find international relations theory strange

REBECCA ADLER-NISSEN

Introduction

Diplomats often find international relations (IR) books strange. If they read – or more likely reread (as many Western diplomats have studied IR theory at some point of their life) – Waltz's *Theory of International Politics*,[1] they shake their heads. When presented with metaphors of the state such as Wolfers's[2] famous billiard ball: "a closed, impermeable, and sovereign unit, completely separated from all other states," they look bewildered. Also non-realist IR scholarship appears odd to most diplomats. Finnemore and Sikkink's life cycle of norms[3] would seem as far from their daily work tasks as Jervis's game theoretical models of cooperation and conflict under anarchy.[4] Diplomats would anytime prefer the gossip in their embassy cables and the *Financial Times* (*FT*) to the models in *International Organization* or *International Studies Quarterly*. Not just because cables and *FT* provide a lighter read but also because they seem closer to what diplomats perceive as the "real world." What lies behind this estrangement between diplomats and scholars of international relations?

I wish to thank Iver B. Neumann, Vincent Pouliot, Ole Jacob Sending, and the other participants at the workshop at the New School for Social Research in September 2012 for their helpful ideas and comments. Moreover, I am grateful to the anonymous reviewers as well as to Julia Frohneberg, Lars Bo Kaspersen, Lene Hansen, and Cynthia Weber for constructive suggestions.

1 Kenneth Waltz, *Theory of International Politics* (Boston: McGraw-Hill, 1979).
2 Arnold Wolfers, *Discord and Collaboration* (Baltimore: The Johns Hopkins University Press, 1962), 19.
3 Martha Finnemore and Kahtryn Sikkink, "International Norm Dynamics and Political Change," *International Organization*, 52(4), 1988.
4 Robert Jervis, "Cooperation Under the Security Dilemma," *World Politics*, 3(2), 1978.

Scholars in diplomatic studies have argued that the reason for the estrangement is to be found within IR theory itself. It is "dangerously reductionist,"[5] "rationalistic,"[6] focusing on macro decisions of superpowers,[7] or simply irrelevant – "locked within the circle of esoteric scholarly discussion" as US diplomat David D. Newson put it.[8] Arguably, IR theory has failed to acknowledge the logic of practice in diplomacy,[9] and it does not capture the bodily experience to being a diplomat.[10] However, the authors of the preceding chapters have demonstrated that the problem is more fundamental: IR scholars have ignored that diplomacy helps constitute world politics. To bring out the ways in which this constitution takes place, this book has employed a relational approach.

In this conclusion, which reflects critically on this approach and its wider consequences, I argue that diplomats are estranged from IR theory – and vice versa – because IR scholars generally subscribe to *substantialism*, whereas diplomats tend to think in terms of *relations*. In fact, a deeper understanding of these relations is a key theoretical take-away point of this book. More specifically, this conclusion argues that relationalism – as a meta-theoretical approach – not only helps us understand the diplomatic production of world politics, relationalism also reflects a particular ontology, which differs fundamentally from the worldview that most IR scholars subscribe to. As I suggest, most IR scholars depart from the social phenomenon they want to study, for example, states, diplomats, soldiers, organizations, treaties, companies, and women.[11] Assuming a

5 Carne Ross, *Independent Diplomat: Dispatches from an Unaccountable Elite* (Ithaca, NY: Cornell University Press, 2007), 146.

6 Harald Müller, "Arguing, Bargaining and All That: Communicative Action, Rationalist Theory and the Logic of Appropriateness in International Relations," *European Journal of International Relations*, 10(3), 2004; Jeffrey Lewis, "The Janus Face of Brussels: Socialization and Everyday Decision Making in the European Union," *International Organization*, 59(4), 2005.

7 Geoffrey Wiseman, "Bringing Diplomacy Back In: Time for Theory to Catch Up with Practice," *International Studies Perspectives*, 12(4), 2011.

8 Newson (2001) quoted in Stephen Walt, "The Relationship between Theory and Policy in International Relations," *Annual Review Political Science*, 8, 2005, 24.

9 Vincent Pouliot, "The Logic of Practicality: A Theory of Practice of Security Communities," *International Organization*, 62(2), 2008.

10 Iver B. Neumann, "To Be a Diplomat," *International Studies Perspectives*, 6(1), 2005.

11 See also Patrick J. Jackson and Daniel H. Nexon, "Relations before States: Substance, Process and the Study of World Politics," *European Journal of International Relations*, 5(3), 1999.

priori the existence of these phenomena (e.g. states or individuals) and ascribing certain characteristics to them, they develop substantive theories. Consequently, diplomacy is reduced to the mechanics of states bumping into each other or a system of reciprocal signaling.

However, most diplomats know, in an embodied but often unarticulated sense, that world politics is deeply relational. Their job is to make those relations "work," and they are convinced that important knowledge can be gained by consulting and meeting with foreign powers, that is, "the other." As such, they subscribe to a relational thinking (shared to some extent by diplomatic scholars). Relationalism takes as its point of departure the idea that social phenomena making up world politics always develop in relation to other social phenomena. Thus, for example, states are not born into this world as fully developed states that then "exist"; states are made in continuous relations with other states and non-state actors. The development, consolidation, weakening (or even disappearance) of states can only be understood in terms of continuous processes that play out in relation to other social processes. These ontological and epistemological differences between much of IR scholarship and diplomatic knowledge and practice are important for how we understand (and construct) world politics, including war, international cooperation, and responses to human and natural catastrophes.

The chapter is organized as follows. The next section illustrates diplomats' relational ontology and construction of national interests with an anecdote from the Danish Ministry of Foreign Affairs and an account from a former US ambassador to France. The third section shows that substantialism may be part of the reason why IR theory, in its realist, liberalist, and constructivist versions, has produced reductionist images of diplomacy. Addressing this problem, the fourth section teases out the relational approach, which is advanced in this book, whereby diplomacy is seen as constitutive (or rather co-constitutive) of other international or transnational practices. The fifth and sixth sections examine the problems and limits of the relational approach adopted in this book, which still insists that diplomacy is the mediation of estrangement: first, the risk of downplaying the consequences of diplomacy's move from representation toward governance and second and the risk of seeing diplomacy as politically "empty" (and thus innocent) practice that can be addressed separately from questions of power. The chapter concludes that if IR theory is to begin closing the gap between the theory and practice of world politics, as scholars such as Walt have called for,[12] it will need to acknowledge other forms of knowledge than the substantialist version dominating political science today.

Diplomacy as "folk relationalism": we would never talk about "win-sets"

The first argument that I wish to make, drawing on the preceding chapters, is that the diplomatic worldview differs from that of IR scholars. This helps explain their mutual estrangement. More specifically, many IR scholars have a substantialist view of world politics, whereas many diplomats subscribe to "folk relationalism."[13] By "folk relationalism," I understand the commonsensical way of carving up the social world in what the anthropologists Ladislav Hóly and Milan Stuchlik call "folk models," that is, people's representations of their own world – stylized schemata of social facts, ideas of relations and social causes that people work by in their everyday lives. They are learned or experienced assumptions about how the world works that help navigate social relationships, conflicts, and needs that they have in ordinary life.[14] Diplomatic action, as I will show, also proceeds based on a particular representation of the world. This has important implications for the construction of national interests, as the following example illustrates.

When I was working as a head of section in the Danish Ministry of Foreign Affairs (MFA; 2010–11), I once showed an academic article on EU foreign policy to a colleague. I was employed full time at the MFA, but I continued to teach the IR undergraduate course at the university, and I was interested in my colleague's thoughts on the article, which was on the students' reading list. My colleague, who was responsible for EU foreign policy coordination in the MFA, read it. In the lunch canteen, he said: "It's too bad your students never learn how diplomacy really works." "What do you mean?" I asked. He answered, "I mean this is so far from reality. We would never talk about 'win-sets' . . . You

[12] Walt, "The Relationship Between Theory and Policy in International Relations."

[13] I thank the editors for this formulation.

[14] See also Iver B. Neumann and Ole Jacob Sending, "The 'International' as Governmentality," *Millennium-Journal of International Studies*, 35(3), 680.

know how Michael [our head of department] likes to put it: 'it's about being within target,'" my colleague said.[15] In the course of my stint at the MFA, I learned that "being within target" was extremely difficult to pin down in words. It was not always based on a calculation of interest, but more a gut feeling. You knew when it sounded right, when you had described our national position in the right terms.

Of course, my colleague's criticism of the article may just reflect his self-construction or professional identity.[16] For instance, few people think about their choice between two supermarkets as related to their indifference curves. Yet, economists have effectively demonstrated that – as abstract and idealized as they may be – indifference curves actually provide an accurate description of consumer behavior. So perhaps my colleague, the diplomat, did not know himself well enough. My colleague, however, insisted that this was not the case. He leaned over and said, "the problem is that he [the scholar] believes that national interests are fixed prior to negotiations. But we always keep brackets."

With "we always keep brackets," my colleague referred to the way we drafted the national position and speech notes for the foreign or prime minister. While the MFA would collect background material weeks ahead of the meetings in Brussels, the paragraph explicating the national position and bullet points for the minister were often kept in brackets or left blank until the very last hours before a meeting.[17]

This anecdote suggests that diplomats think in terms of processes and relations rather than substances. Diplomats know that international negotiations require a certain degree of flexibility and adaption of national positions. As Sending shows in Chapter 9, they draw on intuitive flairs or social skills that help them steer the negotiations in the

15 "*Det handler om at være inden for skiven*" in Danish.

16 For fascinating analyses of diplomatic scripts and reflectivity, see Neumann, "To Be a Diplomat"; Iver B. Neumann, "'A Speech That the Entire Ministry May Stand for," or: Why Diplomats Never Produce Anything New," *International Political Sociology*, 1(2), 2007; Costas M. Constantinou, "Between Statecraft and Humanism: Diplomacy and Its Forms of Knowledge," *International Studies Review*, 15(2), 2013.

17 This is an interesting parallel to Neumann's observation that keeping brackets is a way of wielding influence (Iver B. Neumann, *At Home with the Diplomats: Inside a European Foreign Ministry* [Ithaca, NY: Cornell University Press, 2012], 114).

preferred direction. Of course, some negotiations are based on clearly formulated and fixed goals such as security partnerships, trade rounds, or membership accession agreements, but even such negotiations require a certain degree of subtleness in terms of presentation of positions, timing, and an ability to make compromises. Moreover, national interests may change in the course of the negotiation process as the involved parties learn more about the issue and their opponents and as the negotiations gain their own momentum.

This ever-changing nature of national positions has been accepted to some degree in the bargaining literature. For instance, two-level game approaches acknowledge that domestic politics affects diplomacy continuously. Putnam even admits that

> formally speaking, game-theoretic analysis requires that the structure of issues and payoffs *be specified in advance*. In reality, however, much of what happens in any bargaining situation involves attempts by the players to restructure the game and to alter one another's perceptions of the costs of no-agreement and the benefits of proposed agreement.[18]

Yet Putnam (and others) still assumes that there is such a thing as a national win-set. Putnam needs a priori assumptions and win-sets to make his theory work. In many occasions, however, a negotiation has no clear beginning. This was also the case one century ago. The seasoned diplomat Henry White, reflecting on his experience as US ambassador to France (1906–9) and as representative of the United States at a range of international conferences from the 1880s to the 1910s, explains how negotiations often start with vague ideas. For instance, the International Agriculture Conference, held in Rome in 1905,

> assembled not only with a very vague idea as to what shape, if any, its labors would assume, but with a strong conviction on the part of a majority of the delegates that no result at all was likely to be attained, beyond perhaps a demonstration of good will to the Italian sovereign and nation.[19]

However, as a result of the "zeal and tact of the very able men composing the Italian delegation, encouragement and interest took place of

[18] Robert D. Putnam, "Diplomacy and Domestic Politics: The Logic of Two-Level Games," *International Organization*, 42(3), 1988: 454, my italics. As Putnam writes, "much ambassadorial action ... has precisely this function" (ibid.).

[19] Henry White et al., "The Organization and Procedure of the Third Hague Conference," Proceedings of the American Society of International Law at Its Annual Meeting, 6, 1912, 182.

skepticism and apathy."[20] In the end, the negotiations led to the sharing of information on agricultural products and the establishments of agricultural bureaus across much of the Western world. Diplomacy, in other words, helped construct the national interest, not just represent it. How did IR scholars come to believe in (or feel a need to assume) a pre-given national interest or win-set that determines negotiations?

Bumping billiard balls and signals: two images of diplomacy in IR theory

To get at the core of the problem with most accounts of diplomacy (and why my colleague could not recognize himself in the academic article), we need to address the substantialist thinking inherent in much IR theory. I build here on Mustafa Emirbayer's distinction between substantialist and relational social theory.[21] Within IR, Emirbayer's relational manifesto has influenced Jackson and Nexon's argument about the processual character of world politics,[22] leading them to argue – as diplomats would do – that relations come before states.[23] This brief section cannot do justice to the nuances and sophistication of the different IR theories; instead, it will point to a few basic assumptions that have limited IR scholars' view of diplomacy.

Substantialism dominates much of social science and in particular IR theory. It claims that substances (things, beings, entities, essences) are the "units" or "levels" of analysis and that they exist prior to the analysis. Emirbayer uses Norbert Elias to trace the analytical fondness for substances (things, beings, essences) back to the grammar of

20 Ibid.

21 Mustafa Emirbayer, "Manifesto for a Relational Sociology," *American Journal of Sociology*, 103(2), 1997, 283.

22 Jackson and Nexon, "Relations before States." For an interesting argument about survival units, see Lars Bo Kaspersen and Norman Gabriel, The importance of survival units for Norbert Elias's figurational perspective. The Sociological Review, 56(3), 2008, 370–387.

23 With a different purpose, Albert et al. have argued that large-scale change is only intelligible with a relational ontology, and Guillaume has constructed a relational-dialogical approach to provide a more nuanced understanding of subjectivity and the development of national identities. See Mathias Albert, David Jacobson, and Yosef Lapid, eds., *Identities, Borders, Orders: Rethinking International Relations Theory* (Minneapolis: University of Minnesota Press, 2011); and Xavier Guillaume, "Foreign Policy and the Politics of Alterity: A Dialogical Understanding of International Relations," *Millennium*, 31(1), 2002.

Western languages.[24] One example is the wind, "the wind is blowing." "We speak as if the wind were separate from its blowing, as if a wind could exist which did not blow."[25]

The idea of that a state has (i.e., possesses) a particular national interest as mentioned earlier, is illustrative of IR's substantialism. In a constructivist version that interest is socially constructed, yet at the most fundamental level – "before interaction" – it is the desire to survive that drives states.[26] However, as poststructuralist and feminist IR scholars have demonstrated,[27] while one may show that the state is partially a social construction as Wendt does, many of the processes that construct the state as a subject – including diplomacy – will be left out of the analysis when the essentialist ontology sneaks in.

Self-action: diplomacy as states bumping into each other

According to Emirbayer, there are two substantialist positions: "self-action" and "inter-action." Following a self-action perspective, things are "acting under their own powers" and "there exists things which inherently possess being" (e.g., the soul in Christian theology).[28] In modern social theory, the self-action perspective is expressed in arguments about the existence of the will and methodological individualism. Within IR theory, liberal and rational choice approaches assume that human beings and states act rationally to maximize utility,[29] whereas social identity theorists believe that social status is the main behavioral driver.[30] We also find the self-action perspective in norm-following

24 Emirbayer, "Manifesto for a Relational Sociology," 283.

25 Elias, quoted in ibid., 283.

26 Alexander Wendt, "Anarchy Is What States Make of It: The Social Construction of Power Politics," *International Organization*, 46(2), 1992, 402.

27 For example, Roxanne L. Doty, "Aporia: A Critical Exploration of the Agent-Structure Problematique in International Relations Theory," *European Journal of International Relations*, 3(3), 1997; Jonathan D. Wadley, "Gendering the State: Performativity and Protection in International Security," in Laura Sjoberg, ed., *Gender and International Security: Feminist Perspectives* (London: Routledge, 2010), 44.

28 Emirbayer, "Manifesto for a Relational Sociology," 283.

29 For example, Andrew Moravcsik, "Taking Preferences Seriously: A Liberal Theory of International Politics," *International Organization*, 51(4), 1997.

30 For example, Jonathan Mercer, "Anarchy and Identity," *International Organization*, 49(2), 1995; Rawi Abdelal, Yoshiko M. Herrera, Alastair Iain Johnston, and Rose McDermott, "Identity as a Variable," *Perspectives on Politics*, 4(4), 2006.

individuals or states (pursuing internalized norms).[31] More holistic, structuralist or system-oriented theories seek to avoid assumptions about motives (e.g., Durkheim or Waltz) but assume the existence of the phenomenon they seek to study, that is, society (Durkheim) or the state system (Waltz). From a structuralist realist perspective, diplomacy is close to irrelevant because of the "irreducible" security dilemma.[32] Scholars in the defensive realist camp of structural realism are typically less pessimistic, because they believe that certain forms of soft-line diplomacy can mitigate, although not eliminate, the security dilemma.[33] It is perhaps also in the substantialist approaches that Humes's legacy is most apparent in IR theory: We cannot observe the act of causation; we can only observe that the motion of the first billiard ball is followed by the motion of the second billiard ball. And so we infer causation. Diplomacy then becomes the mechanisms of states bumping into each other.

Inter-action: diplomacy as reciprocal signaling

Following inter-action theory, the relevant action takes place among the entities themselves. At first sight, the inter-action version of substantialism resembles relationalism and allocates a greater role for diplomacy. However, things in inter-action are "in causal interconnection" against one another.[34] Thus, entities remain fixed and unchanging throughout such interaction, each independent of the existence of the others. This is where Jervis's foreign policy signals fit in.[35] The inter-actionist approach is also detectible in diplomatic language itself: deep-rooted expressions such as "normalizing" or "severing" diplomatic ties; the former is a signaling device for approval or recognition, while the latter sends strong signals of dissatisfaction without necessarily any military intentions.[36]

[31] See James Fearon and Alexander Wendt, "Rationalism v. Constructivism: A Skeptical View," *Handbook of International Relations*, 2002, 58.

[32] See also Iver B. Neumann, Chapter 5, this volume.

[33] Charles Glaser, "The Security Dilemma Revisited," *World Politics*, 50, 1997.

[34] Emirbayer, "Manifesto for a Relational Sociology," 285.

[35] Jervis, "Cooperation under the Security Dilemma." For a relational view of the security dilemma, see Ken Booth and Nicholas J. Wheeler, *The Security Dilemma* (Houndmills: Palgrave MacMillan, 2008).

[36] Geoff Berridge, *Talking to the Enemy – How States Without "Diplomatic Relations" Communicate* (London: St. Martin's Press, 1994), 7. The language of diplomacy is rife with references to ongoing production and reproduction of a

The inter-action perspective can also be found in constructivism's symbolic interactionist roots. As Copeland writes in a (critical) review of Wendt, "each actor's conception of self (its interests and identity) is a product of the others' diplomatic gestures."[37] While Wendt reinforced a focus on state interactions, he bracketed off diplomatic and domestic processes.[38] Accordingly, diplomacy became understood as a system of reciprocal signaling that affected state identities and interests.

Liberals in the interdependence tradition tend to replace the signaling with a cobweb, thereby giving diplomacy a greater role.[39] But this complex diplomatic network of negotiation is not in and of itself in need of theorizing; instead, it is the interests of the states that are in focus, together with levels of trust, economic independence, and so on. Globalization and "soft power" scholars come closer to a relational approach, by focusing on the interrelated and connected nature of world politics. Yet substantialist assumptions sneak in. For instance, Nye argues:

> A country may obtain the outcomes it wants in world politics because other countries want to follow it, admiring its values, emulating its example, aspiring to its level of prosperity and openness ... This aspect of power – getting others to want what you want – I call soft power. It co-opts people rather than coerces them.[40]

Soft power clearly is about relations, including diplomatic relations, yet, "values," "models," "prosperity," or "openness" are possessed or represented by the state, according to Nye. None of this includes relations of mutuality or intersubjectivity, and they are seldom put specifically at work in a concrete analysis.

However, in the past two decades, the "new diplomacy" literature has brought attention to the increasing involvement of NGOs, citizens, and private companies in diplomatic negotiations. Diplomatic scholars

mediated international order. See Rebecca Adler-Nissen, "Diplomacy as Impression Management: Strategic Face-Work and Post-Colonial Embarrassment," CIPSS Working Paper Series, 38, Center for International Peace and Security Studies (Montreal: McGill University, 2012).

37 Dale C. Copeland, "The Constructivist Challenge to Structural Realism: A Review Essay," *International Security*, 25(2), 2000, 188.

38 Ibid., 212.

39 Christer Jönsson and Martin Hall, *Essence of Diplomacy* (Houndmills: Palgrave Macmillan, 2005), 17.

40 Joseph S. Nye, *Soft Power: The Means to Success in World Politics* (New York: Public Affairs, 2004), 5.

have identified changes in the relations between, for instance, new and old forms of diplomacy, pointing to the role of companies and NGOs,[41] and have shown that in addition to bilateral and multilateral forms of diplomacy, the "polylateral" (or non-state) form of diplomacy has become more predominant.[42] Moreover, diplomatic scholars have discussed what causes these changes. Some have argued that the changes in diplomatic practices can be explained by external factors such as the end of the Cold War, globalization, shifts in the traditional balance of world power, and regionalization.[43] Alternatively, the change may be termed as a form of "mutual adaption" of diplomacy to new technological, cultural, and political contexts.[44] Following this approach, we can analyze change in specific interests and relative power positions between official state representatives and their relations to multinational companies, NGOs and multilateral arenas, but it is less clear whether and how diplomacy as such is also changing. More radically, in terms of transformation, Sharp concludes that "public diplomacy is merely the latest of a series of waves seeking to transform diplomacy and to point us to a world which will not need it."[45] However, as the editors note, much of the new diplomacy literature remains actor-centric, reflecting more an inter-actionist view of the world. This makes it blind to the processes that produce changes in diplomatic practice.[46]

In sum, in its self-action or inter-actionist versions, IR theory tends to bracket diplomacy away or use particular interests or actors as proxies for diplomacy. IR theory often searches for kicks of exogenous change (since its units are usually left unchanging), leaving the change itself unexplainable. The new diplomacy literature brings us closer to

41 Andrew F. Hocking and Brian Cooper, "Governments, Non-governmental Organisations and the Re-calibration of Diplomacy," *Global Society*, 14(3), 2000.

42 Geoffrey Wiseman (1999), "'Polylateralism'" and New Modes of Global Dialogue." Reprinted in Christer Jönsson and Richard Langhorne, eds., *Diplomacy*, Vol. III. Discussion Papers, No. 59, Leicester Diplomatic Studies Programme, 36–57 (London: Sage, 2004).

43 Pauline Kerr and Geoffrey Wiseman, eds., *Diplomacy in a Globalizing World: Theories and Practices* (Oxford: Oxford University Press, 2013).

44 See Jan Melissen, ed., *Innovation in Diplomatic Practice* (New York: Palgrave Macmillan, 1999).

45 Paul Sharp, "Diplomacy, Diplomatic Studies, and the ISA," *International Studies Perspectives*, 13, 2011, 718.

46 Ole Jacob Sending, Chapter 9, this volume.

diplomacy as a research object – and to the way it changes – but has tended to fall back on inter-actional arguments, evaluating the interaction between state-based and non-state diplomacy. The next section discusses how Emirbayer's alternative, what he calls a trans-action perspective or relational social theory. This perspective is implicit in the way in which this book understands diplomacy.

Relationalism: diplomacy as social entanglement

In relational theory, the terms or units derive their meaning, significance, and identity from the (changing) functional roles they play within that relation. Thus, the relationship is a dynamic unfolding process. Relations become the primary unit of analysis (rather than the constituent elements themselves). Contrary to self-action and inter-action perspectives, with trans-action or relationalism, "systems of description and naming are employed to deal with aspects and phases of action, without final attribution to 'elements' or other presumptively detachable or independent 'entities,' 'essences,' or 'realities,' and without isolation of presumptively detachable 'relations' from such detachable 'elements.'"[47]

Examples of this way of thinking can be found for instance in Marx's understanding of class as a relational (not pre-given) phenomenon. The bourgeoisie exists only in relation to the working class. Another example is Bourdieu's field theory, which shows that social practices are never isolated activities. A human practice, for instance playing golf, cannot be understood in itself and as a practice for its own sake. People may play golf because they like to do so, but playing golf also brings "distinctive gains" (at least in the 1970s) in contrast to, for instance, rugby.[48] Relationalism can also be found in Cynthia Enloe's analysis of diplomats' wives who appear as almost invisible women, but who help promote the national interest abroad and are complicit in the global injustices that produce hierarchies between the Third and the First World.[49] To analytically isolate the wives from our understanding of (the male) diplomats is therefore problematic.

47 Dewey and Bentley, quoted in Emirbayer, "Manifesto for a Relational Sociology," 286.

48 Pierre Bourdieu, "Sport and Social Class," *Social Science Information*, 17(6), 1978, 828.

49 Cynthia Enloe, *Bananas, Beaches and Bases: Making Feminist Sense of International Politics* (Berkeley: University of California Press 1990).

Similarly, this book has shown that diplomacy is not an isolated, detached activity.[50] Tilly famously argued that "states make war and war makes states."[51] This book adds: so does diplomacy. More specifically, diplomacy is co-constitutive of other practices. For example, Barkawi shows that diplomacy and war cannot be separated as easily as diplomatic scholars (and diplomats) suggest. The underlying rationale of the diplomatic profession may be to facilitate orderly and peaceful relations among states,[52] but this is not necessarily done peacefully. As Barkawi demonstrates, the a priori (substantialist) classification of war and the juridical fiction of the state as a unitary actor hinder understanding its true nature, including the way war helps sustain a particular order. The Correlates of War project, which conducts quantitative research into the causes of warfare since the 1960s, builds on a classification of war that makes it possible to argue that the coup against Guatemala's Arbenz in 1954 was not orchestrated by the United States because "interstate war is defined as organized violence between two sovereign states involving at least one thousand battle deaths over the course of a year."[53] The international administration of war is a web of relations.[54] In Hurd's chapter, it is argued that the "essentially state-centric nature of diplomacy could conceivably change if non-state actors become more central to public international law."[55] Similarly, Seabrooke identifies change in the sense that brokers take over a number of diplomatic tasks. Importantly, but this remains more obscure, this change of actors also implies a change in the nature of diplomacy.[56] Indeed, the diplomatic system cannot be defined by its structure, but by "the conflicting relations, which maintain, reproduce, and sometimes transform it."[57] These conflicting relations involve soldiers, lawyers, religious groups, consultants, human right activists,

[50] In many ways, the new diplomacy literature evokes this entanglement but steers away from an explicit theorization of it.

[51] Charles Tilly, "War Making and State Making as Organized Crime," in Peter B. Evans, Dietrich Rueschemeyer, and Theda Skocpol, eds., *Bringing the State Back In* (Cambridge: Cambridge University Press, 1985), 170.

[52] James Mayall, "Introduction," in Paul Sharp and Geoffrey Wiseman, *The Diplomatic Corps as an Institution of International Society* (New York: Palgrave, 2007), 6.

[53] Tarak Barkawi, Chapter 2, this volume.

[54] Ibid.

[55] Ian Hurd, Chapter 1, this volume.

[56] Leonard Seabrooke, Chapter 7, this volume.

[57] James Der Derian, *On Diplomacy: A Genealogy of Western Estrangement* (Oxford: Blackwell, 1987).

citizens, and a range of other people. Diplomacy is deeply entangled with other practices, and it is not separate from the states it helps constitute. Consequently, the distinction between war and diplomacy (which is so central to most theories of diplomacy) is problematic. This brings us back to diplomatic studies' somewhat rosy account of diplomacy, which this book has begun to undermine.

Diplomacy beyond the mediation of estrangement

If diplomacy is as deeply entangled in world politics as this book suggests, it raises the question of whether diplomacy can still be seen as the mediation of estrangement, or if that notion risks concealing more than it reveals. I understand mediation in Der Derian's abstract way as the mediation of distinct identities,[58] not as the concrete practice of third-party mediation between two or more conflicting parties in terms of reconciliation that Neumann analyzes.[59] This book, while steering away from an explicit definition of diplomacy, adopts a mediation perspective on diplomacy, in insisting with Sharp that diplomacy requires a "condition of separateness."[60] Diplomacy is about constituting and representing states as separate units.[61] Indeed, a classic argument in diplomatic theory (and in diplomatic self-understanding) is that diplomats are essentially mediators. Previously, Neumann has described diplomacy as a third culture, that is, a culture for mediation between political entities with diverse cultures.[62] Similarly, Sharp's diplomatic theory of international relations insists on diplomacy

58 Ibid.

59 The starting point for Der Derian's genealogy is the terminology for alienation, which was used first as a noun – the "other," "another" or as a verb *alienare*, which meant "to take away" or "to remove" something. Following Der Derian, necessarily ambiguous identities derive from the fact that the principle of universality (e.g. God, and economic and political rights) is estranged from the beings and they have to "share" this notion also among one another – which necessarily leads to their alienation from one another. This means that they can only recognize themselves or the others completely, if the principle of universality works. The diplomatic process arguably resembles the necessity of mediation between identities being left in the confusion about themselves and others, in which constant cognition and recognition of the actors is in place at all times. Iver B. Neumann, Chapter 5, this volume.

60 Paul Sharp, *Diplomatic Theory of International Relations* (Cambridge and New York: Cambridge University Press, 2009).

61 Ole Jacob Sending, Chapter 9, this volume.

62 Neumann, "To Be a Diplomat."

retaining separateness between entities, individuals, cultures, and states.[63] For Hall and Jönsson, diplomacy is "a timeless, existential phenomenon."[64] It is constitutive of any international society and at the most abstract level, "diplomacy can be analyzed as the mediation of *universalism* and *particularism.*"[65] Somewhat similarly, Sending and Neumann argue that diplomacy "derives its strength in part from allowing disagreement and contestation, also over the appropriate form and content of diplomacy in different situations."[66] As Sending puts it, "diplomacy constitutes a 'thin' inter-subjective space inasmuch as it includes a minimum standard, or expectations, to 'keep on talking.'"[67]

There is a great deal of ambivalence in these different calls for acknowledging diplomacy as a mediating practice, from the English School pluralists (Bull and Butterfield) to Constantinou's poststructuralist calls for humanism in diplomacy.[68] They range from pragmatic system maintenance to more uncompromising attempts to sustain "global hope" and "restore diplomacy as a virtue."[69] In Lynch's account, religio-theological debates give a primary role to diplomacy to mediate and manage the tension between universalist (Christianity) and particularist authority claims (state sovereignty) as well as between the Christian and the non-Christian other.[70] As she demonstrates, the quest for universalism can be envisaged in very different ways (from cosmopolitanism to moral leadership or more pessimistic forms of system maintaining), leading to different forms of mediation (with different moral and political agendas) and consequently different forms of diplomacy.

However, the scholarly defense of diplomacy's (postulated) ability to mediate distinct ideas or world visions is problematic. While mediation

[63] Sharp, *Diplomatic Theory of International Relations.*
[64] Jönsson and Hall, *Essence of Diplomacy*, 3.
[65] Ibid., 25. Emphasis in original.
[66] Ole Jacob Sending and Iver B. Neumann, "Banking on Power: How Some Practices in an International Organization Anchor Others," in Emanuel Adler and Vincent Pouliot, eds., *International Practices* (Cambridge: Cambridge University Press, 2011), 236.
[67] Ole Jacob Sending, this Chapter 9, volume.
[68] Constantinou, "Between Statecraft and Humanism."
[69] Costas M. Constantinou and James Der Derian, "Sustaining Global Hope: Sovereignty, Power and the Transformation of Diplomacy," in Costas M. Constantinou and James Der Derian, eds., *Sustainable Diplomacies* (Basingstoke: Palgrave Macmillan, 2010), 3.
[70] Cecelia Lynch, Chapter 6, this volume.

may sound like a relational idea, it often conceals inter-actionist assumptions, failing to fully access how diplomatic ideas and practices of mediation themselves are productive of particular politics. While we may agree with the importance of separation or respect for differences, we need to dissect carefully the idea that diplomacy always equals mediation of estrangement.

Ambassador White's account may serve again as illustration. Whether the negotiations concerned regulation of sugar trade, imperialism in North Africa, or agriculture, the Ambassador recalls that "a certain amount of kindly hospitality was exceedingly efficacious in *greasing the wheels* of the conference, as I have so often known it to be in the settlement of other diplomatic questions."[71] Ambassador White represented the United States in the Algeciras Conference in 1906, addressing the Tangier crisis (Germany had attempted to prevent France from establishing a protectorate over Morocco). The chief concern of most delegates was that the conference should not break up without an agreement, as this would possibly lead to war. The US ambassador reports the following:

> I felt at the time, and have felt ever since, that it was owing to the perpetual exchange of views which took place day after day between the delegates outside the conference, and consequently, informally, and to the agreeable and intimate personal relations which could hardly fail to be established between a number of men of the world meeting all day long for three months, that all friction at the formal sessions was avoided, in spite of an amount of tension in the atmosphere prevalent almost to the end, and very difficult to realize by anyone who was not present.[72]

For the diplomat, "substance" is important, but in the end "the perpetual exchange of views" is crucial. "Greasing the wheels" is still a fitting metaphor for how diplomats think of their job. This reflects the

[71] White et al., "The Organization and Procedure of the Third Hague Conference," 182, emphasis added. The focus on greasing the wheels helps explain conflicts between line ministries and foreign ministries that disagree on whether "relations to foreign powers" are important, or whether "substance" regarding agriculture, environment, energy – or even security and defense – is more important. Thomas Nowotny, *Diplomacy and Global Governance: The Diplomatic Service in an Age of Worldwide Interdependence*, (New Brunswick, NJ: Transaction Publishers, 2012).

For diplomats, nothing is more important than process.

[72] White et al., "The Organization and Procedure of the Third Hague Conference," 183–184.

diplomat's own understandings, her "folk relationalism," but it does not necessarily give us the full account of diplomacy's entanglement. While "diplomatic studies are closer to their subject – that is, diplomatic practice – than some IR students see as acceptable,"[73] this closeness should not lead diplomatic scholars to "go native."

The practical knowledge of how to do diplomacy does have its own logic that "cannot be reduced to that of theoretical knowledge; that, in a sense, agents know the social world better than the theoreticians."[74] However, the scientist's work consists in making explicit this practical knowledge, in accordance with its own articulations.[75] Indeed, while diplomats may continue to think of themselves as system maintainers concentrating on "being within target," this book effectively shows that there is more to diplomacy than the mediation of estrangement (and that mediation has several meanings). The next two sections discuss the broader consequences of these findings, the problems that come with adopting a folk relationalist approach, and the risks of uncritically overtaking the diplomatic self-understanding as mediator.

Diplomacy from system maintenance to governance

The first limit of the relational approach to diplomacy advanced in this book is that while it successfully shows diplomacy's move to governance, it has difficulty analyzing the way in which diplomats become policy makers. On the one hand, the chapters in this volume demonstrate that the sharp distinctions between diplomacy as representation and governing become untenable when adopting a relational approach. On the other hand, they cannot draw out all the implications because they insist that diplomacy (still) has to do with mediation between distinct identities or states.

For instance, several of the contributors to this volume show that diplomacy does not just involve representation of particular interests but also the construction of a more integrated international political order. If multilateralism has become the dominant form of diplomacy, then diplomacy – even when performed as representation – turns into a

73 Sharp, "Diplomacy, Diplomatic Studies, and the ISA," 723.

74 Pierre Bourdieu, Jean-Claude Chamboredon, Jean-Claude Passeron, and Beate Krais, eds., *The Craft of Sociology: Epistemological Preliminaries* (Berlin & New York: Walter de Gruyter, 1991), 252.

75 Ibid.

form of governance. This is perhaps most evident in Pouliot's account of multilateral "group diplomacy" or PRIO cliques. Pouliot (and several other contributors to this book) approach diplomacy sociologically, identifying strategic moves in a Bourdieusian sense. Consequently, when Pouliot talks about how "multilateral diplomacy involves addressing multiples audiences simultaneously,"[76] he also shows the sociological impossibility of a sharp distinction between representation and governance. A great deal of "information asymmetry" exists in multilateral arenas that have grown increasingly complex and technical. The multilateral scene is secluded from home capitals, and yet it still features diplomats promoting national interests. In the EU, this turns into a form of late sovereign diplomacy.[77] The practice of "joining the consensus" that Pouliot analyzes is not entirely the same as the mediation "that allow[s] life to go on when major differences persist."[78] Instead, permanent representatives in different multilateral venues "develop a stake in the success of multilateralism itself, they seek to help their partners in trouble, and they contribute to the collective effort at compromise."[79] This form of diplomacy, while it involves "keep on talking," transcends national representation. It is in itself a form of global governance. In her analysis of the Concert of Europe and the effect of forum talks – that is, repeated face-to-face diplomacy – Mitzen concludes that even a world state requires a "diplomatic moment."[80] This might have been the case in the nineteenth century, but is it still the case?

Seabrooke begins to answer that question in his analysis of the outsourcing of diplomacy from governments, NGOs, and IOs to private actors. He distinguishes between traditional diplomatic mediation and brokering, the later involving market logics and the creation of new information.[81] Seabrooke's distinction hinges on the assumption that traditional diplomats are mediators who do not "actively create new information problems at the national and international levels."[82] Following this argument, consultancy groups such as Independent Diplomat may increase the heterogeneity of diplomatic actors, but

[76] Vincent Pouliot, Chapter 3, this volume.
[77] Rebecca Adler-Nissen "Late Sovereign Diplomacy," *The Hague Journal of Diplomacy*, 4(2), 2009.
[78] Constantinou, "Between Statecraft and Humanism," 158.
[79] Vincent Pouliot, Chapter 3, this volume.
[80] Jennifer Mitzen, Chapter 4, this volume.
[81] Leonard Seabrooke, Chapter 7, this volume. [82] Ibid.

not necessarily change diplomacy as a practice of representation and mediation (because arguably that's what diplomats do). Seabrooke concludes that outsourcing can help keep politically sensitive topics secret.[83] Indeed, outsourcing provides a perfect way of avoiding domestic scrutiny and legal responsibility.[84] It also makes it possible for diplomats to enter into a tricky game to simultaneously allow international cooperation and communicate a sense of sovereignty to the domestic audience. Diplomacy and diplomats are deeply involved in everything from humanitarian work to economic consultancy.

Hurd shows how international law and foreign policy are mutually constitutive: legal resources exist by virtue of being used by states to justify their policies, and state policies depend on a legal justification.[85] This view of international law as a political and strategic product, which shapes future negotiations (rather than an ordered system), has shaped insights in a range of academic fields, including postcolonial and development studies[86] and historical international relations.[87] However, diplomatic scholars have hitherto not shared such critical views of international law and governance. Perhaps they uncritically accept the diplomatic self-narrative: diplomats "grease the wheels" without ever becoming greasy themselves.

Neumann notes that "diplomacy is about the formulation and pursuit of national interests, and it is about systems maintenance."[88] Yet, as Neumann and the other contributors show, the pursuit of national interests is more complicated than IR usually admits. But so is the international system that diplomats help maintain. It is also not a stable, unchanging system. In fact, system maintenance has evolved, partly under the radar of public attention, to governance. Diplomacy is still focused on living together in difference, but this life together – in its

83 Ibid.
84 Thomas Gammeltoft-Hansen and Rebecca Adler-Nissen, "Introduction to Sovereignty Games," in Rebecca Adler-Nissen and Thomas Gammeltoft-Hansen, eds., *Sovereignty Games: Instrumentalizing State Sovereignty in Europe and Beyond* (Basingstoke: Palgrave Macmillan, 2008).
85 Ian Hurd, Chapter 1, this volume.
86 Balakrishnan Rajagopal, *International Law from Below: Development, Social Movements and Third World Resistance* (Cambridge: Cambridge University Press, 2011).
87 Stephen Hobden and John M. Hobson, eds., *Historical Sociology of International Relations* (Cambridge: Cambridge University Press, 2002).
88 Iver B. Neumann, Chapter 5, this volume.

multilateral and networked forms – has become increasingly demanding for all parties involved. According to Sharp, the modern diplomat moves away from representing the notion of a sovereign state toward engineering new international institutions.[89] As a consequence, "representation – of sovereigns, interests, or ideas – has been replaced by metaphors of constructing and building by which issues were to be managed and problems was to be solved."[90]

This leaves us with a question: who become the losers in this struggle? What ideas, projects, and groups are marginalized when diplomats engage in forum talks, build new institutions, outsource, and engage in military diplomacy? In demonstrating diplomats' ability to not just represent but also produce world politics, this book has been more silent on those that diplomats get to govern, from Iranian civilians to HIV-positive homosexuals in Africa. Moreover, it has not addressed situations where diplomacy is excluded, silenced, or disempowered in world politics (beyond when it is strategically outsourced or when diplomatic tasks are shared with others). Yet, given the potential of the relational approach to address exactly such processes, this is a task that needs to be taken up in future studies. Exploring the non-diplomatic blank spots on the map will be crucial to our understanding of the diplomatic production of world politics.

Diplomacy and power: just greasing the wheels?

The second challenge to the relational approach adopted in this book concerns the way in which questions of power and responsibility become obscure.[91] To see how this plays out, let us return to the

[89] Sharp, "Who Needs Diplomats?"; Kelley observes a move from "diplomacy as an institution" to "diplomacy as a behavior"; see John Robert Kelley, "The New Diplomacy: Evolution of a Revolution." *Diplomacy & Statecraft*, 21(2), 2010, 288.

[90] Sharp in an earlier piece also called "Who Needs Diplomats" writes about the dilemma of diplomats being 100 percent true to the sending state or diplomats being "ambitious internationalists" who act so detached from the state that their action is not authoritative for their sending state anymore; see Paul Sharp, "Who Needs Diplomats? The Problems of Diplomatic Representation," *International Journal*, 52(4), 1997, 610.

[91] For another version of this argument about power and diplomatic studies, see Rebecca Adler-Nissen, "Just Greasing the Wheels? Mediating Difference or the Evasion of Power and Responsibility in Diplomacy," *The Hague Journal of Diplomacy*, 10(2), 2015.

conversation with my MFA colleague about the gap between theory and practice. What did my colleague mean with "being within target"? It is a way of saying that the foreign service is merely the skilled interpreter of a gut feeling, diplomats try to "sense" or "embody" the national interest. As Sending notes, whereas diplomats simply "manage frictions" as professional strangers, "humanitarians can be said to share a substantive commitment that cuts across territorial units"; they act as professional friends.[92] In other words, diplomats are messengers, but the substance is defined somewhere else and by someone else (the minister, the line ministry, or an external consultant).

However, this argument is based on a fiction of a substantive national interest that can be identified and possessed. This fiction, of course, is necessary for most forms of diplomatic negotiations, but it does not always have the kind of vitalism or societal backing that most IR theories implicitly assume. Much of what is promoted as "national interests" is never (and has never been) discussed in parliamentary assemblies or among government ministers as the "information asymmetry" that Pouliot identifies also reveals. Nonetheless, even when they are deeply implicated in global governance projects, diplomats still pass as messengers.

This self-understanding as mediator and messenger – rather than manager and policy producer – can have almost perverse effects. I recall a discussion in the Danish MFA on the EU's response to the refugee crisis following the international intervention in Libya in March 2011. I was working in the MFA when the Arab Spring erupted. (It was not called "Arab Spring" internally in the ministry because everybody was aware of the important differences between the processes in the North African countries.) Whereas the Ministry of Refugee, Immigration, and Integration Affairs called for a review of visa possibilities for selected groups of refugees from Libya, the MFA concentrated on finding a position that could balance domestic concerns and the median position among the EU member states – our partners.

When I asked for a clarification of the MFA's position on the refugee crisis, the response from my superior was that "we follow governmental policy." But the governmental policy had yet to be defined, and the MFA was a party to the negotiations on how to handle the refugee situation. In the end, the Danish foreign minister was equipped with the

[92] Ole Jacob Sending, Chapter 9, this volume.

following speech notes for the Council of Foreign Ministers' meeting: "We support that the general visa dialogue continues with Southern neighbours. Still too early to consider negotiations on visa facilitation and visa liberalization." So we would just go with the flow. This is illustrative of what Neumann identifies as how "system maintainers experience themselves as minor players."[93] It is, however, also a very comfortable position because one can pretend that one is not taking sides.

Yet, every MFA across the world has strategic departments and policy offices handling everything from the Middle East to development policies or international law and human rights. Over the years, these MFA offices and departments have developed their own takes on these issues that they deal with on a routine basis. For instance, it is likely that every MFA in the world has its own position (and institutional memory) on the Israel-Palestinian conflict. Of course, MFAs do produce policy. However, the way that scholars describe diplomacy, it is always about the process and bargaining tactics, but seldom about the production of ideas and policies. This book has begun addressing the ideological and practical work that goes into the diplomatic making of world politics and the engineering of new international institutions, using terms such as "collective intentionality," "commitment," "pure love-ethics," and "the international administration of war."

More broadly, then, the implication of the relational approach adopted in this book is that diplomacy cannot keep the innocence or detachment that some of its practitioners (and theorists) would want it to keep. This book has problematized the understanding of diplomacy as a third culture. Diplomats contribute to defense planning and organization,[94] war making,[95] humanitarianism,[96] conflict management and mediation,[97] polity building and multilateral governance,[98] international law making,[99] and economic reordering.[100] Diplomacy is deeply entangled in the world it helps constitute. On the one hand, as several contributors show, it is becoming militarized to the degree that

[93] Iver Neumann, Chapter 5, this volume.
[94] Krieger, Souma, and Nexon, Chapter 8, this volume.
[95] Tarak Barkawi, Chapter 2, this volume.
[96] Ole Jacob Sending, Chapter 9, this volume.
[97] Iver Neumann, Chapter 5, this volume.
[98] Vincent Pouliot, Chapter 3, and Jennifer Mitzen, Chapter 4, this volume.
[99] Ian Hurd, Chapter 1, this volume.
[100] Leonard Seabrooke, Chapter 7, this volume.

it becomes absurd to define it as the resolution of conflict by peaceful means. On the other hand, "when conflict is diplomatized, it changes the conflict, but it also changes diplomacy."[101]

The editors note: "As far as authority is concerned, what sets diplomats apart from other types of actors is not that they exclusively engage in representation, but that they claim – usually with success – jurisdictional control over it."[102] In other words, diplomats have the ability to officially represent – and act on behalf of – a state or an organization or institution of some sort. However, as we also learn, this is only part of the story. Diplomats keep the conversation going, but in doing so they also help shape it. What makes diplomacy particular is not just that it focuses on formal representation, but that it sees itself as responsible for managing relations, yet often sneaks away from responsibility for the content of these relations. It is now time that the power-diplomacy nexus is explored in more depth,[103] and this requires further research. If diplomacy is as deeply implicated in the making of world politics as this volume suggests, it not only questions IR theoretical understandings of what drives international relations, but it also challenges the idea that foreign policy is decided by (more or less democratically accountable) governments. So how is the diplomatic making of world politics to be held accountable?

Adopting a relationalist view, the answer cannot be framed in terms of a principal-agent logic – whereby accountability equals control with diplomats depicted as power holders. A relational view of power does not see power as a resource or a substance, one that different individuals or states possess in varying quantities. Instead, power is conceptualized as productive energy that simultaneously shapes and is shaped by social interactions. To address the power involved in the diplomatic making of world politics requires us to trace power in practice, that is, the emergent power, which plays out as a never-ending struggle for recognition as competent.[104] Rather than seeking to attribute power in a reified entity – an actor such as a state or political leader – power can be studied by exploring the actual production of world politics.

101 Iver Neumann, Chapter 5, this volume. 102 Introduction, this volume.
103 Sharp, "Diplomacy, Diplomatic Studies, and the ISA."
104 Rebecca Adler-Nissen and Vincent Pouliot, "Power in Practice: Negotiating the International Intervention in Libya," *European Journal of International Relations*, 20(4), 2014, 889–911.

Conclusion

Diplomats and mainstream IR theory have been mutually estranged. Many diplomats find IR scholarship problematic because it presents their job in abstract and reductionist terms. IR theory seldom takes diplomatic knowledge and practice seriously. Diplomacy, according to many realist and liberalist IR scholars, is done by unitary, sometimes even rational, states with more or less fixed national interests that determine negotiations. Alternatively, constructivists interpret diplomacy as inter-action with mutual signaling of values and identities. Both the image of billiard balls bumping into one another and the image of continuous signaling are far from how diplomats experience world politics. Meanwhile, IR theorists complain about the anecdotal character of diplomatic history and ambassadors' memoirs. Basically, diplomatic self-narratives do not reflect the deeper mechanisms of international relations.[105] This is where this volume provides a richer view of how diplomacy works in practice, by showing that diplomacy is much more than the mediation of estrangement.

I have suggested that one of the reasons for the estrangement between IR scholars and diplomats is that much of IR theory is substantialist, while diplomats work with a relational ontology. For the diplomat, the primary unit of analysis is relations (not states) – what I called the diplomatic folk relationalism. The analysis of diplomacy's role in world politics has been hindered by a priori classifications of diplomacy in state focused, actor-centric ways. Diplomats have been interpreted as substantives that act, rather than nouns that come into being.[106] However, as Barkawi insists in his discussion of Iraq and the war in Syria, we cannot think of "Iraq" as some kind of unitary actor (of course this is true for all states). Instead, we need to recall the web of relations sustaining the war in Syria, the international flows of money, people, material, and arms. The association between peaceful means and diplomacy is problematic. More generally, diplomacy is deeply entangled; it is constantly reproduced and reproducing of other social practices in world politics.

[105] See Colin Elman and Miriam Fendius Elman, "Diplomatic History and International Relations Theory: Respecting Difference and Crossing Boundaries," *International Security*, 22(1), 1997.

[106] Ole Jacob Sending, Chapter 9, this volume.

Uncritically taking on the relational ontology of diplomacy has at least two major pitfalls. First is the risk of accepting the view that diplomacy is a meta-relational practice of mediation. Indeed, if we take the diplomats' own account at face value, diplomacy appears almost empty – it is about mediation and representation, not governance. Arguably, others (line ministries, foreign powers, governments, etc.) feed in with political content, but diplomats are not themselves policy makers. A relational approach as the one sketched out in this book should not stop at the analysis of the co-constitution of diplomacy and other aspects of world politics. Further research should look at the way in which responsibility disappears when diplomacy turns into governance. Deeply entangled in wars, treaty making, refugee crises, and so on, diplomacy is much more than the mediation of estrangement. We also need studies that look into the limits of diplomacy when other international practices, peoples, or technologies manage to silence or marginalize the diplomatic production of world politics.

Second, and related to the first, a relational approach should not avoid the question of power. On the contrary, it should promote a different way of assigning responsibility (today, it is usually with governments, rarely with diplomats). The IR discipline is in need of approaches that can address basic questions about power and influence. A relational approach, as the one proposed in this book, insists that diplomacy's system-maintaining functions, the grease on the wheels, is indeed greasy. Moving from units to relations thus involves less attention to national win-sets and other forms of unhelpful reductionism and more attention to the actual making of world politics.

Bibliography

Aalberts, Tanja E., and Rens Van Munster (2008) "From Wendt to Kuhn: Reviving the 'Third Debate' in International Relations," *International Politics*, 45(6), 720–746.

Abbott, Andrew (1988) *The System of Professions* (Chicago: University of Chicago Press).

Abbott, Andrew (1995) "Things of Boundaries," *Social Research*, 62(4), 857–882.

Abbott, Andrew (2005) "Linked Ecologies: States and Universities as Environments for Professions," *Sociological Theory*, 23(2), 245–274.

Abdelal, Rawi, Yoshiko M. Herrera, Alastair Iain Johnston, and Rose McDermott (2006) "Identity as a Variable," *Perspectives on Politics*, 4(4).

Abrahamsen, Rita, and Michael C. Williams (2010) *Security Beyond the State: Private Security in International Politics* (Cambridge: Cambridge University Press).

ActionAid (2012) *A Just Peace? The Legacy of War for the Women of Afghanistan* (London: ActionAid).

Adler, Emanuel, and Vincent Pouliot (2011) "International Practices: Introduction and Framework," in Emanuel Adler and Vincent Pouliot, eds., *International Practices* (Cambridge: Cambridge University Press), 3–35.

Adler, Emanuel, and Vincent Pouliot (2011) "International Practices," *International Theory*, 3(1), 1–36.

Adler-Nissen, Rebecca (2008) "The Diplomacy of Opting Out: A Bourdieudian Approach to National Integration Strategies," *Journal of Common Market Studies*, 46(3), 663–684.

Adler-Nissen, Rebecca (2009) "Late Sovereign Diplomacy," *The Hague Journal of Diplomacy*, 4(2), 121–141.

Adler-Nissen, Rebecca (2012) "Diplomacy as Impression Management: Strategic Face-Work and Post-Colonial Embarrassment," Working Paper #38, Center for International Peace and Security Studies, McGill University.

Adler-Nissen, Rebecca (2014) *Opting Out of the European Union: Diplomacy, Sovereignty and European Integration* (Cambridge: Cambridge University Press).

Adler-Nissen, Rebecca (2015) "Just Greasing the Wheels? Mediating Difference or the Evasion of Power and Responsibility in Diplomacy," *The Hague Journal of Diplomacy*, 10(2), 2015, 22–28.

Adler-Nissen, Rebecca, and Vincent Pouliot (2014) "Power in Practice: Negotiating the International Intervention in Libya," *European Journal of International Relations*, 20(4), 1–23.

Air Force International Affairs, www.safia.hq.af.mil/internationalaffairs specialist, accessed July 6, 2014.

Albert, M., D. Jacobson, and Y. Lapid (eds.) (2001) *Identities, Borders, Orders: Rethinking International Relations Theory* (Minneapolis: University of Minnesota Press).

Albert, Matthias, Lars-Erik Cederman, and Alexander Wendt (2010) *New Systems Theory and International Relations* (London: Palgrave), 99–126.

Alter, J. (2014) *The New Terrain of International Law: Courts, Politics, Rights* (Princeton, NJ: Princeton University Press).

Ambrosetti, David (2009) *Normes et rivalités diplomatiques à l'ONU. Le Conseil de sécurité en audience* (Brussels: Peter Lang).

Andersen, Morten Skumsrud, and Iver B. Neumann (2012) "Practices as Models: A Methodology with an Illustration Concerning Wampum Diplomacy," *Millennium*, 40(3), 457–481.

Anderson, Kenneth (2000) "The Ottawa Convention Banning Landmines, the Role of International Non-governmental Organizations and the Idea of International Civil Society," *European Journal of International Law*, 11(1), 91–120.

Angers, Kathleen (2010) *Intégration européenne et pratique diplomatique. L'expérience autrichienne (1987–2009)*. MA thesis, Université de Montréal.

Appathurai, E. R. (1985) "Permanent Missions in New York," in G. R. Berridge and A. Jennings, eds., *Diplomacy at the* UN (London: MacMillan), 64–108.

Asad, Talal (2003) *Formations of the Secular* (Stanford: Stanford University Press).

Ashley, Richard K. (1984) "The Poverty of Neorealism," *International Organization*, 38(2), 225–286.

Ashley, Richard K. (1988) "Untying the Sovereign State: A Double Reading of the Anarchy Problematique," *Millennium – Journal of International Studies*, 17, 227–262.

Atkinson, Carol (2006) "Constructivist Implications of Material Power: Military Engagement and the Socialization of States," *International Studies Quarterly*, 50(3), 509–510.

Australian Customs and Border Protection Service (ACBPS) (2011) "Strategic Assessment of Counter People Smuggling Communications

Activities, November 2011," www.customs.gov.au/webdata/resources/files/2012-018673_Document04_Released.pdf.

Australian Government, Senate Standing Committees on Foreign Affairs, Defence and Trade, *Inquiry into the Nature and Conduct of Australia's Public Diplomacy, Australia's Public Diplomacy: Building our Image*, Chap. 6, "The Coherence and Consistency of Australia's Public Diplomacy Message," Committee Hansard, 04–11-2007, 15, www.aph.gov.au/Parliamentary_Business/Committees/Senate/Foreign_Affairs_Defence_and_Trade/Completed_inquiries/2004-07/public_diplomacy/report/c06

Autessere, Séverine (2010) *The Trouble with the Congo: Local Violence and the Failure of International Peacebuilding* (Cambridge: Cambridge University Press).

Avant, Deborah, Martha Finnemore, and Susan Sell (eds.) (2010) *Who Governs the Globe?* (Cambridge: Cambridge University Press).

Badie, Bertrand (2009) "The European Challenge to Bismarckian Diplomacy," *International Politics*, 46(5), 519.

Badie, Bertrand, and Guillaume Devin (eds.) (2007) *Le multilatéralisme. Nouvelles formes de l'action internationale* (Paris: La Découverte).

Barkawi, Tarak (2001) "War Inside the Free World: The Democratic Peace and the Cold War in the Third World," in Tarak Barkawi and Mark Laffey, eds., *Democracy, Liberalism and War* (Boulder, CO: Lynne Rienner), 107–128.

Barkawi, Tarak (2010) "State and Armed Force in International Context," in Alex Colas and Bryan Mabee, eds., *Mercenaries, Pirates, Bandits and Empires* (London: Hurst), 33–53.

Barkawi, Tarak (2011) "'Defence Diplomacy' in North/South Relations," *International Journal*, 66(3), 597–612.

Barkawi, Tarak, and Shane Brighton (2011) "Powers of War: Fighting, Knowledge and Critique," *International Political Sociology*, 5(2), 126–143.

Barnett, Michael (2006) "Building a Republican Peace: Stabilizing States After War," *International Security*, 30(4), 87–112.

Barnett, Michael (2011) *Empire of Humanity: A History of Humanitarianism* (Ithaca, NY: Cornell University Press).

Barnett, Michael, and Martha Finnemore (2004) *Rules for the World: International Organizations in Global Politics* (Ithaca, NY: Cornell University Press).

Barnett, Michael, and Raymond Duvall (2005) "Power in Global Governance," in Michael Barnett and Raymond Duvall, eds., *Power in Global Governance* (Cambridge: Cambridge University Press), 1–32.

Barnett, Michael, and Janice Gross Stein (2012) "Introduction: The Secularization and Sanctification of Humanitarianism," in Michael Barnett and Janice Gross Stein, eds., *Sacred Aid: Faith and Humanitarianism* (New York: Oxford University Press), 3–36.

Barnett, Michael, and Janice Gross Stein (eds.) (2012) *Sacred Aid: Faith and Humanitarianism* (New York: Oxford University Press).

Barnett, Michael, and Thomas Weiss (2008) *Humanitarianism in Question: Power, Politics, Ethics* (Ithaca and London: Cornell University Press).

Barnett, Michael N. (2010) *The International Humanitarian Order* (London: Routledge).

Baron, Kevin (2013) "Pentagon's China Guru David Helvey: Friction Is 'Inevitable' but Mil-Mil Relations Are 'as Good as It's Been,'" *Foreign Policy*, May 8, http://foreignpolicy.com/2013/05/09/pentagons-china-guru-david-helvey-friction-is-inevitable-but-mil-mil-relations-are-as-good-as-its-been/, accessed June 15, 2013.

Baron, Kevin (2013) "US Army 'Fences Off' Military Diplomacy from Sequester," *Foreign Policy*, Retrieved from http://e-ing.foreignpolicy.com/posts/2013/05/14/us_army_fences_off_military_diplomacy_from_sequester, accessed May 26, 2013.

Barston, R. P. (2014) *Modern Diplomacy*, 4th edn (London: Routledge), 1, 4–5, 244.

Bauman, Zygmunt (1992) *Intimations of Postmodernity* (London: Routledge).

Baumann, Rony (2012) "Médicins Sans Frontieres and the ICRC: Matters of Principle," *International Review of the Red Cross*, 94(888).

Bergen, Peter (2014) "Obama's High-Stakes Drone War in Yemen," CNN, http://edition.cnn.com/2014/04/21/opinion/bergen-yemen-obama-drone-war/index.html, accessed June 13, 2014.

Berman, Nathaniel (2005) "Legitimacy Through Defiance: From Goa to Iraq," *Wisconsin Journal of International Law*, 23.

Berridge, G. R. (1994) *Talking to the Enemy – How States without 'Diplomatic Relations Communicate* (London: St Martin's Press).

Berridge, G. R. (2010) *Diplomacy* (Basingstoke: Palgrave Macmillan), 207–208.

Betsill, Michelle, and Elizabeth Corell (eds.) (2007) *NGO Diplomacy: The Influence of Non-governmental Organizations in International Environmental Negotiations* (Cambridge, MA: MIT Press).

Biersteker, Thomas, and Sue E. Eckert. UN Targeted Sanctions Consortium at the Watson Institute at Brown University/Graduate Institute, http://graduateinstitute.ch/un-sanctions, accessed April 5, 2015.

Bjola, Corneliu (2009) *Legitimising the Use of Force in World Politics: Kosovo, Iraq, and the Ethics of Intervention* (London: Routledge).

Bjola, Corneliu, and Markus Kronprobst (eds.) (2011) *Arguing Global Governance: Agency, Lifeworld, and Shared Reasoning* (Oxford: Routledge).

Black, Jeremy (2010) *A History of Diplomacy* (London: Reaktion Books), 12.

Blair, Alasdair (2001) "Permanent Representations to the European Union," *Diplomacy and Statecraft* 12(3), 139–158.

Bob, Clifford (2005) *The Marketing of Rebellion: Insurgents, Media, and International Activism* (Cambridge: Cambridge University Press).

Boltanski, Luc (1999) *Distant Suffering: Morality, Media, and Politics*. (Cambridge: Cambridge University Press).

Booth, Ken, and Nicholas J. Wheeler (2008) *The Security Dilemma* (Houndmills: Palgrave MacMillan).

Borchgrevink, Axel (2009) "Aiding Rights? Dilemmas in Norwegian and Swedish Development Cooperation with Ethiopia" *Nordisk tidsskrift for menneskerettigheter* 27(4), 452–466.

Borrie, John (2009) *Unacceptable Harm: A History of How the Treaty to Ban Cluster Munitions Was Won* (Geneva: United Nations Institute for Disarmament Research).

Bourdieu, P., J. C. Chamboredon, J. C. Passeron, and B. Krais (eds.) (1991) *The Craft of Sociology: Epistemological Preliminaries* (Berlin and New York: Walter de Gruyter).

Bourdieu, Pierre (1978). "Sport and Social Class." *Social Science Information*, *17*(6), 819–840.

Bourdieu, Pierre (1990) *The Logic of Practice* (Stanford: Stanford University Press).

Bourdieu, Pierre (2000) *Pascalian Mediations* (Cambridge: Polity Press).

Boussebaa, Mehdi, Glenn Morgan, and Andrew Sturdy (2012) "Constructing Global Firms? National, Transnational and Neocolonial Effects in International Management Consultancies," *Organization Studies* 33(4), 465–486.

Bratman, Michael (1999) *Intention, Plans, and Practical Reason* (Stanford: CSLI Publications).

Brennan, John, Gordon Lubold, and Noah Schachtman (2013) "Inside Yemen's Shadow War Arsenal," *Foreign Policy*, August 7, 2013, www.foreignpolicy.com/articles/2013/08/07/inside_yemens_shadow_war_arsenal, accessed June 8, 2014.

Bridge, Robert (2011) "Tough Talking: Russia and US Discuss European Missile Defense," *RT*, August 31, 2011, http://rt.com/politics/russia-us-missile-defense-embassy-moscow-519/, accessed June 5, 2013.

Brooks, Stephen G., and William C. Wohlforth (2008) *World out of Balance: International Relations and the Challenge of American Primacy* (Princeton, NJ: Princeton University Press).

Brown, Robin (2010) "Diplomacy, Public Diplomacy and Social Networks," Paper presented at the 2010 Annual Convention of the International Studies Association, New Orleans, Louisiana, 6.

Bruner, Edward F. (2007) "CRS Report for Congress: US Military Dispositions: Fact Sheet," www.fas.org/sgp/crs/natsec/RS20649.pdf, accessed May 16, 2013.

Brunnée, Jutta, and Stephen J. Toope (2011) "An Interactional Theory of International Legal 'Obligation,'" *Legal Studies Research Paper*, University of Toronto, #08–16.

Buchanan, Allen (2007) *Justice, Legitimacy, and Self-Determination: Moral Foundations for International Law* (Oxford: Oxford University Press) cited in Henry Shue and David Rodin (2007) *Preemption: Military Action and Moral Justification* (Oxford: Oxford University Press).

Buchanan-Smith, Margie (2003) "How the Sphere Project Came into Being: A Case Study of Policy-Making in the Humanitarian Aid Sector and the Relative Influence of Research," *ODI Working Paper*, 215.

Buchet de Neuilly, Yves (2009), "Devenir diplomate multilatéral. Le sens pratique des calculs appropriés," *Cultures et conflits* 79, 75–98.

Bull, Hedley (1977) *The Anarchical Society. A Study of Order in World Politics* (London: Macmillan).

Burt, Ronald S. (2004) "Structural Holes and Good Ideas," *American Journal of Sociology* 110(2), 349–399.

Byman, Daniel (2006) "Remaking Alliances for the War on Terrorism," *Journal of Strategic Studies* 29(5), 767–811.

Byrnes, Timothy A., and Peter J. Katzenstein (eds.) (2006) *Religion in an Expanding Europe* (Cambridge: Cambridge University Press).

Calhoun, Cheshire (2000) "The Virtue of Civility," *Philosophy and Public Affairs* 29(3), 251–275.

Calhoun, Craig (2010) "The Idea of Emergency: Humanitarian Action and Global (Dis)Order," in Didier Fassin and Mariella Pandolfi (eds.), *Contemporary States of Emergency* (New York: Zone Books), 29–58, 47.

Carpenter, R. Charli (2011) "Vetting the Advocacy Agenda: Networks, Centrality and the Paradox of Weapons Norms," *International Organization* 65(1), 69–102.

Carvalho de, Benjamin, and Ole Jacob Sending (eds.) (2013) *Protection of Civilians in UN Peace Operations* (Berlin: Nomos Verlag).

Carvalho de, Benjamin, Halvard Leira, and John M. Hobson (2011) "The Big Bangs of IR: The Myths That Your Teachers Still Tell You about 1648 and 1919," *Millennium* 39(3), 735–758.

Casanova, José (1994) *Public Religions in the Modern World* (Chicago: University of Chicago Press).

Casanova, José (2008) "Balancing Religious Freedom and Cultural Preservation," *The Review of Faith and International Affairs*, 13.

Castells, Manuel (2008) "The New Public Sphere: Global Civil Society, Communication Networks, and Global Governance," *The Annals of the American Academy of Political and Social Science* 616(1), 78–93.

Castle, Timothy N. (1993) *At War in the Shadow of Vietnam: U.S. Military Aid to the Royal Lao Government 1955–1975* (New York: Columbia University Press), 61.

Center for Constitutional Rights (2011) "CCR Announces Bush Indictment for Convention against Torture Signatory States," http://ccrjustice.org/newsroom/press-releases/human-rights-groups-announce-bush-indictment-convention-against-torture-sign, accessed February 8, 2011.

Chandler, David (2001) "The Road to Military Humanitarianism: How the Human Rights NGOs Shaped a New Humanitarian Agenda," *Human Rights Quarterly* 23(3), 678–700.

Chayes, Abram, and Antonia Handler Chayes (1995) *The New Sovereignty: Compliance with International Regulatory Agreements* (Cambridge, MA: Harvard University Press), 25–26, 119.

Checkel, Jeffrey (2001) "Why Comply? Social Learning and European Identity Change," *International Organization* 55(3), 553–588.

Checkel, Jeffrey T. (ed.) (2007) *International Institutions and Socialization in Europe* (Cambridge: Cambridge University Press).

Chesterman, Simon (2006) "Who Needs Rules? The Prospects of a Rules-Based International System," discussion paper for Institute of International Law and Justice, New York University.

Chesterman, Simon (2008) "An International Rule of Law?" *American Journal of Comparative Law* 5, 331–361.

Chwieroth, Jeffrey M. (2010) *A Capital Idea: The Role of Neoliberalism in the Resurrection of Global Finance in Emerging Markets* (Princeton, NJ: Princeton University Press).

Clinton, Hillary Rodham (2010) "Leading through Civilian Power," *Foreign Affairs* 89(6).

Codevilla, Angelo M. (2008) "Tools of Statecraft: Diplomacy and War," Foreign Policy Research Institute, www.fpri.org/footnotes/1301.200801.codevilla.statecraftdiplomacywar.html, accessed June 3, 2013.

Cohen, Roberta (2012) "From Sovereignty to Responsibility," in W. Andy Knight and Frazer Egerton, eds.,*The Routledge Handbook of the Responsibility to Protect* (London: Routledge).

Constantinou, C. M. (2013) "Between Statecraft and Humanism: Diplomacy and Its Forms of Knowledge," *International Studies Review* 15(2), 141–162.

Constantinou, C. M., and J. Der Derian (2010) "Sustaining Global Hope: Sovereignty, Power and the Transformation of Diplomacy," in

C. M. Constantinou and J. Der Derian, eds., *Sustainable Diplomacies* (London: Palgrave Macmillan), 1–22.

Constantinou, Costas (1996) *On the Way to Diplomacy* (Minneapolis: University of Minnesota Press).

Cooley, Alexander (2008) *Base Politics* (Ithaca, NY: Cornell University Press).

Cooley, Alexander, and James Ron (2002) "The NGO Scramble: Organizational Insecurity and the Political Economy of Transnational Action," *International Security* 27(1), 5–39.

Cooley, Alexander, and Daniel H. Nexon (2011) "'We Are All Georgians Now': Symbolic Capital, Trust, and Authority under Hierarchy." Unpublished ms., https://bc.sas.upenn.edu/system/files/Nexon_04.11.12.pdf, accessed July 3, 2013.

Cooley, Alexander, and Daniel Nexon (2013) "The Empire Will Compensate You: The Structural Dynamics of the U.S. Overseas Basing Network," *Perspective on Politics*, 11(4).

Cooley, Alexander, and James Ron (2002) "The NGO Scramble: Organizational Insecurity and the Political Economy of Transnational Action," *International Security* 27(1).

Cooper, Andrew F. (1997) "Beyond Representation," *International Journal* 53(1), 173–178.

Cooper, Andrew F. (2008) *Celebrity Diplomacy* (Boulder, CO: Paradigm).

Cooper, Andrew F., John English, and Ramesh C. Thakur (eds.) (2002) *Enhancing Global Governance: Towards a New Diplomacy* (New York: United Nations University Press).

Cooper, Andrew F., Brian Hocking, and William Maley (eds.) (2008) *Governance and Diplomacy: Worlds Apart?* (New York: Palgrave Macmillan).

Copeland, D. C. (2000) "The Constructivist Challenge to Structural Realism: A Review Essay," *International Security* 25(2), 187–212.

Cozette, Murielle (2008) "What Lies Ahead: Classical Realism on the Future of International Relations," *International Studies Review* 10(4), 667–679.

Crawford, Neta (2002) *Argument and Change in World Politics: Ethics, Decolonization, and Humanitarian Intervention* (Cambridge: Cambridge University Press).

Crescenzi, Mark J. C., Jacob D. Kathman, Katja B. Kleinberg, and Reed M. Wood (2012) "Reliability, Reputation, and Alliance Formation," *International Studies Quarterly* 55(2), 259–274.

Crocker, Chester, Fen Osler Hampson, and Pamela Aall (eds.) (1999) *Herding Cats: Multiparty Mediation in a Complex World* (Washington, DC: United States Institute of Peace).

Cronin, Bruce (2008) "Conclusion: Assessing the Council's Authority," in Bruce Cronin and Ian Hurd, eds., *The UN Security Council and the*

Politics of International Authority (London and New York: Routledge), 199–214.

Cross, Mai'a K. Davis (2007) *The European Diplomatic Corps: Diplomats and International Cooperation from Westphalia to Maastrich* (London and New York: Palgrave).

Cross, Mai'a K. Davis (2011) *Security Integration in Europe: How Knowledge-based Networks Are Transforming the European Union* (Ann Arbor: University of Michigan Press).

Defense Security Cooperation Agency, www.dsca.mil/, accessed August 5, 2013.

Deitelhoff, Nicole (2009) "The Discursive Process of Legalization: Charting Islands of Persuasion in the ICC Case," *International Organization* 63(1), 33–65.

Deitelhoff, Nicole (2009) "The Discursive Process of Legalization: Charting Islands of Persuasion in the ICC Case," *International Organization* 63(1), 33–65.

Deitelhoff, Nicole, and Harald Müller (2005) "Theoretical Paradise—Empirically Lost? Arguing with Habermas." *Review of International Studies* 31(1), 167–179.

Del Mar, Maksymilian 2011. "Concerted Practices and the Presence of Obligations: Joint Action in Competition Law and Social Philosophy," *Law and Philosophy* 30, 105–140.

Department for International Development, the Foreign and Commonwealth Office and the Ministry of Defence (2011) "Building Stability Overseas Strategy," www.gov.uk/government/uploads/system/uploads/attachment_data/file/67475/Building-stability-overseas-strategy.pdf, retrieved June 15, 2013.

Der Derian, James (1987) "Mediating Estrangement," *Review of International Studies* 13 (2), 91–110.

Der Derian, James (1987) *On Diplomacy: A Genealogy of Western Estrangement* (Oxford: Blackwell).

Der Derian, James (1996) "Hedley Bull and the Idea of Diplomatic Culture," in Rick Fawn and Jeremy Larkins, eds., *International Society after the Cold War: Anarchy and Order Reconsidered* (Houndsmills: Macmillan), 84–100.

Devji, Faisal (2008) *The Terrorist in Search of Humanity: Militant Islam and Global Politics* (London: Hurst).

Dezalay, Yves, and Bryant G. Garth (1996) *Dealing in Virtue: International Commercial Arbitration and the Construction of a Transnational Legal Order* (Chicago: University of Chicago Press).

DFLIC Website "About DLIFIC," www.dliflc.edu/about.html, accessed June 13, 2013.

DOD (2012) *Annual Foreign Area Officer Report*, https://fao.nps.edu/documents/10249/2373fa8b-4446-46d7-baac-954c67554250, accessed September 10, 2013.

Doty, Roxanne L. (1997) "Aporia: A Critical Exploration of the Agent-Structure Problematique in International Relations Theory," *European Journal of International Relations* 3(3).

Doyle, Michael (2008) *Striking First: Preemption and Prevention in International Conflict* (Princeton, NJ: Princeton University Press).

Doyle, Michael, and Nicholas Sambanis (2011) *Making War and Building Peace: United Nations Peace Operations* (Princeton, NJ: Princeton University Press).

DuBois, Marc (2008) "Civilian Protection and Humanitarian Advocacy: Strategies and (False?) Dilemmas," *Humanitarian Exchange Magazine*, issue 39, 1.

Dunoff, Jeffrey, and Mark A. Pollack (eds.) (2013) *Interdisciplinary Perspectives on International Law and International Relations: The State of the Art* (Cambridge: Cambridge University Press).

Earle, Timothy (1997) *How Chiefs Come to Power: The Political Economy in Prehistory* (Stanford: Stanford University Press).

Egeland, Jan (1999) "The Oslo Accords: Multiparty Facilitation through the Norwegian Channel," in Chester Crocker, Fensler A. Hampson, and Pamela Aall, eds., *Herding the Cats* (Washington, DC: U.S. Institute of Peace), 527–546.

Ekengren, Magnus (2002) *The Time of European Governance* (Manchester: Manchester University Press).

Elman, Colin, and Miriam Fendius Elman (1997) "Diplomatic History and International Relations Theory: Respecting Difference and Crossing Boundaries," *International Security* 22(1), 5–21.

Elster, Jon (1995) "Strategic Uses of Argument," in Kenneth Arrow et al., eds., *Barriers to Conflict Resolution* (New York: W. W. Norton), 236–257.

Elster, Jon (1998) "Deliberation and Constitution-Making," in Jon Elster, ed., *Deliberative Democracy* (Cambridge: Cambridge University Press), 97–122.

Emirbayer, M. (1997) "Manifesto for a Relational Sociology," *American Journal of Sociology*, 103(2), 281–317.

ENJJPT, www.sheppard.af.mil/library/factsheetspage/factsheet.asp?fsID=5168, accessed May 27, 2013.

Enloe, Cynthia (1990) *Bananas, Beaches and Bases: Making Feminist Sense of International Politics* (Berkeley: University of California Press).

Epstein, Charlotte (2008) *The Power of Words in International Relations: Birth of an Anti-Whaling Discourse* (Cambridge, MA: MIT Press).

Eriksen, Stein S., and Ole Jacob Sending (2013) "There Is No Global Public," *International Theory* 5(2), 213–237.

Evans-Pritchard, E. E. (1940) *The Political System of the Anuak of the Anglo-Egyptian Sudan*. Monographs on Social Anthropology, no. 4, 164.

Evans-Pritchard, E. E. (1949) *The Nuer: A Description of the Modes of Livelihood and Political Institutions of a Nilotic People* (Oxford: Clarendon).

Evetts, Julia (2013) "Professionalism: Value and Ideology," *Current Sociology*, DOI: 10.1177/0011392113479316.

Eyffinger, Arthur (2012) "Diplomacy," in Bardo Fassbender and Anne Peters, eds., *The Oxford Handbook of the History of International Law* (Oxford: Oxford University Press), 813–849.

Fall, Bernard (1969) *Anatomy of a Crisis* (Garden City, NY: Doubleday).

Fassbender, Bardo, and Anne Peters (eds.) (2012) *Oxford Handbook of the History of International Law* (Oxford: Oxford University Press).

Fassin, Didier (2010) "Heart of Humanness: The Moral Economy of Humanitarian Intervention," in Didier Fassin and Mariella Pandolfi, eds., *Contemporary States of Emergency* (New York: Zone Books), 269–293.

Fassin, Didier, and Mariella Pandolfi (2010) "Introduction: Military Humanitarian Government in the Age of Intervention," in Didier Fassin and Mariella Pandolfi, eds., *Contemporary States of Emergency* (New York: Zone Books), 9–25.

Faulconbridge, James R., and Daniel Muzio (2008) "Organizational Professionalism in Globalizing Law Firms," *Work, Employment and Society* 22(1), 7–25.

Faulconbridge, James, and Daniel Muzio (2012) "Professions in a Globalizing World: Towards a Transnational Sociology of the Professions," *International Sociology* 27(1), 136–152.

Fearon, James (1995) "Rationalist Explanations for War," *International Organization* 49 (3), 379–414.

Fearon, James (1998) "Deliberation as Discussion," in Jon Elster, ed., *Deliberative Democracy* (Cambridge: Cambridge University Press), 44–68.

Fearon, James, and Alexander Wendt (2002) "Rationalism v. Constructivism: A Skeptical View," in Walter Carlsnaes, Thomas Risse, and Beth Simmons, eds., *Handbook of International Relations* (Thousand Oaks, CA: Sage), 52–72.

Federal Department of Foreign Affairs, Human Security Division, last modification: 08.05.2014, www.eda.admin.ch/eda/en/home/dfa/orgcha/sectio/pad/pad4.html.

Ferris, Elizabeth (2005) "Faith-based and Secular Humanitarian Organizations," *International Review of the Red Cross*, 87, 858, 313.

Finnemore, M., and K. Sikkink (1998) "International Norm Dynamics and Political Change," *International Organization* 52(4), 887–917.

Fortes, M., and E. E. Evans-Pritchard (eds.) (1940) *African Political Systems* (New York: Oxford University Press).

Foucault, Michel (2004) *Society Must be Defended* (London: Penguin), 15.

Fourcade, Marion (2006) "The Construction of a Global Profession: The Transnationalization of Economics," *American Journal of Sociology* 112(1), 145–194.

Fourcade, Marion (2009) *Economists and Societies: Discipline and Profession in the United States, Britain, and France, 1890s to 1990s* (Princeton, NJ: Princeton: Princeton University Press).

Galston, William A. (2010) "Realism in Political Theory," *European Journal of Political Theory* 9(4), 385–411.

Gammeltoft-Hansen, T., and R. Adler-Nissen (2008) "An Introduction to Sovereignty Games," in R. Adler-Nissen and T. Gammeltoft-Hansen, eds., *Sovereignty Games: Instrumentalizing State Sovereignty in Europe and beyond.* (New York: Palgrave Macmillan), 1–19.

George, Alexander (1991) *Forceful Persuasion: Coercive Diplomacy as an Alternative to War* (Washington, DC: United States Institute of Peace Press).

Geppert, Dominik (2008) "German and British Ways with the Press," in Markus Mösslang and Torsten Riotte, eds., *The Diplomats' World: A Cultural History of Diplomacy 1815–1904* (New York: Oxford University Press), 133–164.

Ghebali, Victor-Yves (1998), "L'évolution du phénomène des missions permanentes à Genève," in M. A. Boisard and E. M. Chossudovsky, eds., *Multilateral Diplomacy: The United Nations System at Geneva* (The Hague: Kluwer Law International), 39–45.

Gilbert, Margaret (1992) *On Social Facts* (Princeton, NJ: Princeton University Press).

Gilbert, Margaret (2003) "The Structure of the Social Atom," in Frederick Schmitt, ed., *Socializing Metaphysics: The Nature of Social Reality* (Lanham, MD: Rowman and Littlefield), 39–64.

Gilbert, Margaret (2006) *A Theory of Political Obligation* (Oxford: Clarendon Press).

Gilbert, Margaret (2006) "Rationality in Collective Action," *Philosophy of the Social Sciences*, 36(1), 3–17.

Gilpin, Robert (1981) *War and Change in International Politics* (Cambridge: Cambridge University Press).

Givoni, Michal (2011) "Humanitarian Governance and Ethical Cultivation: Médecins sans Frontières and the Advent of the Expert-Witness," *Millennium – Journal of International Studies* 40, 43–63.

Glaser, Charles L. (1997) "The Security Dilemma Revisited," *World Politics* 50, 171–201.
Global Witness (2012) "Seeing the Strings: Global Witness Annual Review 2011" (London: Global Witness Ltd).
Goddard, Stacie E. (2009) "Brokering Change: Networks and Entrepreneurs in International Politics," *International Theory* 1, 249–281.
Goddard, Stacie E. (2012), "Brokering Peace: Networks, Legitimacy, and the Northern Ireland Peace Process," *International Studies Quarterly* 56(3), 501–515.
Goffman, Erving (1967) *Interaction Ritual: Essays on Face-to-face Behavior*. New York: Random House.
Goffman, Erving (1983) "The Interaction Order: American Sociological Association, 1982 Presidential Address," *American Sociological Review* 48(1), 1–17.
Goldsmith, Jack, and Eric Posner (2005) *The Limits of International Law* (Oxford: Oxford University Press).
Goodman, Ryan, and Derek Jinks (2005) "Toward an Institutional Theory of Sovereignty," *Stanford Law Review*, 55.
Gordon, Michael R., Eric Schmitt, and Tim Arango (2012) "Flow of Arms to Syria Persists, to U.S. Dismay." *New York Time*, December 12, www.nytimes.com/2012/12/02/world/middleeast/us-is-stumbling-in-effort-to-cut-syria-arms-flow.html?_r=0.
Gotz, Norbert (2011) *Deliberative Diplomacy: The Nordic Approach to Global Governance and Societal Representation at the United Nations* (St. Louis, MO: Republic of Letters Publishing).
Grandin, Greg (2006) *Empire's Workshop* (New York: Henry Holt).
Gray, Rosie (2013) "How Carne Ross Created a New Kind of Diplomacy," BuzzFeed Politics, July 9, 2013, www.buzzfeed.com/rosiegray/how-carne-ross-created-a-new-kind-of-diplomacy, accessed July 6, 2014.
Gregory, Derek (2004) *The Colonial Present* (Oxford: Blackwell).
Grey, Christine D. (2008) *International Law and the Use of Force*, 3rd edn (Oxford: Oxford University Press).
Grosser, Pierre (2007) "De 1945 aux années 1980: une efflorescence sur fond de Guerre froide et de décolonisation," in Bertrand Badie and Guillaume Devin, eds., *Le multilatéralisme. Nouvelles forms de l'action internationale* (Paris: La Découverte), 23–40.
Gruber, Lloyd (2000) *Ruling the World: Power Politics and the Rise of Supranational Institutions* (Princeton, NJ: Princeton University Press).
Guillaume, Xavier (2002) "Foreign Policy and the Politics of Alterity: A Dialogical Understanding of International Relations," *Millennium* 31(1).
Gulati, Ranjay, Nitin Nohria, and Akbar Zaheer (2000) "Strategic Networks," *Strategic Management Journal* 21(3), 203–215.

Haas, Peter M. (1992) "Knowledge, Power and International Policy Coordination," *International Organization* 46(1).

Habermas, Jurgen (1984) *Theory of Communicative Action*, vol. 2 (Boston, MA: Beacon Press).

Hafner-Burton, Emilie M., Miles Kahler, and Alexander H. Montgomery (2009) "Network Analysis for International Relations," *International Organization* 63(3), 559–592.

Hafner-Burton, Emilie, David G. Victor, and Yonatan Lupu (2012) "Political Science Research on International Law: The State of the Field," *American Journal of International Law* 106(1), 47–97.

Hall, Rodney Bruce (1997) "Moral Authority as a Power Resource," *International Organization* 51(4), 591–622.

Hamilton, Keith, and Richard Langhorne (2011) *The Practice of Diplomacy*, 2nd edn (London: Routledge), 1.

Hammer, Joshua (2004) "Uncivil Military," *New Republic*, March 1.

Hanneman, Robert A., and Mark Riddle (2011) "Concepts and Measures for Basic Network Analysis," in John Scott and Peter J. Carrington, eds., *The SAGE Handbook of Social Network Analysis* (Thousand Oaks, CA: Sage), 340–369.

Harpviken, Kristian Berg, and Inger Skjelsbæk (2010) "Tilslørt Fredspolitikk" *Nytt norsk tidsskrift* 27(4), 379–388.

Harries, Richard (ed.) (1986) *Reinhold Niebuhr and the Issues of Our Time* (London and Oxford: Mowbray).

Harroff-Tavel, Marion (2006) "The Humanitarian Diplomacy of the International Committee of the Red Cross," www.icrc.org/eng/resources/documents/article/other/humanitarian-diplomacy-articles-040310.htm.

Haspeslagh, Sophie (2013) "'Listing Terrorists': The Impact of Proscription on Third-Party Efforts to Engage Armed Groups in Peace Processes – A Practitioner's Perspective," *Critical Studies on Terrorism* 6(1).

Hawkins, Darren G. et al. (2006) *Delegation and Agency in International Organizations* (New York: Cambridge University Press).

Hehir, J. Bryan (2006) "The Old Church and the New Europe: Charting the Changes," in Timothy Byrnes and Peter Katzenstein, eds., *Religion in an Expanding Europe* (New York: Cambridge University Press), 93–116.

Held, David, and Anthony McGrew (eds.) (2002) *Governing Globalization: Power, Authority, and Global Governance* (Cambridge: Polity Press).

Hertzke, Allen D. (2008) "International Religious Freedom Policy: Taking Stock," *The Review of Faith and International Affairs* 17.

Hill, Charles (2004) "Remarks by Charles Hill," *ASIL Proceedings* 98, 329–331.

Hirschfeld, Lawrence A. (1996) *Race in the Making: Cognition, Culture and the Child's Construction of Human Kinds* (Cambridge, MA: MIT Press).

Hobden, S., and J. M. Hobson (eds.) (2002) *Historical Sociology of International Relations* (Cambridge: Cambridge University Press).

Hocking, Andrew F., and Brian Cooper (2000) "Governments, Non-governmental Organisations and the Re-calibration of Diplomacy," *Global Society* 14(3).

Holder, Eric (2012) "Remarks to Northwestern University School of Law," March 5, www.justice.gov/iso/opa/ag/speeches/2012/ag-speech-1203051.html, accessed February 25, 2013.

Holland, Ben (2010) "Sovereignty as Dominium?" *International Studies Quarterly* 54, 449–480.

Holmes, Marcus (2011) *The Force of Face-to-Face Diplomacy in International Politics*, PhD dissertation, Ohio State University.

Holton, Richard (1999) "Intention and Weakness of Will," *Journal of Philosophy* 96(5), 241–262.

Hongju Koh, Harold (1997) "Why Do Nations Obey International Law? *Yale Law Journal* 106(8), 2599–2659.

Hopgood, Stephen (2006) *Keepers of the Flame: Inside Amnesty International* (Ithaca, NY: Cornell University Press).

Hopgood, Stephen (2009) "Moral Authority, Modernity and the Politics of the Sacred," *European Journal of International Relations* 15(2), 229–255.

Hopgood, Stephen, and Leslie Vinjamuri (2012) "Faith in Markets," in Michael Barnett and Janice Gross Stein, eds., *Sacred Aid: Faith and Humanitarianism* (New York: Oxford University Press), 43.

Hurd, Elizabeth Shakman (2007) *The Politics of Secularism in International Relations* (Princeton, NJ: Princeton University Press).

Hurd, Ian (2003) "Labor Standards through International Organizations: The Global Compact in Comparative Perspective," *Journal of Corporate Citizenship*, 11.

Hurd, Ian (2007) "Breaking and Making Norms: American Revisionism and Crises of Legitimacy," *International Politics*, 44.

Hurd, Ian (2008) *After Anarchy: Legitimacy and Power in the UN Security Council* (Princeton, NJ: Princeton University Press).

Hurd, Ian (2011) "Is Humanitarian Intervention Legal? The Rule of Law in an Incoherent World," *Ethics and International Affairs* 25(3), 293–313.

Hurd, Ian (2011) "Law and the Practice of Diplomacy," *International Journal* Summer, 581–596.

Hurd, Ian (2014) "The International Rule of Law: Law and the Limits of Politics," *Ethics and International Affairs* 28(1), 39–51.

Hutchinson, Sharon E. (1996) *Nuer Dilemmas: Coping with Money, War, and the State* (Berkeley: University of California Press).

Huysmans, Jef (1997) "James Der Derian: The Unbearable Lightness of Theory" in Iver B. Neumann and Ole Wæver, eds., *The Future of*

International Relations: Masters in the Making (London: Routledge), 360–383.

ICJ Advisory Opinion (2010) "Accordance with International Law of the Unilateral Declaration of Independence in Respect of Kosovo," www.icj-cij.org/docket/files/141/15987.pdf, accessed February 25, 2013.

Ikenberry, G. John (2000) *After Victory: Institutions, Strategic Restraint, and the Rebuilding of Order after Major Wars* (Princeton, NJ: Princeton University Press).

Ikenberry, John G. (2011) *Liberal Leviathan: The Origins, Crisis, and Transformation of the American World Order* (Princeton, NJ: Princeton University Press).

Inayatullah, Naeem, and David L. Blaney (2004) *International Relations and the Problem of Difference* (London: Routledge).

Ingebritsen, Christine (2002) "Norm Entrepreneurs: Scandinavia's Role in World Politics," *Cooperation and Conflict* 37(1), 11–12.

Ingo, Venzke (2015) "Is Interpretation in International Law a Game?" in Andrea Bianchi, Daniel Peat, and Matthew Windsor, eds., *Interpretation in International Law* (Oxford: Oxford University Press).

International Federation of Red Cross and Red Crescent Societies (IFRC) (2009) *Strategy 2020: Humanitarian Diplomacy Policy* (Nairobi: ICRF), 25.

International Institute of Strategic Studies (2013) "The Military Balance 2012–2013" (London: IISS),www.iiss.org/en/publications/military%20 balance/issues/the-military-balance-2013–2003.

Jackson, P. T., and D. H. Nexon (1999). "Relations before States: Substance, Process and the Study of World Politics," *European Journal of International Relations* 5(3), 291–332.

Jakobsen, Peter Viggo (2009) "Small States, Big Influence: The Overlooked Nordic Influence on the Civilian ESDP," *Journal of Common Market Studies* 47(1), 81–102.

Jervis, Robert (1978) "Cooperation under the Security Dilemma," *World Politics* 30(2), 167–214.

Jinks, Derek (2005) "Toward an Institutional Theory of Sovereignty," *Stanford Law Review* 55.

Johnson, Chalmers (2004) *The Sorrows of Empire* (London: Verso), 131–140.

Johnston, Alastair Iain (2001) "Treating International Institutions as Social Environments," *International Studies Quarterly* 45(4), 487–515.

Johnstone, Ian (2003) "Security Council Deliberations: The Power of the Better Argument," *European Journal of International Law* 14(3), 437–480.

Johnstone, Ian (2004) "US-UN Relations after Iraq: The End of the World (Order) as We Know It?" *European Journal of International Law* 15(4), 813–838.

Johnstone, Ian (2011) *The Power of Deliberation: International Law, Politics and Organizations* (Oxford: Oxford University Press).

Jönsson, Christer, and Martin Hall (2005) *Essence of Diplomacy* (London: Palgrave).

Jönsson, Christer (2002) "Diplomacy, Bargaining and Negotiation," in Walter Carslnaes,Thomas Risse, and Beth Simmons eds., *Handbook of International Relations* (Thousand Oaks, CA: Sage) 212–234.

Kadushin, Charles (2012) *Understanding Social Networks: Theories, Concepts, and Findings* (Oxford: Oxford University Press).

Kaplan, Robert D. (2006) *Imperial Grunts: On the Ground with the American Military, from Mongolia to the Philippines to Iraq and Beyond* (New York: Vintage).

Kaufmann, Johan (1998) "Some Practical Aspects of United Nations Decision-Making, Tactics and Interaction Between Delegates," in M. A. Boisard and E. M. Chossudovsky, eds., *Multilateral Diplomacy: The United Nations System at Geneva* (The Hague: Kluwer Law International), 231–245.

Keal, Paul (1983) *Unspoken Rules and Superpower Dominance* (London: Macmillan).

Keck, Margaret, and Kathryn Sikkink (1998) *Activists Beyond Borders: Advocacy Networks in International Politics* (Ithaca, NY: Cornell University Press).

Kelley, John Robert (2010) "The New Diplomacy: Evolution of a Revolution." *Diplomacy & Statecraft* 21(2), 288.

Kennan, George (1997), "Diplomacy without Diplomats?" *Foreign Affairs* 76(5), 198–212.

Kennedy, Paul (1987) *The Rise and Fall of Great Powers. Economic Change and Military Conflict from 1500 to 2000* (New York: Vintage).

Keohane, Robert O. (1984) *After Hegemony: Cooperation and Discord in the World Political Economy* (Princeton, NJ: Princeton University Press).

Kerr, Pauline L. (2010) "Diplomatic Persuasion: An Under-Investigated Process," *The Hague Journal of Diplomacy*, 5, 235–261.

Kerr, Pauline, and Geoffrey Wiseman (eds.) (2013) *Diplomacy in a Globalizing World: Theories and Practices* (Oxford: Oxford University Press).

Khalili, Laleh (2012) *Time in the Shadows* (Stanford: Stanford University Press).

Kinsella, David (1989) "Arms Transfer Dependence and Foreign Policy Conflict," *Journal of Peace Research* 35, 1.

Kipping, Matthias and Christopher Wright (2012) "Consultants in Context: Global Dominance, Societal Effect, and the Capitalist System," in

Matthias Kipping and Timothy Clark, eds., *The Oxford Handbook of Management Consulting* (Oxford: Oxford University Press), 165–185.

Kissinger, Henry (1957) *A World Restored: Metternich, Castlereagh and the Problem of Peace, 1815–1822* (Boston: Houghton Mifflin).

Kissinger, Henry (2004) *Diplomacy* (New York: Simon & Schuster).

Kleiner, Jurgen (2010), *Diplomatic Practice: Between Tradition and Innovation* (Hackensack, NJ: World Scientific.

Koch, Scott A. (1995) "The Role of US Army Attachés between the World Wars: Selection and Training," *Studies in Intelligence* 38(5), www.cia.gov/library/center-for-the-study-of-intelligence/csi-publications/csi-studies/studies/95unclass/Koch.html accessed June 5, 2013.

Koremenos, Barbara, Charles Lipson, and Duncan Snidal (2001) "The Rational Design of International Institutions," *International Organization* 55(4), 761–799.

Kornprobst, Markus (2008) *Irredentism in European Politics: Argumentation, Compromise, and Norms* (Cambridge: Cambridge University Press).

Koskenniemi, Martti (2000) "Carl Schmitt, Hans Morgenthau, and the Image of Law in International Relations," in Michael Byers, ed., *The Role of Law in International Politics: Essays in International Relations and International Law* (Oxford: Oxford University Press), 17–34.

Koskenniemi, Martti (2004) *The Gentle Civilizer of Nations: The Rise and Fall of International Law 1870–1960* (Cambridge: Cambridge University Press).

Koskenniemi, Martti (2006) *From Apology to Utopia: The Structure of International Legal Argument* (Cambridge: Cambridge University Press).

Kratochwil, Friedrich (1984) "The Force of Prescriptions," *International Organization* 38(4), 685–708.

Krebs, Ronald, and Patrick Jackson (2007) "Twisting Tongues and Twisting Arms: The Power of Political Rhetoric," *European Journal of International Relations*, 13(1), 35–66.

Kristiansen, Kristian (1984) "Ideology and Material Culture: An Archaeological Perspective," in Matthew Spriggs, ed., *Marxist Perspectives in Archaeology* (Cambridge: Cambridge University Press), 72–100.

Kristiotis, Dino (1998) "The Power of International Law as Language," *California Western Law Review* 34.

Kupchan, Charles (2012) *No One's World: The West, the Rising Rest and the Coming Global Turn* (Oxford: Oxford University Press).

Kuper, Adam (1985) *Anthropologists and Anthropology. The British School 1922–1972* (Harmondsworth: Penguin).

Laatikainen, Katie Verlin (2012) "Group Politics at the UN: Conceptual Considerations," paper presented at the 2012 BISA/ISA conference, Edinburgh.

Lafeber, Walter (1993) *Inevitable Revolutions* (New York: W. W. Norton).

Lake, David (2009) *Hierarchy in International Relations* (Ithaca, NY: Cornell University Press).

Lang, Winfried (1994), "Lessons Drawn from Practice: Open Covenants, Openly Arrived At," in I. William Zartman, ed., *International Multilateral Negotiation: Approaches to the Management of Complexity* (San Francisco: Jossey-Bass), 201–211.

Langmore, John, and Jan Egeland (2011) "Distinctive Features of Norwegian Foreign Policy: Possible Lessons for Australia," Paper presented at the Australian Political Science Association Conference, Canberra, September 26–28, 2011.

Lawler, Peter (2005) "The Good State in World Politics: In Praise of Classical Internationalism," *Review of International Studies* 31(3), 427–449.

Le Monde, "Situation Critique à Abidjan, Laurent Gbagbo se Terre Toujours," *Le Monde* 4 July 2011, www.lemonde.fr/afrique/article/2011/04/07/abidjan-la-france-frappe-des-objectifs-militaires-a-la-residence-de-gbagbo_1504070_3212.html#xtor=AL-32280270, accessed September 11, 2012.

Leary, William M. (1995) "The CIA and the 'Secret War' in Laos: The Battle for Skyline Ridge, 1971–1972," *The Journal of Military History* 59, 505–518.

Leczowski, John (2011) *Full Spectrum Diplomacy and Grand Strategy* (Lanham, MD: Lexington Books).

Lederach, John P. (2003) "Cultivating Peace: A Practitioner's View of Deadly Conflict and Negotiation," in John Darby and Roger MacGinty eds., *Contemporary Peacemaking: Conflict, Violence and Peace Processes* (New York: Palgrave MacMillan), 30–37.

Lee, Donna, and David Hudson (2004) 'The Old and New Significance of Political Economy in Diplomacy," *Review of International Studies* 30, 343–360.

Leicht, Kevin T., Tony Walter, Ivan Sainsaulieu, and Scott Davies (2009) "New Public Management and New Professionalism across Nations and Contexts," *Current Sociology* 57(4), 581–605.

Leira, Halvard (2004) "'Hele vort folk er naturlige og fødte Fredsvenner' – Norsk fredstenkning fram til 1906," *Historisk Tidsskrift* 83(2), 153–180.

Leira, Halvard (2011) *The Emergence of Foreign Policy: Knowledge, Discourse, History* (University of Oslo, unpub).

Lewis, Jeffrey (2005) "The Janus Face of Brussels: Socialization and Everyday Decision Making in the European Union," *International Organization* 59(4), 937–971.

Lieber, Keir A., and Gerard Alexander (2005) "Waiting for Balancing: Why the World Is Not Pushing Back," *International Security* 30(1), 109–139.

Lindseth, Peter (2010) *Power and Legitimacy: Reconciling Europe and the Nation-State* (Oxford: Oxford University Press).

Loder, Kåre (1997) "The Peace Process in Mali," *Security Dialogue* 28(4), 409–424.

Lose, Lars (2001) "Communicative Action and the World of Diplomacy," in Karin M. Fierke and Knud Erik Jorgensen, eds., *Constructing International Relations: The Next Generation* (New York: M. E. Sharpe), 179–200.

Lumpe, Lora (2002) "U.S. Foreign Military Training," *Foreign Policy in Focus*, http://tamilnation.co/intframe/SRmiltrain.pdf.

Lynch, Cecelia (2000) "Acting on Belief: Christian Perspectives on Suffering and Violence," *Ethics & International Affairs* 14(1), 83–97.

Lynch, Cecelia (2000) "Dogma, Praxis, and Religious Perspectives on Multiculturalism," *Millenium – Journal of International Studies* 29(3), 741–759.

Lynch, Cecelia (2009) "A Neo-Weberian Approach to Religion in International Politics," *International Theory* 1(3), 381–408.

Lynch, Cecelia (2011) "Local and Global Influences on Islamic NGOs in Kenya," *Journal of Peacebuilding & Development* 6(1), 22.

MacFarquhar, Neil (2013) "U.N. Votes to Establish Peacekeeping Force for Mali." *New York Times*, April 25.

Malkki, Lisa (1996) "Speechless Emissaries: Refugees, Humanitarianism, and Dehistoricization," *Cultural Anthropology* 11(3), 377–404.

Malle, Bertram, and Joshua Knobe (2001) "The Distinction between Desire and Intention: A Folk-Conceptual Analysis," in Bertram Malle, Louis Moses, and Dare Baldwin, eds., *Intentions and Intentionality: Foundations of Social Cognition* (Cambridge, MA: MIT Press), 45–67.

Maoz, Zeev, and Lesley Terris (2006) "Credibility and Strategy in International Mediation," *International Interactions* 32(4), 409–440.

Markell, Patchen (2003) *Bound by Recognition* (Princeton, NJ: Princeton University Press), 110.

Martey, Emmanuel (2009) *African Theology: Inculturation and Liberation* (Eugene, OR: Wipf & Stock Publishers).

Marx, Karl (1965 [1867]) *Capital: A Critical Analysis of Capitalist Production*, vol. 1. Translated from the third German edition by Samuel Moore and Edward Aveling. Edited by Frederick Engels (Moscow: Progress Publisher), 103.

Masters, Roger D. (2012) "World Politics as a Primitive Political System," *World Politics* 16(4), 595–619, www.sharework.net/www/cuny-gc/intl-politics/World-Politics-Primitive.pdf, retrieved August 2, 2012.

Matthews, Jessica (1997) "Power Shift," *Foreign Affairs* 76(1), 50–66.
Mayall, James (2007) "Introduction," in P. Sharp and G. Wiseman, eds., *The Diplomatic Corps as an Institution of International Society* (New York: Palgrave), 1–11.
Mazower, Mark (2013) *Governing the World: The History of an Idea, 1815 to the Present* (New York: Penguin).
Mazzetti, Mark, Michael R. Gordon, and Mark Landler (2013)"U.S. Is Said to Plan to Send Weapons to Syrian Rebels." *New York Times*, June 14.
McDonough, Frank (2002) *Hitler, Chamberlain and Appeasement* (Cambridge: Cambridge University Press).
McEvily, Bill, Vincenzo Perrone, and Akbar Zaheer (2003) "Trust as an Organizing Principle," *Organizational Science* 14(1), 91–103.
McNeill, William (1982) *The Pursuit of Power* (Chicago: University of Chicago Press), chaps. 9–10.
Melissen, Jan (ed.) (1999) *Innovation in Diplomatic Practice* (London: Palgrave Macmillan).
Mérand, Frédéric (2010) "Pierre Bourdieu and the Birth of European Defense," *Security Studies* 19(2).
Mercer, J. (1995). "Anarchy and Identity." *International Organization*, 49(2), 229–252.
Miller, Donald, and Tetsuano Yamamori (2007) *Global Pentecostalism: The New Face of Christian Social Engagement* (Berkeley: University of California Press).
Minear, Larry (2007) "The Craft of Humanitarian Diplomacy," in Larry Minear and Hazel Smith, eds., *Humanitarian Diplomacy: Practitioners and Their Craft* (Tokyo: United Nations University Press), 7–35.
Mische, Ann (2011) "Relational Sociology, Culture, and Agency," in John Scott and Peter J. Carrington, eds., *The SAGE Handbook of Social Network Analysis* (Thousand Oaks, CA: Sage), 81–97.
Mitchell, Christopher (2003) "Mediation and the Ending of Conflicts," in John Darby and Roger MacGinty, eds., *Contemporary Peacemaking: Conflict, Violence and Peace Process* (Houndmills: PalgraveMacmillan), 77–86.
Mitchell, Timothy (1991) "The Limits of the State: Beyond Statist Approaches and Their Critics," *The American Political Science Review* 85(1), 77–96.
Mitzen, Jennifer (2005) "Reading Habermas in Anarchy: Multilateral Diplomacy and Global Public Spheres," *American Political Science Review* 99(3), 401–417.

Mitzen, Jennifer (2006) "Ontological Security in World Politics: State Identity and the Security Dilemma," *European Journal of International Relations* 12(3), 341–370.

Mitzen, Jennifer (2013) *Power in Concert: The 19th Century Origins of Global Governance* (Chicago: University of Chicago Press).

Momani, Bessma (2013) "Management Consultants and the United States' Public Sector," *Business & Politics* 15(3).

Montgomery, Alexander H. (2006), "Proliferation Networks in Theory and Practice," *Strategic Insights* 5(6).

Moravcsik, Andrew (1997) "Taking Preferences Seriously: A Liberal Theory of International Politics," *International Organization* 51(4), 513–553.

Morgenthau, Hans J. (1941) "Positivism, Functionalism and International Law," *American Journal of International Law*.

Morgenthau, Hans J. (with Kenneth W. Thompson) (1985[1948]) *Politics Among Nations: The Struggle for Power and Peace*, 6th edn (New York: Alfred A. Knopf).

Muldoon, James P. (2005) "The Diplomacy of Business," *Diplomacy & Statecraft* 16(2), 341–359.

Müller, H. (2004) "Arguing, Bargaining and All That: Communicative Action, Rationalist Theory and the Logic of Appropriateness in International Relations," *European Journal of International Relations*, 10(3), 395–435.

Muller, Harald (2001) "International Relations as Communicative Action," in Karin M. Fierke and Knud Erik Jorgensen, eds., *Constructing International Relations: The Next Generation* (New York: M. E. Sharpe), 160–178.

Nardin, Terry (ed.) (1996) *The Ethics of War and Peace: Religious and Secular Perspective* (Princeton, NJ: Princeton University Press).

National Endowment for Democracy,"National Endowment for Democracy: Somaliland," www.ned.org/where-we-work/africa/somaliland, accessed July 6, 2014.

Nelson, Scott Reynolds, and Carol Sheriff (2008) *A People at War* (New York: Oxford University Press), 187–213.

Neuman, Stephanie (1986) *Military Assistance in Recent Wars* (New York: Praeger).

Neumann, Iver B. (1998) *Uses of the Other: "The East" in European Identity Formation* (Minneapolis: University of Minnesota Press).

Neumann, Iver B. (2002) "Harnessing Social Power: State Diplomacy and the Land-Mines Issue," in Andrew F. Cooper, John English, and Ramesh Thakur, eds., *Enhancing Global Governance: Towards a New Diplomacy?* (Tokyo: United Nations University Press), 106–132.

Neumann, Iver B. (2002) "Returning Practice to the Linguistic Turn: The Case of Diplomacy," *Millennium – Journal of International Studies* 32(3), 627–652.

Neumann, Iver B. (2005) "To Be a Diplomat," *International Studies Perspectives* 6(1), 72–93.

Neumann, Iver B. (2007) "A Speech That the Entire Ministry May Stand For, "Or: Why Diplomats Never Produce Anything New," *International Political Sociology* 1(2), 183–200.

Neumann, Iver B. (2008) "Globalization and Diplomacy," in Brian Cooper, Andrew Hocking, and WIlliam Maley eds., *Global Governance and Diplomacy* (London: Palgrave Macmillan), 15–28.

Neumann, Iver B. (2011) "Euro-centric Diplomacy: Challenging but Manageable," *European Journal of International Relations* 18(2).

Neumann, Iver B. (2012) *At Home with the Diplomats: Inside a European Foreign Ministry* (Ithaca, NY: Cornell University Press).

Neumann, Iver B., and Ole Jacob Sending (2010) *Governing the Global Polity: Practice, Rationality, Mentality* (Ann Arbor: University of Michigan Press).

New York State Department of Law (2011) Office of the Attorney General, Charities Bureau, Annual Filing for Charitable Organizations, #41–01-83, www.charitiesnys.com.

Nexon, Daniel (2009) *The Struggle for Power in Early Modern Europe: Religious Conflict, Dynastic Empires, and International Change* (Princeton, NJ: Princeton University Press).

Nicolson, Harold (1939) *Diplomacy*, 3rd edn (London: Oxford University Press, [1939] 1963).

Niebuhr, Reinhold (1953) *Christian Realism and Political Problems* (New York: Scribner).

Niemann, Holger (2011) "Justification as a Discursive Practice in the UN Security Council during the 2002/2003 Iraq Crisis," paper presented at the Third General Conference of the International Politics Section of the German Association of Political Science, October 6–7, 2011, Munich.

Nye, Joseph S. (2004) *Soft Power: The Means to Success in World Politics* (New York: Public Affairs).

Nyerges, Janos (1998) "How to Negotiate?" in M. A. Boisard and E. M. Chossudovsky, eds., *Multilateral Diplomacy: The United Nations System at Geneva* (The Hague: Kluwer Law International), 175–180.

Nyerges, Janos (1998) "How to Negotiate?" in Marcel A. Boisard, Evgeny Chossudovsky, and Jacques Lemoine, eds., *Multilateral Diplomacy: The United Nations System at Geneva* (The Hague: Kluwer Law International), 177.

O'Brien, Robert et al. (eds.) (2000) *Contesting Global Governance: Multilateral Economic Institutions and Global Social Movements* (Cambridge: Cambridge University Press).

Onuf, Nicholas (1985) "Do Rules Say What They Do? From Ordinary Language to International Law," *Harvard International Law Journal* 26(2), 385–410.

Orbinski, James (1998) "On the Meaning of SPHERE Standards to States and Other Humanitarian Actors," lecture delivered in London on December 3, 1998.

Orford, Ann (2011) *International Authority and the Responsibility to Protect* (New York: Cambridge University Press).

Pandolfi, Maria (2003) "Contract of Mutual (In)Difference: Government and the Humanitarian Apparatus in Contemporary Albania and Kosovo," *Indiana Journal of Global Legal Studies* 10(1), 369–381.

Paris, Roland, and Timothy D. Zisk (eds.) (2009) *The Dilemmas of Statebuilding: Confronting the Contradictions of Postwar Peace Operations* (London: Routledge).

Payne, Rodger (2001) "Persuasion, Frames and Norm Construction," *European Journal of International Relations* 7(1), 37–61.

Phillips, Janet, and Harriet Spinks (2013) "Boat Arrivals in Australia since 1976," Department of Parliamentary Services, Social Policy Section, Parliament of Australia.

Philpott, Daniel (2001) *Revolutions in Sovereignty: How Ideas Shaped Modern International Relations* (Princeton, NJ: Princeton University Press).

Pigman, G. A. (2010) *Contemporary Diplomacy* (Cambridge: Polity), 138–179.

Placidi, Delphine (2007) "La transformation des pratiques diplomatiques nationales," in Bertrand Badie and Guillaume Devin, eds., *Le multilatéralisme. Nouvelles forms de l'action internationale* (Paris: La Découverte), 95–112.

Posen, Barry (2003) "Command of the Commons: The Military Foundation of U.S. Hegemony," *International Security* 28(1), 8.

Pospisil, Leopold (1958) *Kapauku Papuans and Their Law* (New Haven, CT: Yale University Press).

Pouliot, Vincent (2008) "The Logic of Practicality: A Theory of Practice of Security Communities," *International Organization* 62(2), 257–288.

Pouliot, Vincent (2010) *International Security in Practice: The Politics of NATO-Russia Diplomacy* (Cambridge and New York: Cambridge University Press).

Pouliot, Vincent (2010) "The Materials of Practice: Nuclear Warheads, Rhetorical Commonplaces and Committee Meetings in Russian-Atlantic Relations," *Cooperation and Conflict* 45(3), 294–311.

Pouliot, Vincent (2011) "Multilateral Diplomacy," *International Journal*, Summer 2011.

Pouliot, Vincent (2011) "Multilateralism as an End in Itself," *International Studies Perspectives* 12(1), 18–26.

Pouliot, Vincent (2012) *International Security in Practice: The Politics of Nato-Russian Diplomacy* (Cambridge: Cambridge University Press).

Powell, Robert (2006) "War as a Commitment Problem," *International Organization* 60, 169–204.

Priest, Dana (2000) "The 'Proconsuls,'" *Washington Post*, September 28.

Putnam, R. D. (1988). "Diplomacy and Domestic Politics: The Logic of Two-Level Games," *International Organization*, 42(3), 427–460.

Queller, Donald E. (1967) *The Office of Ambassador in the Middle Ages* (Princeton, NJ: Princeton University Press).

Rajagopal, B. (2011). *International Law from Below: Development, Social Movements and Third World Resistance* (New York: Cambridge University Press).

Ramsbotham, Oliver, Tom Woodhouse, and Hugh Miall (eds.) (2005) *Contemporary Conflict Resolution*, 2nd edn (Cambridge: Polity), 168.

Ranshofen-Wertheimer, Egon Ferdinand (1945) *The Position of the Executive and Administrative Heads of the United Nations International Organizations* (Washington DC: Carnegie Endowment of International Peace), 403.

Rathbun, Brian (2012) *Trust in International Cooperation: International Security Institutions, Domestic Politics and American Multilateralism* (Cambridge: Cambridge University Press).

Rawls, John (1996) *Political Liberalism* (New York: Columbia University Press).

Regnier, Philippe (2011) "The Emerging Concept of Humanitarian Diplomacy: Identification of a Community of Practice and Prospects for International Recognition," *International Review of the Red Cross*, 93(884), 1211–1237.

Reus-Smit, Christian (1999) *The Moral Purpose of the State: Culture, Identity, and Institutional Rationality in International Relations* (Princeton, NJ: Princeton University Press).

Reus-Smit, Christian (2013) *Individual Rights and the Making of the International System* (Cambridge: Cambridge University Press).

Reveron, Derek S. (2004) *American Viceroys: The Military and US Foreign Policy* (New York: Palgrave Macmillan).

Richmond, Oliver P. (2005) *The Transformation of Peace* (Houndmills: Palgrave).

Risse, Thomas (2000) "'Let's Argue!' Communicative Action in World Politics," *International Organization* 54(1), 1–39.

Risse, Thomas, Stephen Ropp, and Kathryn Sikkink (eds.) (1999) *The Power of Human Rights: International Norms and Domestic Change* (Cambridge: Cambridge University Press).

Ross, Carne (2007) *Independent Diplomat: Dispatches from an Unaccountable Elite* (Ithaca, NY: Cornell University Press).

Ross, Carne (2010) *Independent Diplomat: Dispatches from an Unaccountable Elite*, in Carne Ross, *The Leaderless Revolution* (London: Simon & Schuster).

Roth, Abraham Sesshu (2004) "Shared Agency and Contralateral Commitments," *The Philosophical Review* 113(3), 359–410.

Rubin, Jeffrey Z. (1992) "Conclusion: International Mediation in Context," in Jacob Bercovitch and Jeffrey Z. Rubin, eds., *Mediation in International Relations* (New York: Palgrave Macmillan), 249–272.

Ruggie, John (1998) "What Makes the World Hang Together? Neo-Utilitarianism and the Social Constructivist Challenge," *International Organization* 52(4), 855–886.

Ruggie, John Gerard (1992), "Multilateralism: The Anatomy of an Institution," *International Organization* 46(3), 561–598.

Ryall, David (2002) "The Catholic Church as Transnational Actor," in Daphne Josselin and William Wallace, eds., *Non-State Actors in World Politics* (Houndsmills, Basingstoke: Palgrave), 41–58.

Santos, Fernanda (2008) "After the War, a New Battle to Become Citizens." *New York Times*, February 24, 2008.

Satow, Sir Ernest (1917) *Satow's Guide to Diplomatic Practice*, 6th edn (London: Longman, [1917] 2009).

Scharf, Michael P. (2009) "International Law and the Torture Memos," *Case Western Reserve Journal of International Law* 42, 321–358.

Schatzki, Theodore R. (1996) *Social Practices: A Wittgensteinian Approach to Human Activity and the Social* (Cambridge: Cambridge University Press).

Schauer, Frederick (1995) "Giving Reasons," *Stanford Law Review* 47, 633–659.

Schia, Niels Nagelhus (2013) "Being Part of the Parade – 'Going Native' in the United Nations Security Council," *Political and Legal Anthropology Review* 36(1).

Schmid, Hans Bernhard (2008) "Plural Action," *Philosophy of the Social Sciences* 38(1), 25–54.

Schmitt, Carl (2006) *The Nomos of the Earth in the International Law of Jus Publicum Europaeum* (Candor, NY: Telos Press).

Schmitt, Eric (2003) "Boom Times for U.S. Military Recruiters." *International Herald Tribune*, September 22, 8.

Schmitt, Eric (2014) "U.S. Officers Kill Armed Civilians in Yemen Capital." *New York Times*, May 9, 2014.

Schmitt, Eric (2014) "U.S. Signs New Lease to Keep Strategic Military Installation in the Horn of Africa." *New York Times*, May 5, 2014.

Scholte, Jan Aart (2001) *Globalization: A Critical Introduction* (New York: Palgrave Macmillan).

Schroeder, Paul (1994) *The Transformation of European Politics, 1763–1848* (Oxford: Oxford University Press).

Schwartz, General Nordy, Chief of Staff of the Air Force, a speech delivered to The Atlantic Council, April 9, 2012, www.atlanticcouncil.org/news/transcripts/the-future-of-the-united-states-air-force-4-09-12-transcript.

Scott, Shirley V. (1994) "International Law as Ideology: Theorising the Relationship between International Law and International Politics," *European Journal of International Law* 5, 313–325.

Sea Shepherd International, www.seashepherd.org/whales/, accessed February 25, 2013.

Seabrooke, Leonard (2011) "Economists and Diplomacy: Professions and the Practice of Economic Policy," *International Journal* 66, 629–642.

Seabrooke, Leonard (2014) "Epistemic Arbitrage: Transnational Professional Knowledge in Action," *Journal of Professions and Organization* 1(1), 49–64.

Seabrooke, Leonard, and Emelie Rebecca Nilsson (2014) "Professional Skills in International Financial Surveillance: Assessing Change in IMF Policy Teams," *Governance: An International Journal of Policy, Administration and Institutions* 27.

Seabrooke, Leonard, and Eleni Tsingou (2009) "Revolving Doors and Linked Ecologies in the World Economy: Policy Locations and the Practice of International Financial Reform," Centre for the Study of Globalisation and Regionalisation, working paper 260, no. 09, University of Warwick.

Seabrooke, Leonard, and Eleni Tsingou (2014) "Distinctions, Affiliations, and Professional Knowledge in Financial Reform Expert Groups," *Journal of European Public Policy* 21(3), 389–407.

Seabrooke, Leonard, and Duncan Wigan (2013) "Emergent Entrepreneurs in Transnational Advocacy Networks: Professional Mobilization in the Fight for Global Tax Justice," GREEN Working Paper No. 42, Centre for the Study of Globalisation and Regionalisation, University of Warwick.

Searle, John (1995) *The Construction of Social Reality* (New York: The Free Press).

Security Assistance Management Manual, updated July 18, 2013, www.samm.dsca.mil/listing/chapters.

Sending, Ole Jacob (2002) "Constitution, Choice and Change: Problems with the 'Logic of Appropriateness' and Its Use in Constructivist Theory," *European Journal of International Relations* 8(4), 443–470.

Sending, Ole Jacob (2011) "United by Difference: Diplomacy as a Thin Culture," *International Journal* 66, 643–659.

Sending, Ole Jacob (2015) *The Politics of Expertise: Competing for Authority in Global Governance* (Ann Arbor: University of Michigan Press).

Sending, Ole Jacob, and Iver B. Neumann (2006) "Governance to Governmentality: Analyzing NGOs, States, and Power," *International Studies Quarterly* 50, 651–672.

Sending, Ole Jacob, and Iver B. Neumann (2011). "Banking on Power: How Some Practices in an International Organization Anchor Others," in Emanuel Adler and Vincent Pouliot, eds., *International Practices* (Cambridge: Cambridge University Press), 231–254.

Shaffer, Gregory, and Tom Ginsburg (2012) "The Empirical Turn in International Legal Scholarship," *American Journal of International Law*, 106(1).

Shanker, Thom, and Eric Schmitt (2013) "Ties with Egypt Army Constrain Washington." *New York Times*, August 16, 2013, www.nytimes.com/2013/08/17/world/middleeast/us-officials-fear-losing-an-eager-ally-in-the-egyptian-military.html, accessed September 10, 2013.

Sharp, Paul (1997) "Who Needs Diplomats? The Problem of Diplomatic Representation," *International Journal* 52(4), 609–632.

Sharp, Paul (1999) "For Diplomacy: Representation and the Study of International Relations," *International Studies Review* 1(1), 33–57.

Sharp, Paul (2004) "Who Needs Diplomats? The Problem of Diplomatic Representation," in C. Jönnson and R. Langthorne, eds., *Diplomacy,* Volume III. *Problems and Issues in Contemporary Diplomacy* (London: Sage).

Sharp, Paul (2009) *Diplomatic Theory of International Relations* (Cambridge and New York: Cambridge University Press).

Sharp, Paul (2011) "Diplomacy, Diplomatic Studies, and the ISA," *International Studies Perspecitves* 13, 718.

Shea, Timothy C. (2005) "Transforming Military Diplomacy," *Joint Forces Quarterly* 38, 50.

Shklar, Judith N. (1964/1986) *Legalism: Law, Morals, and Political Trials* (Cambridge, MA: Harvard University Press).

Shue, Henry, and David Rodin (eds.) (2010) *Preemption: Military Action and Moral Justification* (New York: Oxford University Press).

Skånland, Øyvind H. (2010) "Norway Is a Peace Nation: A Discourse Analytic Reading of the Norwegian Peace Engagement," *Cooperation and Conflict* 45(1), 34–54.

Slaughter, Anne-Marie (2004) *A New World Order: Government Networks and the Disaggregated State* (Princeton, NJ: Princeton University Press).

Slim, Hugo (2003) "Humanitarianism with Borders? NGOs, Belligerent Military Forces and Humanitarian Action," paper for ICVA Conference on NGOs in a Changing World Order: Dilemmas and Challenges Geneva, February 14.

Small, Melvin, and J. David Singer (1982) *Resort to Arms* (Beverly Hills, CA: Sage), 326.

Smith, Perry M., and Daniel M. Gerstein (2007) *Assignment Pentagon: How to Excel in a Bureaucracy*, 4th edn (Washington, DC: Potomac Books).

Smith-Simonsen, Christine (2014) "Eritrea-initiativene – En forløper for Den norske modellen innen fred og forsoning," *Internasjonal politikk* 72(2), 175–197.

Sofer, Sason (1997) "The Diplomat as Stranger," *Diplomacy and Statecraft* 8(3), 179–186.

Spiro, Peter (2004) "What Happened to the New Sovereigntism?" *Foreign Affairs* July 28.

STATT (2013) "Afghan Migration in Flux," *Synapse*, issue 10, http://www.unodc.org/cld/bibliography/2013/afghan_migration_in_flux.html.

STATT, http://statt.net/category/home/, accessed July 6, 2014.

Steffek, Jens (2003) "The Legitimation of International Governance: A Discourse Approach," *European Journal of International Relations* 9(2), 249–275.

Steinmetz, George (2008) "The Colonial State as a Social Field: Ethnographic Capital and Native Policy in the German Overseas Empire before 1914," *American Review of Sociology* 73, 589–612.

Steller, Verena (2008) "The Power of Protocol: On the Mechanisms of Symbolic Action in Diplomacy in Franco-German Relations, 1871–1914," in Markus Mösslang and Torsten Riotte, eds., *The Diplomats' World: A Cultural History of Diplomacy 1815–1904* (Oxford: Oxford University Press)

Stevenson, Charles (1973) *End of Nowhere* (Boston: Beacon Press), chaps. 1–3.

Støre, Jonas Gahr (2010) "Norway's Conflict Resolution Efforts – Are They of Any Avail?" *Speech at the House of Literature*, Oslo, June 11, 2010.

Strachan, Anna Louise (2013) *Interests, Identity and Nordicity. Explaining Norwegian Mediation Efforts*, PhD thesis, S. Rajaratnam School of International Studies, Singapore.

Stuenkel, Oliver (2012) "How Many Diplomats Does an Emerging Power Need?" *Post-Western World*, www.postwesternworld.com/2012/10/14/how-many-diplomats-does-an-emerging-power-need/, accessed September 10, 2013.

Swidler, Ann (2001) "What Anchors Cultural Practices," in Theodore R. Schatzki et al., eds., *The Practice Turn in Contemporary Theory* (London: Routledge), 74–92.

Swistek, Göran (2012) "The Nexus between Public Diplomacy and Military Diplomacy in Foreign Affairs and Defense Policy," *Connections: The Quarterly Journal* 11(2), 82.

Tamanaha, Brian (2004) *On the Rule of Law: History, Politics, Theory* (New York: Cambridge University Press).

Tamanaha, Brian (2006) *Law as a Means to an End: Threat to the Rule of Law* (Cambridge: Cambridge University Press).

Taylor, Charles (1993) "... to Follow a Rule," in Craig Calhoun, Edward Lipuma, and Moishe Postone, eds., *Bourdieu: Critical Perspectives* (Chicago: University of Chicago Press), 45–60.

Teitel, Ruti G. (2011) *Humanity's Law* (New York: Oxford University Press).

Telegramme from Beijing, 31 March 1971, Norwegian National Archives, MFA, ad-doss 25 4/33, II.

Teschke, Benno (2003) *The Myth of 1648: Class, Geopolitics, and the Making of Modern International Relations* (London: Verso).

The Ambassador Partnership, www.adrgambassadors.com, accessed July 6, 2014.

The Guardian (2014) "Ukraine Crisis: Diplomacy Fails to Yield Result as Russia Stays Put in Crimea," www.theguardian.com/world/2014/mar/05/ukraine-crisis-russia-nato-talks-live accessed May 21, 2014.

The International Commission of Jurists (2003) March 18, http://jurist.org/paperchase/2003/03/international-commission-of-jurists.php, accessed September 10, 2012.

Thérien, Jean-Philippe, and Vincent Pouliot (2006) "The Global Compact: Shifting the Politics of International Development?" *Global Governance* 12(1).

Thévenot, Laurent (2001) "Pragmatic Regimes Governing Engagement with the World," in Theodore R. Schatzki et al., eds., *The Practice Turn in Contemporary Theory* (London: Routledge), 56–73.

Thomas, Dietz, and Jill Steans (2005) "A Useful Dialogue? Habermas and International Relations," *Review of International Studies* 31(1), 127–140.

Thomas, Scott M. (2000) "Taking Religious and Cultural Pluralism Seriously: The Global Resurgence of Religion and the Transformation of

International Society," *Millenium – Journal of International Studies* 29(3), 815–841.

Thuysbaert, Prosper (1994) *L'art de la diplomatie multilatérale*. Brussels: Vander.

Tilly, Charles (1985) "War Making and State Making as Organized Crime," in P. B. Evans, D. Rueschemeyer, and T. Skocpol, eds., *Bringing the State Back In* (Cambridge· Cambridge University Press), 169–191.

Tilly, Charles (1998) "International Communities, Secure or Otherwise," in Emanuel Adler and Michael Barnett, eds., *Security Communities* (Cambridge and New York: Cambridge University Press), 397–412.

Tilly, Charles (2002) *Stories, Identities, and Political Change* (Lanham, MD: Rowman & Littlefield).

Tollefson, Deborah (2002) "Collective Intentionality and the Social Sciences," *Philosophy of the Social Sciences* 32(1), 25–50.

Toope, Stephen J. (2001) "Emerging Patterns of Governance and International Law," in Michael Byers, ed., *The Role of Law in International Politics* (Oxford: Oxford University Press), 91–108.

Trenin, Dmitri (2013) "Rice and the Russians," *Foreign Policy* June 7.

Tuomela, Raimo (2005) "We-Intentions Revisited," *Philosophical Studies* 125, 327–369.

UNSC Resolution 2100 (2013) www.securitycouncilreport.org/atf/cf/%7B65BFCF9B-6D27-4E9C-8CD3-CF6E4FF96FF9%7D/s_res_2100.pdf, accessed May 22, 2013.

US Department of Defense (2009) "Unified Command Plan (2009)," www.defense.gov/home/features/2009/0109_unifiedcommand/, accessed June 15, 2013.

US Department of Defense Knowledge Base (2012) Defense Manpower Data Center, www.dmdc.osd.mil/appj/dwp/dwp_reports.jsp, accessed May 30, 2013.

US Department of Defense Knowledge Base (2013) "US Defense Budget Proposal Released For Fiscal Year 2014," www.defense.gov/news/2014budget.pdf.

US Department of Justice, Registration Statement, Pursuant to the Foreign Registration Act of 1938, registration no. 5860-Exhibit-AB-20090720-5, registered on 07-09-2009, www.fara.gov/.

US Department of Justice, Registration Statement, Pursuant to the Foreign Registration Act of 1938, registration no. 5860-Exhibit-AB-20080403-1, registered on 03-25-2008, www.fara.gov/.

US Department of Justice, Registration Statement, Pursuant to the Foreign Registration Act of 1938, registration no. 5860-Exhibit-AB- 20130408-12, registered on 04-08-2013, www.fara.gov/.

US Department of State, Bureau of Political and Military Affairs Website, www.state.gov/t/pm/, accessed June 2, 2013.

Van Dusen, Henry P. (ed.) (1960) *The Spiritual Legacy of John Foster Dulles: Selections from His Articles and Addresses* (Philadelphia: The Westminster Press).

Velleman, J. David (1997) "How to Share an Intention," *Philosophy and Phenomenological Research* 57(1), 29–50.

Vettovaglia, Jean-Pierre (1998) "De la coordination comme instrument essentiel de la négociation multilatérale intergouvernmentale," in M. A. Boisard and E. M. Chossudovsky, eds., *Multilateral Diplomacy: The United Nations System at Geneva* (The Hague: Kluwer Law International), 247–255.

Vincent, John (1986) *Human Rights and International Relations* (Cambridge: Cambridge University Press).

Vine, David (2009) *Island of Shame* (Princeton, NJ: Princeton University Press).

Von Clausewitz, Carl (1976) *On War* (Princeton, NJ: Princeton University Press), 605.

Wadley, Jonathan D. (2010) "Gendering the State: Performativity and Protection in International Security," in Laura Sjoberg, ed., *Gender and International Security: Feminist Perspectives* (London: Routledge), 44.

Wæver, Ole (1994) "Resisting the Temptation of Post Foreign Policy Analysis," in Walter Carlsnaes and Steve Smith, eds., *European Foreign Policy: The EC and Changing Perspectives in Europe* (London: Sage), 238–277.

Walker, R. B. J. (1992) *Inside/Outside: International Relations as Political Theory* (Cambridge: Cambridge University Press).

Walker, Ronald A. (2011) *Manual for UN Delegates: Conference Process, Procedure and Negotiation* (Geneva: UNITAR).

Walt, Stephen M. (2005). "The Relationship between Theory and Policy in International Relations," *Annual Review Political Science* 8, 23–48.

Waltz, Kenneth N. (1979) *Theory of International Politics* (New York: McGraw-Hill).

Ware, Vron (2012) *Military Migrants* (London: Palgrave Macmillan).

Warner, Daniel (2013) "Henri Dunant's Imagined Community," *Alternatives* 38(1), 3–28.

Warren, Mark E. (2006) "What Should and Should Not Be Said: Deliberating Sensitive Issues," *Journal of Social Philosophy* 37(2), 163–181.

Watson, Adam (1984) *Diplomacy: The Dialogue between States* (London: Methuen).

Watson, Adam (1992) *The Evolution of International Society* (London: Routledge).

Weick, Karl E. (1995) *Sensemaking in Organizations* (Thousand Oaks, CA: Sage).

Weiner, Tim (2007) *A Legacy of Ashes* (New York: Random House).

Wendt, Alexander (1992) "Anarchy Is What States Make of It: The Social Construction of Power Politics," *International Organization* 46(2), 391–425.

Wendt, Alexander (1994) "Collective Identity Formation and the International State," *American Political Science Review* 88(2), 384–396.

Wendt, Alexander (1999) *Social Theory of International Politics* (Cambridge: Cambridge University Press).

Wendt, Alexander (2003) "Why a World State Is Inevitable," *European Journal of International Relations* 9(4), 491–542.

Wendt, Alexander (2004) "The State as Person in International Theory," *Review of International Studies* 30(2), 289–316.

Wheeler, Nicholas J. (2000) *Saving Strangers: Humanitarian Intervention in International Society* (Oxford: Oxford University Press).

White, Harrison C. (2008) *Identity & Control: How Social Formations Emerge*, 2nd edn (Princeton, NJ: Princeton University Press).

White, Henry et al. (1912) "The Organization and Procedure of the Third Hague Conference," *Proceedings of the American Society of International Law at Its Annual Meeting* 6, 182.

Wight, Martin (ed. Hedley Bull) (1977) *Systems of States* (Leicester: Leicester University Press).

Wilson, Erin K. (2012) *After Secularism: Rethinking Religion* (New York: Palgrave Macmillan).

Wines, Michael (2006) "South Africa: Anti-Mercenary Law Passed." *New York Times*, August 20.

Wiseman, Geoffrey (2005) "Pax Americana: Bumping into Diplomatic Culture," *International Studies Perspectives* 6(4), 409–430.

Wiseman, Geoffrey (2011) "Distinctive Characteristics of American Diplomacy," *The Hague Journal of Diplomacy* 6, 255.

Wolfers, Arnold (1962) *Discord and Collaboration* (Baltimore: The Johns Hopkins University Press).

Wong, Wendy A. (2012) *Internal Affairs: How the Structure of NGOs Transforms Human Rights* (Ithaca, NY: Cornell University Press).

Wright, Christopher, Andrew Sturdy, and Nick Wylie (2012) "Management Innovation through Standardization: Consultants as Standardizers of Organizational Practice," *Research Policy* 41(3), 652–662.

Yoo, John (2003) "International Law and the War in Iraq," *American Journal of International Law* 97(3), 563–575.

Young, Iris Marion (2000) *Inclusion and Democracy* (New York: Oxford University Press).

Zartman, I. William (1994) "Introduction: Two's Company and More's a Crowd: The Complexities of Multilateral Negotiation," in I. William Zartman, ed., *International Multilateral Negotiation: Approaches to the Management of Complexity* (San Francisco: Jossey-Bass), 1–10.

Zartman, I. William (ed.) (1994) *International Multilateral Negotiation: Approaches to the Management of Complexity* (San Francisco: Jossey-Bass).

Zartman, William, (1989) *Ripe for Resolution: Conflict and Intervention in Africa* (New York: Oxford University Press).

Zartman, William and Saadia Touval (1985) "International Mediation: Conflict Resolution and Power Politics," *Journal of Social Issues* 44(2), 27–45.

Žižek, Slavoj (2006) "Philosophy, the "Unknown Knowns" and the Public Use of Reason," ***Topoi*** 25(1–2), 137–142.

Zolberg, Aristide (2008) *A Nation by Design* (Cambridge, MA: Harvard University Press).

Zorn, Dick (2004) "Here a Chief, There a Chief: The Rise of the CFO in the American Firm," *American Sociological Review* 69(3), 345–364.

Interviews

Confidential interview with military staff officer with extensive combat experience in Iraq, Washington, DC, May 19, 2013.

Interview with a senior pilot and officer executing a Red Flag exercise, May 23, 2013.

Interview with a senior ranking international strategy official within the Department of Defense, May 21, 2013.

Interview with Captain Kevin Kenney, USAF pilot at Lakenheath AB, England and Red Flag Team Chief for Operation, May 2013.

Interview with Colonel Michael Fleck, chief, Strategy and Plans Division, Deputy Under Secretary of the Air Force for International Affairs, Washington, DC, May 19, 2013.

Interview with Colin Kahl, former deputy assistant secretary of defense (DASD) for the Middle East (2009–2011).

Interview with Dan Livermore, DFAIT, former Canadian ambassador to Guatemala, Waterloo, September 29, 1999.

Interview with experienced US Navy flight instructor, May 17, 2013.

Interview with former director of strategy and plans for the US Office of Security Cooperation Iraq, Washington, DC, May 19, 2013.
Interview with former head of section, July 9, 2010.
Interview with Hans Jacob Frydenlund, June 22, 2010.
Interview with head of section, June 4, 2012.
Interview with head of the section for peace and reconciliation, April 23, 2010.
Interview with mid-level naval officer with extensive Middle East experience, May 19, 2013.
Interview with mid-level US Marine Corps FAO, May 19, 2013.
Interview with senior naval officer with 15 years of experience in acquisitions, May 20, 2013.
Interview with the director of STATT, December 2012.
Interview with the director of the Brussels Office of Independent Diplomat, August 2012.
Interview with the director of the London Office of Independent Diplomat, September 2012.
Interview with US Defense official, Washington DC, May 3, 2013.
Interview, former UNIDIR official, September 2012.
Interview, MFA official Oslo, Norway, March 8, 2011.
Interview, MFA official, Norway, February 2011.
Interview, MFA official, Oslo, Norway, May 10, 2011.
Interview, MFA official, Oslo, Norway, January 20, 2011.
Interview, MFA official, Oslo, Norway, September, 2012.
Interview, official at Norwegian Refugee Council, Oslo, Norway, February 10, 2011.
Interview, official with Norwegian Peoples Aid, Norway, February 16, 2011.
Telephone interview with former OCHA official, September 12, 2012.

Index

CAMBRIDGE STUDIES IN INTERNATIONAL RELATIONS

131 *Jonathan D. Caverley*
Democratic militarism: Voting, wealth, and war

130 *David Jason Karp*
Responsibility for human rights:
Transnational corporations in imperfect states

129 *Friedrich Kratochwil*
The status of law in world society:
Meditations on the role and rule of law

128 *Michael G. Findley, Daniel L. Nielson, and J. C. Sharman*
Global shell games:
Experiments in transnational relations, crime, and terrorism

127 *Jordan Branch*
The cartographic state:
Maps, territory, and the origins of sovereignty

126 *Thomas Risse, Stephen C. Ropp, and Kathryn Sikkink (eds.)*
The persistent power of human rights:
From commitment to compliance

125 *K. M. Fierke*
Political self-sacrifice:
Agency, body and emotion in international relations

124 *Stefano Guzzini*
The return of geopolitics in Europe?
Social mechanisms and foreign policy identity crises

123 *Bear F. Braumoeller*
The great powers and the international system:
Systemic theory in empirical perspective

122 *Jonathan Joseph*
The social in the global:
Social theory, governmentality and global politics

121 *Brian C. Rathbun*
Trust in international cooperation:
International security institutions, domestic politics
and American multilateralism

120 *A. Maurits van der Veen*
Ideas, interests and foreign aid

119 *Emanuel Adler and Vincent Pouliot*
International practices

118 *Ayşe Zarakol*
After defeat: How the East learned to live with the West

117 *Andrew Phillips*
War, religion and empire: The transformation of international orders

116 *Joshua Busby*
Moral movements and foreign policy

115 *Séverine Autesserre*
The trouble with the Congo:
Local violence and the failure of international peacebuilding

114 *Deborah D. Avant, Martha Finnemore, and Susan K. Sell*
Who governs the globe?

113 *Vincent Pouliot*
International security in practice:
The politics of NATO-Russia diplomacy

112 *Columba Peoples*
Justifying ballistic missile defence:
Technology, security and culture

111 *Paul Sharp*
Diplomatic theory of international relations

110 *John A. Vasquez*
The war puzzle revisited

109 *Rodney Bruce Hall*
Central banking as global governance:
Constructing financial credibility

108 *Milja Kurki*
Causation in international relations:
Reclaiming causal analysis

107 *Richard M. Price*
Moral limit and possibility in world politics

106 *Emma Haddad*
The refugee in international society:
Between sovereigns

105 *Ken Booth*
Theory of world security

104 *Benjamin Miller*
States, nations and the great powers:
The sources of regional war and peace

103 *Beate Jahn (ed.)*
Classical theory in international relations

102 *Andrew Linklater and Hidemi Suganami*
The English School of international relations:
A contemporary reassessment

101 *Colin Wight*
Agents, structures and international relations:
Politics as ontology

100 *Michael C. Williams*
The realist tradition and the limits of international relations

99 *Ivan Arreguín-Toft*
How the weak win wars:
A theory of asymmetric conflict

98 *Michael Barnett and Raymond Duvall*
Power in global governance

97 *Yale H. Ferguson and Richard W. Mansbach*
Remapping global politics:
History's revenge and future shock

96 *Christian Reus-Smit*
The politics of international law

95 *Barry Buzan*
From international to world society?
English School theory and the social structure of globalisation

94 *K. J. Holsti*
Taming the sovereigns: Institutional change in international politics

93 *Bruce Cronin*
Institutions for the common good:
International protection regimes in international security

92 *Paul Keal*
European conquest and the rights of indigenous peoples:
The moral backwardness of international society

91 *Barry Buzan and Ole Wæver*
Regions and powers:
The structure of international security

90 *A. Claire Cutler*
Private power and global authority:
Transnational merchant law in the global political economy

89 *Patrick M. Morgan*
Deterrence now

88 *Susan Sell*
Private power, public law:
The globalization of intellectual property rights

87 *Nina Tannenwald*
The nuclear taboo:
The United States and the non-use of nuclear weapons since 1945

86 *Linda Weiss*
States in the global economy:
Bringing domestic institutions back in

85 *Rodney Bruce Hall and Thomas J. Biersteker (eds.)*
The emergence of private authority in global governance

84 *Heather Rae*
State identities and the homogenisation of peoples

83 *Maja Zehfuss*
Constructivism in international relations: The politics of reality

82 *Paul K. Ruth and Todd Allee*
The democratic peace and territorial conflict in the twentieth century

81 *Neta C. Crawford*
Argument and change in world politics:
Ethics, decolonization and humanitarian intervention

80 *Douglas Lemke*
Regions of war and peace

79 *Richard Shapcott*
Justice, community and dialogue in international relations

78 *Phil Steinberg*
The social construction of the ocean

77 *Christine Sylvester*
Feminist international relations: An unfinished journey

76 *Kenneth A. Schultz*
Democracy and coercive diplomacy

75 *David Houghton*
US foreign policy and the Iran hostage crisis

74 *Cecilia Albin*
Justice and fairness in international negotiation

73 *Martin Shaw*
Theory of the global state: Globality as an unfinished revolution

72 *Frank C. Zagare and D. Marc Kilgour*
Perfect deterrence

71 *Robert O'Brien, Anne Marie Goetz, Jan Aart Scholte, and Marc Williams*
Contesting global governance:
Multilateral economic institutions and global social movements

70 *Roland Bleiker*
Popular dissent, human agency, and global politics

69 *Bill McSweeney*
Security, identity, and interests: A sociology of international relations

68 *Molly Cochran*
Normative theory in international relations: A pragmatic approach

67 *Alexander Wendt*
Social theory of international politics

66 *Thomas Risse, Stephen C. Ropp, and Kathryn Sikkink (eds.)*
The power of human rights:
International norms and domestic change

65 *Daniel W. Drezner*
The sanctions paradox:
Economic statecraft and international relations

64 *Viva Ona Bartkus*
The dynamic of secession

63 *John A. Vasquez*
The power of power politics:
From classical realism to neotraditionalism

62 *Emanuel Adler and Michael Barnett (eds.)*
Security communities

61 *Charles Jones*
E. H. Carr and international relations: A duty to lie

60 *Jeffrey W. Knopf*
Domestic society and international cooperation:
The impact of protest on US arms control policy

59 *Nicholas Greenwood Onuf*
The republican legacy in international thought

58 *Daniel S. Geller and J. David Singer*
Nations at war:
A scientific study of international conflict

57 *Randall D. Germain*
The international organization of credit:
States and global finance in the world economy

56 *N. Piers Ludlow*
Dealing with Britain: The Six and the first UK application to the EEC

55 *Andreas Hasenclever, Peter Mayer, and Volker Rittberger*
Theories of international regimes

54 *Miranda A. Schreurs and Elizabeth C. Economy (eds.)*
The internationalization of environmental protection

53 *James N. Rosenau*
Along the domestic-foreign frontier:
Exploring governance in a turbulent world

52 *John M. Hobson*
The wealth of states:
A comparative sociology of international economic and political change

51 *Kalevi J. Holsti*
The state, war, and the state of war

50 *Christopher Clapham*
Africa and the international system:
The politics of state survival

49 *Susan Strange*
The retreat of the state:
The diffusion of power in the world economy

48 *William I. Robinson*
Promoting polyarchy:
Globalization, US intervention, and hegemony

47 *Roger Spegele*
Political realism in international theory

46 *Thomas J. Biersteker and Cynthia Weber (eds.)*
State sovereignty as social construct

45 *Mervyn Frost*
Ethics in international relations: A constitutive theory

44 *Mark W. Zacher with Brent A. Sutton*
Governing global networks:
International regimes for transportation and communications

43 *Mark Neufeld*
The restructuring of international relations theory

42 *Thomas Risse-Kappen (ed.)*
Bringing transnational relations back in:
Non-state actors, domestic structures and international institutions

41 *Hayward R. Alker*
Rediscoveries and reformulations:
Humanistic methodologies for international studies

40 *Robert W. Cox with Timothy J. Sinclair*
Approaches to world order

39 *Jens Bartelson*
A genealogy of sovereignty

38 *Mark Rupert*
Producing hegemony:
The politics of mass production and American global power

37 *Cynthia Weber*
Simulating sovereignty:
Intervention, the state, and symbolic exchange

36 *Gary Goertz*
Contexts of international politics

35 *James L. Richardson*
Crisis diplomacy:
The Great Powers since the mid-nineteenth century

34 *Bradley S. Klein*
Strategic studies and world order:
The global politics of deterrence

33 *T. V. Paul*
Asymmetric conflicts:
War initiation by weaker powers

32 *Christine Sylvester*
Feminist theory and international relations in a postmodern era

31 *Peter J. Schraeder*
US foreign policy toward Africa:
Incrementalism, crisis and change

30 *Graham Spinardi*
From Polaris to Trident:
The development of US Fleet Ballistic Missile technology

29 *David A. Welch*
Justice and the genesis of war

28 *Russell J. Leng*
Interstate crisis behavior, 1816–1980: Realism versus reciprocity

27 *John A. Vasquez*
The war puzzle

26 *Stephen Gill (ed.)*
Gramsci, historical materialism, and international relations

25 *Mike Bowker and Robin Brown (eds.)*
From cold war to collapse: Theory and world politics in the 1980s

24 *R. B. J. Walker*
Inside/outside: International relations as political theory

23 *Edward Reiss*
The strategic defense initiative

22 *Keith Krause*
Arms and the state: Patterns of military production and trade

21 *Roger Buckley*
US-Japan alliance diplomacy 1945–1990

20 *James N. Rosenau and Ernst-Otto Czempiel (eds.)*
Governance without government: Order and change in world politics

19 *Michael Nicholson*
Rationality and the analysis of international conflict

18 *John Stopford and Susan Strange*
Rival states, rival firms: Competition for world market shares

17 *Terry Nardin and David R. Mapel (eds.)*
Traditions of international ethics

16 *Charles F. Doran*
Systems in crisis: New imperatives of high politics at century's end

15 *Deon Geldenhuys*
Isolated states: A comparative analysis

14 *Kalevi J. Holsti*
Peace and war:
Armed conflicts and international order 1648–1989

13 *Saki Dockrill*
Britain's policy for West German rearmament 1950–1955

12 *Robert H. Jackson*
Quasi-states: Sovereignty, international relations, and the third world

11 *James Barber and John Barratt*
South Africa's foreign policy:
The search for status and security 1945–1988

10 *James Mayall*
Nationalism and international society

9 *William Bloom*
Personal identity, national identity, and international relations

8 *Zeev Maoz*
National choices and international processes

7 *Ian Clark*
The hierarchy of states:
Reform and resistance in the international order

6 *Hidemi Suganami*
The domestic analogy and world order proposals

5 *Stephen Gill*
American hegemony and the Trilateral Commission

4 *Michael C. Pugh*
The ANZUS crisis, nuclear visiting and deterrence

3 *Michael Nicholson*
Formal theories in international relations

2 *Friedrich V. Kratochwil*
Rules, norms, and decisions:
On the conditions of practical and legal
reasoning in international relations and domestic affairs

1 *Myles L. C. Robertson*
Soviet policy towards Japan:
An analysis of trends in the 1970s and 1980s